Voices

From the Field

Voices

From the Field

DEFINING MOMENTS IN COUNSELOR AND THERAPIST DEVELOPMENT

Edited by

Michelle Trotter-Mathison, Julie M. Koch, Sandra Sanger,
and Thomas M. Skovholt

Routledge
Taylor & Francis Group
New York   London

In accordance with the American Psychological Association's Ethical Principles of Psychologists and Code of Conduct (2002) the editors and the authors of the defining moments included in this book have made every effort to protect the confidentiality of clients and other individuals included in the narratives. When necessary, identifying information; including names, locations, age and other factors have been changed to protect confidentiality.

Routledge
Taylor & Francis Group
270 Madison Avenue
New York, NY 10016

Routledge
Taylor & Francis Group
27 Church Road
Hove, East Sussex BN3 2FA

© 2010 by Taylor and Francis Group, LLC
Routledge is an imprint of Taylor & Francis Group, an Informa business

Printed in the United States of America on acid-free paper
10 9 8 7 6 5 4 3 2 1

International Standard Book Number: 978-0-415-99574-0 (Hardback) 978-0-415-99575-7 (Paperback)

Library of Congress Cataloging-in-Publication Data

Voices from the field : defining moments in counselor and therapist development / Michelle Trotter-Mathison ... [et al.].
   p. cm.
Includes bibliographical references and index.
ISBN 978-0-415-99575-7 (pbk. : alk. paper) -- ISBN 978-0-415-99574-0 (hardcover : alk. paper)
   1. Counseling. 2. Therapeutics. I. Trotter-Mathison, Michelle. II. Title.

BF636.6.V65 2010
158'.3--dc22
   2009032777

Visit the Taylor & Francis Web site at
http://www.taylorandfrancis.com

and the Routledge Web site at
http://www.routledgementalhealth.com

To Carl and Jean Trotter, my dear grandparents.

Michelle Trotter-Mathison

To Katie, Pecos, and Maggie! Of course.

Julie M. Koch

To Bryson, my sunshine.

Sandra Sanger

To Annie and Iztchel with gratitude and love.

Thomas M. Skovholt

Contents

Foreword   ix
Confidentiality Statement   xiii
About the Editors   xv
About the Contributors   xvii
Acknowledgments   xxv

1   Introduction to Defining Moments   1

2   The Lay Helper Phase   13

3   The Beginning Student Phase   49

4   The Advanced Student Phase   97

5   The Novice Professional Phase   173

6   The Experienced Professional Phase   199

7   The Senior Professional Phase   221

8   Defining Your Own Journey   261

Using *Your* Voice... Articulating Your Defining Moments   267

Foreword

The willingness of clients to address their vulnerability and weaknesses while also recognizing their strengths and resources is an essential ingredient of optimal counseling and therapy. Similarly, practitioners' recognition of their own limitations, while also seeing the potential for transcending them, characterizes optimal professional development. Clients need to be engaged in meaningful and emotional ways for constructive change processes to occur. In a similar vein, experienced counselors and therapists must resist the temptation to experience their work as routine. By continually engaging themselves meaningfully and emotionally in their work they can grow professionally and help clients optimally. In these basic ways, there are fundamental similarities between how clients and practitioners learn and change. *Voices From the Field: Defining Moments in Counselor and Therapist Development* is a strong testimony to the personal aspects of being a counselor or therapist. The book is grounded in the wonderful idea of asking contributors to scan through experiences in their training and professional lives in order to come up with the most engaging and important moment. The result is a collection of deeply meaningful and engaging stories by 87 practitioners who have shared tales of defining moments in their personal and professional lives. I will briefly share some reflections while reading the book manuscript.

Research has convincingly demonstrated that, when asked what has impacted their professional development the most, counselors and therapists answer as with one voice: interpersonal experiences. This voice of *interpersonal experiences* emerged powerfully in the narratives in this book, just as they have emerged in qualitative interviews of American counselors and therapists (Skovholt & Rønnestad, 1995; Rønnestad & Skovholt, 2003) and in a large-scale survey study of approximately 5000 therapists from more than 20 countries (Orlinsky & Rønnestad, 2005). The generality of this finding is demonstrated by the consistency that emerged when separate analyses were made for profession, experience level, therapists' theoretical orientation, gender, and nationality (Orlinsky & Rønnestad). In both studies above, the general picture is that clients are seen as major teachers throughout the professional lifespan. This may not be surprising when you take into account that the practitioner spends by far most of their work time with clients. Supervision and personal therapy were ranked as the second or third, and personal life by many as the fourth most important source of influence in the survey study. So the interpersonal experiences of relating to clients, supervisors, personal therapists, and to others, such as family members, friends and colleagues are rated as most impactful for professional development. The book *Voices From the Field* adds rich, moving, and engaging narratives to this literature.

Although research using traditional research designs has not demonstrated that supervision improves the quality of professional work, supervision is still considered a highly treasured learning activity for students and practitioners (Orlinsky, Botermans, & Rønnestad, 2001). Large proportions of practitioners seek supervision beyond the formal requirements of training, licensure, and post-graduate education, which attests to the value of this classic educational activity. But, just as therapy can be "for better or for worse," so can supervision. *Voices From the Field* contains rich descriptions of constructive learning experiences emerging from interacting with supervisors and seniors who have provided support and guidance, but also tales of supervisors who have violated rules of professional conduct.

Therapists' self-reflexivity, insight, self-knowledge, self-understanding, and self-awareness are some of the concepts that underscore the personal aspect of professional work. Many interpersonal settings are fertile grounds to increase one's self-understanding. This book is saturated with stories in which practitioners give accounts of how professional and personal life facilitated a deeper understanding of themselves. It is also interesting to note that writing the defining moments appeared to be therapeutic for the authors. We are reminded of the learning potential that ensues from vacillating between the immediate experience and the more distant and remote view of one's experiences.

In addition to reading about experiences with clients, we are informed of experiences and dialogues with friends, family, colleagues, clients, and others. From the perspective of a researcher of personal therapy, the classic activity to enhance one's self-understanding, I was surprised that few mentioned experiences in personal therapy as a defining moment. Why is this? In the survey study mentioned above (Orlinsky & Rønnestad, 2005) about 80% of therapists and counselors reported at least one course of personal therapy. Are the practitioners providing these defining moments less inclined to have sought personal therapy? This does not seem likely. Rather it appears that when the most important experience, the defining moment is selected, other experiences are simply more prominent.

The defining moments for Chapters 2–7 of this book are organized according to phases of professional development (Rønnestad & Skovholt, 2001, 2003; Skovholt & Rønnestad, 1995, 2003, 2010). Many of the narratives fit such a structure, while others do not. Some cut across developmental phases, while others served to integrate earlier (e.g., childhood events) and later experiences (e.g., as a senior practitioner). Although practitioners were recruited from all levels of experience, proportionally the most stories came from the graduate student years, stories that were well remembered and had a lasting impact even for senior practitioners. We are reminded that much is at stake for graduate students. The stories bear witness to the vulnerability of the graduate student, and also of the developmental potential in recognizing one's vulnerability.

An important feature of the book is the editors' discussion on how this book of defining moments can be used as a training tool. Practical points are provided for use at the undergraduate level, graduate level, in supervision, and for practitioners. It has already been tried, and it works. In comparison to others' books on the topic of practitioner development, what stands out profoundly is the deep personal nature of being a counselor or therapist. The book thus contrasts attempts to make the practitioner a technician, a provider of techniques and methods. The book is a highly readable and important continuation and extension of the earlier work published by Skovholt and McCarthy (1988) on critical incidents in the lives of counselors and counselor educators. We know that professional development can be continuous or erratic. These stories inform us of the suddenness of change, but they are also tales of the paramount importance of reflecting upon these deeply meaningful experiences. This book on defining moments adds to the literature on related perspectives such as transforming life events, limitation–remediation scripts, and epiphanic moments. With powerful illumination, the stories inform us well of the vulnerability of student and novice practitioners. These stories also transcend the life of the beginner as they cover the entire lifespan. More than anything, though, these gripping narratives are a testimony to practitioners' commitment to professional development during their entire career. You will be stimulated by the reading. Enjoy being a reflective practitioner.

Michael Helge Rønnestad
Oslo, Norway

REFERENCES

Orlinsky, D.E., Botermans, J.F., & Rønnestad, M.H. (2001). Towards an empirically grounded model of psychotherapy training: Four thousand therapists rate influences on their development. *Australian Psychologist, 36,* 139–148.

Orlinsky, D.E., & Rønnstad, M.H. (2005). *How psychotherapists develop: A study of therapeutic work and professional growth.* Washington, DC: American Psychological Association.

Rønnestad, M.H., & Skovholt, T.M. (2001). Learning arenas of professional development: Retrospective accounts of senior psychotherapists. *Professional Psychology: Research and Practice, 32,* 181–187.

Rønnestad, M.H., & Skovholt, T.M. (2003). The journey of the counselor and therapist: Research findings and perspectives on professional development. *Journal of Career Development, 30,* 5–44.

Skovholt, T.M., & McCarthy, P. (1988). Critical incidents: Catalysts in counselor development. *Journal of Counseling and Development, 67,* 69–73.

Skovholt, T.M., & Rønnestad, M.H. (1995). *The evolving professional self: Stages and themes in therapist and counselor development.* Chichester: Wiley.

Skovholt, T.M., & Rønnestad, M.H. (2003). Struggles of the novice counselor and therapist. *Journal of Career Development, 30,* 44–58.

Skovholt, T.M., & Rønnestad, M.H. (In press, 2010). The path toward mastery: Stages and themes of development. In Skovholt, T.M., *Becoming a therapist: On the path toward mastery.* New York: Wiley.

Confidentiality Statement

In accordance with the American Psychological Association's Ethical Principles of Psychologists and Code of Conduct (2002), the editors and the authors of the defining moments included in this book have made every effort to protect the confidentiality of clients and other individuals included in the narratives. When necessary, identifying information, including names, locations, age, and other factors, have been changed to protect confidentiality.

REFERENCE

American Psychological Association. (2002). Ethical principles of psychologists and code of conduct. Retrieved August 11, 2009, from http://www.apa.org/ethics/code2002.html

About the Editors

Michelle Trotter-Mathison, PhD, is a psychologist at Boynton Health Service and a lecturer, both at the University of Minnesota. She is a licensed professional counselor in the state of Minnesota. Dr. Trotter-Mathison completed an MA and PhD at the University of Minnesota in the Counseling and Student Personnel Psychology program. She completed her predoctoral internship with Counseling and Psychological Services at Montana State University. Dr. Trotter-Mathison is coauthor of the second edition of the forthcoming book *The Resilient Practitioner* with Dr. Skovholt.

Julie M. Koch, PhD, is an assistant professor at Oklahoma State University in the School of Applied Health and Educational Psychology. She holds a BA in Japanese language from the University of Massachusetts, an MEd in counseling from the University of Texas, and a PhD in counseling psychology from the University of Minnesota. Dr. Koch is a licensed school counselor in Oklahoma and Texas. Her predoctoral internship was completed with the Student Counseling Center at Texas Tech University.

Photo by Mitch Harrison

Sandra Sanger, MA, is a doctoral candidate in the Counseling and Student Personnel Psychology program at the University of Minnesota and a licensed professional counselor. She completed an MA in counseling at the University of Denver and is currently completing her predoctoral internship at Personal Counseling and Testing Services at the University of St. Thomas; she also maintains a small private practice in St. Paul, Minnesota.

Thomas M. Skovholt, PhD, is a professor of educational psychology at the University of Minnesota and a licensed psychologist. He has been a part-time practitioner for many years. He is board certified by ABPP and a fellow of APA. Dr. Skovholt has been a Fulbright Lecturer in Turkey and taught in Singapore. He is coauthor of *The Resilient Practitioner; Master Therapists, Helping Skills and Strategies;* and *The Evolving Professional Self.*

About the Contributors

Sarah M. Backes-Diaz, MA, is a career counselor at the University of California–Berkeley Career Center.

Kelly A. Bailey, MA, is a graduate assistant therapist at West Virginia University Carruth Center for Psychological and Psychiatric Services and a PhD student in counseling psychology.

James M. Benshoff, PhD, is a professor in the Department of Counseling and Educational Development at the University of North Carolina at Greensboro.

Carolyn Bershad, PhD, is the associate director for clinical services at Northern Illinois University's Counseling and Student Development Center.

Ruth Chu-Lien Chao, PhD, is an assistant professor of counseling psychology at the University of Denver.

John Chambers Christopher, PhD, is a professor of counseling in the Department of Health & Human Development at Montana State University.

Julie Dorton Clark, PhD, is an assistant professor of counseling and counseling psychology and associate director of the Counseling Psychology Clinic at Oklahoma State University.

John C. Dagley, PhD, is an associate professor of counseling psychology at Auburn University.

John Danna, MA, is a graduate student in Duquesne University's clinical psychology program, an adjunct instructor at George Washington University, and is doing clinical work under supervision in Washington, D.C.

Claytie Davis III, PhD, is the director of training in Counseling and Psychological Services at the University of California–Berkeley.

Edward A. Delgado-Romero, PhD, is an associate professor in the Department of Counseling and Human Development Services at the University of Georgia.

Daniel F. Detzner, PhD, is a professor in the Department of Post Secondary Teaching and Learning and is on the graduate faculty in the Family Social Science Department in the College of Education and Human Development at the University of Minnesota.

Bryan J. Dik, PhD, is an assistant professor of counseling psychology in the Department of Psychology at Colorado State University.

Vasudev N. Dixit, MA, is a second-year counseling psychology doctoral student at Seton Hall University in South Orange, New Jersey.

Pat Donahoe, EdD, is director of Counseling and Psychological Services at Montana State University.

Changming Duan, PhD, is an associate professor of counseling psychology at the University of Missouri–Kansas City.

Sara M. Fier, PhD, is an assistant professor of counseling at Counseling and Testing Services at Southwest Minnesota State University.

Jenelle C. Fitch, PhD, is an assistant professor of counseling psychology in the Department of Psychology and Philosophy at Texas Women's University.

Elizabeth A. Garcia, PhD, is a counseling psychologist at Northern Illinois University's Counseling and Student Development Center.

Marco Gemignani, PhD, is an assistant professor of clinical psychology in the Department of Psychology at Duquesne University in Pittsburgh, Pennsylvania.

Samuel T. Gladding, PhD, is a professor of counseling at Wake Forest University.

Michael Goh, PhD, is an associate professor, director of training, and multicultural teaching and learning fellow in the Counseling and Student Personnel Psychology program at the University of Minnesota.

Jim Guinee, PhD, is director of training and adjunct professor at the University of Central Arkansas Counseling Center and Department of Family and Consumer Sciences.

Sally M. Hage, PhD, is an assistant professor in the Division of Counseling Psychology at the State University of New York–Albany.

Marcia Hanlon, MSW, is director of counseling services at Aurora University.

Matthew R. Hanson, PhD, is a psychologist in the University Counseling and Consulting Services at the University of Minnesota.

Sarah L. Hastings, PhD, is an assistant professor in the Psychology Department at Radford University.

Mary J. Heppner, PhD, is a professor of counseling psychology in the Department of Educational, School and Counseling Psychology at the University of Missouri.

Mary Kathleen Hill, PhD, is a postdoctoral fellow in psychology at Children's Medical Center–Dallas.

Aida Hutz, EdD, is an assistant professor of counselor education in the Department of Counselor Education at Boise State University.

Moshe Israelashvili, PhD, is an associate professor in the Department of Human Development and Education, School of Education, at Tel Aviv University in Israel.

Julie A. Jackson, PhD, is a psychologist at the Zablocki VA Medical Center in Milwaukee, Wisconsin.

Len Jennings, PhD, is an associate professor in the Graduate School of Professional Psychology at the University of St. Thomas.

Chad V. Johnson, PhD, is an assistant professor of human relations, clinical assistant professor in the Department of Psychiatry, and project director of the Center of Applied Research for Nonprofit Organizations at the University of Oklahoma, Schusterman Center.

Sandra Kosse Kacher, MSW, is in private practice in Minneapolis. She also consults with the Resiliency Training Program at the Penny George Institute for Health and Healing.

Annette S. Kluck, PhD, is an assistant professor of counseling psychology at Auburn University.

Nicholas Ladany, PhD, is professor, Counseling Psychology Program coordinator, and director of doctoral training at Lehigh University.

Valerie Stephens Leake, PhD, is an assistant professor of counseling psychology in the Department of Psychology at Radford University.

Régine Leclerc, MA, is a school counselor and head of Learning Support and Counseling Services at the International School of Paris, France.

Wei-Chien Lee, PhD, is a psychologist and counselor faculty in the Counseling Services at San Jose State University.

Richard A. Lenox, PhD, is associate director and director of training at the Texas Tech University Student Counseling Center.

Harriet Lerner, PhD, is a psychologist in private practice in Lawrence, Kansas. She is the author of numerous books, including *The Dance of Anger, Women in Therapy,* and, most recently, *The Dance of Fear.*

Amina Mahmood, PhD, is a research assistant at the University of Iowa Hospitals and Clinics.

Guy J. Manaster, PhD, is retired from the Department of Educational Psychology at the University of Texas–Austin, where he is the Charles H. Spence Professor Emeritus in Education.

Sharon M. McLennon, MSEd, is a rehabilitation consultant and therapist for Ultimate Consultation and Evaluation and a PhD doctoral candidate in the counseling psychology program at Seton Hall University in South Orange, New Jersey.

Cynthia McRae, PhD, is a professor of counseling psychology in the Morgridge College of Education at the University of Denver.

Laurie B. Mintz, PhD, is an associate professor at the University of Missouri and practicing licensed psychologist. She is the author of the self-help book, *A Tired Woman's Guide to Passionate Sex.*

Michael Mobley, PhD, is an associate professor at Rutgers, the State University of New Jersey in New Brunswick.

Anissa L. Moody, PhD, is a postdoctoral fellow at Princeton House Behavioral Health.

Monicah Muhomba, PhD, is a staff psychologist at the Vanderbilt University Psychological and Counseling Center.

Susan Allstetter Neufeldt, PhD, is a writer and practitioner in Santa Barbara and former clinic director and lecturer at the University of California–Santa Barbara.

Melanie A. Nuszkowski, PhD, is a psychologist at the West Virginia University Carruth Center for Counseling and Psychological Services.

Roberta L. Nutt, PhD, is professor emerita and a former director of training in counseling psychology in the Department of Psychology and Philosophy at Texas Women's University.

Timothy A. G. Osachuk, PhD, is a clinical psychologist, associate professor, and the director of internship training at the Student Counselling and Career Centre at the University of Manitoba.

Catherine L. Packer-Williams, PhD, is an assistant professor of counselor education in the Department of Educational Studies at the University of South Carolina.

Jeeseon Park, PhD, is an assistant professor of counseling psychology in the Department of Educational and Counseling Psychology at McGill University.

Megan Phillips, PsyD, is a postdoctoral resident at the Kaiser Permanente Department of Psychiatry.

M. Carole Pistole, PhD, is an associate professor of counseling psychology in the Department of Educational Studies at Purdue University.

Richard F. Ponton, PhD, is director of human services in the Township of Ocean.

Mark Pope, EdD, is a professor and chair of the Division of Counseling and Family Therapy at the University of Missouri-Saint Louis.

Senel Poyrazli, PhD, is an associate professor of counseling psychology at Pennsylvania State University–Harrisburg.

Amanda Lienau Purnell, PhD, is a clinical psychologist at the VA Medical Center in St. Louis.

Ryan J. Quirk, PhD, is a psychologist with the Washington State Department of Corrections.

Salina Renninger, PhD, is director of training and a senior psychologist at University Counseling and Consulting Services at the University of Minnesota.

Ruth Riding-Malon, PhD, is an assistant professor of counseling psychology in the Department of Psychology at Radford University.

Jeffrey A. Rings, PhD, is a postdoctoral psychology fellow with the Department of Veterans Affairs at the Eastern Colorado Health Care System.

John L. Romano, PhD, is a professor of educational psychology in the Counseling and Student Personnel Psychology program at the University of Minnesota.

Mark B. Scholl, PhD, is an assistant professor of Counselor Education in the Department of Counselor and Adult Education at East Carolina University.

David McGraw Schuchman, MSW, is director of Immigrant and Refugee Behavioral Health at the Volunteers of America Minnesota.

Paul J. Schwartz, MA, is a faculty crisis counselor at New York City College of Technology (City University of New York) and a student counselor at Nyack College Manhattan Campus.

Kimber Shelton, PhD, is a postdoctoral fellow at the Georgia State University Counseling and Testing Center.

Dustin K. Shepler, MA, is a PhD student in counseling psychology at Ball State University.

Janet Shriberg, EdD, is an assistant professor in the International Disaster Psychology Program, Graduate School of Professional Psychology at the University of Denver.

Laura E. Sobik, PhD, is a licensed clinical psychologist and training director at James Madison University in Harrisonburg, Virginia.

Abdalla M. Soliman, PhD, is a professor of counseling psychology at Cairo University in Egypt.

Arnold R. Spokane, PhD, is a professor of counseling psychology in the College of Education at Lehigh University and a board-certified counseling psychologist.

Michael T. Starkey, MA, is a psychological intern at the University of Maine in Orono and doctoral candidate at the University of Minnesota in the Counseling and Student Personnel Psychology Program.

Jill C. Thomas, PhD, is an assistant professor and assistant director of student counseling at SUNY Upstate Medical University.

Ling-Hsuan Tung, PhD, is studying French in Montreal, Canada, in order to obtain psychology licensure in the province of Quebec. She recently received her PhD in counseling psychology from the University of Minnesota and completed her predoctoral internship at the Center for Multicultural Training in Psychology at the Boston Medical Center/Boston University School of Medicine.

Yuh-Jin (Jean) Tzou, PhD, is a postdoctoral fellow in Counseling and Consultation Services at the University of Wisconsin–Madison.

Tammi Vacha-Haase, PhD, is an associate professor of counseling psychology in the Department of Psychology at Colorado State University.

Barbara M. Vollmer, PhD, is a clinical associate professor and director of the Counseling Psychology Training Clinic at the University of Denver.

Andrew C. Weis, PhD, is a clinical psychologist at the Carleton College Wellness Center.

James L. Werth, Jr., PhD, is a professor of psychology and director of the doctor of psychology program in counseling psychology at Radford University in Southwest Virginia.

Acknowledgments

We would like to first acknowledge our families, friends, and loved ones, who have supported us through the development of this project. Their love, support, and presence contribute to who we are as counselors and scholars and make our work feel worthwhile. We are also so grateful to the Counseling and Student Personnel Psychology program at the University of Minnesota for bringing us together and for beginning bonds of friendship and collaboration that we look forward to continuing.

We would like to thank Dr. Pat McCarthy Veach and Dr. Thomas M. Skovholt for compiling the original critical incident narratives in the *Journal of Counseling and Development*. Their work was the inspiration for this book and the foundation upon which we have built. Thank you to Dr. Helge Rønnestad for sharing the thoughts and wisdom he gleaned over the years on the process of counselor development. We would also like to acknowledge Dana Bliss, Chris Tominich, and Tara Nieuwesteeg, the professionals at Routledge who provided expert guidance and diligently helped to shepherd this book into print.

We are honored and touched and extend our sincere gratitude to all of the contributors for making this project, a dream conceived of years ago, into a reality. The contributors shared parts of their work and of themselves, and for this we are truly grateful.

Finally, we would like to acknowledge the clients mentioned in these stories, and all clients, who honor us with their trust in their search for personal growth and understanding.

Michelle Trotter-Mathison
Julie M. Koch
Sandra Sanger
Thomas M. Skovholt

1

Introduction to Defining Moments

I n 1988, Tom Skovholt and Patricia McCarthy published a series of brief, story-like articles from the counseling profession in a special issue of the *Journal of Counseling and Development*. The narratives were called "critical incidents" and were written by counselors, therapists, and counselor educators from a diverse array of backgrounds. Years ago as first-year doctoral students in the Counseling and Student Personnel Psychology Program at the University of Minnesota, three of us (Michelle Trotter-Mathison, Julie M. Koch, and Sandra Sanger) had the opportunity to explore these critical incidents as a part of our doctoral seminar.

In the field of clinical supervision, Heppner and Roehlke (1984) have defined a *critical incident* as an incident or "turning point" that results in change in a professional's perception of himself or herself. Several authors, including McCarthy Veach, Bartels, and LeRoy (2002a, 2002b), have used the term *defining moment* to signify these kinds of catalysts for growth or development. For the purposes of this book, we have chosen to use this term, *defining moments*, because we believe it captures the essence of the experience—one that plays a key role in counselors' subsequent development—without the negative connotations that are sometimes attached to the word *critical*.

A defining moment can be positive or negative but has a significant influence on professional identity. When we read the narratives in the *Journal of Counseling and Development* as graduate students, we were drawn in by the intimate accounts of the ways counselors were inspired by their clients, discovered something meaningful about themselves, or uncovered what the true essence of counseling was for them. The stories were written about topics ranging from crisis counseling to a practitioner's personal experiences with mental illness. We were struck by how candidly the writers spoke of their personal and professional experiences; they expressed both their struggles and the ways they had grown.

Our reactions to having read through these critical incidents, or defining moments, ranged from relief to surprise. We found that we weren't as alone as we believed in our struggles with the challenges and surprises of working with clients. We were also surprised that a similar resource had not presented itself earlier in our training. Throughout graduate school, we found ourselves thirsting for the kinds of "real-world" experiences that seemed to enlighten us by leaps and bounds beyond what we could pick up in a text.

The first sentences spoken to us by our first "real" clients and our first, seemingly fumbled responses have etched themselves deeply in our memories. Interactions with clients have shaped our development in ways that coursework never could. Yet there were only so many clinical experiences we could have at one time. Reading the vivid firsthand accounts provided by new and seasoned clinicians gave us an opportunity to vicariously experiment with ideas beyond our direct experience. We learned about encountering a homicidal client for the first time without needing to directly stomach the anxiety that comes with the threat of violence. We also glimpsed secondhand the unique effects of certain life experiences, such as the birth or death of a child, upon one's professional life. Reading the narratives gave us a flavor, as students, of what it is like to be a professional in the field. It also revealed to us that the distinction between student and professional is not quite as sharp as we had once believed.

The overarching messages that we gleaned from the defining moments we read were that all therapists grapple at times with difficult clients, difficult reactions, and difficult emotions and that to do so is only human. Beyond these more concrete struggles, however, we also came to understand that there is one specific area of development that demands focus as a therapist, that screams out to us for attention. The message from the defining moments is about reaching out to tolerate ambiguity. We may not be able to reach out to tolerate ambiguity with grace. That is asking a lot of students who are struggling with … well, a lot of things. The plate is usually full, sometimes overflowing. Accepting ambiguity with humility is made more possible by reading the defining moments of others' struggles. We are grateful to have had the chance to lay the foundations for these lessons before we left graduate school, and we hope that others will have similar experiences in taking comfort in, and learning from, the experiences of others offered here.

Skovholt and McCarthy's (1988) collection of critical incidents was a meaningful training tool for our doctoral seminar. It inspired each of us to reflect on our counseling education and to spontaneously compose our own narratives. Some of us explained the significant moment when we were "called" to the field of psychology, when we knew this was the profession in which our talents and interests intersected, while others wrote of our first experiences as beginning counselors. Through this sharing of defining moments, we felt motivated to seek out others' stories and ultimately came to the decision to compile a new collection of stories related to counselor and therapist development. It is our hope that this collection of defining moments will build upon those published two decades ago in contributing to training counselors, therapists, and other helping professionals and in facilitating personal and professional growth.

Now, through recent years as we have worked to become more competent practitioners, we find ourselves similarly engrossed, moved, and inspired by the stories shared in this current collection of narratives. The authors in this collection invite us into their inner lives. They share with us from the inside what happens when a catalyst for change or development, a defining moment, occurs in their lives. In this book, you will read a story of how the death of a loved one forever changed one man's life and his counseling practice. You will step inside the mind of a predoctoral intern while she sorts out her conflicted feelings related to her client's suicide. You will read about how being a mother influences one woman's work as a therapist and teacher. In fact, you will find a whole book of engaging narratives. We hope this collection will draw you in and inspire you in the same way it inspired us. We hope that reading these stories will allow you to tap into your own motivation to pursue what we consider a meaningful, noble, and valuable career field of counseling and therapy. We hope the defining moments in this book create new energy and renew excitement for your education and work.

DEFINING MOMENTS AND THE REFLECTIVE PRACTITIONER

In training to be counselors and therapists we are taught to be reflective practitioners. In our classes and professional lives a major task is to examine our motivations, biases, strengths, and weaknesses—essentially to know ourselves. The notion of being a "reflective practitioner" is not new to our profession. It is something that sets us apart from other professions as our work as counselors involves art, science, and ourselves among the primary tools. To effectively use all of these tools, we must continually examine and reflect upon ourselves as therapists, educators, and researchers as an integral part of our professional practice and responsibilities.

Hubble, Duncan, and Miller (1999), in *The Heart and Soul of Change*, tell us that relationship factors account for approximately 30% of the variance in counseling outcome. This drives home the point that it is essential for us to look deeply at our personal and professional selves and to examine who we are as helpers and how this affects our ability to build meaningful relationships with clients. One way of doing this is by reflecting on significant events that have influenced our development as counselors. The process of identifying and articulating these developmental pieces is a way for us to get a more complete picture of who we are as practitioners, what we bring to the counseling relationship, and what we value in our lives, our relationships, and the counseling process. By retelling stories of our most influential and meaningful moments, it is possible that we will find new meaning, learn something about why they were meaningful to us to begin with, and potentially hear feedback that helps us to expand our view of our developmental impasses. Stories of professional and personal development are powerful. It is a gift that so many are willing to share their stories and to allow others to learn vicariously from them. The writers who contributed to this book were brave, insightful, and willing to challenge themselves when composing their own defining moments.

CREATING COMMUNITY

Reading and reflecting upon defining moments is one way to get a deeper look at the inner lives and thoughts of other professionals and trainees in the field. In this way, we can aspire to support and guide each other through the ups and downs of working as counselors. Through sharing our stories, our community of counselors can train each other. Counseling is often a solitary profession, and sharing defining moments is a way for us to create community, a way for students and professionals in the field to create a mechanism for sharing integral moments of meaningful learning with each other. Parker Palmer (2004), in his book *A Hidden Wholeness: The Journey Toward an Undivided Life,* writes:

> Of course, solitude is essential to personal integration: there are places in the landscapes of our lives where no one can accompany us. But because we are communal creatures who need each other's support—and because, left to our own devices, we have an endless capacity for self-absorption and self-deception—community is equally essential to rejoining soul and role. (p. 22)

The counselor's office can be a lonely place for practitioners. The space between therapist and client is filled with the weight of the client's despair, dreams, and desires. As practitioners we may find ourselves perpetually sitting perfectly still, poised to listen and absorb, with barely a chance at the end of the 50-minute hour to reflect, take a breath, and reset our frame of mind to prepare for the next incoming client with a different story, a different need, and a different way of being. In between clients, we write notes, return phone calls, and address billing issues. The hours stack up on one another, end to end, until another day has gone by without a chance to engage with another person in a simple, nonprofessional manner.

Those of us who work in the academic community as faculty members, students, or researchers also grapple with the presence of solitude as a career hazard. It may be all too easy for us to become holed up in our offices, trying to secure that next grant, to prepare for classes, and to polish off that manuscript we keep meaning to attend to. Add to this countless committee meetings, likely far removed from the initial reasons we pursued this work, that often spiral off into unproductive gripe sessions riddled with the nuances of office politics. Soon the outside world may start to fade away, as the endless tasks continue to mount. Even in those instances when we have the opportunity to meet face to face with our colleagues, we may easily lose sight of the community that is sorely needed to sustain us all.

At the end of the day, we all know this work can be particularly isolating and draining because of the aloneness of it. Ethical codes and standards upholding the confidentiality of clients' disclosures prohibit us from sharing the specifics, and sometimes even the broad generalities, of our days with those who are important to us. Hectic schedules crammed back to back with meetings, classes, and precious little research and writing time can preclude our attempts to build a working community with our colleagues. For practicing therapists, clinical supervision becomes one of the few places where we can unburden ourselves of some of our secrets, not only those we are bound to keep about our clients, but also those that reveal aspects of our own selves as therapists and people that we are sometimes reluctant to examine or disclose. Similarly, peer consultation groups can serve as a forum for educators, researchers, and practitioners to solicit feedback from and to provide support to others. Of course, supervision and peer consultation may fall short at times, as supervisors and supervisees alike are busy. Anxiety about scrutiny from an authority figure or peer may also cause us to stop short of disclosing *everything* that goes on in the counseling office or classroom.

Another resource available to helping professionals—outside of supervision, peer or otherwise, and the kind of didactic learning that occurs in graduate school—is the accumulated and polished wisdom of students and practitioners who have gone before us. Case studies are an often sought out resource that provide what novice therapists often crave: *real* examples of how clients might present, the issues they may bring to the table, and the means by which seasoned clinicians interact with these clients. The study of defining moments extends the potential represented by case studies and supervision for enriching one's practice beyond the realm of purely clinical material to include, for example, issues that crop up around personal life experiences and complexities in academic life. Novice therapists can benefit from knowing that there are others out there who have walked paths similar to their own among the numerous dimensions that make up counselors' beings. We believe that in addition to students, experienced therapists and faculty can also connect with the authors of these stories and benefit from remembering that even those with more experience under their belts are human.

COUNSELOR DEVELOPMENT AND DEFINING MOMENTS

In addition to serving as prompts for counselor self-reflection, defining moments also have the potential to assist novice and trainee counselors in traversing the developmental arc along which all beginners progress as they find their way into the realm of the professional. Many trainees report that the single factor contributing most potently to their development as counselors is practical experience in the field (Furr & Carroll, 2003). One large international study found that, of eight sources, experience with clients was the most influential source of development for therapists overall (Orlinsky & Rønnestad, 2005). Novices rated it second only to clinical supervision. This does not require any kind of intuitive leap to understand; learning by doing allows for the integration of previously learned didactic content with the necessary process of seeing clients, bringing the seemingly dimensionless content alive. However, practical experiences in counseling can be difficult to come by for the neophyte whose only previous exposure to the helping field consists of earlier attempts in assisting friends and family, a process that is qualitatively different from offering professional help. Role plays with other counseling trainees, which are known by trainers to be key in promoting development of the use of basic counseling skills, in our experience are often dismissed by trainees as lacking realism. While we certainly do not suggest that such an essential tool be discarded by trainers and supervisors, we do believe that the reading of and reflection upon defining moments written by other practitioners can provide another means by which trainees may be exposed to "real-world" situations in the helping field without compromising client treatment.

Of course, development as a clinician does not occur solely within the boundaries of graduate training. Congruent with theories of lifespan development, which do not limit development to the early years, we come into knowing about how to be therapists, as well as who we are as therapists, gradually, over time, and within the context of repeated interactions with clients and other professionals. The defining moments offered here can apply to the growth of therapists at all stages in their careers.

Rønnestad and Skovholt (2001, 2003; Skovholt & Rønnestad, 1995, 2003, in press) offer a model of counselor/therapist development that is based upon the results of a large qualitative investigation. Their model describes the evolution of therapists' development across the entire spans of their careers—from trainee to senior professional.

In Phase 1, *The Lay Helper Phase*, novices offer nonprofessional help to acquaintances and family; they can be prone to quick problem identification, advice giving, and boundary issues. High school or undergraduate students who enjoy "helping others," possibly through volunteer work or peer tutoring, might be classified as lay helpers.

Individuals enter Phase 2, *The Beginning Student Phase*, when they begin graduate school in a counseling-related field. It signals a time of high dependency, vulnerability, and anxiety in trainees as they seek out the "right way" to counsel. Much of their technique is modeled upon that of expert clinicians. For example, a master's-level practicum student might write down everything her supervisor says or recommends and use those notes word for word in session.

In Phase 3, *The Advanced Student Phase*, students have established a basic level of professional competency but tend to vacillate between feelings of increased comfort on one hand and insecurity and vulnerability on the other. They continue to value support and validation from senior clinicians. Advanced practicum students and interns may value time not only to discuss skill development, but also to process how they are feeling about their experiences, supervision, and their own personal development.

Following graduate training, individuals move into Phase 4, *The Novice Professional Phase*. At this time, the demands of graduate school and constraints of supervision are left behind, but in their wake, therapists often discover that graduate school has not prepared them as well as hoped or expected for the exigencies of more independent practice. In this phase, therapists learn to increasingly incorporate their own personalities into treatment.

As counselors gain more experience, they move into Phase 5, *The Experienced Professional Phase*. They begin to focus on establishing authenticity as a primary developmental task. Experienced professionals nearly universally recognize the centrality of the therapeutic relationship in contributing to client change. They also become increasingly comfortable with the necessary ambiguity present in counseling interactions.

Following the accumulation of more than 20 years of experience, counselors enter Phase 6, *The Senior Professional Phase*. At this level, therapists have built a practice based on their own authentic, idiosyncratic approaches to the field. Self-confidence is often tempered by acknowledgement of the real limitations of their impact on client change with an increased focus on the "client as hero." Loss plays a primary role in this phase, with clinicians addressing and coping with nearing retirement as well as the fading of their own professional mentors.

In addition to identifying these six phases, Rønnestad and Skovholt (2003) have also adopted a bird's-eye view of the development process to identify broad qualitative themes in counselor/therapist development. The themes describe the nature and process of change across the career span, some mechanisms underlying change and development, and important sources of learning. The authors posit that continuous reflection, especially upon challenges, is paramount for promoting learning and professional development (Theme 3). Furthermore, a commitment to learn drives movement across the developmental arc (Theme 4).

Professional development is a lifelong process (Theme 7; Rønnestad and Skovholt, 2003) that is sometimes erratic and cyclical (Theme 6). Even though the process may be slow and long, therapists enjoy an increasing sense of competence and mastery as they develop (Theme 6). Practitioners gain knowledge and further their development first and foremost through interpersonal sources of influence, including clients (Theme 9), "professional elders," professional peers, friends, and family (Theme 11). Personal life experiences often influence professional development (Theme 10).

As therapists develop from novices to senior professionals, they learn to more fluidly integrate their personal and professional selves (Theme 1; Rønnestad and Skovholt, 2003). They also move from relying on external expertise as novices to relying on internal expertise as seasoned practitioners (Theme 5). While beginning counselors are often fraught with anxiety, over time, anxiety decreases and is generally mastered (Theme 8). Over time, therapists also shift their focus from "self as hero" to "client as hero" (Theme 14; p. 38). Novice therapists are profoundly impacted by their interactions with "professional elders" (e.g., supervisors, personal therapists, professors, mentors); as they shift away from graduate school, they often experience some disillusionment related to their graduate training (Theme 12). Poignantly, as therapists accrue more time in the field, their "extensive experience with suffering" affords them "heightened recognition, acceptance, and appreciation of human variability" (Theme 13, p. 37).

DEFINING MOMENT CHAPTERS

This book contains a compilation of experiences that counseling trainees and professionals have noted as defining moments in their development. They are written in the words of those who experienced them; while the defining moments have been authored by unique individuals, as Skovholt and McCarthy (1988) have noted, they often fall into similar categories, speaking to the more universal aspects of our development as therapists. In soliciting contributions, we provided potential contributors with prompts for crafting their own defining moments. We asked them to reflect on the most powerful or impactful moment in their development as therapists and to describe their experiences in the form of a defining moment narrative. Some prompts we asked authors to consider included the following:

- What led to your decision to pursue a career in counseling?
- What personal or professional experiences have you had that have influenced your development as a counselor (or as a person)?
- How have you changed across the span of your work as a counselor (personally or professionally)?
- How have cultural issues, your worldview, or your systems (or those of your clients) influenced your development as a counselor?

- What ethical dilemmas or taboos have you encountered that have influenced your development?
- How have you avoided burnout in your professional development?

These questions served as a starting point for authors to begin their reflective processes; what emerged went far beyond the scope of our questions. That said, we have chosen to break down the book as follows.

This chapter provides an introduction to the nature of defining moments and their role in counselor and therapist development. We discuss a generalized model of counselor development. We also talk about creating a community of professionals through shared experiences to enhance practitioners' understanding of, and belonging to, the profession. Finally, we discuss proposed uses for the book within graduate level coursework and as a tool for augmentation of counselors' development across their careers.

Chapters 2 through 7 use Rønnestad and Skovholt's (2001, 2003; Skovholt & Rønnestad, 1995, 2003, in press) model of counselor development as a structural framework for organizing the compiled defining moment narratives. The model includes six stages of counselor development: Phase 1: The Lay Helper Phase; Phase 2: The Beginning Student Phase; Phase 3: The Advanced Student Phase; Phase 4: The Novice Professional Phase; Phase 5: The Experienced Professional Phase; and Phase 6: The Senior Professional Phase. At the beginning of each chapter we include a brief description of the developmental phase to set the stage for the narratives included in the particular chapter.

Finally, in Chapter 8 we draw conclusions from the compiled defining moments. We present general themes that have emerged from this particular collection of stories and direct readers toward articulating their own defining moments.

USING *VOICES FROM THE FIELD*

We have discussed the usefulness of defining moments as a training tool, not only for formal coursework and supervision experiences, but also for those practitioners who value self-reflection as a means to enrich personal and professional growth. To assist with this self-reflection, we have developed some stimulus questions related to the defining moments in each chapter that we hope will prompt further discussion, introspection, and questioning of one's own preconceived notions regarding what counseling is "supposed to" look like, be like, or feel like. We believe that these defining moments can be used in a number of ways, at the undergraduate and graduate levels, in a supervisory context at the postgraduate or professional level, or for exploration of one's personal and professional self. The following are examples of how this book can be used.

At the Undergraduate Level

In undergraduate courses in psychology or social work or other helping professions, instructors can use this book as a supplement to give students an idea of what "helping" actually looks like in practice. Larger classes can be broken into small groups to discuss reactions to the defining moments and to answer the discussion questions provided. One defining moment could be assigned as reading for each class session. Alternatively, the instructor could assign a group of readings or a chapter of the book for a certain class session, with students then participating in a broader discussion of how to make sense of the defining moments and what these readings imply about the helping professions.

At the Graduate Level

In a graduate program in counseling psychology or counselor education or in another helping field, faculty can choose to use this book in a number of ways. The book can be applied across courses, drawing upon relevant chapters or individual defining moment narratives. For instance, narratives addressing multicultural or cross-cultural counseling experiences could be assigned in a multicultural counseling course, while narratives discussing experiences with clients could be used in a beginning counseling skills course. The book can also be used as a supplemental text for a course devoted to professional issues and development, at either the master's or doctoral level. Defining moments can be assigned individually, in thematic groups of two or three, or in larger "chunks" for small- or large-group discussion. Instructors might assign reaction papers for two or three of the readings, using the discussion questions as writing prompts, or might ask students to maintain a "reaction journal," to be handed in on a regular basis. In addition, instructors might ask students to write their own defining moments (see the guidelines on page 267 at the end of the book) to facilitate students' self-understanding. Instructors could give students the opportunity to share their incidents with the class on a voluntary basis.

In Supervision

Voices From the Field could provide discussion fodder for supervision sessions in practicum, fieldwork, and internship experiences. A supervisor may ask a supervisee to complete certain readings that are particularly relevant to the type of clients being seen, supervisee learning goals, or key areas of growth and development. The defining moments may be used as a way to broach a subject that is sensitive or difficult to discuss. Supervisees may be asked to explore their reactions in supervision, in a journal, or through writing their own defining moments (see the guidelines on page 267 at the end of the book). The discussion questions can be used, or supervisees can consider how they might handle a similar situation.

For Practitioners

Outside of the academic realm, we hope that practitioners will use the book to explore their own professional development. The defining moments could be used in a peer supervision or consultation group. We recommend starting a "defining moments" book group with colleagues, in which a different defining moment narrative is discussed each week, the discussion questions are considered, or new questions are developed and posed. If you are interested in writing your own defining moment, see the guidelines at the end of the book for ideas.

SUMMARY

In editing this collection of defining moments, we were given the opportunity to enter into the professional and personal inner worlds of counselors and therapists—some graduate students, some new professional therapists, some faculty members, and others who are highly experienced senior members of the field. All of the authors described intense, meaningful experiences. We were touched by being invited into the inner lives of these individuals. In an academic setting, we rarely read published articles that examine how a therapist may have erred or the series of meaningful self-examinations that lead to a particular clinical decision. Our title uses the phrase "voices from the field"—in the pages that follow we hear counselors' words coalesce into their own voices and their own unique ways of recounting events that significantly changed their personal and professional lives. The reality is that defining moments are very personal—what may be a developmental marker for one may be a normal day at work for another. All of the contributors articulate and make meaning of their defining moments in their own ways. In a profession where there are more questions than answers, we struggle to face the reality of ambiguity that marks the human existence. Stories from others can help us to live the questions together to try to make meaning for ourselves in the face of human suffering. All counselors, researchers, professors, and counselors in training have stories to tell about what brings meaning and purpose to their work and how they are changed and shaped by their work with clients or events in their personal lives. We invite you to share in the following stories. As you read, we invite you to also think of the moments that have shaped your own personal and professional development!

REFERENCES

Furr, S.R., & Carroll, J.J. (2003). Critical incidents in student counselor development. *Journal of Counseling & Development, 81*, 483–489.

Heppner, P.P., & Roehlke, H.J. (1984). Differences among supervisees at different levels of training: Implications for a developmental model of supervision. *Journal of Counseling Psychology, 31*, 76–90.

Hubble, M.A., Duncan, B.L., & Miller, S.D. (1999). *The heart and soul of change: What works in therapy.* Washington, DC: American Psychological Association.

McCarthy Veach, P., Bartels, D.M., & LeRoy, B.S. (2002a). Defining moments: Catalysts for professional development. *Journal of Genetic Counseling, 11*, 277–280.

McCarthy Veach, P., Bartels, D.M., & LeRoy, B.S. (2002b). Defining moments: Important lessons for genetic counselors. *Journal of Genetic Counseling, 11*, 333–337.

Orlinsky, D.E. & Rønnestad, MH. (2005). *How psychotherapists develop: A study of therapeutic work and professional growth.* Washington, DC: American Psychological Association.

Palmer, P.J. (2004). *A hidden wholeness: The journey toward an undivided life.* San Francisco: Jossey-Bass.

Rønnestad, M.H., & Skovholt, T.M. (2001). Learning arenas for professional development: Retrospective accounts of senior psychotherapists. *Professional Psychology: Research & Practice, 32*, 91–98.

Rønnestad, MH., & Skovholt, T.M. (2003). The journey of the counselor and therapist: Research findings and perspectives on professional development. *Journal of Career Development, 30*, 5–44.

Skovholt, T.M., & McCarthy, PR. (1988). Critical incidents: Catalysts for counselor development. *Journal of Counseling & Development, 67*, 69–130.

Skovholt, T.M., & Rønnestad, M.H. (1995). *The evolving professional self: Stages and themes in therapist and counselor development.* New York: John Wiley & Sons.

Skovholt, T.M., & Rønnestad, M.H. (2003). Struggles of the novice counselor and therapist. *Journal of Career Development, 30*, 44–58.

Skovholt, T.M., & Rønnestad, M.H. (in press). The long textured path from novice to senior practitioner. In Skovholt, T.M. and Trotter-Mathison, M., *The resilient practitioner: Burnout prevention and self-care strategies for therapists, counselors, teachers, and health professionals.* 2nd edition. New York: Routledge.

2

The Lay Helper Phase

*M*any of us as counselors and therapists can tell stories of times when we have helped others, long before our training or credentials made the role official. The lay helper is a novice who helps others in a nonprofessional setting. Lay helpers are friends, coworkers, parents, sisters, and brothers. People seek them out for advice, or they are quick to offer it. Lay helpers have not received any formal training in counseling, and they tend to rely upon their own solutions to similar problems as the basis upon which they offer advice. At times, lay helpers may identify so strongly with others' struggles that they become overinvolved, asserting specific and strong advice that may or may not be appropriate. Typically, an individual in the lay helper phase of counselor development "identifies the problem quickly, provides strong emotional support, and gives advice based on one's own experience" (Rønnestad & Skovholt, 2003, p. 10). Oftentimes, individuals' experiences as lay helpers catalyze their entry into the helping professions and related fields such as teaching and nursing.

Reference

Rønnestad, M.H., & Skovholt, T.M. (2003). The journey of the counselor and therapist: Research findings and perspectives on professional development. *Journal of Career Development, 30,* 5–44.

A THERAPY FAILURE
Richard A. Lenox

As a gay adolescent male growing up in the Midwest in the late '70s and early '80s, I struggled, as many of my kind did, with self-acceptance. A lack of visible, healthy role models resulted in significant depression for me, with occasional thoughts of suicide. My parents, not knowing any better and simply wanting my pain to go away, were directed to conversion therapy by a consulting psychiatrist. Interestingly, participating in conversion therapy to change my sexual orientation during my undergraduate years was not an unpleasant experience. Once a week,

I would drive 30 minutes from campus out to an idyllic country setting where my psychologist's practice was located. I don't recall there ever being an overt moral component to his therapy. In his therapeutic philosophy, he was simply trying to help me "unlearn" my attraction to men.

The fact that he was conducting conversion therapy and was not embracing of my diversity were not the aspects of the experience that have stayed with me over the years. I can attribute his approach as a function of the times (1980s), to being in a very conservative part of the country, and to the therapist being of a different generation. I can hope only that he changed his philosophy over time. Rather, it was the message I received about my efforts in therapy that I recall most vividly today.

While I had made some behavioral changes over the course of therapy (with considerable effort, I might add), my sexual attraction to men had not changed at all. We mutually decided to end therapy after a year and a half. I recall being told that I had not put forth enough effort to achieve change. While I don't believe he ever uttered the word *failure*, I heard it loudly and clearly. I had failed. For a 20-year-old overachiever who was compensating for both a perceived flaw in my sexuality and for messages about "laziness" received in childhood, this message was devastating. I don't recall any suggestion that his therapeutic methods may have been suspect. Was he an unkind man? Not at all. Did he use harsh words? Probably not, but I do believe he missed the mark in not recognizing the impact our parting had on me.

My history as an "achiever" goes back to early childhood and was deeply ingrained by that time. I am certainly not unusual in being a gay individual of my generation who racked up success over time to compensate for a perceived personal flaw. I somehow managed to compartmentalize my life in such a way during high school and college that I was able to maintain a high grade point average and maintain significant extracurricular involvement while struggling with depression, self-loathing, and alcohol abuse. Add to this that my family culture was one that clearly valued "doing" over "being," and it created the perfect storm for me. Am I still an achiever today? Absolutely, but I like to think that my achievements now simply bring me a sense of satisfaction for a job well done rather than serve as statements about my worth as an individual.

As I work with clients and clinicians in training today, I find myself thinking carefully about therapy "success" and "failure" (the quotation marks are intentional) and what these mean to both the therapist and the client. Moreover, I am concerned about how this is communicated to, and received by, the client. What does it suggest if agreed upon goals are not met? Several possibilities can be considered. Is readiness for change an issue for the client? In this case, redefining success may be necessary. Is there an inherent flaw in the therapeutic goal, as I believe there was in my situation? This scenario may involve significant exploration on the part of the therapist and possible referral for the client. Regardless, I have been left with an acute awareness that my communications, both spoken and unspoken, to clients about their efforts must be chosen carefully, as they could very likely have a lasting impact. I've learned over time that any discussions with clients about treatment progress, whether at midtreatment or at termination, must be processed fully.

This means that in addition to hearing clients' thoughts on progress and providing them with my impressions, I ask them to share their reactions to my feedback. This gives me the opportunity to clarify any misinterpretations or misunderstandings they might have.

My sensitivity to clients' perceived therapy success also comes into play when starting therapy with individuals who have had previous therapy experience. I want to understand fully how the individual feels about this previous experience. Certainly, if it was positive, I'd like to be able to replicate some of the aspects that made it successful for the client. But, if the experience was not a positive one, I want to clarify the client's understanding about what contributed to its being unsuccessful. Sometimes clients will dispassionately talk about their unwillingness to work at the time, a poor client–therapist fit, or a therapeutic approach that did not work for them. This is certainly helpful information for our work together, but I'm more concerned about emotionally laden reactions to previous therapy (e.g., shame, anger, embarrassment). These clients are often very wary of therapy, are hypersensitive to therapist comments and interpretations, and likely have reentered therapy only as a last resort. Typically, I downplay the power differential in therapy and attempt to collaborate with all my clients in a team effort toward healthy functioning. For clients with negative therapy histories, I will more actively highlight this collaborative effort and invite ongoing feedback from them.

Did I come to value this approach on my own? Not completely. I must give credit where credit is due. During my predoctoral internship, I chose to return to therapy to address my anger at the perceived injustices to which I had been subjected over the years. Here, I do not mean just this earlier therapy experience. I am referring to multiple experiences related to living as a gay man. Although I was hesitant about making myself vulnerable in this arena again, I recognized that my obsessive anger was becoming a problem. And as a neophyte therapist who was learning to assist others in recognizing when they needed to ask for help, I didn't want to be a hypocrite. My therapist wisely recognized that what I needed from her was a corrective, healing environment. Looking back, I can honestly say that she reparented me. Undoubtedly, this therapy experience was significantly more painful than my conversion therapy experience. The difference was that it was a pain I entered into willingly, but only after I could trust that my therapist was willing to go there with me and wouldn't let me fall. I remember feeling raw, exposed, exhausted, and both entering and leaving her office in tears. I have a deep sense of gratitude for the healing environment she provided for me. The content of what we discussed is only a vague memory now, probably very important at the time, but its usefulness is in the past. What has stayed with me is the precious feeling of being valued, regardless of what I achieved. I believe that these personal therapy experiences have served as a catalyst for my current work as a therapist. I want all of my clients to feel a sense of appreciation for the efforts they put forth in therapy, even if it is simply for their willingness to walk through my door.

THE HEALING POWER OF FORGIVENESS
Ling-Hsuan Tung

Human nature is fascinating to me, and helping people has always intrigued me. My family and life experiences have contributed to my passion for helping. The defining moment for me was when I finally, truly forgave my father and how my own experiences with forgiveness have shaped my work as a counselor.

Growing up in a conservative society in a single-parent family helped me become a strong person with a tender heart because I was often discriminated against. I was raised by my mother in Taiwan as an only child. Her sacrifices for others planted the seed of helping in my mind. Her courage and achievement inspired me to be brave, to undertake challenges, and to pursue my goals. My parents were divorced before I was 1 year old. People gossiped about my family and thought that my mother was a bad woman because of the divorce. Taiwanese society tends to consider children from single-parent families as potential troublemakers and as people with potential psychological problems. I was usually among the only one or two students from a single-parent family in my class of 50–60 students. I felt like I had to keep my family background secret. I found the only way to earn others' respect for my mother was to get good grades so that other people would admire how well she taught me and consider me a good student instead of a troublemaker. At the same time, people tended to pity us and to place me in a victim role. The victim role provided extra attention, which I enjoyed as a kid, but it also prevented me from forgiving my father earlier.

My biggest struggle was my relationship with my father. My father did not care about me much when I was little. Before I was 8 years old, he seldom called me or visited me. I did not know about my parent's divorce until I finally asked my mother when I was 6 years old. It was very hard for me to accept that they were divorced, and I became jealous toward other kids. Secretly, I hoped that my father would come back and take care of us. Then I realized that it was impossible because he was remarried. My feelings toward him gradually changed from love to hatred. At first, I desired his love and care. After feeling disappointed so many times, I decided to hate him and to let him experience the feeling of not being wanted. Later on, I realized that I was hurt so deeply and felt so abandoned by him that it negatively affected my sense of security.

My father started to call me and invite me to spend time with his family when I was 10 years old. I went out with them a few times before I decided to end the relationship. Beginning at age 12, I always turned down his invitations. I felt the power of revenge, but I also felt sad. I found myself in a dilemma—I expected his phone calls and hoped he cared about me but was cold and unapproachable when he did call me. Also, I was angry and sad when he often forgot which grade I was in when he called me. Looking back, I was often immersed in the strong mixed feelings of love and hatred toward my father. This kind of situation continued until I was a freshman in college.

There was one big turning point in my life, a defining moment. This was when I dropped out of the university during my second semester as a freshman. During that semester off from school, I faced my biggest struggle—my relationship with my father. I hurt myself deeply by hating him because he left us and did not care much. Although my mother reminded me constantly that the first person I would hurt by hating others is myself, I could not help hating my father. Also, my Christian faith emphasizes that you should love your enemy. However, before I was 19 years old, I could not accept the idea of forgiving my father because I thought he was such a bad person. I also could not forgive myself because I thought I was not generous and compassionate enough toward my father. I was struggling with the decision of whether to forgive. When I realized that I hurt my mother by dropping out of school, I started to think that maybe I needed to give my father a second chance in the same way that I hoped my mom would forgive me. Also, I decided to try to set myself free from feeling hurt and being paralyzed in the victim role. I started my forgiveness journey by contacting my father and building a new relationship with him and his family.

When we first started to meet, my father apologized for abandoning me. I also confronted him about the divorce and expressed my feelings of hurt and anger. After knowing him more, I encountered another challenge—the difference between my ideal father and real father. I became angry at him again because he lied about what had happened and tried to split my mother and me. Then I decided to forgive him again and try to accept him as a person and not stick to my own version of the ideal father.

Acting in a scene "Forgiving Father" from the play *Coming out of the Shadows* as a senior in college greatly helped me feel ready to forgive my father again. Our drama teacher helped us create the characters and write the play. I wrote a few scenes of the play, including the scene "Forgiving Father." My character in the play was a paranoid patient who was hurt by her father. She practiced confronting her father with a friend and found the inner strength to grow and become strong again. A few lines that really touched me were

- "I want to stand up again and let bygones be bygones. Sometimes I think about you and try to think from your point of view, and I find that you may also suffer a lot of pain. For this, I pity you."
- "Let's forget about fault! Father, I get tired of hating you! Besides, if I keep on hating you, I cannot recover from the horrible experience. The only way for me is to forgive you and let it go!"
- "Father, I miss the outside world. I want to love others again. I want to walk into the crowd. I don't want to be afraid anymore."

Fortunately, I did experience healing and gain strengths from writing the scripts, rehearsing the play, and actually performing onstage. Again, I felt I could forgive my father. I did not want to torture myself anymore, and I wanted to set myself free. I realized that I had used anger to make my father feel guilty, to help myself feel safe, and to keep myself in the victim role. I had also used anger to give myself a feeling of control, but, ironically, I experienced real control and power only after I forgave my father. I experienced the healing power of forgiveness and enjoyed a new freedom without anger and hatred.

My experiences with forgiveness have contributed to my work as a counselor. I believe that we counselors need to experience and explore what we encourage our clients to do. It is important for us to face our own situations and ourselves honestly. It is also pivotal to continue working through our challenges and self-reflecting. My experiences with forgiveness have helped me to see how complex and difficult it may be and how much healing and freedom it could provide. I have watched many clients struggle with the decision about whether to carry hurt indefinitely or to forgive. I am able to be patient with my clients and to help them to explore their feelings and painful experiences and what might be helpful for them. My painful experiences have helped me to relate to my clients' pain and to be more empathic and compassionate. I have seen the healing impact that deciding to forgive can have. When clients tell me they finally, truly forgive another, they describe feeling free. What happened still matters, but it helps them to free themselves from being hurt. However, it is important to recognize it is not easy and not to prematurely push clients to forgive. Deciding to forgive can give clients a sense of power and control. However, for clients who are questioning if they have truly forgiven the other person because they do not want to tell or interact with the other person, or for those who are afraid to forgive because they think forgiveness must involve reconciliation, we may explain that people have different kinds of choices and that forgiveness does not equal reconciliation. I am grateful to my life experiences because they have prepared me to become a better counselor. I welcome continued growing experiences.

THE VOICE OF A GRANDMOTHER
Kimber Shelton

As a child, whenever I was asked the question, "What do you want to be when you grow up?" I responded that I wanted to be a surgeon or a psychologist. After seeing a televised surgery, however, my enthusiasm for psychology quickly surpassed medicine. Although I had an early interest in becoming a psychologist, it has been only in recent years that I have come to understand how the relationship I had with my grandmother shaped who I am as a helping professional today. My grandmother taught me to be both an advocate and a leader and sparked my desire to work with oppressed populations.

Originally from West Virginia, I moved with my parents to upstate New York when I was a child. Although far from my grandmother, I saw her often during the year and spent two months out of the summers with her. I have nostalgic memories of spending summers building club houses, swinging from grapevines, and picking blackberries. I learned not only practical lessons during those summers, such as to stay away from plants that have three leaves, but also, unfortunately, of the hardships that come along with a minority identity. My carefree recollections are overshadowed by memories of watching my grandmother struggle to survive in a world that belittled her for being Black, uneducated, and poor. Even as a child, I noticed a subtle disdain in the tone in which others addressed my grandmother, faint sighs of exasperation to my grandmother's questions, and a quiet invisibility to my grandmother's presence. Like air, my grandmother breathed in these daily messages of denigration, and the disease of discrimination stole my grandmother's strength and distorted her self-perception.

At the time, I couldn't understand my grandmother's self-doubt and broken spirit because I saw her as a beautiful woman with unlimited strength. As the matriarch of our family, she supported and raised her children and her grandchildren, and she took care of others even when she couldn't take care of herself. Her nature was honest, and she was rarely sparing of the feelings of those close to her. The delivery of her infelicitous opinion lacked any resemblance of diplomacy or sophistication; in fact, her statements were harsh and unfounded to the point of being comical. If you made the mistake of focusing on her words, it would be easy to disregard or ridicule my grandmother. But if you listened to the pleading in her eyes, attended to the anguish in her clasped hands, and concentrated on the shapes made by her lips, you were privy to a moment in time that was rich with immeasurable wisdom and truth. The timeliness and powerful delivery of my grandmother's stories left recipients of her words longing for more. Therefore, I grappled to understand the coexistence of blaring muteness: How could my grandmother be silent to the world, when her presence was so loud to those close to her?

I grew furious with the dismissive glances and deferential treatment directed toward my grandmother. Being a little Black girl, there was only so much I could do, and at times I felt powerless. But my feelings of powerlessness could not compare with the anguish I felt when my grandmother was humiliated in front of me. It wasn't a conscious decision at the time, but I made sure I used the one power I did have to eradicate such humiliation: my voice. I was too young to articulate these acts as racism, sexism, and classism, but I was old enough to start asking questions and to make requests: When will the doctor be in to see us? Why are you trying to rush us? Tell me the reasons you are unable to fulfill our request. Let me speak to the manager. I found myself quickly becoming an advocate for my grandmother at community businesses and organizations where she was often a target of prejudice and discrimination.

As I grew older, I found myself challenged by more difficult questions: Why are people treated differently because of what they look like or the possessions they have? Why is so much energy put into perpetuating hate? Why did no one try to help my grandmother? Who is responsible for making changes? The defining question that influenced who I am today as a helping professional came from asking myself how I could help.

It is amusing to consider that my professional development as a psychologist began as a child, but retracing my journey, it only makes sense that I would find a career that allows me to ask daily, "How can I help?" I realize that my grandmother's experience is not uncommon; many people experience oppression from factors such as their race, gender, socioeconomic status, educational attainment, or sexual orientation. I love that each day I ask individuals, couples, and groups how I can be of service to them. Additionally, I hope my work as a clinician results in fewer and fewer people asking, "Why is no one trying to help me?" I appreciate my role as a counselor because it also entails helping people find solutions and build resistance to internalizing self-hatred and discrimination. As I wished someone would have helped my grandmother see her true reflection, I like to think that I am helping others see the strengths and beauty they possess.

Those hot days and warm nights in the West Virginia mountains solidified my dedication to working with minority groups. Witnessing such oppression during my childhood and being a voice for my grandmother taught me to stand up for injustice. The once timid and angry voice of a little Black girl is now seasoned with experience, education, and empathy. The power associated with a degree, combined with the inheritance of my grandmother's quick tongue, affords me the privilege and flexibility to teach, counsel, research, and advocate for marginalized persons who, like my grandmother, have been silenced and have internalized the messages society ascribes to them.

It shames me to admit that some of the questions I had as a child placed blame on my grandmother. Rightly so, I was angry at systemic discrimination, but I was also frustrated with my perception of my grandmother's inaction. I found myself wondering, "Why do you let people talk to you like that?" or "Why are you being so weak?" I now realize that my grandmother gave up her voice so that I could find mine. The times when I thought she was being weak, she was actually teaching me to be strong. The times she faltered were lessons for me to press on. This is so clear to me today because when I speak, my grandmother's voice is reflected in the words I say.

TRANSFERENCE: A PATH TO GROWTH AND INDIVIDUATION
Régine Leclerc

When I entered psychotherapy as a client in the late summer of my life, the psychologist asked me, "Do you love your parents?" What a silly question. "Of course I love them," I promptly replied, with, I remember, a certain difficulty in articulating those words.

It seemed too benign a question coming from a seasoned psychologist. What was he after? I was a novice client, so I took the question at face value and hardly thought before I replied. What would he possibly dig up from a relationship that had seemed perfect to me? "Perfect," I realized after, because I had never actually examined it.

Do we often, or ever, look at our upbringing before something or someone makes us look at it? And even then, are we willing, or able, to do so? The psychologist's question had introduced a certain level of uneasiness into my mind. It was hard to know why at the time. It seemed like the first time I was verbalizing feelings of love toward my parents. During my upbringing, not vocalizing expressions of love to one's parents or children was a cultural given to which my family adhered. It did not seem to be necessary to say it or to hear it. It was felt. It was rarely contemplated or expressed. The "love question" posited that maybe my sense of love for my parents was more sophisticated than I had previously thought. The impact of that question endures to this day.

The 2 years that followed that first session initiated a powerful and unexpected voyage into troubled yet purifying waters. I started to revisit my roles in life and to consider why I had, for as long as I could remember, wanted to please others and to achieve harmony at any cost—whether it was as a child, a friend, a wife, or a mother. Physically, it felt like the liberating tearing of a veil. Psychologically, a nagging residue of guilt held me back yet paradoxically kept on providing me with material for growth.

My therapy came to be much more than an individuation process. It led to a shift in my career path and brought a new meaning to my life. The first chapters of my life would not have consciously pointed to the counseling career that I later embraced. Yet, looking back, those first chapters created the foundation for my dreams and life choices, all of which were related to healing, teaching, and providing.

I was raised in a family in which taking responsibility, caring, and providing for family members was the cultural paradigm. Both children and adults complied with family expectations and demands; it is no surprise that I did too, as the precepts of my upbringing were nonnegotiable. The unspoken message of needing to give back to "given love" developed in me a sense of family obedience and faithfulness, concern for others' well-being, and, also, some self-censure of my own needs.

My parents' story, loaded with their own happy and tragic moments, was instrumental in my identity formation. They both had experienced the German occupation of France during the Second World War, with all of the accompanying trauma and hardship. This was especially true of my mother, who had felt she had been sacrificed for the well-being of the whole family, having to work from age 14 while her siblings all continued their studies.

I had to be the perfect daughter—the one who would live the life that my mother had not, the one who would be loved more than my mother ever felt she was, the one who had to make the right choices to not be victimized. Choices I made that were unworthy in her eyes were "fine," but often not quite good enough. So she loved me—for myself and for the person that she would have liked to be. And she showed contempt for the person that she did not recognize—the actual self I was painstakingly trying to be. Perhaps it was a version of the person she wanted to be but could not.

It was hard to reject or say no to what was lovingly expected of me. Gradually and pervasively, through my family's nuclear culture and my mother's unconscious expectations of me, I came to fill a role, or roles, that I never questioned consciously until I started psychotherapy. The roles I assumed and my lack of questioning were culturally and transgenerationally coherent.

These roles shaped the next 20 years of my adult and marital life and continued to sow the seeds of a counseling career, though I remained unaware of it. France had resisted Sigmund Freud for decades, and my family epitomized that resistance. To them, the field of psychology was at best an esoteric science and at worst nonexistent. People worked out their problems by themselves. I remember my father saying that gaining insight into one's psyche is a risky game he would not want to play. My mother frequently talked about all these "psypersons" as being the fashionable healers of a society that was sick.

I married an Englishman at 20. At the time, Northern England without family, friends, a phone, car, or career, seemed the ultimate adventure on the other side of the world. It never occurred to me that I might have been escaping my loving, smothering mother.

For the next 20 years, I flew from one culture to the next—France to England to Spain—without ever really landing or feeling at home. Then I came to live in the United States. I was in the *Land of the Individual*. I had five children by then, one of whom my husband and I had adopted in Brazil when he was 8 years old. Our seemingly enlightened, multicultural family did not support our adopted son in ways I now wish we would have. I now know that I was neither enlightened nor good enough. Feeling alone in my struggles to cope with my son, and encouraged by the local culture, I called a psychologist.

That call came to be a turning point in my personal and professional lives. It was the first step in moving away from my parents' distrust of psychology. It was my own initiation into the field, and from that very first question about love, I embraced it with all the paradoxes it could create: resistance, disbelief, passion, enlightenment. As it happened, the work I was doing in therapy was supported by a thought-provoking graduate course in Intercultural Relations that I was taking concurrently.

The ensuing family and couples therapy led to healthy shifts in family dynamics, especially for my son. I came to realize that my adopted son had unwillingly carried, and had suffered from, my own struggles in my intimate partnership.

The couples therapy put me through the wringer. The therapy sparked in me doubts and deep interrogations, which, if not always pleasant, were always a move toward individuation and healing. The therapist sure had some nerve to suggest I was self-absorbed and unwilling to change! How dare he suggest that I forgive myself for making some choices that I questioned later in my life? Why was he relentlessly questioning my perception of oppression and sense of victimization?

I often thought at the time that I was not heard by our therapist. It hit home and felt familiar; I became immersed in transference. As the therapy advanced and as I perceived the therapist as mostly aligning with my partner, I became angry about not feeling understood or believed, and I was desperate to be heard and loved. With its positive and negative components, the therapeutic alliance became both a struggle and a huge learning ground. I absorbed every word the therapist pronounced; I scrutinized, dissected, and explored the content and meaning of his language. I examined his gestures, tone of voice, and body language. I questioned his interpretations, fascinated by the intellectual challenge that the therapy offered, and I forcefully resisted what I saw as a new form of oppression and abuse.

I read endless psychology books to restore rationality into my emotionality and turmoil. My intellectual curiosity and admiration prompted me to want so badly to become my own therapeutic executioner. I was motivated and impelled to look right where it hurt. I became both the client and my own "therapist." As the client, I let go and accepted the therapeutic process. As the "therapist," I gave myself the power to make my own decisions and to recraft my sense of self.

Regardless of the grueling moments, I discovered psychotherapy to be a beautiful art in its capacity to metamorphose and to give meaning to hurt and the narratives describing my life. I was astonished that this transformation relied solely upon a meeting of minds and therapeutic dynamics. I learned to question, comfort, and accept uneasy feelings and conflict as a part of healthy growth. I learned to not always please and to not always try to make peace, to paradoxically become more accessible. I viewed my relationship with my parents in a different light, becoming more aware of their own stories and trying to not get lost in that exploration. My partner and I chose to continue different life paths.

My experiences in therapy prompted me to transfer from the intercultural program to the counseling psychology program. I moved from being a novice client to becoming a novice therapist with the same sense of vulnerability, occasional naïve acceptance, and readiness and willingness to understand.

FROM MY EYES: COMING OUT OF THE DARK
Sharon M. McLennon

My visual world is dark, but I see so bright! I hear the magical glow of the birds in the sky, the whistling of the leaves through the trees on a cool fall day, the effervescent sound of gentle, relaxing musical notes that are arranged into a magnificent, harmonious sound. My favorite sound of all is the delightful voices of people from around the world speaking with their distinct accents and inflection of tones. I intensely smell the roses. The ocean breeze has about 10 different fragrances to me. I feel the multitude of textures that are naturally created or manmade in hopes of finding something that feels soft, cuddly, and warm to me. I too really enjoy tasting the rich flavors that true home-cooking has to offer. Dining out in restaurants for an evening or two is also quite delightful. By now, you are probably thinking that this counselor must be crazy! Not too crazy, only a very creative, totally blind female who has been a certified rehabilitation counselor since 1998.

I am a native New Yorker and grew up in Brooklyn. Growing up in Brooklyn with a disability provided me with a rich and diverse experience. I acquired a visual disability at age 6 that resulted in total blindness. Completing educational goals and extracurricular activities, making and having friends, and developing my potential were definitely concepts encouraged and supported by my parents. However, these processes were extremely challenging to a developing young child diagnosed with a painful, progressive, incurable eye disease. All the fun and excitement of early childhood soon was lost to understanding the medical process, struggling with comprehending "why me," while yearning to still be accepted by my teachers, peers, neighbors, and even some members of my own family. My parents said, "Yes, you have a visual disability, but this disability should not limit you from pursuing and obtaining your vocational dreams and aspirations." They elected to place me in Roman Catholic academic instruction for both elementary and secondary school.

To this date, there is no known cause of my visual problem. I guess that this is my cross to bear in life! And what a cross to bear: My world was finally totally dark by age 21 and continues to be without light. I had to find the path, my true and guiding light, to lead me to a life of "normalcy." My academic and spiritual preparation enabled me to become a well-rounded individual with qualities of caring, honesty, compassion, understanding, dedication, and loyalty to my convictions. I grew up in a family that blessed me with an extremely wonderful mother who is a registered nurse, a father who was a small business owner, a second cousin who is a surgeon, and an aunt who is a teacher. Having these role models truly propelled me to push myself out of the darkness of pity to another place.

This place was a place of hope. It is very easy to stay in the place of pity. To constantly ruminate on why this disability happened to me would foster an environment composed of anger. The anger was fueled by the realization, as a child, that I was labeled as someone with a disability. I had the letter "D" placed on my head because now I was seen as different. This label can be quite arduous for anyone to handle. Fortunately, my family and inner spirit guided me to an alternative direction.

Don't be mistaken: I did have my moments of "It sucks to be blind!" But, at the same time, I wanted to be productive. I wanted the world to see me as a contributing member of society. I wanted the world to see me as a working person who pays federal and state income taxes!

All through my early academic years, I wanted to become a mental health provider. I thought that I had the gift of gab! Seriously, I truly believed that I was given a special gift to listen, understand, and counsel people. This gift became especially evident when I engaged in community-based activities. I can remember my first counseling-type experience. I was 17 years old. I was working for a mission group in my local church that provided assistance to elderly citizens in my Brooklyn neighborhood. I was assigned to visit two elderly women who required help with daily living activities, food support, and basic companionship.

I remember my initial visits were about my listening to what these women had to say about their lives. They wanted to share their worldly experiences with me. They wanted someone to take the time to really listen to what they had to say. At that time, I was a good, but novice, listener. As the relationship progressed, I even had some good things to say to them. Initially, I was scared to talk to them because I did not know if they would accept my visual disability and my youth. But they did. Over time, I realized that all people worry about being judged for individual characteristics. Learning how to understand and accept my personal dilemma gave me the inner perspective to truly listen and to work with clients and their problems.

This mission experience stoked my desire to attend college to pursue study in biology and psychology. I wanted to learn about human behavior and to eventually become a counselor. I thought that as a woman who was blind, I could effectively use my communication and listening skills to help people. Additionally, I could use my social and academic knowledge and creative skills to further work with others who might have even greater limitations than those I faced each day.

According to the American Foundation for the Blind (1995), approximately 70% of persons who are visually impaired are unemployed despite having formal postsecondary and graduate education and training. This could be attributed to societal stigma and discrimination associated with blindness in the workplace. I am happy to say that since I became a trained counselor, I have been gainfully employed.

Over the years, I have been granted the working opportunity to counsel individuals from diverse backgrounds and disenfranchised groups. I have worked with persons from different ethnicities, persons with disabilities, persons with diverse religious and political beliefs, and persons with diverse sexual orientations and convictions. I have worked as a counselor, senior counselor, and program coordinator and supervisor. These previous employment opportunities gave me a chance to provide clinical supervision services to full-time and part-time employees as well as to graduate students who were completing internships at Hunter College and New York University.

This experience enabled me to grow, as I trained future clinicians in the ethical codes, guidelines, practices, and decorum needed by all counseling professionals. Providing these weekly clinical supervision sessions consisting of role modeling, role-play exercises, resources, and counseling techniques helped to prepare these clinicians to work more effectively with clients from diverse backgrounds and with significant functional limitations. Learning even more about myself, as I coaxed new workers in our field to trust their talent, allowed me to further develop as a practitioner. It is so important to provide salient insight to future clinicians about what it is like to work with a client who puts his or her trust in you, as the counselor.

Three years ago I decided to pursue a doctoral degree in counseling psychology. I want to become a full-time teacher and researcher. I plan to teach the next generation of clinicians how to be effective, multicultural professionals. I think that it is imperative to prepare psychologists and counselors to work with all clients, including clients with disabilities. The essential fact to keep in mind is that all of us are one step away from having some type of disability.

I hope that my personal story inspires you each day to find the hope and pride in what you do as a counseling professional. Thus far, this has been a wonderful and rewarding career for me. I would recommend it to anyone who really cares about people. Such an individual must be willing to analyze his or her own behavior and to make the changes that can promote good personal and emotional health. We owe this to our clients.

Reference

American Foundation for the Blind. (1995). Blindness Employment Statistics. Retrieved May 19, 2009, from http://www.afb.org/Section.asp?DocumentID=1529&SectionID=7

PEOPLE ARE EXACTLY THE SAME; PEOPLE ARE VERY DIFFERENT: THE PROFOUND EXPERIENTIAL LESSON OF MY PEACE CORPS YEARS
Roberta L. Nutt

I said in my Society of Counseling Psychology presidential address in 2006 that my Peace Corps service was "the single most defining experience of my life," but I had little time then to explain in detail the true meaning of that phrase.

I spent 1966 and 1967 on the East Coast of the Malaysian peninsula teaching mathematics and running a secondary school library when both the Peace Corps and I were young. I immersed myself in a multicultural society. My friends were Malays, Chinese, and Indians. I ate and learned to cook the foods of all three cultures, I dressed in the clothing of all three cultures, and I learned the customs of all three cultures.

This deep immersion in another country for 2 years deeply affected my life, both personally and professionally. It was life changing. I had grown up in a family that respected and observed the very different customs of both my parents' families of origin, but the Peace Corps service built upon and deepened this respect. I learned, at an experiential level, to appreciate the paradox of the simultaneous differences between peoples and their core similarities.

To get myself into a mindset to think about my Peace Corps experience 40 years ago, I picked up a book of Peace Corps essays (Coyne, 1994) for inspiration. In the book, Richard Lipez says, "Whatever we were before, and none of us can quite remember, that's all gone. Peace Corps life tempers one by its sheer and irresistible intensity" (p. ix). Coleman Lollar remarks, "I found ... confirmation of a long-held suspicion that in no place on earth would I ever feel entirely the stranger" (p. x). And Harris Wofford writes, "Peace Corps Volunteers know how not to be strangers. Their experience allowed them to reach through the barriers of culture and tradition and touch other lives" (p. x). They carry that ability thereafter.

It is somewhat difficult to put into words what I mean by the paradox of simultaneous differences and core similarities because it is an experiential concept, but I will try. When I was leaving Malaysia, some of my local friends asked me what I thought were the most important things I had learned. Upon reflection, I talked about the many ways we were similar. We cared deeply about the same things: our families, friends, personal values and standards, hopes for our futures, and appreciation for art. I spent many afternoons with my friends in the teachers' hostel drinking tea, experimenting with foods, and talking about our lives and plans. We understood each other's wants and desires. Although I appreciated these similarities, I was not blind to the subtly different textures and tones within these similarities. These different textures and tones create interest and make life more fascinating and exciting. It reminds me of the multicultural conversations in this country. We call the person who overemphasizes similarities colorblind and the one who overemphasizes differences prejudiced or racist. Somehow, you have to experience and celebrate both the similarities and the differences.

My Peace Corps experience removed many cultural obstacles in my ability to connect with others. This has impacted my relationships with clients, students, and friends. With clients, it has certainly increased my ability to accept them where they are and to allow them to progress and grow at their own pace. I am reminded of a particular client who had suffered abuse within her family. Her friends had repeatedly urged her to break off connections with her family. They could not understand why she refused. This client came from a communal culture in which family is extremely important and in which children do not cut off connection with parents under *any* circumstances. Our therapy relationship worked because I never suggested that she cut off her relationship with her family, although I did suggest that she renegotiate it to create some protection for herself. Eventually, in very small steps, she created more and more distance from her family, at her own pace. Our therapy worked, I think, only because I understood the parameters of her communal culture.

The sheer and irresistible intensity, to use Lipez's words, of my Peace Corps years made me much more open to the diversity of human experience—in fact, more enthusiastic about and fascinated by that diversity. My international clients and students have particularly appreciated my Peace Corps experience. I can think of a graduate student who told stories of being made fun of as an immigrant elementary school student because she was different. One way she reacted was to abandon everything from her country of origin and to exaggerate her adoption of everything American. By the time she entered graduate school, she was beginning to question the conflict between her two cultures. She was receiving pressure from her family to adopt some family norms. One week, I showed up in class (with her permission) wearing the native dress of her homeland (which I happened to have, courtesy of my Peace Corps travels) and asked her to explain the various pieces to the class. After all, she was the expert. It was a valuable reversal of her elementary school experience and seemed to set her on a new course that eventually led her to visit her country of origin. More importantly, it helped her begin a new integration of both cultures into her own identity as a person.

I would not trade my Peace Corps experience for anything. It opened up my life to the world as nothing else could. It made me feel like a citizen of the world as no other experience could have. It has, in Wofford's words, allowed me to feel like never quite a stranger anywhere, and that feeling allows a wonderful permissiveness to reach out to others. I hope, as a corollary, it has made me more approachable for others.

Reference

Coyne, J. (Ed.). (1994). *Going up country: Travel essays by Peace Corps writers.* New York: Macmillan.

HOW MY CAREER CHOSE ME
Harriet Lerner

Before finishing kindergarten, I decided to become a clinical psychologist—a decision I never veered from. Perhaps my early career choice had something to do with the fact that my mother put me in therapy before the age of 3. I later joked that my mother would send me to a therapist if I came home from school with anything less than a B plus. I was exaggerating, but only a little bit.

Unlike other parents of the day who viewed therapy to be a last resort for the mentally ill, my progressive Jewish mother considered therapy to be a learning experience. For much of my adult life I resented my mother for always sticking me into therapy for no good reason that I could tell. Then, when I was 43 years old, I cornered my mother in the kitchen of my home in Topeka, Kansas, and confronted her with the big question: Why had I been put in psychotherapy from the time I was barely out of diapers? Surely I was no crazier than any other kid on the block.

My mother beamed. "I got it for a dollar," she said.

"You got what for a dollar?" I asked, not registering that she had just answered my question.

"The very best therapists for you and Susan!"

My mother explained that she had obtained a special health insurance policy that allowed my sister, Susan, and me to go to weekly therapy sessions for $1. Susan's psychiatrist was nationally acclaimed in psychoanalytic circles; mine was her disciple. This was definitely a bargain.

"Did I have problems?" I pursued uncertainly.

"Of course," my mother responded reasonably. "Doesn't everyone?"

Giving her children an early start in therapy obviously reflected more than my mother's love for a good bargain. Family therapist Monica McGoldrick, an expert on culture ethnicity, notes that Jews enter therapy more readily than any other cultural group and stay longer, viewing it as an opportunity to understand. In this regard, my mother was true to stereotype.

My mother also went for the best of what she believed to be most important. Although we were poor during much of my growing up years in Brooklyn, my mother made sure that Susan and I had the following four things:

1. A therapist.
2. Good shoes (I don't mean stylish).
3. Firm, quality mattresses.
4. A top pediatrician (none other than Dr. Benjamin Spock, who was also a bargain).

My mother was confident that these four things—along with the values and principles she passed down to us—would provide her daughters with the foundation we needed to "be somebody" and not just "find somebody" as was culturally prescribed at the time.

From an Individual to a Systems Perspective

My mother's penchant for putting me in therapy was surely a factor in my career choice, but not because I had positive experiences. My best therapist before I entered adulthood was a clinical psychologist I started seeing when I was 13. He was kind and empathic, the first adult man who had ever truly listened to me with attention and respect. But he was clueless about the family events that were fueling my problems. Therapists back then focused narrowly and exclusively on the internal conflicts of one "problem person" in the family, in this case, me.

My mother found this therapist for me after she was diagnosed with advanced endometrial cancer at the age of 47. Earlier symptoms had been misdiagnosed as menopause, and she was given a very poor prognosis when the correct diagnosis was finally made. This was the '50s, a time when children were "protected" from painful information and nobody knew what was going on in anyone else's home. No facts were provided about my mother's health problem, although she looked like she was dying.

One reason that secrecy and silence can wield so much negative power is that parents can hide crucial facts from children but not the intensity of feelings surrounding these facts. In my family, for example, my mother's cancer diagnosis could be concealed, but the survival anxiety was in the air. When children sense a disturbance in the field but do not feel free to ask questions, they flounder in unconscious fantasies that cannot be put to rest. In the shadow of secrecy, children are especially vulnerable to acting out or developing symptoms. I certainly volunteered for the job.

In the aftermath of the diagnosis, Susan managed her anxiety by *overfunctioning* (to use the language of family systems theory) and I managed mine by *underfunctioning*. Over time our positions became polarized and rigidly entrenched. The more Susan overfunctioned, the more I underfunctioned. It went like this.

Susan, then a freshman at Barnard College, travelled 3 hours each day on a subway between Brooklyn and Manhattan, returning home to cook, clean, and do everything that needed to be done without complaint. If she felt scared, vulnerable, angry, or bitter, she hid these feelings, even from herself. I, on the other hand, expressed enough of the feelings for the entire family. I became as bad as she was good—creating various scenes, making impossible demands for clothes my family couldn't afford, and messing things up as quickly as my sister was able to clean and straighten them. I engaged in a bit of shoplifting and acted up in school. My parents were informed that I would never be "college material."

My father distanced (a typical male pattern of managing stress), and my mother handled her anxiety by focusing on me. Almost 100 percent of her worry energy went in my direction. She became preoccupied with the thought that I wouldn't make it if she died (Susan, she concluded, would do fine). Although the word *cancer* was never mentioned, I overheard my mother on the phone more than once telling her sister in-law that she was a "fighter" and that for my sake she would not die.

And die she did not, at least not until the age of 94. When asked how she stayed alive against all medical odds, she always gave the same answer. "You see," she explained, as if the answer was logical and merited no further explanation, "I could not die at that time. Harriet needed me. She was such a mess!"

Of course, I resisted any efforts my therapist made to straighten me out. I remained a mess until I felt confident that my mother was out of the woods, not that I made a conscious plan to keep her alive in this way. My point is not that my being a mess really allowed my mother to survive, because many mothers with cancer desperately want to stay alive for their kids and can't. My point is simply that I took on the job in the family of keeping my mother alive by being a mess, just as my sister Susan believed that the integrity of the family depended on her being the all-good daughter who would hide any sign of vulnerability and pain.

None of us, as individuals or as a family, had the benefit of productive therapy so we could talk about what was real. I was the only family member in treatment, and my therapist was clueless about my mother's illness and the anxious family process surrounding my acting out. My mother, for her part, was locked into a position of unutterable isolation and loneliness because even the word *cancer* was unmentionable back then.

This tiny slice of painful family history is obviously a very partial and subjective perspective on how my career chose me. No doubt my deciding to become a clinical psychologist when I was only a few years out of diapers spoke to something quite peculiar in my nature. And countless factors have certainly shaped my career choice. But I do believe that quite early in my life I wanted to fix not only my family, but also the whole business of "treatment" as I knew it firsthand.

The thread that unites all of my work is my desire to help people to speak wisely and well about the most difficult subjects and in the most difficult circumstances. I teach people to identify and understand the relationship patterns that bring us pain, so that we can change our part in them, rather than diagnosing one "problem person" in the system. It's no accident that my academic and popular books take a wide-angle view, pulling back the lens from a narrow focus on individual pathology to take into account the facts of the nuclear family, the extended family, and the culture in which the family is embedded. For this, I owe feminism, Bowen family systems theory, and my own family of origin a great intellectual and emotional debt.

ABANDONING THE FAITH AND DISCOVERING A NEW DIRECTION
Barbara M. Vollmer

Majoring in physics in college was a predictable choice, given my cultural, familial, and personal circumstances. These were the years we watched the *Captain Video and his Video Rangers* on TV, as he and his rangers explored space, and the country heard President John F. Kennedy speak of reaching the moon within a decade, elevating the historical and cultural importance of science.

My parents had encouraged my education, possibly because neither had finished high school. My mom sometimes voiced her disinterest in traditionally female jobs such as teaching. "Who would want to do that?" she would say.

I attended an all-female secondary school run by Hunter College that supported girls' achievement and pursuit of nontraditional careers. In high school, I excelled in and liked math and science. I took an experimental physics course with a textbook that totally engaged me, as it emphasized how ideas were developed and read like a detective story. I became the president of both the math and physics clubs. In hindsight, the fact that I initiated career exploration trips for the physics club and a student survey for the math club may have portended my eventual career.

When I began my undergraduate education at Harpur College, I was looking to study a field that had discovered answers. I looked to experts for their opinions about what direction I should take. I was frustrated when my academic advisor answered my question about whether to take a psychology or physics class with the response, "That is an interesting question!" The definitive answer to my question came when I was waiting in line to register and some upper-class students told me they thought physics was a better major than psychology.

While I pursued this academic path, I also addressed some personal questions. I struggled with my religious and political beliefs, finding many opportunities in my classes and with other students to develop ideas that were different from my parents'. I felt that I was behind in my social development and was dismayed that many of my friends had found a long-term boyfriend or girlfriend within the first month of college! These experiences were unsettling, but I realized that many other students were dealing with similar problems. College life was challenging.

My struggles motivated me to help other students navigate these challenges. I eagerly joined some students in my cohort during the end of my junior year in developing an orientation program for new students. We lamented that we had not been given an orientation to college as new students. In fact, the only thing I remembered was a dean speaking to us. He told us to look to our right and left and predicted that one of the students seated next to us would not graduate! We put together a plan and presented our program to the administration. We were surprised and pleased when we were asked to conduct the college's first orientation program. I loved the experience of joining with others to develop a program that supported students through the transition process that had been so difficult for me.

That same year, I was hired as a residence hall assistant. As a peer helper, my role was to assist students with adapting to dormitory living by answering questions, providing informal counseling, and dealing with crises. One such crisis that occurred my second week on the job was a student's suicide attempt—she borrowed aspirin from everyone on the floor and proceeded to take them while her roommates watched. I was wholly unprepared for anything like this and became newly aware of both my desire to help and my limited skills. I wanted to learn more.

As I approached graduation, I found myself unsure of my future. I had enjoyed my scientific studies, but sometime during my junior year I realized physics did not have all the answers. Courses like atomic physics had begun to feel more like alchemy than truth. I felt no desire to teach physics to students who expressed no interest in it. And as much as I admired one of my professors who wanted to develop a grand unified theory, I did not see myself figuring out some of physics' remaining puzzles.

At the time there was no career guidance offered to students at my university, so I brought my dilemma to the library with the hope that I would find something in physics or a related field that would once again excite me. I remember feeling at home at the library and was delighted that a large section on careers could be found in a sunny section of the second floor. As I pored over the career books, I became disconcerted that nothing in the physical sciences appealed to me. Then I noticed a book about careers in psychology. I had taken a course in psychology as a sophomore and had learned a great deal by training my rat in our weekly lab, but I had not wanted to take additional courses because of the department's emphasis on experimental animal studies. I was told that the psychology faculty thought theories and knowledge about human behavior were not sufficiently scientific to warrant any courses.

As I read about psychology careers, I came across a chapter on graduate programs in college student personnel and counseling. I had no idea such a field existed; the student personnel at my small college were limited to nurses at an infirmary and residence hall directors. The profile of options in this field seemed consistent with my extracurricular activities and my own personal journey in college. At the time, it had not occurred to me that these experiences were paving the way for a career. Working with and supporting students taught me that I was motivated to help others, that I liked creating programs for this purpose, and that I enjoyed working with a team. My slowly unfolding revelation culminated in my realization that I had also liked many of the social science courses I had taken. Ironically, in searching for answers, I had learned not only to tolerate but also to develop an interest in the questions themselves, the process of asking. It seemed to me that it was acceptable and worthwhile to study a subject that posed significant questions about human behavior that had not been answered.

However, I was anxious about considering a change that felt akin to "abandoning the faith." I had devoted so much energy to my major, and physical sciences were still the most applauded disciplines to study. I was nervous about telling others about my ideas about changing my career direction. My physics advisor was supportive and confided that, as a department head, he was more of a college administrator than a pure scientist. My family, who knew little about graduate school, as usual assumed that I knew what I was doing.

The following year, my graduate work in counseling psychology and student personnel work began at Ohio State University. Fortunately, the director of the program, Maude Stewart, had been a mathematician and understood my motivation about changing career direction. I found I enjoyed the experience of counseling, that it was just as absorbing as any physics problem had been. My personal experiences in college had motivated me to want to work with students as a lifelong goal.

That moment in the library jump-started my more than 40 years of experience as a psychologist. I have worked as a counselor, a supervisor, a director of two university counseling centers (and at times career centers), and presently, a counseling psychology faculty member. When I made the transition to an academic position, I created a training clinic with a reflecting team and began two long-term research projects on questions that had aroused my curiosity as a counselor and supervisor.

I am continually inspired by the ideas and projects of my colleagues. Belonging to professional associations and attending workshops and trainings further my passion and my growth as a counselor and educator. Working with others on a team has made developing programs and research projects especially enjoyable.

Since that day in the library, I have not looked back with regret at the physics career I might have had, though I still enjoy learning about advancements in the field. My work now addresses such questions as how client choice of therapy affects outcome, how to assist clients in emotionally abusive relationships, and not surprisingly, how women take on nontraditional gender roles. These questions lead not only to answers but, often, also to more questions. I find that very satisfying.

ONE HOUR OF CAREER COUNSELING AND 30 YEARS OF INFLUENCE
Cynthia McRae

I began the doctoral program in counseling psychology at the University of Iowa in 1980, having had one boring undergraduate class in psychology more than 10 years earlier, where I scraped by with a low B. What was I doing in this doctoral program in psychology?

My qualifications consisted of good undergraduate grades (aside from the aforementioned psych class and a C in swimming), good Graduate Record Examination (GRE) scores, reasonable social skills, and knowing professors in the program because I was a secretary at the University Counseling Service (UCS) at Iowa. Did my marginal secretarial skills increase my attractiveness as a potential student because if I left they could find a better one? I never inquired.

When I decided to go back to graduate school in music in 1979, I began work as a secretary at UCS to pay for school. There I was exposed to the world of counseling psychology. I was not a great secretary, but I did enjoy the counseling environment, respecting the clients who came for help and the psychologists and practicum students who offered services. I learned a lot as I copied articles and typed all sorts of things for staff. The environment reminded me of my previous life as a clergy wife and the years I had already spent listening to and caring for people, albeit in another capacity.

When I realized that getting an advanced degree in playing the flute was not going to provide the stable financial future that I needed for my family, I asked Ursula Delworth, director of UCS at the time, if I could take some of the vocational tests I saw other people taking. As a secretary I knew lots of students came in for career counseling, and I assumed it was effective. It was available, it seemed interesting, and I could use some help. I had every confidence in my academic ability, and I knew my calling did not lie in being a secretary for very long, so I had nothing to lose and everything to gain. After I took the Strong–Campbell Interest Inventory, as it was known then, the person interpreting the results suggested that my interests on the profile matched the interests of persons in psychology or counseling. She asked if I minded going to school for a long time! At that time in my life, I thought one of my only strengths was in the realm of academics, so going to school for years was a great match for me. I had considered medical school, which meant at least 2 years of undergraduate science courses, so I thought that getting a PhD would be the shorter route. Little did I know! After considering my options, I applied to the counseling psychology program and was accepted.

This one session of career counseling was a "defining moment" for me. In the short term, this moment led to my applying to the counseling psychology program at Iowa. It showed me that vocational assessment could indeed provide helpful information and be of great benefit to a person seeking guidance. I also realized that having a caring, knowledgeable person to interpret results and provide information and support was very valuable.

During graduate school, I had the privilege of being a teaching assistant for Dave Jepsen, the faculty member who specialized in vocational psychology. Over 4 years, I taught many sections of an undergraduate class titled "Making a Vocational/ Education Choice." I loved it! And as Dave said, I'd had many careers by the time I taught the course. I had been a musician, teacher, clergy wife, mother, secretary, and graduate student. I found that teaching this class was very helpful in many ways. For example, through administering and interpreting the Strong every semester for all those classes, I learned that my Holland code indicated I had *no* interests or strengths related to "C," Conventional. No wonder I had been such an ungifted secretary!

When I began as an assistant professor at the University of Denver (DU) in 1988, I initiated a career course for undergraduates modeled on the one at Iowa. With Dave's help and the support of the College of Education at DU, I created the course to meet the needs of the students there. It continues to be fully enrolled each quarter it is taught.

Although the focus of my research and career over the years has been in the area of health psychology rather than vocational psychology, my early defining moment continues to play an important part in my life and career. In 2008 I was asked to host a man from Uganda who was visiting Denver to attend a conference for development officers of international universities. I was told he was vice president of his university. I was happy to have him as a guest, and during his several days with me, I learned about his university and about their master's in counseling psychology program. Because his wife has a master's degree in counseling, he was well informed about the professions of counseling and psychology in Uganda and what is needed to build up the counselor training program at his university. In particular, he mentioned the need for training in the area of career counseling in Uganda. The wheels began turning as I thought back to my defining moment and about my long-term interest and experience in career counseling and vocational choice. As we continued to talk, he remembered that the director of the counseling psychology program was in the United States at the same time. A few days later I received a call from the director, who just happened to be in Denver visiting friends. She came to my office later that afternoon, and we discussed the possibility of my coming to teach career counseling to master's students in Uganda.

Now I am tentatively scheduled to go to Uganda during my sabbatical in 2010 to teach career counseling and to make other research and teaching contributions. Having taught briefly in Uganda 2 years ago, I know that I need to learn more about how to teach this subject in a way that will be useful and meaningful to the students. That's part of the adventure, isn't it? This privilege of continuing to learn and grow and teach and share began with one defining moment in 1980. It has shaped my life, and I am very grateful.

ON BEING CALLED TO COUNSELING
Bryan J. Dik

My journey into counseling is laden with ironies. Perhaps the most significant is that the focus of my counseling work—helping clients identify and pursue their callings in life—grew out of significant challenges I experienced identifying my own calling. As an undergraduate student, I was interested in all kinds of things. I knew that I wanted to help people, I enjoyed writing, and I didn't mind school. However, to say I had difficulty narrowing things down would be an understatement. I don't remember actually getting letters from the registrar saying that I was overdue in declaring a major, but that might have happened. I was chronically undecided. Many undecided college students struggle to identify things they intrinsically enjoy. I had the opposite problem: I couldn't bear the thought of having to decide against options that were really appealing to me, and a *lot* of options were really appealing to me. As a person of faith, I was primed to approach career decision making as part of a process of discerning God's will for my life. Yet after months of bathing the matter in prayer, I had not received the burning-bush–type sign I had expected. I made an appointment for career counseling. The experience, strange though it was, had a focusing effect on my career path. Part of my discussion with the counselor included an interchange that went something like this:

Counselor: We can look at test results, but think about my job for a minute. I get
 to be creative and help people all day long. What do you think about
 what I do?
Me: I've been considering it.
Counselor: Do you have a good grade point average?
Me: I've been doing pretty well.
Counselor: Why not get your PhD in counseling psychology?

Twenty minutes later I was in my dorm room calling my parents to tell them I had decided what I was going to do with my career. This was perhaps the last strategy I would ever recommend a counselor use with clients—in retrospect it seems bizarre—but it gave me what I needed at the time: permission, assurance, a vote of confidence. I had spent plenty of time investigating psychology in general and counseling psychology in particular—this was not an uninformed choice that was made out of the blue. Yet I needed the extra nudge to make it. Of course, part of what I knew about counseling psychology was that people do all sorts of different things with the degree, so choosing this path actually meant delaying the "real" decision for another several years. I cannot deny that this was part of my motivation at the time. Thus, I set out on the path toward becoming a counseling psychologist, and discerning my calling continued to be a central developmental task in my life.

While starting to see clients with career concerns as a graduate student counselor, I repeatedly heard expressions of wanting to find meaning in work. Many clients used the word *calling* as they explored these concerns. I threw myself into helping these clients with their career decisions—some of them directionless college students, many of them middle-aged workers miserable with their career paths—and simultaneously I was acutely aware of my own struggles with discerning the next steps in my career. Initially, it felt very unsettling to be working so hard to help others navigate the very issues I struggled with so mightily. I vacillated between feeling fraudulent on the one hand and recognizing my special insight into their challenges on the other. (How's that for a reframe?) Increasingly, I began to resonate with the "wounded healer" motif. Like a family therapist with a dysfunctional family or a dysthymic specialist in depression, I could help people find their way even as I felt like I was stumbling around in the dark in my own career path.

A defining moment for me occurred in an unexpected place. I had started to delve into the psychological literature on calling and vocation. I undertook this task for my clients, sure, but also for myself. There was surprisingly little there—a few theoretical essays, a few brief empirical studies, one *Journal of Research in Personality* article (Wrzesniewski, McCauley, Rozin, & Swartz, 1997) that got a lot of press but that, naturally, raised more questions than it answered. I was frustrated. One night I started to read a worn copy of a 1990 paperback by philosopher Lee Hardy called *The Fabric of This World: Inquiries Into Calling, Career Choice, and the Design of Human Work*. It may be an overstatement to say that an academic book could ever change the direction of a person's life in one reading, but in retrospect, this may well have happened to me. I vividly remember pacing back and forth in the galley kitchen of the small apartment I shared with my wife, book in hand. I poured over Hardy's work: his overview of the role of work in human life; his description of how historic approaches to calling and vocation could translate into the design of human work today; his treatment of job choice and critique of modern management theory. These ideas resonated with me. I marked up the margins so much my pen nearly dried out. The book's spine started to crack in the chapters to which I kept coming back. I was absorbed and intensely focused; my sense of time was distorted—Csíkszentmihályi (1990) could have used this event to illustrate his concept of *flow*.°

Inexplicably, I began to generate an unfamiliarly large volume of ideas for how calling might fit within the context of theory and research in vocational psychology and for how calling could be incorporated into career counseling. I couldn't write them down as fast as they entered my mind. It was so effortless I honestly cannot take credit for it. It was invigorating. As my hypomania started to abate and my stream of creative consciousness gave way to my usual plodding thoughts, I was left with a very clear sense of purpose. My own calling started to crystallize. David Myers (2007), a social psychologist, has described some of his book projects as the result of a question: If I didn't write it, who would? I found myself asking a similar question: If I didn't initiate research on calling and vocation or work out calling-based counseling strategies, who would? So I decided I should take my scientist–practitioner identity into the academic world.

My primary role is as a faculty member, but I still maintain a part-time practice that specializes in vocational assessment and counseling. From the time of my defining moment onward, my work with clients improved. I became a more grounded clinician. Before, my work probably consisted of a loosely theoretically guided process of trial and error, but I now had context. The process was no longer about doing what I could to help people steer themselves away from indecision and toward resolution. Instead, I viewed the process as helping clients identify their gifts and use their strengths to experience meaning in their work—and maybe to make the world, in big or small ways, a better place.

° Csíkszentmihályi (1990) describes flow as a state marked by energized focus and full psychological involvement, typified by nine indicators: clear goals, intense concentration and focus, decreased self-consciousness, a distorted sense of time, direct and immediate feedback, balance between ability and challenge, a sense of mastery, a high level of intrinsic reward, and the experience of absorption.

References

Csíkszentmihályi, M. (1990). *Flow: The psychology of optimal experience*. New York: Harper and Row.

Hardy, L. (1990). *The fabric of this world: Inquiries into calling, career choice, and the design of human work*. Grand Rapids, MI: Eerdmans.

Myers, D. G. (2007). Teaching psychological science through writing. *Teaching of Psychology, 34*, 77–84.

Wrzesniewski, A., McCauley, C., Rozin, P., & Schwartz, B. (1997). Jobs, careers, and callings: People's relations to their work. *Journal of Research in Personality, 31*, 21–33.

MINDFULNESS AND MY SEARCH FOR MEANING
John Chambers Christopher

I took my first yoga class when I was a sophomore at the University of Michigan in Ann Arbor. It blew my mind. In that first class, our instructor, Luis Sfeir-Younis, led us through a conscious relaxation exercise. In the middle of the relaxation I felt a rush of energy through my body moving upwards until it felt as if my head was exploding. The sensation was accompanied by a wave of joy so powerful that tears began to stream down my face. I had no words or concepts to describe what was happening, but it didn't matter. What mattered was the sense of connection, the sense of unity, the sense of peace, the sense of rightness. I don't know how long the state lasted, whether 2 minutes or 5, but I emerged from it with the certainty that this was something I had been looking for and needed to pursue, and in retrospect, this was a defining moment. I began taking yoga classes four times a week.

The style of yoga that I had started with was much slower and more meditative than much of the yoga currently taught in America. In addition, it focused on teaching the complete eight limbs of yoga, which include philosophy and meditation, and not just asana practice (postures). I found, somewhat to my surprise, that my life began to change in ways I had longed for but could not have articulated. More importantly, I began to experience an unexpected sense of hopefulness. This hopefulness increased with the growing ability to observe or witness my thoughts and emotions. Through the practices I began to first experience and then to identify with a part of myself that was conscious of my body, feelings, and thoughts but that was deeper than any of these.

I had struggled with depression since junior high school. This struggle manifested as both self-loathing and as a kind of despair about the world, an experience, I later learned, that Victor Frankl (1967) termed the "existential vacuum." My awareness of the larger world around me started to develop in the early 1970s when my age began to be measured in double digits. Not unlike the current times, the United States was then facing multiple problems that seemed to pervade every area of life. From Vietnam to Watergate to pollution and environmental degradation, the energy crisis, and the economy, there were few indications that America was headed in a positive direction. I experienced the meaninglessness of both the upper middle-class American lifestyle and the sociopolitical status quo and longed for a way of living that was more compelling, more in balance, and more sustainable. To deal with these problems and to try to bring about social change,

I dedicated myself to studying other cultural traditions to see if they might offer resources for thinking about meaning and healing.

I found that the yoga, meditation, and other mindfulness practices began to ease my depression; bouts of depression were neither as deep nor as long as they had been. I started to take my depressive thoughts and feelings less seriously, and I was able to rouse myself out of the heaviness of depressive energy and at least do some activity, like hatha yoga. I also found that my chronic back pain became easier to tolerate and that I became a better student. I noticed that I was able to concentrate when I was studying or attending class, resulting in being a more efficient and effective student. All of these experiences deepened my commitment to mindfulness practice and left me wanting to share what I had learned with others. To this end I pursued yoga teacher training.

At the time, I didn't see room for things like yoga and meditation in the world of counseling. Between the marginalization of mindfulness practices by mainstream psychology until recently and the fact that my own experiences with a psychiatrist and a social worker had been quite disappointing, it did not occur to me for some time to enter counseling as a profession. Eventually, when I did join the profession, it was with the intent of focusing on issues of identity and meaning from an existential perspective. As I was going through graduate school, first at Harvard and then at the University of Texas, my spiritual practices remained important to me—a way of practicing self-care—but they were, with few exceptions, not a part of my life that I could bring into my classes or clinical training. Leading stress-reduction groups as an intern was something of an exception, but I felt that the exercises were watered down in comparison with the power of indigenous mindfulness practices in their unadulterated form. So, for me, mindfulness practice and psychotherapy remained in two separate worlds. Although they were connected internally by my own awareness of how both could foster meaning, transformation, and healing, I did not see a way to integrate or introduce mindfulness practices into my psychotherapy practice or into my training of counseling students.

Mindfulness practices were, however, related to my scholarship in cultural psychology and theoretical and philosophical psychology. I found that my experiences with mindfulness practices, coupled with my experiences with traditional healers in non-Western parts of the world, gave me a vantage point to critique the individualistic and dualistic underpinnings (e.g., mind–body, fact–value, subject–object, self–culture–society, reason–emotion) of Western psychology and to work toward developing alternatives that were more culturally sensitive and inclusive.

As an interpersonally oriented therapist, I was concerned that if I introduced yoga or meditation or *qigong*° into my therapy sessions, I would be cast into a teacher role. I felt this shift could interfere with the interpersonal dynamics and my clients coming to trust their own emerging inner voices. Mindfulness practices, however, did affect how I thought about the therapy process and the ways I was present in the room. Perhaps most importantly, mindfulness practices helped me

---

° Qigong is ancient Chinese practice of which Tai Chi is a specialized form. Qigong means the cultivation and circulation of qi (or chi), which is the vital life force that is central to Chinese medicine and cosmology.

to sit with my clients, to be fully present with them in the midst of their pain and suffering. I found that I could watch my own reactivity in session and not act on it. I became increasingly better able to tolerate the ambiguity and uncertainty that is such a large part of counseling and to just observe my own tendencies to believe I should always know what is going on or that it is my responsibility to do something to end the client's pain. But even more, I think that when a counselor is more fully present, clients have the space to explore themselves and to allow new experiences to emerge. Winnicott (1965) describes "good enough mothering" as avoiding the twin perils of abandonment and intrusiveness (impingements). Therapy seems akin in that we provide space while maintaining contact.

Mindfulness practices also provided me with ways of taking care of myself and preventing burnout. I learned through meditation that I could just allow experiences to move through me. I do *not* mean "moving through" in the sense of moving through to get rid of. Rather, moving through in the sense of not resisting, not putting up walls around seemingly negative experiences and emotions, but giving them space and being a good host, to use the mystic poet Rumi's metaphor from "The Guest House" (Barks, 2005). At the end of those days or sessions that felt tiring, burdensome, deadening, I would allow myself some time for the residuals that seemed stuck in my body to manifest themselves and to have access to my consciousness. Often this would be accompanied by tears, but then a sense of having been cleansed, of the heaviness lifting. Through yoga I learned when I was "efforting" or unnecessarily expending energy or tension to accomplish something. Noticing the state of my body when sitting with clients gave me indicators of when I was becoming tense, when I was trying too hard in session, when I was getting attached to a particular outcome. Mindfulness practices helped to foster the kind of openness to the client's experience that we hold out as an ideal in therapy but often don't have good ways of teaching our counseling students how to do—the best students seem to already have that ability and often the weaker ones never develop it.

Ten years ago, the external separation between my psychotherapy and spiritual practices dramatically changed. Sheila Devitt, a nurse at Student Health Services at Montana State University, took the professional training in mindfulness-based stress reduction (MBSR) by Jon Kabat-Zinn and Saki Santorelli. Sheila ran into a good friend of mine from graduate school who told her she should look me up when she returned. Sheila called me and after a very brief introduction said, "I think we're supposed to work together." Naturally, this grabbed my attention, and as soon as she explained how MBSR used a group format to teach mindfulness practices, I was hooked. Sheila and I began running MBSR groups at the Bozeman Hospital. Then one of my colleagues pointed out that in our counselor training program (as in most others), we do not address student self-care and that I might consider developing a class around the MBSR approach. The course, Mind–Body Medicine and the Art of Self-Care, has been more successful in terms of impact on the students than I could have dreamed. As a result, I began a new line of research into the effects of mindfulness practices on counselor training (Chrisman, Christopher, & Lichtenstein, 2009; Christopher, Christopher, Dunnagan, & Schure, 2006; Newsome, Christopher, Dahlen, & Christopher, 2006; Schure, Christopher, &

Christopher, 2008). These two disparate passions in my life, mindfulness practice and counselor training, have come together in ways I could never have predicted. And this journey began with one defining moment, what I later learned was the *peak experience* (Maslow, 1968) that occurred in my first yoga class with Luis.

References

Barks, C. (2005). *Rumi: The book of love: Poems of ecstasy and longing*. New York: Harper.

Chrisman, J.A., Christopher, J.C., & Lichtenstein, S.J. (2009). Qigong as a mindfulness practice for counsleing students: A qualitative study. *Journal of Humanistic Psychology*, 236-257.

Christopher, J.C., Christopher, S.E., Dunnagan, T., & Schure, M. (2006). Teaching self-care through mindfulness practices: The application of yoga, meditation, and qigong to counselor training. *Journal of Humanistic Psychology*, 494-509.

Frankl, V.E. (1967). *Psychotherapy and existentialism: Selected papers on logotherapy*. New York: Touchstone Books.

Maslow, A.H. (1968). *Toward a psychology of being*. New York: D. Van Nostrand.

Newsome, S., Christopher, J.C., Dahlen, P., & Christopher, S. (2006). Teaching counselors self-care through mindfulness practices. *Teachers College Record*, 1881-1900.

Schure, M. B., Christopher, J., & Christopher, S. (2008). Mind-body medicine and the art of self-care: Teaching mindfulness to counseling students through yoga, meditation, and qigong. *Journal of Counseling & Development*, 47-56.

Winnicott, D.W. (1965). *The maturational process and the facilitating environment*. Madison, CT: International Universities Press.

FENWAY
Michael T. Starkey

For my dad.

I was 11 years old and watching batting practice at a Boston Red Sox game when a foul ball struck me in the head. Moments earlier, my dad had left to buy us hot-dogs, and I descended the stairs, friends at my side, eager to scoop up as many autographs as possible. The ballpark was alive with baseball—the crack of the bat, the smell of freshly cut grass, vendors yelling, "Hot dogs! Cracker Jack! Peanuts!" I brought my mitt that day to catch any foul ball that came my way. I could tell it was going to be a good day.

When it happened, I was leaning over the fence, excitedly watching my favorite players, eyeing Roger Clemens for a chance to ask for an autograph. The next thing I knew, I was on the floor, looking up at a crowd of players and fans, my dad at my side, and then I blacked out again. I briefly remember waking up in the ambulance asking for my dad, my voice barely above a whisper. He acknowledged his presence—"I'm right here, son"—and squeezed my hand as I slipped back into unconsciousness. I spent three days in intensive care with a cracked skull and bleeding in my brain. The voices of doctors and nurses boomed over the intercom; the vital signs monitor beeped at my side. It was one of the only reminders that I was still alive. I spent my days in and out of computed tomography (CT) scans, listening to the whirr of the machine as it took pictures of my brain. I heard talk that the doctors planned to operate on my brain, to evict the stubborn clot. I was scared. I couldn't put words to this fear, but I knew I wanted very badly to live, that I didn't like the sense of unknowing that circulated around me.

That day—June 4, 1989—haunted me for years. After I recovered, I would try to make sense out of death. My early adolescent years were filled with fear. It was not the kind of fear you experience when startled, when walking alone in dark woods. The breaking tree branches and leaves that crunch below your feet give rise to intensified alertness, a pounding heart, and increased respiration. But, as you emerge from the woods, this fear dissipates; it excites even. My fear was different; it was fear that struck at the core of my being; it was dread, and it was constant. I now knew, really knew, that life ended, and I could not shake that anxiety. I feared sleep even, worried that if I closed my eyes I'd never wake up again. Every night, I kept a glassful of water next to my bed, splashing my face if I felt my eyes getting heavy. Those nights were long and lonely, and it was only after sheer exhaustion that I would crash into sleep. The debilitating terror slowly resolved itself—I'm still unsure what led to its resolution—but I was forever affected. Not until I was an adult did I realize the impact of this experience on me. I began to see that life, in the face of death, is vibrant, mysterious, and meaningful.

What happened to me when I was 11 years old is just one part of my complex life narrative, that collection of stories that make up who I am. As humans, we all have stories to which we have given meaning, and it is the culmination of these that weave together the fibers of our being. That particular story, though, largely informed how I chose to view life, how I dealt with pain, and how I chose my vocation. At times, I felt like an outsider: I did not think my friends shared my fears; my parents and my brother slept soundly while I forced insomnia, and everyone around me seemed content. And I was too scared to ask if my concerns were normal. So I kept them quiet.

During those years, I asked life's questions: Why do we die? Why do we live? Does this all really matter? I demanded answers, but none came. The more I asked, the more I searched, it seemed like the more the answers eluded me. But I kept searching, and I searched for a very long time. My search brought a passion for psychology as an undergraduate and a concentrated effort to get into graduate school. It was there I found what I was looking for: existential psychotherapy. I learned that the fears I experienced as a child—death, isolation, meaninglessness—were common and even root concerns for every person. I learned that no one is immune to our existence's harsh realities and that psychic pain manifested from a confrontation with death, freedom, isolation, and meaninglessness. I finally felt normal. This discovery spawned an intense passion for doing psychotherapy.

I feel privileged to be a psychotherapist. When we listen closely to each other's stories, we bear witness to what it means to be alive, and every session with a client allows me that witness. I have listened to countless stories, each one pulsating with life. One client told me about the shame that comes with being an unwanted child; another shared the unspeakable grief over a best friend's death; another, the terror of cancer and the glory of conquering it. Their stories are of struggle, of strife, of triumph, of joy. My clients' stories inspire me, enlighten me, frighten me. They remind me of my own humanness, my own state of being.

One of the most powerful things I offer my clients is to sit with them, listening to and understanding their stories. If I really listen, really understand, my clients know they matter to me, that their stories—and their beings—have value. This is where my life narrative comes into play: I can truly understand another person's stories of suffering, joy, hardship, and triumph, because I have my own similar stories. Our stories—the universality of them—are what connect us. Indeed, existential psychotherapist Irvin Yalom (1989) writes, "We are, all of us, in this together" (p. 14). I find this sense of the universal incredibly satisfying. And that is why I am a psychotherapist.

Reference

Yalom, I.D. (1989). *Love's executioner.* New York: Basic Books.

AN UNOBSTRUCTED VIEW
Anonymous

Ten years ago I tried to end my life. Not many people know this about me.

Attempting suicide did not directly influence my later decision to become a therapist. But it did alter my perspective—as a person and as a clinician—in a way that I cannot take back. It taught me from the inside out about the fragile balance that depressed individuals sometimes maintain between life and death, hope and despair, moving forward and ceasing all motion. Gaining distance from the attempt taught me that depression can be insidious and that it lies. It tells people that all hope is lost, that there is no meaning in life, that there is no point in going on, that no one understands.

I struggled with depression off and on throughout my adolescence and into adulthood. In the past, depression cast a shadow over my life, at times obscuring my view, not only of the future but also of the vista spread out right in front of me. Being depressed was like stumbling through a dense fog, barely able to make out my hands in front of my face. I bumped into an awful lot of things along the way because I just couldn't see straight.

When I went to college, the slow burn of depression that had constituted the undercurrent of my teenage years flared up into a conflagration that threatened to obliterate me. It felt at once foreign and familiar. Depression reassuringly slung its arm over my shoulder like an old companion and reminded me that I was used to feeling this way—that sadness, loneliness, and hopelessness are a part of life, or of my life at least. At the same time, this particular bout with a familiar demon felt different. It was more intense, and it had me in a chokehold before I knew what had happened. Depression lodged itself firmly in my line of sight, narrowing my vision to a dark tunnel until I started to think, "I will never feel better. This is too much. If this is life, I don't want any part of it. I want out. I want to die."

That last one caught me unawares. It's not that I hadn't thought about suicide previously. I had, but it had been bound up with teenage angst and, as with most things teenaged, was therefore more drama than substance. This time the thoughts stared me down and would not leave. I couldn't stop thinking about killing myself.

At my boyfriend's urging, I made an appointment with a therapist at the university counseling center. Meeting with a therapist for the first time can be a bizarre experience. The general expectation to spill your guts to a complete stranger, although not necessarily accurate, is present and daunting. Eventually I told my therapist about feeling depressed, about the energy it took to achieve what should have been the simplest of tasks, of my urgent thoughts about suicide. One day he looked at me and said, "Laura, you're profoundly depressed." His words dropped like anvils in my lap. They felt *heavy*. Though I don't remember precisely how I responded, I imagine I backpedaled that day, strongly in the habit of softening my moods for others. But his words stayed with me. They also allowed me to let go of some of the guilt I was carrying for not being able to beat depression on my own. It was oddly freeing.

I got better. I went on to graduate school, got married, and found a good job at a university library. And then, as often is the case with the cyclical beast of depression, I got worse. When asked how he went bankrupt, a character in Ernest Hemingway's *The Sun Also Rises* explains that it happened gradually, then suddenly. The reappearance of depression in my life was like that. I struggled more and more to keep it together in front of my friends and colleagues and eventually became inundated with thoughts of suicide. And then one day, everything fell apart—gradually, then suddenly. I stayed home from work, wrote a brief note to my husband, swallowed every pill I could find, and laid down on the couch.

I woke up in the ICU.

People seem to be fond of saying that it's always darkest before the dawn. I usually cringe at these kinds of pat metaphors, so it's with some difficulty that I admit that this was (eventually) the case for me. I traveled a bumpy road to recovery following my suicide attempt, but with time I learned to anticipate depression before it fully reared its ugly head. I learned how to temper it, how to tame it. For me, the metaphorical dawn came years down the road when I decided that I could do more good in this world as a therapist than as a librarian. Making this decision infused my life with new meaning.

There are some who will say that having attempted suicide uniquely disqualifies me from practicing as a mental health professional—that my judgment will be too clouded, or perhaps my own mental health too compromised to be able to competently help others. Or that I have chosen to pursue this line of work for the sole purpose of working out my own issues. I can't deny that I have sought to learn more about depression and suicide through research and my clinical work.

There are also others who might say that my experiences with depression and my suicide attempt afford me a heightened sensitivity or increased capacity to understand the despair and hopelessness that can go hand in hand with depression. Like every other imperfect clinician, I try not to let my own past issues stand between my clients and effective treatment. My clinical supervisors and peer consultants have helped me to be watchful for potential countertransference issues. I have also periodically sought my own therapy over the years, in part to help me remain mindful of everything that I bring to the therapeutic relationship.

Living with a suicidal depression and attempting suicide has obviously influenced my own work with clients. In some ways, I think it instilled in me a deep calm. Clients have remarked to me that I have a calming presence amidst the chaotic mishmash of depression, anxiety, and suicidal thoughts that they sometimes bring to our sessions. The long process of succumbing to and then emerging from the other side of a suicide attempt also taught me that, in some ways, the ability to see clearly can be antithetical to feeling depressed.

Looking back, I recognize that when I was depressed, I suffered from the kind of myopia that caused me to miss the forest, not because I was focused on individual trees but because I was scrutinizing the same square foot of bark in front of my face over and over again. When I attempted suicide, I surrendered to this shortsightedness wrought by depression. It had obstructed my view to the point where all alternatives, other than self-destruction, were excluded. Though I didn't know it at the time, I couldn't see clearly.

Edwin Shneidman (1996), the premier suicidologist, aptly called this kind of depressive tunnel vision *cognitive constriction*. It is now a familiar presence in my sessions with depressed clients. I hear them utter versions of "There is nothing worth living for" and "I'm never going to feel better," and I recognize the voice of depression speaking through them. I see the map for therapy with these clients as consisting of two major portions: (1) building a connection and (2) making room for multiple perspectives, multiple possibilities. For the client who is convinced that she is unable to connect with others, there is room for the possibility that there are indeed others who care about her. For the client who believes that the only way to deal with his emotional pain is through suicide, there is room for the possibility that he will not always feel this way. I don't try to reason others out of their despair. Remembering how healing it can be to simply feel heard, I listen to and empathize with their pain. And I challenge them to allow for the possibility that there is something more, or something different from what they are currently thinking or feeling. Together, we work to seek out exceptions and alternate plots within their lives.

For me, this process of learning to see clearly meant learning how to step outside of myself long enough to appreciate that depression is neither omniscient nor omnipresent. It is not, nor has it ever been, the essence of me. Learning to see clearly meant coming to the conclusion that I can experience suffering without allowing it to consume me, that these things ebb and flow. Therapy and training in mindfulness meditation helped a lot with this. So did envisioning someone outside of my head looking in and sorting through my thoughts: These are influenced by depression; these are not. More than one cognitive therapist (and more than one Buddhist) has observed that just because you think a thought doesn't mean it's true. It took me a long time to learn this, longer to understand it, and I'm still working on living it. It's one of the fundamental lessons I try to impart to my clients.

I learned a lot about life after I approached death—more than I can write about in this short narrative. Right now I can say that, when I was feeling out of sorts, I learned to try to back up and change my perspective. I'm not sitting in the cheap seats anymore, the ones with the obstructed view. Most days I can see a lot more clearly. I have a sharper appreciation for little things, like the feeling of warm sunlight on the back of my neck or the chance to snuggle up with my child to read a story. To me, this is clarity. And I feel honored, as a therapist, to help others seek out their own versions of clarity.

Reference

Shneidman, E.S. (1996). *The suicidal mind.* New York: Oxford University Press.

CHAPTER SUMMARY

The Lay Helper phase, or the period of time before actually entering the counseling profession as a student, is representative of a wide array of experiences. Sometimes in this phase, we see the first little signs that one is destined to be a helper—a lay helper can be the 8-year-old child who tries to comfort another child on the playground or the 50-year-old grandparent who delivers meals to the homebound through church. At other times, there is the decision one makes to enter the counseling field, thus leading to the transition to the Beginning Student phase—a lay helper can be a physics major or a veterinary technician who is considering a career change. While this phase showcases greater diversity than many of the other phases, there seem to be some common themes. These themes become evident as the authors reflect on experiences prior to starting their paths to becoming counselors.

The Context

One of the most prevalent themes in this phase seems to be related to a larger social, cultural, political, familial, and historical context. Almost every author in this chapter provides a setting, or background, for his or her narrative. Some provide information about the historical and sociopolitical happenings of the time of their own defining moment to set the scene. Christopher mentions Vietnam and Watergate. Nutt shares her experience as a Peace Corps volunteer in the mid '60s. Shelton discusses observing racism, sexism, and classism in West Virginia, and Vollmer attributes her interest in physics partially to hearing Kennedy speak about reaching the moon.

Some provide information about their own cultural backgrounds that helps us understand their experiences. Leclerc says that her parents, who experienced the German occupation of France, "epitomized" the resistance of Freud and psychotherapy. Lerner talks about growing up in a poor Jewish family in Brooklyn. Lenox shares that he grew up gay in the conservative Midwest in the late '70s and early '80s. Shelton provides a vivid image of being a child and seeing her grandmother "belittled for being Black, uneducated, and poor," and Tung talks about growing up the child of a single parent in conservative Taiwanese society. It seems that this phase, more than the others, takes the authors "back" to a time that was different enough from today, or different enough from current mainstream U.S. culture, that they need to clarify for us how this influenced their development. Because the Lay Helper phase encompasses the early years of childhood and adolescent development, those whose defining moments are in this phase may need to share the importance of a different cultural period in time with us.

The Family

Family influences also seem to have a significant impact on authors who focused on this phase of their development. Leclerc mentions her family's disapproval of psychology. Lerner shares how her mother felt that therapy was very positive for a child—a "learning experience" and a bargain. Lenox was encouraged by his parents to attend therapy. Shelton discusses how growing up close to her grandmother helped her "find her voice." Tung writes about her relationship with her father, finding the ability to forgive and applying that in therapy. Perhaps we can attribute this emphasis on family dynamics to the fact that the lay helper is typically (but not always) younger—or perhaps the family is most influential in this phase, when the person may not yet have entered college.

The Meaning and the Calling

Lay helpers, again possibly due to the typically younger age, may experience existential concerns and a desire to find meaning, to make meaning, or to find a calling. In this chapter, two authors discuss how the search for meaning influenced their development. Christopher writes about his journey to find meaning that was spurred by the first yoga class he ever took. Starkey was inspired to explore existential psychology because of a close call with death as a child. He discusses how "trying to make sense" of life and death came from a specific childhood event.

A few authors wrote of finding "a calling" in counseling. McRae and Dik write of career counseling sessions that helped pinpoint counseling as a vocation worth pursuing. One author, Vollmer, did not have career counseling assistance but found a book in the library that opened her eyes to counseling psychology. Yet others, such as Lerner and Shelton, knew from childhood that they were destined to be counselors.

The Client

One of the most striking themes that arose for the lay helper in this chapter is that of experiencing therapy as a client or of dealing with one's own issues related to mental health. Several authors describe their own personal experiences as clients—the good, the challenging, the disappointing. We have an anonymous contributor who shares experiences related to depression and a near-death experience that continues to shape her ability to work with depressed clients. McRae and Dik experience career counseling as life changing. Lenox talks about his experience with conversion therapy and being labeled a "failure." Leclerc says that one question from a psychologist had an impact "that endures to this day."

QUESTIONS

1. Some authors in this chapter knew from early childhood that they wanted to be therapists; others found their calling to the field of counseling through career counseling sessions. Many make their way to counseling as a profession after years of journeying and exploration. How did you make the decision to pursue a career in counseling?

2. (For personal reflection only; sharing in a class environment should be voluntary and optional.) Several authors discuss their own personal challenges and mental health issues. If you have participated in therapy as a client, how did this affect your personal or professional development as a counselor?

3. Several authors mention family dynamics in their narratives in this phase. How has your family influenced (or not) your decision to be a counselor? How have family dynamics influenced who you are as a person and a therapist?

4. Lenox writes about feeling like a therapy "failure" when he was a client. How do you discuss (or not) goal setting and achievement of goals with clients? Is it important for clients to feel that they are successful in therapy?

5. Nutt discusses her experience in the Peace Corps as life changing and enhancing her ability to see both "differences and core similarities" in people. Have you had any cross-cultural experiences that were influential? How do they affect your work as a therapist?

3

The Beginning Student Phase

*T*he beginning student is starting his or her professional training career in a helping field. This is an exciting and vulnerable period in the development of counselors. Entry into graduate school is coupled with the growing acknowledgment that the methods of the lay helper phase are perhaps no longer appropriate or valid. Eager to master newly learned theories and skills, beginning students tend to model their behaviors on those of experts. Accordingly, during the beginning student phase of development, trainees are often especially attuned to, and reliant upon, professors' and supervisors' feedback. Whether it is accurately perceived, even subtle criticism can feel crushing to beginning students. Trainees at this phase often attach their self-confidence to their supervisors' encouragement or criticism. As a result, they are strongly dependent on their supervisors. Negative experiences in supervision can also be detrimental to beginners' development as counselors and therapists.

Apprehension and anxiety are the emotions that dominate the beginner's early experiences in providing clinical services to clients. The beginner also tends to feel vulnerable and lack strong feelings of competence. Keen to buffer these sometimes overwhelming feelings, beginning trainees often hold fast to straightforward, structured theories of counseling, with the hope that the techniques can be applied to all clients. Their fears may be somewhat allayed by explicit, positive feedback from supervisors and clients; this feedback is sometimes elicited directly by the therapist-in-training.

Individuals at this phase of development are nurturing an emerging, yet uncertain, identity as a counselor. As their awareness of the complexities and challenges inherent in practicing as a therapist grows, so does the importance of adopting an open attitude toward all that is new and unfamiliar. The potential for long-term professional development hinges upon trainees' openness to new experiences. When their attitudes are restricted or closed, students are much more likely to begin heading down the narrow road of professional stagnation.

PRACTICUM PAIN, PROFESSIONAL GAIN
Len Jennings

When I was a fledgling therapist in my first master's-level practicum, I had a run-in with my supervisor. It was not good. As we know, the first practicum for many of us is brimming with self-doubt and anxiety. So the last thing I wanted to do was annoy my supervisor. But unwittingly I did. Even now, when sorting out just what went wrong, the memory of this experience still haunts me.

I really tried to please him. People-pleasing and conflict avoidance were strong parts of my psychological makeup back then. But soon the tension began. A major source of our tension was theoretical differences. He espoused cognitive-behavioral therapy (CBT), but Carl Rogers and person-centered therapy wowed me. At first, I began feeling subtle pressure to conform to his theoretical worldview. I felt, though never said, "Why can't I work with clients in a way that develops my own personal style of therapy?" But I sat in silent protest. I am the soft-spoken, encouraging, sensitive, Rogerian type. Albert Ellis I'm not. In the beginning, we were fairly cordial about these apparent differences, but as time wore on, he likely noticed my resistance to applying CBT interventions. We probably would have muddled through our supervision relationship the way many mismatched supervising relationships do if there had not been the "difficult client." Unfortunately, I was assigned to work with a client who struggled with severe pathology. As an aside, I am not sure why counseling agencies assign these difficult clients to practicum newbies. Shouldn't the best therapists be assigned to the most difficult clients? A better plan is to set the therapist-in-training up for success by aiming for a reasonable match between therapist skill level and the client's level of pathology. Not only is this strategy fairer to clients, it helps build the novice therapist's confidence at a time when this trait is surely lacking. I hope it is not some sort of rite of passage or power play such as, "Let's keep the YAVIS (young, attractive, verbal, intelligent, successful) clients and pass the rest on to the lowly practicum student."

At any rate, I did not do a good job with the difficult client. The more my supervisor required me to take a cognitive-behavioral approach with this client, the more I became anxious and less able to carry out his instructions. My inability to perform CBT techniques may have been seen as intentionally disregarding his supervisory authority. And I am guessing that my ability to perform CBT techniques was hampered by my less-than-enthusiastic embrace of CBT theory. Whatever the reasons, I believe he may have felt that mutiny was at hand. His escalating irritation further triggered my feelings of inadequacy as a therapist.

The main difficulty was, I believe, a poor supervisor–supervisee match. Both of us seemed inflexible and ineffectual at addressing our tension. When my supervisor got visibly angry with me, my stress level skyrocketed. It was getting serious and personal, too. I was in the free fall of what Orlinsky and Rønnestad (2005) describe as double traumatization. This is when the novice practitioner experiences a lack of client improvement coupled with a critical supervisor. I tried to endure by holding onto this one hope: "If only I can survive this mess, next semester I will be assigned a new supervisor."

Unfortunately, things got much worse for me. I was devastated and humiliated when I discovered that I did not pass my practicum. When I received the news, I felt the ground beneath my feet sway and roll. My foundation was shaken to the core. I profoundly questioned my goodness of fit for this profession. And my worst fear, that a counseling authority would doubt my readiness, was now a reality.

Fortunately, there were two people who really believed in me. One was the director of the University of Missouri at Kansas City's (UMKC) counseling center, where I was doing my practicum. The other person was the director of UMKC's placement center who had worked closely with me on many career services projects. They both advocated for me and helped implement a remediation plan that included taking on extra counseling hours during our school's holiday break. This way I could improve my grade and continue with my practicum. Their faith in me inspired me to do whatever it took to improve my counseling skills. They believed in me, even when I was at my lowest!

This crisis was obviously a pivotal moment in my counseling career and forced me to take an honest look at myself. Above all, I realized how important the field of counseling was to me and that I had to work hard at skills that I lacked. I learned that, for me, a client-centered approach is more than empathy statements and paraphrasing. To be a truly skilled client-centered therapist meant that I needed to work on my own congruence, authenticity, and willingness to be vulnerable. Although the client-centered approach is still the bedrock of my theoretical orientation, it is not enough when it comes to working with certain types of client pathology. I discovered that I needed other skills in my "toolkit." To paraphrase Abraham Maslow (1966), "If you only have a hammer, you treat everything like a nail." My first supervisor was not clueless, after all, in that I did need to learn how to employ CBT techniques to help clients take action and challenge dysfunctional thinking. However, in my case, his message was lost because he seemed to be forcing me to do a certain type of therapy versus encouraging me to explore a variety of therapies that fit for me. This pressure greatly inhibited my ability to cope and adapt due to my performance anxiety. Although we never saw each other again, I wonder what we could learn from each other if we could process that experience today.

From this ordeal, I learned several important lessons that currently influence my supervisory work with therapists in training. First, I think the power of positive reinforcement and encouragement goes much further than criticism, especially with first-year practicum students. The primary question that guides my supervisory work is, "How can I support my students' strengths so that they can believe in themselves and find their own way?"

Second, I strive to help supervisees feel as safe and relaxed as possible. Because performance anxiety is a pervasive part of the practicum experience, anxiety often ambushes supervisees' best efforts. Performance anxiety is due to more than just being a beginner. Counseling professionals frequently teach that the "person of the therapist" is our main "tool" in our work. Therefore, the supervisee may conclude that when things go poorly in the session, the deficit lies within the supervisee's personhood. So helping the student feel safe and relaxed under these conditions is no easy task.

Third, I realized the importance of a good supervisor–supervisee relationship. Just like the therapeutic alliance with clients, a productive, caring, and empathic relationship with the supervisee is required for good work. Equally important, a poor supervisor–supervisee match, especially one tinged with negative feelings, requires early and vigorous intervention. There should be no surprises at the end of the semester; otherwise, the supervisory relationship has failed.

Finally, as a supervisor I hold the supervisees accountable. Supervisees must address their growth edges. Ideally, within a culture of encouragement, trouble spots are identified early, and the student is given ample opportunity to remediate. With an emphasis on both safety and challenge, I believe that I help create an optimal environment for the supervisee's growth.

Looking back, I realize that I have gained so much professionally from this challenging and agonizing experience. At the time of the difficult client, my unsuccessful performance, and the critical supervisor, I never imagined that, decades later, I would consider my practicum pain to be a "blessing in disguise."

References

Maslow, A. (1966). *The psychology of science.* New York: Oxford University Press.
Orlinsky, D.E., & Rønnestad, M.H. (2005). *How psychotherapists develop: A study of therapeutic work and professional growth.* Washington, DC: American Psychological Association.

GROWING MY PERSPECTIVE BEYOND THE "SECRET KNOWLEDGE" MINDSET
Andrew C. Weis

I have encountered people, including some within our profession, who view psychotherapists as repositories of secret knowledge. We therapists are often presumed to have special insight into human nature, the way of the world or society, or the how and why of an individual's inner workings. Those who hold this view seem to expect psychotherapists to dole out enough of this secret knowledge to help clients achieve their goals.

As a novice practicum counselor, I believe that I encountered this secret knowledge mindset in one of my first group supervision sessions. I had just explained to my peers and supervisor how I had started my most recent therapy session. My seasoned supervisor chided, "This is the stupidest thing I have ever heard."

What had I done in therapy that seemed so stupid? I had sat side by side with a client, who had long struggled with bulimia, and had reviewed a list of treatment approaches. She and I compared and contrasted the underlying theories and technical elements of her therapy options. That therapy session helped set a tone for an intentional, transparent, and open-minded collaboration.

Reflecting on my supervisor's disdain, I concluded that my supervisor expected me to be the authority on matters such as selecting a treatment option. That authority, presumably grounded in specialized knowledge, had been bestowed upon me via my graduate studies. Perhaps as my supervisor saw it, my approach to reviewing treatment options had compromised my authority and spilled some of the secrets of our profession.

I had a very different view. The young woman struggling with bulimia had parents, athletic coaches, and past providers who were often telling her what to do, what to think, and how to feel. She felt disempowered. Were I to simply tell her how we were going to work, I would have perpetuated an experience central to her extended struggle with bulimia.

While being chastised in supervision, however, I seriously wondered if I had acted stupidly. After the reprimand, I reflected deeply on my choice. I sought clarity in the clinical literature. And, despite feeling shamed by my supervisor, I consulted further with him and other supervisors. Along the way, I concluded that I had acted competently, in good faith, and to the benefit of the client. I also learned much about how I grow, how I experience therapy, and how I best use supervision.

I learned through this supervision experience that my professional growth depends on my willingness to seriously consider opposing views. Had I held on to my initially defensive posture, I could have dismissed my supervisor's feedback. I could have gotten stuck in my defenses much like the client seemed to be stuck in her defense of bingeing and purging. I could have missed out on what proved to be an important catalyst in my personal and professional development.

I have grown as a clinician, colleague, spouse, parent, and friend through taking seriously the opposing perspectives of others. I still pause when my ego gets bruised, but instead of readying defenses I usually focus on the opportunity for growing my perspective. I say "usually," because sometimes I balk. Even then, however, I eventually address and resolve the disparity of views.

That challenging moment in supervision also began a deeper understanding of my experience of therapy. I now see better the place for sharing knowledge that need not be kept secret. I also see better the place of the working relationship and direct experience in therapy. Awareness of that place for each has enriched and helped to define my practice: I try to offer clients (and supervisees) a relationship and experience in which they can empower themselves.

Expanding personal power or agency through counseling and psychotherapy can help clients deeply engage life. I believe that knowledge empowers, so clients and I explore knowledge of our biological, psychological, and social worlds. Clients benefit from understanding the essentials for a balanced and integrated life. It is no secret that the body thrives with good sleep, a wholesome diet, time in nature, and regular physical activity. It is no secret that the mind thrives with a balance between challenge and renewal, between discernment and deciding, between focused attention and open awareness. It is no secret that the human spirit thrives with loving, with daring to live in concert with our highest values, and with making a meaningful contribution to more than oneself. It is no secret that our relationships with each other can define us, support us, and encourage us through life's many challenges. But sometimes that knowledge is not shared, or is forgotten, or is lost in translation. As a result, we lose our balance, and we lose our way.

Clients can sense that imbalance, that gap between reality and possibility, between path and practice. The knowledge we share with clients can help them close that gap and realize their full potential. The knowledge we share and apply with our clients is not secret but is grounded in public and constantly evolving empirical and contemplative traditions. We therapists are not repositories of a secret knowledge but conduits of an evolving and essential knowledge that can be hard to notice or take seriously in our busy and often distracted lives.

Knowledge, however, rarely can suffice when seeking or coping with significant life change. Direct experience is also essential to such change. This is why our discipline relies so much on the supervision process and relationship. Supervision is primarily experiential. It affords experiences that help us use our knowledge with wisdom. The supervision experience can translate into a therapy experience that, in turn, helps clients use their knowledge with wisdom.

With the client I noted earlier, I believe that the experiences in our therapy sessions were more critical to her progress than the knowledge shared in our sessions. We certainly dedicated much to expanding our knowledge of herself and her world and her options for engaging it, and as a result her resilience blossomed. But at least as important was how she experienced the therapeutic process. I believe I offered her the experience of acceptance, authenticity, genuine concern, understanding, and a willingness to be fully present. As she experienced these essentials to a therapeutic relationship, she gradually began to adopt them herself. She ultimately gained a richer, gentler, and more open-minded experience of herself.

Only years later, during predoctoral internship, did I come to fully appreciate parallels between supervision and therapy relationships. My internship supervisor modeled the rich and balanced relationship essential to clinician and client growth. That supervisory experience was challenging yet so fulfilling! Words cannot convey sufficiently my experience or my gratitude. I hope every therapist has that kind of relationship and experience in supervision: no secret knowledge mindset, just two people wholly invested in a relationship that is dedicated to awareness, understanding, and skill in creating change.

HYPOTHETICALLY SPEAKING
Claytie Davis III

I began my first practicum placement at the age of 23 as a graduate student, 1 year after graduating with a BA in psychology. The training took place in the university counseling center, on the same campus from which I had just graduated. Similar to the other students in my practicum cohort, I was extremely excited to be working with college students rather than patients at the local state hospital or community mental health agency. I believed I would have an easier time helping clients in a university counseling center compared with clients in the other options—since I had more in common with that population (i.e., I was part of the population). Now, almost 15 years later, I remember one of my first assigned clients, and I doubt I will ever forget her. Yolanda (pseudonym) was my first long-term client; however, that is not why I remember her or our work together. I remember Yolanda because I was attracted to her. Before each session I felt both anxious and excited due to this attraction.

Yolanda was of average height and weight and normally presented in casual attire (e.g., jeans, T-shirt, flip-flops). Early in our work together, as I learned about her academic interests as well as her personal hobbies, I thought of her as someone with whom I had much in common and who would be *fun to hang out with*. Stated differently, I wondered what would have happened if I had met her at a café or at a social gathering rather than in a therapy office. I was never sexually attracted to her but definitely remember thinking she was cool and someone who I wanted to share more of myself (e.g., be able to say, "I do that too"). A few weeks into our work some of our sessions seemed similar to that of two friends, albeit one-sided.

At that point in my graduate program I had received only limited training regarding how to deal with feelings of attraction toward clients. I realized the fantasies I had of meeting her at one of the cafés she frequented was not an option; however, I was stuck wondering what to do with my varied thoughts and feelings about her. How was I supposed to help her when I was distracted during part of the session wondering, "What if?" I wondered what it said about me as a therapist that I looked forward to seeing this client more than other clients. I wanted to know how other therapists dealt with these types of dilemmas. In sum, I felt trapped and unsure of what to do. The only thing I knew for certain was that I would *not* be sharing my thoughts and feelings about this particular client with my supervisor. Unfortunately, holding onto this secret only exacerbated my feelings of guilt and uncertainty about my ability to be a good therapist.

As our work progressed Yolanda made progress in spite of my lack of willingness to address my attraction toward her in supervision. Supervision sessions focused on discussing other clients, and if Yolanda's name came up we discussed only the various techniques I was attempting to use (e.g., empty chair technique). I never brought an audiotape of our work for fear that my supervisor might identify some clue that I liked this client more than others. I worked with Yolanda for about 5 months, and when we terminated I remember feeling a sense of both loss and relief.

It was not until the following semester, when I was assigned a new supervisor, that I had enough courage to discuss the topic of attraction to clients. I asked, "*Hypothetically speaking*, what do you do when you have feelings of attraction and would rather be friends with a client than provide them with therapy?" My supervisor, an older White male, smiled and reassured me that attraction to a client is a normal phenomenon and that it would be more problematic if I never felt (acknowledged) some form of attraction to a client in the course of my career. He helped me understand that this type of countertransference occurs and that I should use my feelings (and the experience) to learn more about myself as a therapist. It was clear that ignoring these feelings prevented my work with Yolanda from being as productive as it could have been. For example, it was difficult for me to challenge Yolanda in the same way I challenged other clients. Too much of my attention in session was focused on wondering if she liked me or thought I was a good therapist.

As I reflect back on this experience, almost 15 years later, I wonder what might have facilitated openness on my part to discuss these feelings with my supervisor, or anyone for that matter. There were many factors at play—I was a young, African

American man conducting therapy with a young, White woman (in the South); my supervisor was a middle-aged White woman, and we were working at a predominately White university where I was the only African American male on the counseling center staff (albeit as a trainee). In addition, I had never engaged in my own individual therapy, was new to providing "real" therapy, and had never been supervised or evaluated by someone outside of my academic program. In many ways there seemed to be very few extrinsic reasons to discuss my feelings of attraction in supervision. While there were men with whom I similarly connected, I believe the fact that this client was a woman made the topic seem more taboo for me to bring to supervision, given these cultural issues. This begs the question: What did I need at that time, from those involved in my training (e.g., supervisor, practicum coordinator, academic program), to take a risk in disclosing my thoughts and feelings? Discussions about multiple relationships, countertransference, and the evaluation process are a few topics that might have helped lead to my disclosing my feelings about Yolanda sooner. I believe the first two issues are especially critical for beginning therapists working on college campuses. It is incumbent upon supervisors to discuss attraction to clients early in supervision, similar to discussions about diversity. This would serve the purpose of normalizing the experience (on the front end) and has the potential to serve as an invitation to the supervisee to mention this in supervision when the situation occurs. It also serves as a reminder that bringing this topic up would not jeopardize a positive evaluation.

More than anything, this experience has influenced my own supervisory work. Early in the supervisory relationship I ask my interns and postdoctoral fellows if they have ever been attracted to a client, and I push back when I hear the inevitable "no" or "what do you mean." I attempt to normalize that we all find some clients attractive in some manner (e.g., sexually, intellectually, physically) and that there is nothing wrong with the feelings. At times I have shared my experience with Yolanda, and at other times I have shared more recent experiences and how I have appreciated the feedback colleagues have provided. Those in training need to know that supervision is the place to discuss feelings of attraction, which would hopefully free them from the anxiety and guilt I experienced.

ALIEN: THE EXPERIENCES OF AN INTERNATIONAL STUDENT IN COUNSELOR TRAINING
Michael Goh

Aliens. Nonresident aliens. That's how the U.S. Department of Homeland Security officially categorizes non-U.S. citizens. I have always been amused by the choice of words used to describe foreign visitors to the United States, but actually feeling *alien* or *alienated* as an international student and experiencing daily epiphanies about why the word might be used is often anything but funny. International students experience the word as both an adjective and a noun.

Growing up in multiracial Singapore with myriad religions, languages, cultures, and traditions did not prepare me for multicultural America. As an international student and sojourner who began my counselor training in Indiana, I often felt without a home. I was far away from Singapore, and the United States did not easily become a home away from home. I quickly became familiar with racism in the United States. Several incidents shaped a sense of marginalization and contributed critically to my development as a counseling professional.

In my first week in the United States, while biking to class, I was startled when someone in a passing pickup truck shouted, "Hey Chink … take your boat and go home." I soon learned the derogatory meaning of the word *Chink* as well as the misconception that I was a Vietnamese "boat" refugee. This awakening prefaced the next 10 years of my higher education experience in the Unites States. As I accumulated more and more experiences of racism, discrimination, and marginalization, what also grew was my empathy toward the minority experience. Nevertheless, I constantly felt caught between my official status and identity as an international scholar and my emotional experience as a minority in the United States.

I experienced many incidents that illustrate what being caught in between looked like. I recall being in the earlier stages of culture shock, slipping toward the bottom of the U-shaped curve of adjustment. During those moments, I remember walking between classes and trying to engage in a conversation with a gentleman who looked of Chinese descent, erroneously assuming the person to be an international student from Singapore, Hong Kong, Malaysia, China, or Taiwan. I was proud of my cross-cultural sophistication in not assuming the person to be from my homeland Singapore, only to be embarrassed by the discovery that he grew up in Chicago. I also recall my attempts to identify with minority students in my counselor training program. In classes or practicum, it was often clarified by students and faculty, "Oh, he is not a minority; he is an international student." And while I comprehended the meaning of that distinction, I was often frustrated by the lack of appreciation for the similarities of my emotional and psychological experience as a nonmajority person in the United States. It was as if the discrimination and racism I experienced were less severe or scarring.

Even though I grew up speaking English in my family and learning British Queen's English throughout the education system in Singapore (with Mandarin Chinese as a compulsory second language), I somehow could not get it right when trying to adapt to the different English accents and pronunciations in the United States. Lorries were now *trucks*, lifts were called *elevators*, and car parks were now *parking lots*. American football was *football,* and what the rest of the world called football America called *soccer.* I played *squash*; Americans played *racquetball*. Little nuances chipped away at my confidence. In Singapore, I had become a leader in school, in youth programs, at work, and even as an officer and platoon commander during my compulsory military experience. It was therefore a shock to my sense of self-efficacy to often be asked to repeat my words and sentences, to be asked what I meant, and ultimately to be corrected from British to American English.

Language is central to our work as counselors, and navigating new words, accents, and colloquialisms took a lot of time and emotional energy. I had pursued this field because of my natural helping ability in Singapore and countless successful helping relationships, but this learning curve made me feel inadequate and accentuated my sense of being a novice. To reduce the frequency of being corrected, I spoke less in class and interacted less with my classmates. I seldom enjoyed others' favorite conversation icebreakers such as baseball, football, the Indianapolis 500, the Little 500, and basketball (quite a task at Indiana University with larger-than-life basketball coach Bobby Knight).

The defining moments for me occurred in two parallel events in the second year of my master's program at Indiana University. One of my professors asked me to contribute to a panel presentation of three international students she had organized for her introduction to counseling course. We were to speak about counseling in our countries. We were from Singapore, Taiwan, and Malaysia. The recognition that we had something worth sharing with our peers and faculty, the diversity of views and stories shared, and the ensuing discussion that followed that presentation was a huge turning point for me. Suddenly the other students talked to us differently. And for some of us, the important part was just the fact that they now talked to us at all. It seemed so simple yet powerful that we needed a professor to help us bridge a cultural divide. Beyond this presentation, this professor was as consistent and persistent in her interest in our countries of origin as she was interested in our well-being and adjustment. Two decades later, it was fitting that this professor was an external reviewer for my successful process to obtain tenure.

The parallel event involved one of my other professors inviting me to do a counseling role-play that he could use for a training workshop in Malaysia that he was to conduct. My role-play was with another Singaporean student. Even though we both spoke English as a first language, I felt that I struggled—not because of English but because of the unique language of therapy and the nonverbal communication associated with the therapeutic alliance. I concluded that I was very unnatural, unhelpful, and incompetent and that the video role-play was likely to be used as a teachable moment—also known as a negative example. I was therefore surprised when my professor returned from Malaysia to report that the audience was amazed that I was *only* a novice student because they considered my skills to be proficient. My professor said he agreed.

These two moments were simple but critical affirmations that I could do this work and that I could manage the growth trajectories needed to succeed, just like any other U.S. student. In fact, the cross-cultural nuances that I encountered suggested to me that there was a lot more that I wanted to learn and research around international issues in counseling and the application of my education and experiences from the United States to Singapore. In search of a more culturally diverse community as well as a program and faculty that could take me to my next stage of cultural learning, I landed in Minnesota for my PhD At the University of Minnesota, I found a rare collection of faculty that had Fulbright and other international experiences, as well as the Minnesota International Counseling Institute (Skovholt, Hansen, Goh, Romano, & Thomas, 2005), created to help faculty, students, and graduates navigate the unwieldy process of applying counseling theories and practices from the United States to other parts of the world.

I am afraid to imagine what my career journey might have looked like if I had not come across the two professors at Indiana University or the faculty at the University of Minnesota. In the absence of these positive experiences, my early negative encounters and resultant lack of affection for the United States, perhaps to the extent of feeling bitter, might have festered, as it does for many other international sojourners. I probably would have never continued my PhD studies in Minnesota, and I would have returned home to Singapore recommending that others avoid embarking on this very disenchanting experience.

After graduating in 1995, I returned to be a professor in Singapore. While in Singapore, I encouraged numerous students to pursue an overseas education and served as a consultant and speaker at forums that prepared students to study in countries such as the United Kingdom, Australia, New Zealand, and the United States. In 1999, I returned to be a faculty member at the University of Minnesota. Given my own history of culture shock and the adjustment process, I try to share my experiences with other international students, creating conversations earlier rather than later in their sojourns.

Every international student's sojourner script will be unique. But I still try to help other international students avoid disorienting encounters and unnecessary deviations from their personal and professional goals.

Reference

Skovholt, T.M., Hansen, S.S., Goh, M., Romano, J.L., & Thomas, K.A. (2005). The Minnesota International Counseling Institute (MICI) 1989–present: History, joyful moments, and lessons learned. *International Journal for the Advancement of Counseling, 27,* 17–33.

THE POWER OF INFORMAL MENTORING IN COUNSELOR DEVELOPMENT
James M. Benshoff

There are many types of mentors, and I have been very fortunate to have benefited from mentoring by different people along my career path. One of these mentors, though, stands out for having served as a teacher–mentor, helping me learn new ways of understanding and working with groups that have been critical to every aspect of my work as a counselor and counselor educator. Although mentoring can be multifaceted, its value also can be measured in small moments such as those casual comments and connections that cut through the barriers and complexities inherent in student–faculty relationships. One conversation, or even just the right few words at a critical moment, can make more difference in students' lives than any class they might take.

My first mentor appeared to me at the very beginning of my graduate counseling program. Gloria was an extraordinary teacher and group facilitator par excellence, but not at all the "warm, fuzzy" counselor or teacher type. She seemed tough and formidable, with very high expectations for her students. In fact, Gloria was not a counselor at all but was an educational psychologist by academic training and a group facilitator by professional experience. As an excellent and experienced teacher she had an "eye" for students with potential—and, fortunately, I was one of those students in whom she saw possibilities.

Her influence on me started early, in just the second course I took in my master's program. As a returning adult student and someone who had been a pretty marginal undergraduate student, I was highly motivated to do well in my graduate courses. Her course was a basic human development course that included my first exposure to a group approach to learning. The course required a major paper, developed over the course of the semester. Although this was supposed to be a 25-page paper, mine became more than 50 pages—longer than anything I had ever written.

One day, Gloria and I walked out of class together. I was astounded when she not only commented very favorably on my paper but also suggested I should consider doctoral work. Here I was, just hoping I could make it through a master's program successfully, and an admired professor already was suggesting that I could be doctoral material. I am not easily flattered, but this was one of the biggest compliments I had ever received. I began to think seriously about how I could get my doctorate and the implications of that degree for my career opportunities.

I learned from this encounter how powerful that kind of affirmation or suggestion can be for students (as well as for clients), how planting that seed really can make a difference in people's lives and aspirations. This ability to see potential in clients and students—and to help them see and cultivate that—is a key tool in being an effective counselor or counselor educator.

Gloria ended up giving me an even bigger gift, though. Through her group counseling course—in particular the instructor-led experiential group—I learned clearly and deeply the profound power of process, in both group and individual work. For Gloria, facilitating the process was an art form and was a very powerful way of seeing and working in the world. Observing her ability to work in the here and now, to help group members focus on difficult issues, and to use process interventions to guide group members to deeper levels provided me with an extraordinarily powerful learning process. After the initial group course, Gloria invited me to colead the group with her the following semester. There were many aspects to this invitation, but most important was the fact that she had confidence I could do this.

For me, this was a rich learning opportunity since I had the chance not only to colead the group but also to process and plan group sessions with her. It was the opportunity to apprentice with a master, to be able to get inside her head to see how she thought about and intervened intentionally in groups. Although I could not know it at the time, this experience would dramatically alter my counseling and teaching styles. As I have continued to develop and hone these group facilitation skills over the years, they have become the basis for everything I do, including teaching, counseling, and professional leadership. A deep appreciation of, and respect for, the process of experiences also has extended into my personal life and my relationships. It's not just what I do—it's become a core part of who I am.

As I reflect on my experiences with Gloria, *mentoring* is the best word I can find to capture the nature of the relationship and the impact it had on me. Most definitions or descriptions of mentoring emphasize the variety of roles that mentors can play in the lives of their mentees. One university guide to mentoring graduate students suggests roles such as *guide, counselor, advisor, consultant, tutor, guru,* and *teacher.* The role that Gloria took with me, though, was primarily one of *guru,* or wise, experienced master teacher. Interestingly, I had to look elsewhere for good models for success in academia, research, or professional service and leadership. Gloria's unique gifts to me were about being a master teacher and an extraordinarily skilled group facilitator.

This is what I learned from Gloria: how to offer intuitive, well-timed support and encouragement in ways that have the potential to impact on students' lives; how to appreciate, create, and manage the process aspects of learning; and how to be an effective group facilitator, regardless of the type of group or group setting. Along the way, she helped me discover some core parts of myself and to explore possibilities for how I could use these to be a more effective counselor, teacher, leader, and eventually a mentor myself.

I doubt that Gloria would have ever labeled our relationship as mentoring. Her influence, although very powerful, was subtle in many ways and reached me mostly because of the tremendous respect and admiration I held for her. I do not know whether she knew how closely I was watching her—*how* she managed groups, *how* she responded to students who were struggling to master course content, *how* she was able to make use of the process dimension to create self-awareness and change. Shortly before I graduated from my master's program, Gloria left the university, having been denied tenure (my lesson about the importance of research and scholarship for faculty survival). Except for one or two instances, we went separate ways after that, and I moved on to be mentored by others and, in turn, learned to become a mentor for my own graduate students.

Part of Gloria's legacy, for me, is the reminder that the most important learning does not necessarily take place in the classroom, and how important it is to value the opportunities for facilitating learning that come in the moment, in the context of open and real relationships between me and my students and clients. This is one important way that who I am as a counselor informs who I am as a counselor educator: The power of the relationship is the foundation of both for me.

There are moments when you can slowly begin to see something you have never before paid attention to, moments when the point of view shifts and your way of seeing and being in the world is forever altered. Thanks, Gloria, for showing me how to see and understand the shadows moving just beneath the surface of the words and actions in every kind of group setting. Thanks also for teaching me how to use the intricate and underlying patterns of interactions to help others go deeper into their own lives as well as share more fully the experiences of others. Gloria's gift is now one that I strive to share and pass on to my students through teaching and mentoring.

BECOMING AUTHENTIC: ONE COUNSELOR'S PROFESSIONAL EPIPHANY
Sarah M. Backes-Diaz

In August 2003, I entered graduate school without really knowing what to expect. I was filled with abundant anticipation, excitement, and a small dose of nerves buried deep within the pit of my stomach. Still, my elation and eagerness trumped the nervous twinges, and I managed to initially repel those early negative thoughts as

I forged into a new realm of academic challenge and professional growth. Having been a dedicated student all of my life, I was under the impression that learning to become a counselor would be a "piece of cake." I imagined it would involve studying theory, memorizing strategies, and perfecting techniques, similar to the learning process that took place during my undergraduate experience. Essentially, my expectation was that if I completed all of my reading and diligently studied hard for every midterm, eventually a mental "switch" would be flipped, and miraculously I would become a "good counselor."

In retrospect, I chuckle at my naïveté as this structured view of counselor development was quickly shattered during my first-year practicum class. I struggled during counseling sessions, felt overwhelmed by ambiguity, and faced intense internal pressure to "say the right thing" to my struggling clients. My simplistic view of the counselor development process had been basically thrown out the window, and I was left to pick up the pieces, scrambling to reconstruct a new vision for my professional identity and for my future educational experience. Once the initial shock and pain wore off, and especially after consulting with many of my peers who were going through similar transitions, I was able to sew new threads of hope and jump back on track. This harsh awakening felt quite abrupt, but at the same time I am glad it occurred early in my graduate school experience and while I was surrounded by caring, supportive professors and peers.

During one of my first individual supervision sessions with my professor, Dr. P., we played one of the counseling tapes I had recorded earlier in the week at my internship site—a local university career counseling center. The student I was working with possessed career goals that were in immense conflict with those of his parents, and he presented with extreme anxiety and fear. Currently, he was supposed to be applying to law school, the plan his family had engrained into his brain from a very young age. Yet his true dream and passion was to work on a vineyard, connected to the earth, the sunshine, and the natural world. My gut urged me to reach out and hug this student as I saw tears forming in his eyes. I longed to ease his pain and to validate the difficulty of his situation. Instinctively I empathized with how it can feel to have your dreams minimized and stifled, especially by the people whom you love the most.

Yet at that moment, for some strange reason, I held back, scanning my brain for what I felt a "good counselor" would say or for the most "professional" response. Within a matter of a few seconds, I was engaged in an internal mental battle with some imaginary, contrived "perfect counselor" in my head and was pushed face to face with my genuine, raw feelings and reactions. Was it okay to actually share the thoughts, feelings, and questions I was experiencing as a true human being? I challenged these natural feelings and instincts, believing that I needed to share something much more clinical and specific, much like a doctor would prescribe a certain medication to cure a patient's ailment. That perfect counselor wedged somewhere in the crevices of my gray matter was challenging the natural and empathic reply my heart longed to express. I felt an overwhelming pressure to deliver a perfect, professional, legitimate, show-stopping response that would suddenly make my client feel heard and healed. But all I could conjure up was some contrived, generic response such as, "So why don't you want to go to law school?"

I felt embarrassed, confused, and stifled, wallowing in self-doubt and questioning my abilities to ever succeed as a professional counselor. This was not the first time I felt this way (nor was it the last!), but it was the first opportunity I had to publicly express these conflicting thoughts with my professor.

At that moment Dr. P. stopped the tape, as she could see the confusion and pain in my eyes, and I was quickly brought back to the present reality. "What did you really want to say to him at that moment, Sarah?" my professor asked. I replied, "I wanted to say that I really felt for him and that I empathize with his feelings of isolation, frustration, and disappointment. I wanted to tell him that I can see how hard it is for him to follow his dreams without his parents' support. I wanted to acknowledge and validate his desire to reach out for help and to commend his ability to be so open about his current struggles. And lastly, I really wanted to grab his hand and acknowledge the passion I see in his eyes when he talks about the vineyards, and I would ask him to tell me more about his passion." I looked up at Dr. P., quite emotional and overwhelmed myself. In response, she smiled and replied, "Then, Sarah, that is exactly what you should have said."

The conversation that followed was a pivotal moment in my counselor development. My professor explained to me that my greatest gift as a helper—my deepest and truest strengths and resources—could never be learned from a textbook or memorized from a theory. I suddenly realized that I had been trying way too hard to fit myself into a preconceived mold of what I thought defined good counseling. Instead, I now understood that my best strategy for truly connecting with my clients was rooted in my instincts and genuineness. This was a professional epiphany, if you will, and a moment I will never forget. While on one hand our graduate programs provide us with a solid foundation and a theoretical framework upon which to base our practice, what truly makes a counselor good and effective is purely authentic and comes from the heart. From that moment on I began to view my work from a completely new perspective.

The following is a quote taken from a journal that I kept religiously during this tumultuous period of my life and development:

> I realized today that learning how to become a counselor is HARD! Because not only are we learning effective counseling skills and strategies, but because we are forced to look deep within ourselves and to analyze our strengths, limitations, biases, personality traits, and basically pick ourselves apart! It leaves me feeling very vulnerable, confused, scared, and alone. I feel like nobody truly understands what I am struggling with in my life right now, like an abandoned ship in the middle of a dark night ocean. But alas, I have hope and I can feel the twinges of a new wind creeping into my sails. This program has helped me to grow and mature in more ways than I ever thought possible; but that insight and self-exploration does not come without its share of struggle and strife. It is hard for me to admit this, but I am seriously struggling with my development as a counselor. Specifically, this struggle means that it is quite hard for me to find a way to express my true, authentic self, while at the same time being able to implement all the counseling skills and knowledge I am learning and adding to my toolbox each and every day. I hope that eventually I can find a way to integrate my natural, authentic, empathic SELF into my

counseling style, remaining professional and personal at the same time. I feel like I have learned so much and I already know that I am a caring person.…. but am I a good counselor? Am I progressing the way that I should in graduate school? What do my students think about me during and after a counseling session? How can I both connect with and help my clients, while also staying true to myself?

As I reflect upon these memories, I realize that yes, becoming a counselor is hard. But it is also an amazing, insightful, emotional journey that has changed the course of my life forever. Looking back on my time in graduate school, I now realize that I needed to struggle through all of that confusion to peel away the external layers of expectations, fears, and preconceived notions that were limiting my ability to become truly authentic. Today I believe that I am a good counselor, but I am far from perfect. I know that some clients may never "like" me, and my style may not be the best fit for others. And that is okay. Each and every day provides new opportunities to learn more about myself and the world, and my clients continue to challenge me and push me out of my comfort zone. What gives me continued hope is the knowledge that I am still a relatively young professional with a long way to go in my journey of professional development and self-discovery. And while the road will undoubtedly become winding and tumultuous at times, I am excited about what lies ahead.

THE TRANSFORMING MOMENT WITH DAVID
Timothy A. G. Osachuk

I had been in graduate school for several years and had all but completed my PhD in experimental psychology, specializing in psychoneuroimmunology. I was part of a research team demonstrating the ability to condition natural killer cells—immune cells involved in eradicating cancer. I had become a critical thinking researcher. My training was grooming me for academia.

I knew something was missing in my life. There were other skills that I intuitively knew I had. In me, there was a deep recognition that I was meant to develop and use these skills. Some years before, I had worked as an orderly in a hospital for two summers. I enjoyed working with the patients and interacting with other staff in the hospital. I guess it came naturally as my mother was a practicing nurse for many years. I had also served as the undergraduate student advisor in psychology, assisting other students in planning their careers. This experience validated for me that I could listen, communicate well, and be helpful to others. I knew I was sensitive and had the skills to become a good therapist.

Despite the advice of my advisor at the time, I took a large risk. I did not complete the experimental PhD Instead, I applied for and was accepted in the clinical psychology program at the same university. Then began a new task: the need to validate for myself and everyone else who knew me previously as a researcher that I could become a skilled therapist. I was driven, compelled to become a competent therapist, and simultaneously uncertain as to whether I could do so.

I invested heavily in my first psychotherapy course in client-centered therapy—taught by David, a skilled clinical psychologist and icon in our program. In the course, we read and were examined on all of the material within a month and spent the remainder of the course in role-plays with classmates practicing client-centered therapy skills à la Carl Rogers. I remember trying so very hard during the role-plays to practice and integrate the skills we learned in the course. I felt so awkward and uncomfortable, like I was having to completely unlearn patterns of communication inherited from my family and to learn a new way of being. Still, I remained committed to becoming a skilled therapist. The intensity of my determination to learn to become a competent therapist was, however, a double-edged sword. It drove me forward, yet I was so focused on doing things right that I was not fully hearing and understanding what my classmates as role-play clients were saying. My paraphrased responses and empathetic reflections were repetitive, stilted, and wooden. My intensity was getting in the way of a smoother reciprocal interchange in which role-play clients could feel comfortable, relaxed, and heard. I continued to learn, practicing the skills learned in the course, and successfully passed the course.

Like many of the new clinical students, I hoped to be supervised by David in my first practicum as I knew he would be the key in helping me to unlock the skills and potential I knew I had. I felt like a diamond in the rough that needed a great deal of polishing. We all submitted our requests for supervisors, and I requested David. I was disappointed when I was assigned to another supervisor. However, my other supervisor was patient, kind, gentle, encouraging, and affirming, and with a great deal of effort, through reviewing videotapes of sessions and practice, I grew in skills and confidence, successfully passing this practicum.

It came time to begin my second practicum, and I again requested and hoped to have David as my supervisor. My request was granted. David remembered me from his psychotherapy course. Early in my practicum, during videotape review of my therapy with clients, he was pleased to see the improvement of my skills since the course. Being a new therapist, I was still learning and feeling clumsy and awkward, and I hung on every word of his feedback in supervision, as I was in awe of the depth of his skills and continually wanting to improve. Developmentally I also really needed external affirmation and confirmation of my potential to become a skilled therapist and was hoping at some point to receive this from David in supervision. It was as if David saw the potential in me, believed in me, that I would be all right.

The affirmation and confirmation I was hoping to receive came during a subsequent clinical supervision session. It seems like such a small thing, but it was so important to me at the time. David had shared with me that he had spoken about my growth in a telephone conversation with one of his adult daughters. In essence he shared that initially he was uncertain about how I would do based on his memory of me from the time I was in his psychotherapy course, and he was pleased, actually pleasantly surprised, about the development of my skills since that time. He further shared with me what he anticipated he might experience with me in supervision. He was initially dreading my being his supervisee. He shared his memory of my forced intensity and anxiety while in his psychotherapy course and that it was difficult to be in my presence. He said he was not looking forward to having to work through this with me in supervision. While he did not elaborate, I had the sense that he anticipated that supervising me would personally be very taxing.

The reason he was now pleased was that these qualities were largely absent and that my interactions were no longer forced. He said I had made great strides in being present, hearing my clients, and making empathetic reflections. I was thrilled to hear that. Of course I was still very much a beginner, and that's why I was being supervised. This conversation was a defining moment for me. I was finally able to relax and accept that I was going to be a therapist, that I had made the right choice. This experience would be the first of many further affirming experiences of my chosen profession, my craft.

In retrospect, this moment with David was a crucial formative developmental experience. It paved the road for me to participate in an advanced psychotherapy seminar in client-centered therapy, to travel to San Diego and meet colleagues in Carl Rogers's inner circle, and to have many other opportunities. I have no doubt that this experience set me on the path to my current destination. I am now a doctoral-level registered clinical psychologist, clinical supervisor, and director of internship training of a Canadian Psychological Association and American Psychological Association accredited predoctoral internship within a university counseling service. I now regularly pass on what I learned with David, during supervision, to our psychology interns. Providing clinical supervision is my joy of joys, and I frequently hear David's voice ringing in my ears when I provide feedback to our interns.

I left a promising future in experimental psychology with a specialization in psychoneuroimmunology and jumped into the unknown of being a therapist. I worked so hard to validate for myself, and for everyone else who knew me previously as a researcher, that I could become a skilled therapist. I was driven and simultaneously uncertain. In that one magical transforming moment in supervision, David helped me move beyond my uncertainty. In receiving the gift of his confidence, I was able to be confident in myself, for which I am forever grateful.

THERAPIST? OR MAMA?

Julie M. Koch

I had the brilliant thought this morning that to really "get into the mood" to write about my defining moment, I should do it at home. Now I look down on my kitchen table and see the little spot of dried milk from my daughter's breakfast that is making my laptop sticky. I know she has left her unrinsed cereal bowl in the kitchen sink. And on the table there is one lone, forgotten, unnaturally blue Crunch Berry. To my right is the big storage closet that my children have claimed as their play space. On the door hangs a sign that says, "Katie's Undersea Café: Open when we are here, Closed when we are gone." There is a drawing of a happy crab with googly eyes, eating a sandwich. Inside the closet—sorry, *café*—hang little illustrations of sharks, fish, mermaids, and jellyfish. The café is furnished with a tiny blue wooden table, chairs, and a yellow wooden kitchen set that my grandfather built for me when I was a child.

These are the signs that I am a mom. Mama, mother, mommy, and sometimes even "Wedgie Woman" (the evil character from Dav Pilkey's *Captain Underpants* series). Upstairs, my 10-year-old son is playing a math game on our computer. My youngest daughter, 8 years old, is cleaning out her hamster's cage. (At first, we had two hamsters: Pancake and Waffles. Poor Waffles met his maker, and now we have just Pancake.) My oldest daughter, now 12 years old, is reading quietly in her room.

Other signs of motherhood: I have lectured my children about how there are children going hungry in other countries and therefore they should never complain about food. I have been told by a teacher that one of my children was "belching loudly in the cafeteria." I have dried tears when one wasn't invited to a birthday party for a friend. I have heard the hilarious, disbelieving laughter of my daughter when she was 4 years old and a *man* told her that he liked the color pink. I have gone sleepless when I had to take my son to the emergency room via ambulance in the middle of the night. I have cried at the sight of him, so big now at age 10, sleeping with his stuffed animal chipmunk. I have snapped at a nurse for telling me it was "just the hormones" when I was upset about her giving my newborn daughter formula instead of breast milk when she was in the neonatal intensive care unit.

And through most of this motherhood experience, I have been a graduate student in counseling or working as a counselor.

I started my master's program in school counseling when Katie was one and a half. In November of that year, I learned that I was pregnant; I waddled from class to class and was forced to haul my books and materials in a rolling backpack. Pecos was born in May, at the end of that first year. The second year of my master's program, I had little Katie and newborn Pecos, took fewer classes, and studied while they slept. The third year of my master's program, I learned that I was pregnant again; I pulled out the rolling backpack and received sympathetic looks (and some looks of "Are you nuts?"). Maggie was born 1 month after I completed my master's thesis and graduated. I worked as a school counselor for a few years, and when I entered my counseling psychology doctoral program at the University of Minnesota, my children were 3, 5, and 7.

At that time, I was the only mother in my cohort of six women. I think the rest of my cohort (in addition to the general public) thought I was a little deluded for attempting to complete such a challenging degree with three children in tow. I was often asked, "How do you do it?" What they didn't know: Children are the best grounding tool *ever*. They help me remember what is truly important. They counter any perfectionistic tendencies I have or any sense of control I ever thought I had. I could delude myself into believing I was writing the most brilliant research proposal ever and be brought back to Earth by an invitation to Maggie's baby doll's "birthday party" with an Easy Bake Oven cake and homemade lemonade. My children were my self-care. I did school during the day, children afternoons and evenings, and studied at night after they were in bed. I sat outside on my deck on weekends, grading papers or reading or writing, while my children ran around in our backyard with other kids from the neighborhood having a mud fight, catching grasshoppers, or just playing on the swing set.

Being a mother is such a strong part of my identity that it's hard to remember who I was before. I am no longer just "Julie"; I am "Katie's mom." Some of my children's friends even get my attention by saying, "Excuse me? Katie's Mom?" But when I began my counseling psychology program, I thought it was important to try to compartmentalize my motherly-ness and be as professional as possible while at school or work. I was also trying to find a way to supplement my identity as a school counselor with that of a counseling psychologist. I did plenty of counseling as a school counselor, but much of it was crisis oriented, briefer than brief, and often involved a large amount of advocacy and consultation. In the schools in which I worked, school counseling was *therapeutic* but did not allow for one session-a-week *therapy*. I envisioned counseling psychologists as being more client centered, as going "with the flow," as using more intuition, as my professor said, "allowing the structure to unfold." Some of my strengths as a former teacher and school counselor were my attention to detail and organization skills. So being "looser" was a challenge for me, but one that I felt was important and that truly matched my humanistic–existential viewpoint about work with clients and how to effect change.

I mentioned this goal—of letting go of my directive self and leaving my mother-self at home—to both of my supervisors during my first year of doctoral practicum. So I was fairly surprised when, at different points throughout the year, they both encouraged me to bring my "mothering" skills into my counseling practice. I'm not even sure, now, what spurred those conversations. I don't remember their intent, and I don't remember talking about it for more than a minute or two. All I remember is that one semester my supervisor Matt and another semester my supervisor Cynthia both made offhand remarks about me obviously enjoying my children and something about transferring some of that mothering into my approach to therapy. It was never a focus of our supervision—just something mentioned in passing. I'm not sure I fully heard their message, but I do remember being floored! "What?!" I thought. "I am trying to *not* be a mother here. I want clients to come to their own decisions, not give advice or be motherly." I was completely baffled and wondered how I was supposed to reconcile this. Being a mother is a pretty directive activity at times. "I'm sorry, but you chose to write on the wall in crayon, and now you have to clean it off." "No, you may *not* have a kitten." "Austin can come over Friday but not Saturday." "No, you may *still* not have a kitten, even if they're free."

Yet my supervisors both suggested that I could bring some of my mothering skills into the therapy space. I reflected on this more and thought if two people—neither of whom had consulted with the other—felt this was important, I should give it some thought. I pondered how being a mother would fit with a humanistic approach to work with clients. I wondered how these two different identities could be merged within me. Then the defining moment came to me: It wasn't about the directiveness or nondirectiveness; it was about the unconditional positive regard and love that I have for my children. The same unconditional love that my parents and grandparents gave me when I was a child. The love that says, "It's okay to make mistakes; I'll be here with you through it." The love that says, "I can't do this for you, but I will support you all the way."

In *The Prophet*, Khalil Gibran (1923, 1985, p. 17) speaks of children:

> Your children are not your children.
> They are the sons and daughters of Life's longing for itself.
> They come through you but not from you,
> And though they are with you yet they belong not to you.
> You may give them your love but not your thoughts,
> For they have their own thoughts.
> You may house their bodies but not their souls,
> For their souls dwell in the house of tomorrow, which you cannot visit,
>   not even in your dreams.
> You may strive to be like them, but seek not to make them like you.
> For life goes not backward nor tarries with yesterday.

I realized that the unconditional love I have for my children is parallel to unconditional positive regard with clients. I can "give them my love but not my thoughts, for they have their own thoughts." I may "strive to be like them, but seek not to make them like me." This is the love that allows me to simultaneously care for, and be frustrated with, the client who returns to an abusive relationship. It is the love that does not allow clients the easy answers they seek when they ask, "What would you do?" And it is even the love that allows me to gently help them consider all of the potential pros and cons of getting a kitten while fighting my own internal voice that says, "Don't do it!"

For some clients, especially those whose parents were absent or particularly demanding, I have found this love to be reparative in nature. In my experience, providing this kind of unconditional positive regard allows clients to be more open with me, to trust that I will not abandon them, and to hope that they can find this kind of love from others in their lives. For me, this realization allows me to be truly genuine and congruent in my work. I don't have to separate the professional "me" from the mother "me." Occasionally it means that I behave in ways with my clients according to what they *need*, which sometimes deviates from the norm. Sometimes it means a hug. Once it meant giving a stuffed animal bunny to a client upon termination.

As I write this, I have now transitioned to my office environment. My desk is free of milk and Crunch Berries, but there is a photo of three children on my desk. The photo shows these children playing in the snow. There are big smiles on their faces as they enjoy building a snowman. I remember that day well. I helped them find a scarf, sticks for arms, and various necessities for eyes and a nose, but I did not put them on the snowman for them. When they were finished, I brought out the hot chocolate with marshmallows, and we all celebrated their accomplishment together. It's not too different in therapy, really. I can watch from the sidelines, saying, "That looks great!" or "How creative!" or "Wow—how did you do that?" I can help clients problem solve, explore options, and consider what might happen if they do x versus y. When the snowman melts, I can mourn with them. And through it all, I do it with love.

Reference

Gibran, K. (1923, 1985). *The prophet.* New York: Alfred A. Knopf.

CARING FOR THE SELF WHILE CARING FOR ANOTHER: A MAN'S EXPERIENCE WITH SECONDARY TRAUMA
Dustin K. Shepler

During my master's internship, my director, realizing I had few women on my caseload, assigned me to conduct an intake with a young woman who had been raped. My first thought was, "Why would I, a man specializing in GLBT [gay, lesbian, bisexual, and transgender] issues, want to work with a heterosexual woman who had been raped? Besides, wouldn't that client prefer a female counselor?" At the end of the intake, the young woman, Ann (pseudonym), said she would prefer to work with me. Ann was added to my caseload. I was scared.

My supervisor was a specialist in sexual assault; her knowledge and support became invaluable assets. During a crash course in how to work with survivors of rape, my supervisor recommended a method of treatment that involved my helping Ann by supporting her while she reexperienced her rape—for Ann to recall every horrific and frightening detail of her experience. My supervisor further explained that this method is intended to work like systematic desensitization—that by repeatedly asking Ann to expose herself (and me) to her trauma, she would become desensitized and be able to create new meaning for her experience. "I can handle that," I thought. I sat and listened, heard about every moment of the worst night of Ann's life. Sat, was present, empathized, and felt pain *with* Ann. Sat and watched tears roll down her face. Sat and did everything my supervisor told me to do.

While I frequently have strong emotional reactions (usually sympathy) to some of my clients and their problems, something about working with Ann was different. With Ann, that reaction was consistent self-doubt mixed with some anger. I doubted my own ability to work with Ann but took comfort in knowing that my supervisor was constantly there to guide me. I was angry that Ann, who I thought was an amazing person, had to experience being raped. I began thinking about all of the friends that I have had who have told me about their rape experiences. I thought about my niece who would have to grow up in a world where women are harmed. I became angry—not just about Ann's rape but about all rape, and how being raped affects rape victims. I became aware that I, as a man, had never worried about being raped, had never even considered taking all of the precautions to prevent being attacked—all of the precautions that failed Ann.

One day it became too much. I met with Ann at our normal time. By this point in her treatment, we had gone past discussing the superficial and cold facts of what Ann had experienced and were well on our way to exploring the feelings Ann experienced each moment of being raped. Ann began remembering details that had never before surfaced, thoughts she had suppressed. Ann told me about what it was like to be thrown against a wall, to have her clothes ripped and pulled off her, to be thrown down onto a bed, to be paralyzed while a strange man was violating her body, to see the man's roommate walk in, not be able to call for help, and watch the roommate close the door and leave her to be raped. Thankfully, Ann realized that her intoxicated attacker had ceased expecting Ann to fight him, and she was able to throw him off her and run out of the room. It was too late though; Ann had been raped. Ann and I sat and talked about the feelings of terror, of help-lessness, of weakness and vulnerability that were previously foreign emotions for Ann. After what seemed like the longest day on Earth, I went home. That night, when I finally went to sleep, I dreamed about Ann. In my dream I was sitting in a counseling room with Ann. Ann was crying, and I was unable to speak. I had no words to comfort her; in my dream, I sat frozen, watching Ann cry. I was helpless and unable to help all in the same moment.

The next day came after a restless night. Luckily I had supervision and was comfortable sharing my concerns for Ann with my supervisor. My supervisor, being an astute observer, asked if I was doing okay. At first I was confused. What did she mean, "*Was I okay*?" Not fully understanding what was being asked of me, I simply moved on and shared that I was not sure that counseling was "my thing." I explained that I loved working with clients and helping people and honestly felt obligated to use my training to help others, including Ann, and to work through the most difficult parts of their lives, but I questioned my own ability to handle all of the stress that followed me home when working with certain clients. After listening attentively to my admittedly tangential concerns, my supervisor took the opportunity to tell me about "secondary trauma" and how to avoid it. Ironically, my answer to the question I did not fully understand about my own well-being was exactly the opportunity my supervisor used to teach me more about trauma work and the skills needed to be successful as a counselor. Secondary trauma, the way my supervisor explained it, is the experiencing of trauma symptoms by a counselor after having been exposed vicariously to the trauma the client experienced. She further explained that because counselors open themselves up to clients and feel with their clients, they sometimes experience trauma symptoms (e.g., disturbing dreams, anxiety) as well. Before that moment it had never occurred to me that being a counselor could harm me. I was told not only that learning to deal with intense emotions was part of the developmental process in learning to work with trauma clients but also that it was crucial that I be open to exploring what parts of Ann's experience affected me the most. I also needed to be open to talking about what it was like for me to hear about Ann's experience. I was told that keeping a balance of types of cases (i.e., cases that differ diagnostically) would help me main-tain interest in the work I was doing. It would also help me manage my emotions by having time to sort through the feelings I had about working with sexual assault survivors while not overwhelming myself with more than I could feasibly handle at that point in my training.

While Ann slowly began to regain confidence and to redefine herself as a sur-vivor I was reminded of how amazingly resilient people can be. By being present and open to Ann's experience, I was able to help her heal. It mattered little that I was a man working with a woman. What mattered much more was that I was a person who was willing to sit, listen, and support another person. As I gained confidence and learned how to better manage my emotions by examining my work with Ann, I began working with other sexual assault survivors, both women and men. By working with Ann I learned not only about sexual assault work, however, but also that to function as a counselor, to be able to help others, I also had to take care of myself. I found support in a valuable supervision relationship, took time to process what I had experienced, and became aware that my clients had a great impact on me, just as I hoped to have on them. A year later, I have found that consultation and supervision are still two of the most valuable resources available to me. Though life as a doctoral student in counseling psychology is busy, I still take time to think about how my work with clients affects me. Taking this time to reflect allows me to continuously monitor my own well-being and to be cognizant of how I am responding to clients' stories. Perhaps this lesson, the lesson of self-awareness and self-care, is the greater lesson I learned from working with Ann. I, like Ann, needed someone to hear and support me, to make sure I could take care of myself before I tried to help others take care of themselves. Knowing this has made me a better counselor by motivating me to take care of my own mental health by talking to supervisors about tough cases and managing emotions I experience from working with certain clients.

HOW TO FAIL
Sandra Sanger

When my group supervisor at the community mental health center where I was completing my master's practicum presented Grace's (pseudonym) case for disposition, she prefaced it by saying that none of the staff was available to work with this client. What she didn't say outright, but was clear about in her description, was that none of the staff *wanted* to work with this client. Grace had a long history of bipolar disorder and substance abuse. Her drug of choice was heroin. She had seen the revolving door of inpatient drug treatment more than once and was holding tenuously onto a few weeks of sobriety. In this sense, she didn't necessarily stand out from many of the other clients we served at the clinic. But, as I would learn over time, Grace also had a history of burning bridges, with family members and therapists alike. She was quick to lash out in anger and just as quick to apologize beseechingly. She seemed to feel like the world owed her something, and she was determined to exact whatever that was from those around her.

Looking around the room at my peers, it was evident that no one was jumping to work with Grace. It sounded like a lot of work. With only a little reluctance, I allowed my desire to please my supervisor and my novice "I'm gonna save the world one client at a time" attitude to prevail. I agreed to work with Grace. I didn't know at the time that I was bound for failure.

It's been more than 5 years since I last saw Grace. I'm at a point in my career when individual clients are beginning to naturally blur into composites in my memory, but I still remember Grace's first and last name, as well as the anxiety and sometimes frustration, that often rose up in my chest when I met with her.

When we met for the first time, after a volley of back and forth phone calls and multiple initial appointment no-shows, I already knew that I was in over my head. Grace presented her life as one ongoing crisis; she recounted failed relationships, urges to use heroin, and recurrent thoughts of suicide in a voice that pitched up into a startling crescendo while tears streamed down her face. She spoke so quickly that I was amazed she wasn't constantly tripping over her words. "Breathe," I told her gently. "Breathe!" I told myself, a little more urgently, as I tried to sort out in my head where to begin. I had next to no experience working with dually diagnosed clients and felt nervous about figuring out how to best support Grace's recent sobriety while also attending to her mood disorder and relationship instabilities. The fact that she had uttered the "s" word (suicide) so many times only elevated my pulse further into the aerobic activity zone.

After our first session ended and I had time to regroup and consult, I decided on what seemed like reasonable therapy goals: safety planning, relapse prevention, mood and affect management, bolstering interpersonal skills. As it turned out, it didn't really matter what treatment goals I had chosen, since I don't recall ever having had the chance to really discuss them with Grace. Each time we met there was a new crisis that needed attending to. Not knowing much better at the time, I faithfully followed Grace down the path of each crisis, helping her to put out fires but failing to help her prevent new ones. The chaos engendered by this crisis management strategy (or lack thereof) was compounded by the fact that we met so sporadically. It was difficult to construct much continuity between our sessions. Grace probably attended about one session for every three that we scheduled. She never called to cancel when she missed, and I was left guessing as to the cause of her absences. Our work often felt like an unending case of "hurry up and wait." I hurried to return her frantic phone calls, to help her schedule an appointment with the psychiatrist, to advocate on her behalf with housing authorities. And then I waited while she no-showed for our appointments, neglected to take her medications, and showed up an hour late for her housing meeting. It was really frustrating!

Despite all of this, we eventually managed to forge what felt like a workable therapeutic relationship. She seemed to trust me. I admired her repeated efforts to engage in a life that had kicked her down so many times in the past. I imagine that, from Grace's perspective, my dogged and naïve persistence to *be there* for her in whatever way she needed was comforting and relationship enhancing. But it also contributed to growing resentment and emotional exhaustion on my part. It took me awhile to learn that when I feel like I'm doing more work than my client, it's time to coexamine the therapy process. At the time, I couldn't disentangle myself enough to see that my work with Grace had "overinvolvement" written all over it.

Grace taught me as a beginner that progress in therapy can be slow, sporadic, and difficult to define. At times, it's imperceptible. It's like one of those flip books that, when paged through rapidly, shows a horse fluidly galloping across the landscape. But, sometimes, the pages catch on your thumb, and the horse stops and starts with a jerk. If you stop on each individual page, the change from one page to the next is almost impossible to discern. Doing therapy with Grace was like flipping through the pages one at a time. Even when I strained, I could barely see any forward movement, even though there was some evidence of change. Over time, she started opening up more in therapy to discuss the big picture—her relationship with her mother, her view of herself, her disappointments and regrets—even while her crises continued. These disclosures, together with our developing therapeutic bond, were progress, but I didn't realize it until much later because it wasn't what I was looking for initially.

When Grace relapsed during the final week of my practicum, my thumb slipped entirely off the edge of the pages of the book. She landed in the hospital, manic, and it seemed as if we hadn't made any forward movement at all. Our last meeting took place on the haphazardly arranged, threadbare couches on the inpatient unit. Grace thanked me for our work together and then asked if I had brought her new underwear like she had asked. I had not. She hugged me. That was it. I walked out feeling devastated. I felt like I had failed.

At times in my work with Grace it felt as if I were trying to balance on a narrow precipice between two deep chasms. On one side was a well of boundless and naïve optimism that, given enough time and effort, I could help anyone. On the other side was a pit of cynicism and hopelessness, into which I sometimes tumbled after losing my footing. When I was in the pit, I felt powerless to do anything. In the middle was that elusive middle ground called reality, in which both extremes had a hint of truth to them.

This sort of nondualism was a new concept for me. Erich Fromm (1968) described a version of it in *The Revolution of Hope* when he said, "To hope means to be ready at every moment for that which is not yet born, and yet not become desperate if there is no birth in our lifetime" (p. 9). I had a lot of hopes for Grace—too many, in fact—and this left me vulnerable to feelings of desperation when those hopes weren't realized.

It took a couple of years of supervised clinical practice for me to realize that there are a lot of ways to set yourself up to feel like a failure with clients and that I had hit on just about all of them in my work with Grace. Here are some:

- Have unrelentingly high expectations—for your clients and yourself.
- Harbor the belief that you can help anyone, everyone, if you only try hard enough.
- Allow your own notions about "success" and "progress" to supersede your client's ideas about the same.
- Expect your clients to act in certain ways.
- Rely on external sources of positive feedback.
- Take on more than you can handle.
- Forget to take care of yourself.

I'm glad that some of the lessons we must all learn as therapists came early in my career: that success and failure are relative, that progress is nonlinear, that there are limitations to what we can offer, that offering hope is always important. I still feel regret that I couldn't help Grace more. I think of her from time to time when I notice my expectations getting out of hand or when I feel overwhelmed in my work with a particular client. I hope that, even though *I* felt like a failure, I didn't fail *her* entirely. I imagine that she has been making her way through the flip book of her life, at her own pace. I hope that she is well.

Reference

Fromm, E. (1968). *The revolution of hope*. New York: Harper & Row.

SUFFERING NEAR THE END OF LIFE
James L. Werth, Jr.

I have been involved in HIV-related prevention and intervention activities since 1989. Back in the late 1980s, it was not uncommon for people to find out they were infected with HIV and to die soon thereafter. In fact, anyone living more than 2 years after an AIDS diagnosis was considered a long-term survivor. This fact made me fearful that some of my college graduating class might not be around for our 5- or 10-year reunion, so when I was an undergraduate I focused on educating my peers about HIV disease; once I started graduate school in counseling psychology I added a direct service component. Although the journey associated with my HIV work led to many moments that impacted me greatly and taught me important lessons, the one series of interactions that has had the longest lasting impact on me personally and professionally involved my opportunity to work with a man I'll call Thomas and his wife, Katherine. Before talking about Thomas and Katherine in particular, I must lay a foundation to explain why my work with them was so powerful.

When I decided I wanted to do direct service work with HIV–positive individuals, I attended a training sponsored by the local HIV services organization. I had the facts about HIV and knew people who were HIV–positive, but up to this point I had not worked clinically with anyone and therefore had only superficial knowledge about the psychosocial effects of HIV. At the training, the social worker who was leading the session talked about his work with clients and specifically mentioned that one client had said that if he went blind he would kill himself. The social worker talked to us about his struggle associated with this revelation. This made me realize that there was the possibility that some people might come to the conclusion that suicide is a better option than dying of HIV-related conditions. As a psychologist in training and former suicide hotline volunteer, this idea went against all I had learned about suicide prevention. Therefore, I began exploring the idea of "rational suicide" (i.e., that people could make a well-reasoned decision that death is the best option). I wrote an article on the topic that was published in a professional journal (Werth, 1992), which led to my dissertation. In the midst of all this thinking about rational suicide I met Thomas and Katherine.

Thomas became a client of the HIV services organization after he was fired from his job as a janitor in a medical setting. He had become sick and was unable to work. This had led to extensive testing, which had not led to a diagnosis; so as a last resort he had an HIV test done. When it came back positive he tried to figure out how it had happened. The only conclusion he could come to was that he had been infected by a contaminated needle that had been thrown in a trash can. His wife was not infected.

Because he was already ill when he came to the organization, our focus was on trying to keep him as healthy as possible for as long as possible and to keep his wife from becoming infected. He and I both felt a connection quickly when he came into the office for the first time, so I worked with him. Because I was a graduate student who was volunteering for the organization, not working under the supervision of a licensed professional, I didn't do counseling per se but instead was like a "buddy" for him, providing emotional and practical support for him and his wife. As a result of this relationship, I visited Thomas and Katherine in their home, brought them groceries and supplies, and advocated on their behalf with various agencies.

Each time Thomas went into the hospital, I was called by either his wife or someone from the HIV organization. Usually, he was in the hospital for a little while and then released home with treatment for a different condition. However, during what ended up being his last hospitalization, it became clear that things were different. Even after various tests and attempted treatments, the physicians could not seem to determine what was wrong and how to help. As time passed, Thomas's pain increased and his lucidity decreased (probably both as a result of the pain medication and the HIV or other diseases affecting his brain).

Two aspects of this situation are emblazoned in my mind and heart. The first is Thomas's obvious discomfort. Whenever I visited I found Katherine by his side while he moaned—both when he was conscious and when he was sedated. I learned that Katherine had pleaded with the physicians and nurses to do something about the moaning, but to no avail. As Thomas and Katherine's advocate I, too, tried to get him some relief. What his physicians eventually told us was that the moaning was a result of the pain he was experiencing; however, they were unwilling to increase the pain medication or add any other analgesics because they did not want the treatment to accidentally hasten his death. No attempt at reason by me or begging by Katherine had any effect on their decision.

The second aspect that I will forever remember is that part of the reason the physicians took this position was that Thomas did not have any form of advance directive. Even though the agency's social worker and I had talked with him and Katherine about making a living will (a document in which Thomas would state his treatment wishes in the event that he became incapable of making decisions for himself) and a durable power of attorney for health care (a document naming Katherine as the person legally empowered to make medical decisions as if she were he), he had said that he did not want to prepare them yet because he thought there would be plenty of opportunities later. Unfortunately, by the time everyone realized that Thomas was on a downhill course and was losing his ability to make decisions, it was too late. In fact, I believe we were about 1 day too late. By the time we had the forms completed and signed, indicating that he wanted maximum pain relief and naming Katherine as his surrogate, the physicians were convinced that he was no longer capable of making legal decisions and therefore would not honor the forms. They believed they were the ones who should make the medical decisions—hence, the limitations on pain medication.

Thomas died over a week later, the whole time moaning while his wife was in anguish over his suffering. She refused to leave his side, fearful that he might die while she was gone, even though it was agonizing for her to hear him in pain. After he died, she remained in a deep depression, full of guilt over her inability to provide what she believed to be the proper care. I do not know whether she ever came out of the depression.

The entire process of this final hospitalization was incredibly frustrating for me and, clearly, devastating for Katherine. We both felt as if we had failed Thomas, and I felt as if I had failed her as well. The powerlessness and hopelessness we felt were pervasive and palpable. Obviously, her feelings were infinitely deeper than mine, but I still constantly questioned what I could have or should have done differently. My volunteering was not a part of my graduate school experience so I tried to keep it separate, but I am sure that my preoccupation with the misery Thomas and Katherine were experiencing affected my class work and my interactions with my peers. Fortunately, I could talk with my fellow volunteers, which helped tremendously. Unfortunately, once Thomas died, Katherine withdrew from everyone and cut her connections with the organization, so I had to respect her wish to not be contacted by me or anyone else associated with the agency.

I continue to feel some guilt about not being able to help Thomas and Katherine more, but I also have realized that disappointment and emotional pain are a fundamental aspect of this type of work. My time with Thomas and Katherine was truly life changing because it altered my personal and professional outlooks on life. Being a witness to this process led me to want to explore end-of-life decisions and treatment. Since then I have devoted much time and energy to studying and writing about these topics as well as to working with people who are HIV–positive and those who are dying. I am more fully committed to being an informed and assertive advocate for those who are disempowered and disenfranchised. Further, I live my life differently now so that I appreciate each day more and attempt to minimize the "what ifs" and "if onlys." I make decisions in my life based on what my dying clients have taught me about the importance of caring for people and not putting off until tomorrow what can and should be said today. This has made me a better person and a better counselor.

Reference

Werth, J.L., Jr. (1992). Rational suicide and AIDS: Considerations for the psychotherapist. *Counseling Psychologist, 20*, 645–659.

ONLY ROGERS, EVERYWHERE AND ALL THE TIME? NO.
Senel Poyrazli

I started my journey into counseling psychology in Turkey. I completed an undergraduate degree in psychological guidance and counseling and then started graduate school. A year into my master's program, I decided to come to the United States and to complete both the master's and doctorate there. A defining moment in Turkey and a validating moment in the United States both led me to develop as an international counseling psychologist.

Defining Moment in Turkey

My clinical training in Turkey heavily focused on existential–humanistic approaches, mostly Carl Rogers's theory. Many of the Turkish professors who influenced the field of counseling were trained in the 1960s in the United States within an existential–humanistic framework. They carried this knowledge back to Turkey and trained many of their students with these theories. Fulbright professors from the United States in counseling also taught Rogerian methods. Some of these professors, and others who were taught by them, became my instructors and clinical supervisors when I was a student in Turkey.

As an undergraduate senior student, I was required to complete an internship and see clients. Supervision was provided by the course instructor at the university. During this internship, I developed awareness that offering counseling based on Carl Rogers's model caused me to feel stuck after the third or the fourth session. I thought the reason for feeling stuck was because I didn't have advanced training in counseling. As a result, I started the graduate program in counseling.

The program was structured as 1 year of class work and clinical training and another year of thesis work. During my master's internship, I again was disappointed to see that I continued to feel stuck with my clients after a few sessions. I was doing my best to apply what my professors and supervisors were teaching us. I was being empathic, was unconditionally accepting my clients, was providing positive regard, and was being congruent. I was focusing on their emotions. Yet I was feeling inadequate and ineffective as a counselor.

As for my clients, initially they seemed to enjoy being listened to and unconditionally being accepted, but it seemed that they wanted more after a while and felt bored when I did not give them what they needed. In one particular case, one of my clients was Kurdish, and in counseling he expressed the oppression to which he was being subjected. I brought this to my professor's attention in group supervision. I wondered how I could help this client and not feel inadequate. Unfortunately, I was instructed by my professor to tell him, "We do not discuss politics in counseling; we are here to discuss your feelings." However, it was clear to me that I was to discuss any feeling and any event with the client as long as they were not related to this oppression.

I was puzzled. I expressed my confusion and indicated that perhaps we needed more than Rogers and Fritz Perls with particular clients, that it seemed that for some clients their ethnicity played an important role. The professor did not like that I was not satisfied with the theories she was teaching. I was disappointed that oppression was off–limits but also felt that I did not have any choice but to repeat to my client what my professor said. Needless to say, my client dropped out of counseling. *This class discussion was a defining moment for my career.* I made the decision to come to the United States, where the psychology training was the best in the world. I knew that I needed to learn about other theories, to receive advanced training, to learn to help clients from different backgrounds, to become a more effective counseling psychologist, and to carry this knowledge back to Turkey.

After I made this decision, while I was still in Turkey, I decided to trust my "gut feelings" a little bit more, to provide a little bit more structure in the session, and to try to give what my clients seemed to need. I was seeing another client, Filiz (pseudonym), a 10th grader who presented with low self-esteem and self-confidence. Following my supervisor's instructions, initially I applied what I was taught within the existential–humanistic framework and focused on Filiz's experiences and feelings. In two sessions, I was able to bring out that she felt embarrassed in front of her classmates and thought that everyone was always looking at her. She had internalized some of the negative feedback she received from her sister. She believed that her ears were too big, her legs were crooked, and her breasts were uneven. Filiz limped when she walked so that no one would notice her crooked legs. She always wore her hair down so that no one would notice her big ears. She pushed her shoulders out and her chest in so that no one would notice her uneven breasts.

Filiz was facing another dilemma: She had to pass all of her classes. If she did not, her sister was going to send her back to the family's village and not allow her to come back to the city to finish high school. Filiz was passing all of her classes except philosophy. The teacher, fortunately, had given the students the option to take an oral exam in class to receive extra credit. Filiz wanted to take the oral exam, but she had to stand up in class. The thoughts of everyone looking at her and noticing her big ears and uneven breasts were terrifying to her. As Filiz was telling me in the session of her intense fears, I was having my own dilemma. Should I continue to focus on the client's emotions with the hope that empathy and unconditional acceptance would eventually help her break through her problems, or should I follow my gut feelings, provide a little bit more structure and direction in the sessions, and try to change the client's perception so that she could gather her strength to take the oral exam?

My conclusion was that Filiz had to change her inaccurate perception. I needed to get her to see that her negative perceptions about her ears, her legs, her breasts were not accurate. And I had very little time! She came to the conclusion that if her ears were that big, they would stick out from underneath her hair. When she received feedback from me and her friends that her legs were as straight as anybody's can be, she stopped limping. When she received a physical exam from a physician, she learned that her breasts were not uneven and that they were developing normally. Within 2 weeks, she stopped limping and started walking straight. She gathered her courage and took the oral exam. She was thrilled when she learned that she had passed the exam and the class and, therefore, could come back to the city to finish high school. When Filiz gave me the good news that she had stood up in class to take the oral exam, I knew one more time that I needed to receive advanced training. I wanted to keep learning ways of becoming effective with my clients.

Validating Moment in the United States

When I initially arrived in the United States, I first studied English as a second language and then started taking counseling classes at the graduate level. One of the first courses I took was cross-cultural counseling with Dr. Clement E. Vontress at George Washington University. In our first meeting, Dr. Vontress told us that we would focus on different ethnicities, races, and cultures and how a person, depending on his or her culture, might present with different experiences and needs. He also told us that we would be focusing on shortcomings of major theories, that these theories were not inclusive of many multicultural categories, and that many of these theories would not be applicable to different cultural settings. Hearing this knowledge from a professor validated my questioning of the existential–humanistic theories with some of my clients in Turkey. This discussion also helped me see that the counseling psychology education in Turkey could benefit from this multicultural perspective. Similarly, I thought that counseling and psychotherapy education in the United States could also benefit from learning how other cultures in the world operate and how clients' cultural backgrounds could be included in the counseling process. *This particular class discussion was a validating moment for me; I knew that the path I decided to take was the right one and that I should continue examining the applicability of Rogers's theory, especially in cross-cultural settings.* I also knew that I should try to facilitate knowledge exchange between Turkey and the United States so that both cultures could advance the field of psychology and counseling.

Within this particular class, Dr. Vontress encouraged me to write a paper about the validity of Rogerian therapy in a Turkish context. I later published this article in the *Journal of Humanistic Counseling, Education, and Development* (Poyrazli, 2003). In the article, I pointed out that while the theory could be used with some individuals who might be brought up in a more individualistic culture, the theory may not be applicable to the majority of the Turkish population, which practices collectivist values and has an authoritarian structure of relationships.

My hope, with this article, was to facilitate a discussion in Turkey about the cultural limitations of counseling theories and the importance of an individual's cultural background for counseling effectiveness and also to reach others who might be going through the same confusion and feelings of being stuck that I experienced.

In my attempt to facilitate the process of knowledge exchange between the United States and Turkey, I became involved in the American Psychological Association's Division 52—International Psychology. There, I realized that this knowledge exchange should be expanded to include many other countries and cultures in the world. My own defining moment in Turkey and later the validation I received from Dr. Vontress helped me learn more about different ways of healing and cultural practices. This personal development also helped me to be a better instructor for my students. In all of the counseling classes I teach, I expose my students to different helping models from around the world and different cultural backgrounds that their clients might represent. I strongly believe that this knowledge helps my students to be more culturally competent and more effective helpers. I did not know, at the time, that those early feelings of being inadequate and ineffective as a counselor would bring such positive results. Such a nice surprise!

Reference

Poyrazli, S. (2003). Validity of Rogerian therapy in Turkish culture: A cross-cultural perspective. *Journal of Humanistic Counseling, Education and Development, 42*, 107–115.

HEALING AFTER TRAGEDY*
Jill C. Thomas

Although my formal career is only beginning, it has already been a long journey—one that started well before my training in clinical psychology. Prior to graduate school, I worked in community mental health as a case manager, offering clients practical assistance with housing, financial, work, family, and medical issues as well as personal support, gentle challenging, and advocacy. It was during this time that I experienced perhaps the most defining moment of my ongoing development.

My client, Bill (pseudonym), was a 30-year-old, charming, yet very tortured man. He was in an almost constant state of emotional turmoil, suspicion, and pre-occupation with perceived wrongdoings and malintent. Since childhood Bill was "difficult," according to his mother. From early on, his relationships with family members were strained, combative, and sometimes violent. Ever since he could recall, Bill felt fundamentally mistreated and unloved, especially by his mother. He responded with anger, blaming her, rightly or wrongly, for all of his misfortune and misery. Throughout his adult life, including the time I knew him, Bill desperately sought ways to alleviate his pain—he abused drugs, begged for shock treatments, and screamed in anguish via daily letters and calls to his parents until they were terrified and wanted no further contact, finally getting a restraining order.

Bill thought his parents were "toying" with him. As was his pattern, Bill had contacted them seeking financial rescue when he was alone, desperate, and severely depressed, with no medication or money. Instead of sending money, his parents brought him home, promising that once he straightened himself out, they would help him get back on his feet. From the time Bill got home, his goal was to leave. He saw the treatment on which his parents insisted as a means to financial support and escape, not as a means to mental health. He saw treatment as a "game" and felt that he was "playing the game" but that his parents were not living up to their end of the deal. From day one, though I liked Bill, I felt like a pawn in his game—the objective of which was to get me to convince his parents he was "fine."

I resisted Bill's attempts to manipulate me, instead trying to help him to really *be* fine. But Bill sabotaged most such efforts—though I think part of him really did want help. Instead of getting better, he became increasingly angry and fantasized about shooting and killing his family. Though I had resisted before, I decided then to make the call Bill wanted me to make—however, not to convince his parents but to warn them. After speaking to his mother, I was heartbroken. I could see that, rather than the evil monster he thought her to be, she, like Bill, was in incredible pain. She was also terrified because Bill had recently broken into their home and left threatening letters. Thus, it seemed they had already been warned, by Bill himself.

---

* I would like to thank Brian Zalick for his comments on an earlier version of this essay.

Since the police would not take Bill into custody for violating the restraining order and he could not be involuntarily held on a psychiatric unit, I did everything I could to prepare my colleagues before leaving on vacation so that they would take action on any further threats.

When I returned, my worst nightmare began. While away I constantly worried that Bill would be dead when I came back. My first morning back, I was just waiting for someone to tell me it happened. Instead, one of my colleagues told me Bill had come in the day before demanding to see a psychiatrist and that, while waiting, he had talked about buying a gun from the catalog he was browsing. Everyone said he was very agitated, leaving in a fury when the psychiatrist refused to see him without an appointment. As my colleagues recounted these events, I felt panicked and repeatedly asked what they had done to intervene. They had done nothing. I couldn't believe they had done nothing.

Soon after, the phone rang. It was a woman who ran the housing facility where Bill lived when we first met. The police had just called to tell her Bill was dead from an apparent suicide. Her card was in his wallet. As I tried to process this, more news came. Before shooting himself in the head, Bill had shot his sister once and his mother 18 times. The violence of Bill's actions stunned me—even though he had communicated in many ways that this was exactly what he was going to do. As I sat there in my cubicle and focused on his last moments, I finally truly grasped the intensity of Bill's pain and hatred for his mother. I felt incredibly sad for the loss of his life and for the suffering he had inflicted on his family. When I heard that his mother was taken to the hospital by helicopter, I was overwhelmed by the fear that she would die too.

Immediately, I wanted to go home to sleep, thinking it might all be gone when I awoke, like a bad dream. A flurry of activity was going on around me, but I felt heavy and sluggish as I sobbed at my desk. I was surrounded by people, but I felt utterly alone.

Later, at home, I curled up on the couch, covered myself with a blanket, and cried myself to sleep. When I awoke, I turned on the news. I was scared but desperate to know everything that had happened. I needed to know that Bill's family was okay. I learned that Bill's body was found on a landing halfway up the stairs to the second floor of his parents' home. He was dead when the police arrived after receiving a call from neighbors about gunshots. His mother was collapsed at the top of the stairs near her bedroom, bleeding from her gut. His sister was also found upstairs, shot in the leg. That morning, Bill had somehow rented a car and driven to his parents' house, where the car was still sitting. At the scene, the police found Bill's journal detailing his anger and pain. Reporters showed and read clippings from it. They also showed Bill's body as it was removed from the home. He was wheeled out on a gurney. He was covered with a maroon blanket, but I could see the bottoms of his gym shoes.

Still, it all seemed so unreal.

I remember thinking that Bill would have been proud that his story made headlines but also very angry about the picture being painted. He wanted to show the world what an evil woman he believed his mother was. Instead, in his final act he became the villain. As angry as it made me to view such a sensationalized and simplified version of the story that portrayed Bill *only* as evil and crazy, I could not stop watching because I needed to see him. I felt incredibly sad and angry that I had not gotten to see him one last time before he died. He knew I was returning that morning. He killed himself around 7 a.m. I returned to work at 8.

Initially, I convinced myself that Bill's suicide was inevitable, that I couldn't blame myself for being on vacation because I couldn't have prevented his suicide forever. Instead of blaming myself, I blamed others. Bill was dead, and I blamed everyone who had seen him the day before and done nothing. My anger grew as the days went on and I learned more about the events leading up to Bill's death—about more missed opportunities for intervention, both in my office and other places where Bill sought help that day.

I wanted to reach out to Bill's family, out of guilt and grief, but I was scared of their reaction, and I didn't know what to say. Eventually, I sent a card. There was no funeral or service for Bill. I don't know what happened to his family or whether, or how, they recovered from their physical and emotional injuries. I still think about them, and I still think about Bill. It has been many years since his death, yet, even as I write this today, I still feel the loss and experience the memories as if they happened yesterday.

For several years, I tried to understand what led to this tragedy and actively processed my feelings, which grew much more complex over time, so I could move forward. These efforts at healing involved personal exploration, through writing and therapy, and also shaped my early training focus. In graduate school, I began an intense study of the suicide literature and returned to the community mental health system to conduct formal research. I interviewed clinicians and suicidal clients to try to find ways to prevent similar tragedies—to avoid missing opportunities to intervene by trying to understand suicide from a client's perspective and barriers to intervention from a clinician's perspective. I also researched the suicide survivor literature and spoke at a professional convention about being a survivor of client suicide. Though I wrote in detail about my experience as part of this process, I have never publicly shared my narrative. I am grateful to be able to share this experience now.

THE STORY OF A NAME
Wei-Chien Lee

Every identity has at least two sides: "identifying with" and "expression of." People may express a part of themselves through a necklace, a tattoo, or a hairstyle, but each choice communicates to others, "This is what I identify with and choose to show. Can you read me, decipher it, or hear me?" I had never imagined, but surprisingly found, that the name I allowed people to call me had been the most visible front of my identity development in a multicultural context.

Call Me Anything

As a new immigrant and a master's student in a counseling program, I noticed that people could not remember or pronounce my name, even after several interactions. I therefore started suggesting people call me "Way" or "anything." My cultural values dictated me to actively avoid causing people any inconvenience or embarrassment, to respect others, and to create harmony; modifying my name voluntarily was my way to achieve these objectives.

Like many Asian Americans, I have learned to use intentional and considerate behaviors to communicate my respect for self and others. These behaviors are intricate, subtle, and highly contextualized, with a meta-message of "The humbler and more considerate one behaves, the greater one is." The rule of engagement was, "I will accommodate to others' needs before they ask (so they do not even have to ask), and others will do the same for me." Modifying my name and giving people who had a hard time pronouncing or remembering my name the permission to call me "anything" served two purposes. It allowed me to express my virtues— my capability of humbling myself to make others feel more comfortable or to help them "save face." It also invited others to ask me about my name—in a culture in which not calling people their real names is considered rude behavior, you know that when people say, "Call me anything," they are communicating, "I am encouraging you to ask again." I didn't realize until much later, however, that my statement, "Sorry that my name is difficult to pronounce; you can call me anything" was often interpreted drastically differently from my intention.

Fairness and Respect

I continued allowing people to call me anything and was trained to react to sounds such as "Mm…," "Chiny," "Wee," or "Lee," until my off-site practicum supervisor challenged me during our first meeting. She asked me warmly, "Teach me how to pronounce your name." "No, that's okay; call me anything," I replied. I was in shock; she seemed to be serious. Gently and assertively she said, "You respect us enough to learn our names, and we should learn your name." I felt uneasy about "teaching my supervisor," but the ideas of fairness and respect spoke to me.

Through my practicum year, my supervisor always called me Wei-Chien, and she assertively coached others to do the same. During that year, I also learned from my supervisor that multiculturalism is not just a concept but also an action; multiculturalism is about not only truly respecting, understanding, and communicating about "differences" but also recognizing and reducing oppression, through different paths and even in "small" ways such as learning to pronounce a two-syllable name. I stopped using "anything" as my name midway through my practicum.

An "American" Name?

During my doctoral training, I asked my classmates to call me Wei-Chien. They were thoughtful and willing to learn and always called me Wei-Chien. However, challenges to my identity took a different form. During one group supervision class, I attempted to contribute to the class discussion by humbling myself. I shared with my class that one of my scheduled intakes had requested to see an American therapist before meeting with me. My classmates jumped in to help: "You should get an American name." "Maybe you should focus on seeing international students." "Try to use Ms. Lee instead of your full name." I listened to the discussion. However,

I did not say a thing, because I had been the unique voice in that class. Similar to many other minorities, I have learned that to "survive" as a minority, I have to know my "place," pick my battles, or deal with the consequences of speaking my voice. I learned to pick up little clues for how I should behave in different contexts to avoid being "punished" (e.g., isolated, shut down). At the beginning of the semester, many of my comments about cultural issues were invalidated by the instructor or classmates. For example, when I tried to explain why their small, seemingly well-intentioned, and "supportive" feedback hurt me, I was told that I was too sensitive. I was also told that I was "too emotional" or "coming on too strong" on issues related to multiculturalism. More than once I heard, "You always talk about multiculturalism; we get it, we all are different." I knew my place. I tried to change the environment by voicing out, challenging different beliefs, and inviting people to see things from different angles. However, after losing many battles, staying silent at times seemed to be the only thing I could do, and it helped me avoid rejection or judgment.

My advisor kept me strong and centered during my doctoral training. Numerous times I ran into his office for wisdom, compassion, support, and skills. He taught me that multiculturalism is about examining the validity of observations and assumptions. He acknowledged his privileges as a Caucasian male. He validated the inequalities and challenges I had to deal with. He learned my name before our first meeting and patiently earned my trust. He constantly encouraged me to acknowledge and start using my power and strengths to deal with challenges. "Power?" I wondered. "Do I have any power as a minority immigrant female? How could I use it? What or whom would I become if I start using my 'power'?"

The Doors to Freedom

The tidal wave of change came during my internship. My supervisors assertively and consistently informed me that my bilingual and multicultural backgrounds were extremely valuable. They said, "Wei-Chien, you need to put your bilingual and bicultural background in your vita. These are assets for our students." Really? Nobody had ever said anything like that to me directly. My supervisors pointed out that clients appreciated my "differences," stating, "Have you noticed that you open doors to different worlds for your clients and give them the freedom of being themselves?" My clients did say that they realized that many rules, judgments, and perceptions were arbitrary and context dependent, and they frequent cited my "signature" statement: "This behavior would be considered perfectly normal or super in X culture at Y time, but we need to find the skills and knowledge to help you to achieve this goal effectively in this culture at this time."

As the multifaceted and gestalt nature of identity became clearer to me, "being different" became "being unique in this context for this group in this culture at this time." I started exploring and experimenting with ways to use my powers. I thrived, became powerful, and felt whole. I also started telling people what "Wei-Chien" means ("a handsome and great hero").

During my postdoctoral year, I finally gathered enough courage to argue with the California Department of Motor Vehicles (DMV); they had insisted that

"Chien" was my middle name and "Wei" was my first name. During one of the arguments, a manager, apparently trying to be nice, stated, "I don't understand why your name is so important to you; it's just a name. Why don't you get an American name?" My Asian American parts asked me to back away, telling me, "You do not embarrass people; you avoid disrupting harmony." But other voices came to my heart—students who had considered me a role model, my mentors who taught me about multiculturalism, and people who had fewer privileges and less power to defend or fight for themselves. With these voices, I made a conscious decision about what I wanted to do. I gently asserted my request, cited relevant regulations, evoked empathic understanding, and focused on my goal. I won. Tears flooded out of my eyes as I walked out of the DMV.

The crystallizing event of my growth was a new employee self-introduction I made to more than 100 health professionals in an agency, where people had called me "Chin" since I had started. I hadn't "corrected" anyone about my name yet, because I was waiting for a most effective and positive way to communicate my preference. After my name was announced ("Dr. Lee"), I walked up to the podium, smiled, introduced myself, and said, "Please call me Dr. Lee or Wei-Chien. Wei-Chien is my first name. I do not cut your first name in half, so please do not cut mine in half." I pointed at the director. "For example, this is Mark, or should I call him 'Ma' or 'rk'?" The audience laughed and applauded, and I achieved my goal of transferring a small multicultural competence to the staff. I was confident, powerful, and gently assertive. A couple of Asian American employees later came to me and expressed their appreciation of what I had done.

Use Your Power

I imagine my supervisees, students, and clients would smile as they read about these moments. I ask people what they would like to be called and what their names mean to them. I encourage people to make contextualizing statements, such as, "This behavior or knowledge is not effective for achieving this objective at this time within this culture." I actively seek out those "quiet" or "different" students to empower them to find themselves. I always "yell" at my trainees that "multiculturalism is a verb!" I cringe when I hear psychologists or supervisors say to their clients, "You are a credit to your race," or "You are doing pretty well for a ...." I value acknowledging challenges and empowering and empathizing with and trusting others. I point out different levels of injustice by asking, "Do you think it's really all your fault? Would you feel differently if our society were not so ...?" I gently and assertively ask people to "recognize and use your power" to generate compassion and understanding, to acknowledge privileges, and to reduce oppression.

What should you call me now? I am back to the "You can call me anything" stage but for a different set of reasons. People are at different places of identity development, have different identities, and have different levels of cultural competency. People also have learned different "rules" or preferences about what to call others in different contexts at different times. I will work with you at your comfort level and help both of us learn from each other. It will be a beautiful journey.

PARADOXICAL EMPOWERMENT: FINDING A VOICE IN BICULTURAL NAVIGATION
Jeeseon Park

I was a second-year doctoral student in a counseling psychology program, completing my practicum at the university's counseling center. At the time, I was still recovering from the counterculture shock that I had experienced during my trip back home to Korea. After having spent a year as an Asian international student on a predominantly White campus in central Pennsylvania, I rejoiced at the thought of being surrounded by people who looked like me and spoke my language. My blissful anticipation was soon replaced by the painful realization of how much I had already grown apart from my family and friends. I was with "my people," yet I was not one of them anymore. I felt like a stranger in my home country. I left Korea with pangs of sadness and a profound sense of confusion.

My feelings of confusion only intensified when I returned to Pennsylvania, where I stood out like a sore thumb everywhere I went. I did not belong to either place. I had no place that I could call home. I had never felt so lonely and lost in my life.

My confusion filtered its way into my clinical work. I lost my voice as a clinician; I silenced my intuitions, conceptualizations, and reactions to my interactions with my clients, as I constantly questioned which of my two worlds was speaking louder at any given moment. I passively let my clients take charge of the counseling process. Then came the defining moment that set me on the path to finding my voice.

In the second semester of practicum, I was paired up with a new supervisor, who informed me in our first supervision meeting that her supervision style was heavily influenced by the feminist approach. She enthusiastically emphasized that the main focus of her supervision work was the empowerment of her supervisees. She further explained that she tried to achieve that goal by letting her supervisees decide the content of supervision according to their self-identified needs. I sat silently through my supervisor's introduction, attentively listening to her, although my mind was filled with a cacophony of conflicting voices: What a relief that my supervisor is clearly laying out what is expected of me in supervision! Empowerment of supervisee? That sounds quite encouraging and uplifting, but what does it really mean? Do I really get to have a say in what I want to discuss in supervision? How am I going to figure out what I need? Can't she just tell me what I need to do to hone my clinical skills? Isn't she supposed to know what I need at this stage of my training? Even though everything that my supervisor suggested sounded good in theory, it did not fit well with the schema of the evaluative relationship that I had in my mind. Having grown up in a hierarchal culture where paying respect to authority figures was considered an essential virtue, I had a hard time picturing myself as an equal partner in the egalitarian supervisory relationship that my supervisor was describing.

Despite all these questions and doubts, when my supervisor asked me what I thought about her suggestions, I politely told her that they all sounded good to me. It was almost a reflexive response. In my confusion, my mind must have automatically resorted to the acquiescent behavior that had been programmed into me through my upbringing in Korea. At the end of the supervision session, my supervisor held the door for me as we both left the room. I hesitated, but my supervisor insisted that I leave the room first. Despite my feelings of discomfort, I reverted to obedience once again, and I preceded her through the doorway. My supervisor's wonderful sense of humor helped to dissipate the awkwardness that I felt in that moment, and we both burst out laughing.

The following week, my supervisor appeared more subdued than she had the previous week. She asked me what it was like for me to hear what she had to say about the ground rules of our supervision. She said that she had noticed my hesitation to walk through the door when she held it open for me at the end of the session and that this had prompted her to think about my comfort level with adopting American values. She wondered whether her suggestions about having me guide the content of our supervision—suggestions that were meant to empower me—had unintentionally disempowered me. She apologized for imposing her ideas about supervision on me without first asking me about the nature of the supervisory relationships that I had experienced in Korea and the type of supervisory relationship with which I would feel most comfortable.

Suddenly, it felt as if a thick fog had lifted. I was very humbled by my supervisor's openness and honesty about her potential mistake. That was something that I never witnessed in my supervisors in Korea, where rules about saving face are deeply entrenched in social interactions (Zane & Yeh, 2002). I really appreciated the risk that my supervisor was taking by letting go of her assumption that the supervisory style she had proposed would fit with my style. Ironically, by admitting that she might have made a mistake by not assessing my needs, she showed a great deal of sensitivity. I could feel that she was genuinely concerned about my needs as a supervisee. In a very paradoxical way, she practiced what she preached. The congruence between her words and behaviors made me feel understood and cared for as a supervisee. Also, my supervisor's honesty made me want to reciprocate with the same level of candor about my reactions.

The interactions that my supervisor and I had in our first supervision sessions certainly "stretched" me to my limits (Skovholt & McCarthy, 1988). However, the positive feelings that I experienced as a result of my supervisor's humbleness, openness, and congruence helped me move beyond the boundary of my limits and enabled me to give voice to my confusion and doubts about the ground rules of our supervision. Our discussion paved the way for an in-depth exploration of what it would mean to me, as an Asian woman, to embrace a feminist approach. My supervisor's attitude of "not knowing" and her inquisitiveness about my unique experience as an Asian woman studying counseling psychology on a predominantly White campus enabled me to process the internal conflicts I felt while navigating between Korean and American cultures. Even though several years passed before I became somewhat fluid in navigating between the two cultures, this defining moment in supervision helped me catch a glimpse of possibilities beyond an either–or dichotomy.

All these positive experiences in supervision brought forth positive changes in my clinical work. I began to find my voice as a clinician. I became more comfortable about giving voice to my doubts and confusion when my clients' narratives about their experiences did not make sense to me. I came to trust my gut feelings during counseling sessions and started to feel more confident about using them to help my clients gain insight into their interpersonal dynamics. Instead of trying to figure out which part of my two worlds was speaking louder at a given moment, I tried to be present in the moment. This helped me be more spontaneous in counseling sessions and make more meaningful connections with my clients. Furthermore, I became less worried about making mistakes in my clinical work. My experience in supervision taught me that what really matters is how you recover from your mistakes.

I can see now that my journey of finding my own voice in bicultural navigations fostered my development as a clinician in important ways. I echo Olsen's (1988) observation that bicultural experiences force people "to be sensitive to the way others may be viewing *their* world" (p. 92, italics in original). Also, my bicultural experiences afforded me the perceptual acuity that one can obtain only as an outsider. I learned over the years that an outside observer's perspective, combined with empathy and positive regard for clients, could provide a solid sounding board against which clients could explore their issues. I am grateful to my supervisor for helping me find my voice in bicultural navigation.

References

Olson, T. (1988). Bifocality—And the space between. *Journal of Counseling and Development, 67*, 92.

Skovholt, T.M., & McCarthy, P.R. (1988). Critical incidents: Catalysts for counselor development. *Journal of Counseling and Development, 67*, 69–72.

Zane, N., & Yeh, M. (2002). The use of culturally-based variables in assessment: Studies on loss of face. In K.S. Kurasaki, S. Okasaki, & S. Sue (Eds.), *Asian American mental health: Assessment theories and methods* (pp. 123–138). New York: Kluwer Academic/Plenum.

THE GAP
Vasudev N. Dixit

Pursuing my interests in the field of psychology has been a challenge in more ways than one. It is a field that was previously unknown to my parents, who earned their PhDs in chemistry in India before immigrating to America. Thus, when I announced that I would be majoring in psychology, they received the idea with great fear and anxiety. After years of being guided toward the physical sciences, I was breaking out of my mold. This undertaking, along with school and work, led me to pursue an advanced degree in psychology.

While my parents and their families have their educational grounding in the "hard sciences" such as chemistry, engineering, and computer technologies, I chose to study a field of knowledge not traditionally found in my family. We have never openly discussed "tradition" as it pertained to my career choice, but it was salient.

My parents wanted me to be successful, which meant pursuing a career that was proven to be not only lucrative but also stable. However, their perceptions of what careers were lucrative and stable were limited to what they knew through their family, their friends, and their own experiences.

I enjoyed being the pioneer in my family. Many interesting conversations were started when relatives came to learn of what I studied. However, the pursuit of studying psychology came with a price. As a child, I wanted to be a good son, to follow their lead, and to be their pride. As a student, I wanted to explore all possibilities and go where no one had been before. Yes, my dreams were lofty, but they were (and continue to be) real for me. It seemed that my sentiments and my dreams were at a fork in the road of my life. In a strange way, I was forced to make a choice between viewing the world in a way my parents had not conceived and going the "safe way" of what was known.

As a child, my parents would explain the physical science behind anything I observed. Anything from a rainbow to the human body was explained in terms of hard science. When they realized that I was not going to continue along a similar path as they had, there was some kind of intellectual disconnect. It was as if a legacy was broken by my choice to broaden my horizons. It was clear that the intellectual bridge between my parents and me was drawn closed—only a gap remained.

Perhaps this was my fear all along. While I wanted to pursue my own self-directed interests and carve my own niche instead of treading the beaten path, I did not want a disconnection of any sort to take place. As I write this, I realize that this was the inevitable developmental challenge, a rite of passage that indicated the commencement of my adulthood. It was also the beginning of releasing my intellectual identity as it was previously defined by my family's culture, and of reinventing it.

As I went forward with my interests, my parents found that they could not tutor me or even intellectually relate to my studies. Now that I reflect, it was scary for me that my parents were no longer the experts. It may have been even scarier for my parents to watch their first son gain awareness to a world in which they had no formal training.

My parents eventually became interested in what I studied as I progressed through my master's program and eventually my doctorate program. For the first time, in social circles where parents would talk about their children's successes, they would proudly mention my career objectives.

Growing up as a first-generation Indian American has led me to construct my identity from both my Indian roots as well as Western culture. I have shared many of the challenges of defining myself with peers who have their roots in this country. However, I had not only the pressures of fitting in at school but also the compelling force of maintaining traditional values at home.

For example, adolescents in America are generally expected to behave independently and subsequently are given freedom to make decisions on their own. Hence, when I began to assert my independence, as many of my friends did, my parents felt as though I was disrespectful to them and the Indian culture as a whole. Clearly, these "cultural clashes" created miscommunication between my parents and me. This included my decision to study psychology as opposed to medicine. Such challenges have molded my identity; being raised in a culture different from that of my parents has allowed me to understand the perspective of immigrant parents raising their children in a foreign culture.

This experience, along with my education in psychology, not only has made me receptive to the disparities between Asian and Western cultures and their effect on forming identity but also has developed my character by giving me a perspective of both cultures. While I have my roots in the Indian culture, I have assimilated some Western values after being raised in a Western society. In a nature–nurture sense, I am bicultural.

As a first-generation Indian American, I have had the challenge and privilege of being raised in two different cultures. Negotiating cultural values as Indian with my family and as an Indian *American* with my peers has presented a series of unique challenges that have given me a unique perspective. As I observe my younger brother go through a similar process, I realize the heightened level of concern that my parents have about being strangers in a strange land. After 31 years of living in this country, they often feel out of place. At the same time, I see a reflection of myself as I observe the cultural challenges my younger brother faces. While cultural clashes sometimes create friction, I consider my bicultural experience a privilege, as it has offered me the opportunity to take the best of both cultures and blend them into my life.

As I gain experience and learn to apply theory as a clinician in training, I realize much of what I have learned as a student of psychology is not universal. When I compare my cultural experiences with some of my past experiences in academia, I see the gaps in our field's understanding of immigrant populations.

It is my personal mission to increase cultural awareness in the field of mental health and to make our services more accessible to immigrants and their children. As mental health professionals become more sensitive to the unique issues immigrants face, approaches will develop *around* each client as opposed to pushing clients through a system that was never intended for them. It is my dream to see immigrant populations that have traditionally been overlooked by the mental health field consider our services as viable options for improving their lives.

This has driven my research related to multicultural issues such as the effects of acculturation on families, including stressors on immigrant couples, challenges parents face when raising their children in a foreign country, and identity formation in immigrant or first-generation children. These issues must be considered within the therapeutic setting as well as program development in schools and communities if we are to build a truly inclusive and unified society. If we are to be the catalyst for change in society, we must first meet each individual *where he or she is* because change is a self-propagating phenomenon that starts with one person.

In reflecting on my experiences, I don't think my parents will ever know what it feels like to be a therapist in a counseling room. I'm not sure if we will ever draw that bridge across the intellectual gap that seemed to develop when I chose to follow my passion in psychology. What I do know is that I am committed to a field that has broadened my understanding of people. In the same brushstroke, it is a field that has given and continues to give me the tools to give back to a world that has so much potential. It is strange to think of the possibility that I may not have been an aspiring psychologist, were it for me to choose the "safe way." However, I choose my path not in spite of the cultural challenges I have endured but *because* of them.

As I contemplate the path of my life, I am drawn to the inevitable gaps I have overcome. Whether it is drawing attention to culture in traditional psychological perspectives, reaching common intellectual ground with my family, or pulling together my Indian and American identities, I find myself building bridges across gaps. One may consider this to be an arduous task, but it is no different from this moment, as it comes to me from the space between my breaths.

It is at every point along my journey that seemed to be a chasm that I have drawn my strongest bridges and found my purpose. When I look behind me and reflect on the bridges I've built and crossed, I realize that the gaps were never so wide. In fact, there never was a gap in the path, only one in my understanding.

Breaking Boundaries—A Philosophical Note

It is difficult to say for certain that there is any one defining moment in my life that helped me break through the boundaries I've faced in studying psychology. Life is like a single thread that weaves itself under and over a series of other threads. As I observe this orchestrated flow, it becomes apparent that life *is* a Moment. The quality of the quilt that is woven through our existence reflects the lessons we have learned in this great Moment of a life. As I bear this in mind, I continue to learn through my experiences and understand myself as not only an aspiring psychologist but also a constantly evolving human being.

CHAPTER SUMMARY

Beginning students are emerging. They are entering into a period of development that is at once exhilarating and exposed and vulnerable. Students in this stage have often been called to this profession because of a desire to help people and have likely had some positive early helping experiences. However, trainees at this stage are often anxious and not yet adept or sure of themselves or their professional identities.

Importance of Supervision and Mentoring

Beginning students often look to supervisors for encouragement and guidance. When they do not get the support and guidance they seek, the impact can be overwhelming to their developing sense of professional competence. Jennings writes of an early supervision experience in which he described feeling "devastated and humiliated." Fortunately, he found support from other mentors and now uses this experience to guide his interventions with his students and supervisees. Weis heard the dreaded words from his supervisor: "This is the stupidest thing I have ever heard." Although he was initially overwhelmed, he went on to make meaning of the incident for himself, adopting the view that he values helping clients to expand their personal power instead of holding the power as the therapist.

Davis uses his experience of being attracted to a client as a beginning student to inform his subsequent supervisory work. He writes, "It is incumbent upon supervisors to discuss attraction to clients early in supervision, similar to discussions about diversity." As an international scholar, Goh describes the value of his professors' "critical affirmations," as they valued his contributions and perspectives, gestures that changed the trajectory of his career. Benshoff describes the importance of an early mentoring experience for him. He benefited from being able to "apprentice with a master," to grow his group facilitation skills, and to be seen as a capable and effective student.

Exploring an Emerging Sense of Identity

Beginning counselors often feel a strong need to "do it right." For example, Backes-Diaz tells us how she so desperately wanted to be a "good counselor" and how her initial attempts to do so seemed to get in the way of her natural instincts as a helper. Through validating supervision and ongoing self-reflection, she continues on her quest toward becoming an "authentic" practitioner. Osachuk also tells us of how he was "trying so very hard" to be a competent therapist and focusing on "doing things right." Beginning students also work to define who they are as professionals. Koch writes of feeling ambivalent about integrating her mothering abilities into her work as a therapist and finding, to her surprise, that her two identities as therapist and mother could come together.

How Much Can We Help?

Beginning students in this chapter describe experiences in which they question their fit for this profession or whether they are really helping their clients. After working with a client around past trauma, Shepler recalls telling his supervisor that he didn't know if counseling was "his thing." Sanger describes how she felt like a failure with a client and only now, after several years of experience, does she understand that notions of "success" and "failure" are relative. Werth tells us of how he felt as though he failed. He describes feeling powerless and hopeless, though his experience advocating for Thomas and Katherine forever altered his outlook on life and ultimately his career choice. Poyrazli discusses "feeling inadequate and ineffective as a counselor" as he employed a theoretical approach that did not meet all of his needs. He later decided to trust his "gut feelings" and to provide more structure to his counseling sessions with clients and began to feel more effective in his work. Thomas highlights the questions that were raised for her after having experienced a tragedy in a clinical setting; she continues to work to make sense the meaning of this event as she grows as a clinician and person.

Multicultural Experiences and Professional Development

Multicultural identity development and growth as a multiculturally competent practitioner can happen at any phase of counselor–therapist development. However, individuals in the beginning student phase face unique challenges and opportunities related to these processes. As they start to see clients for the first time, they experience exposure to others' worldviews in the novel counseling setting. At the same time, they are likely still becoming aware of their own values and biases. All of this is happening when students are developing a sense of confidence in their abilities as therapists. Paired together, this can present distinctive opportunities for development and growth.

Lee writes about how she experienced tension between her own cultural value of creating harmony and an early supervisor's assertion that she ask others to learn to pronounce her name rather than to defer to others about what to call her. Resolving this tension represented a step forward on her multicultural journey. Park describes her experience of not feeling as though she fit in anywhere—not her home country of Korea or the United States where she was completing her doctoral work. She speaks of how this dearth of belongingness filtered into her clinical work and how she felt as though she lost her voice as a clinician. She later found her voice through the help of a transformative supervisory relationship. Dixit describes being drawn to build bridges across what he describes as gaps and, along the way, realizing that the gaps existed only in his understanding.

Reading the collection of defining moments that occurred for individuals when they were beginning students, one is struck by both the turmoil evident in this phase and the rich opportunities for growth and professional development that exist amidst this turmoil. The questions that are raised for beginning students—about how to practice, who they are as practitioners, in fact what this work is all about—are many. But the potential for valuable learning, especially at the hands of competent, caring supervisors is also great. Learning might take time and reflection to gel, but once it does, it appears to have a lasting impact.

QUESTIONS

1. Davis writes of being attracted to a client. He shares that he now uses this experience to inform his supervisory work. If or when you are or were attracted to a client, would you feel comfortable bringing this up in supervision? In a consultation group of your peers? If not or if so, what factors contribute to your discomfort or comfort? How might a supervisor or consultation group create an environment in which it is safe to bring up such a topic?

2. Sanger writes of how she felt as though she failed her client. Years later, she is able to reflect on the therapeutic relationship and see ways she might have been overinvolved or "working harder than the client." In your work as a therapist in training or therapist, are there times when this has happened to you? If so, what did you take away from those experiences?

3. Lee uses the story of asking people to call her by her name and to pronounce it correctly as a metaphor for her own multicultural journey. What have you learned about your multicultural identity through your work as a counselor?

4. Jennings and Weis both write of early supervision experiences in which they felt invalidated in some way; however, each seems to have challenged himself to make some meaning of the event. How might you use or how have you used a difficult supervisory experience as a catalyst for growth and development?
5. Backes-Diaz describes her strong desire to be a "good counselor" and "do it right." In your own professional development, have these themes come up for you? If so, how have they impacted your work with clients or your professional development process?

4

The Advanced Student Phase

A dvanced students are able to function as professional helpers at the basic level. They feel more comfortable with their clinical skills, and their self-confidence is on the rise. Their beginning training is behind them, visible in the rearview mirror as they look ahead to the process of gaining further clinical experiences through advanced practicums and internships. Even so, individuals at this phase of development still experience considerable vulnerability and insecurity; they continue to actively seek confirmatory feedback from supervisors and peers. Similar to beginning students, advanced students also rely upon modeling as a form of learning, and experiences in supervision may provide strong fodder for defining moments at this level of training. However, unlike beginning students, advanced trainees apply a more critical eye to models of counseling or therapy. They carefully consider model components, rejecting some parts and keeping others, according to their unique assessment criteria.

All told, advanced students function in an in-between space: in between beginner and professional status, in between a predominantly external and a predominantly internal focus, and in between vulnerability and confidence. As they embark upon advanced training experiences, they begin to realize that they have established basic competencies in counseling, even as their awareness of what they do not know grows. This can be very unsettling. They learn how to work with unique populations that have not yet been encountered in their growing professional experience. More complex concepts, such as the dynamics of transference and countertransference, become increasingly salient at this phase of development. Advanced students also experience a growing appreciation for the intricacies related to multicultural counseling, along with the realization that learning to work with diverse populations must be an ongoing process. In contrast to beginning counselors, who can be preoccupied with anxious feelings during sessions, advanced students' internal experiences have generally quieted enough so that they can begin to use their feelings as sources of data rather than of distraction.

LEARNING WHAT NOT TO DO: LESSONS FROM LOUSY EDUCATORS AND SUPERVISORS
Nicholas Ladany

Not long ago I met a Buddhist nun who told me that "mean people offer us the fertilizer to help us grow." Her contention summarizes well some of my best learning experiences from my graduate school training. In particular, in the final 2 years of my doctoral work I learned a great deal about psychological suffering (mine and others) and how that suffering could be turned into a career as a counselor educator. Three educators and supervisors taught me lessons about the field of counseling that I still carry with me. One supervisor employed his primary, and seemingly favorite, supervisory intervention of not showing up for supervision. Another supervisor demonstrated racism that would have made Jesse Helms blush. Still another supervisor's own incompetence overwhelmed him so greatly that his only recourse was to lash out at anyone who appeared more competent than he (which meant a lot of lashing out!). In all, these experiences cultivated and offered fodder for large swatches of my research agenda, specifically my work on secrets in supervision, supervisor disclosure, multicultural issues, and supervisory ethics.

In my fifth year of doctoral training I was afforded the position of counseling coordinator of a supplemental unit at the university counseling center called Middle Earth. The center was initially created as a counterculture center for students in the 1960s and was primarily a hotline for students experiencing mental health concerns. A component of Middle Earth offered face-to-face counseling to students, who, for a variety of reasons (many quite sane), chose not to go to the university counseling center. It was this counseling component that I coordinated, and, in turn, I supervised the other counselors, thereby gaining my first supervision experience (sans any real training). Like J. R. R. Tolkien's more well-known Middle Earth, the center was filled with counselors who, with their wizardry, magically helped their clients. It also had supervisors and administrators/educators who resembled golems, the troll-like creatures of the underbelly, a bit too much. I had two supervisors, one of whom supervised my supervision and the other who supervised my counseling. To protect reputations of people with similar names, I will call them Dr. No-Show and Dr. Don't-Know. Dr. No-Show served his pseudonym well. I may have seen him three times in the fall semester, and, at some point during the spring semester after not seeing him for a couple of months, I learned through a party invitation that he had retired. It's true that you can learn an awful lot about what you know when you work without a safety net, but it is not the way I had hoped to learn. As I mentioned earlier, to that point, and really to this day, I had no training in supervision apart from the research I had done (please don't tell anyone!). Somehow though, I muddled through it, and through the natural skills of the counselors on staff, our center continued to offer counseling services that I believe were better than those offered through the counseling center. Dr. No-Show's lack of attendance was one of my first disillusionment experiences in graduate school and perhaps better prepared me for my next disillusionment experience with Dr. Don't-Know.

The incident that encapsulated my experiences with Dr. Don't-Know occurred during a case conference meeting in the spring semester. It was the staff psychiatrist's turn to present, and during his presentation he referred to one of his clients as his "fat chick" and another client as his "Island Princess" (a slang term for Jewish women from Long Island, New York). Perhaps more disconcerting than his comments were the reactions among the staff, including Dr. Don't-Know. They all laughed. Perhaps naïvely, but certainly boldly, after the case conference I went to the psychiatrist's office and let him know that I was uncomfortable with his comments. With a caring tone in his voice he let me know that over time I would eventually learn that "sometimes you need to see clients as niggers, kikes, and spics." Angry and upset I left the meeting with him and, later that day, talked with Dr. Don't-Know about my feelings regarding this entire incident.

There's an old Gestalt expression that goes something like, "Anything before a 'but' is a lie." Fulfilling the Gestalt prophecy, after expressing my dismay over the psychiatrist's comments, my supervisor offered a concerned look toward me, gave the minimal encourager "Hmm..." and said, "That's not a great thing to say, but ... he is a good psychiatrist. And really, why does that bother you so much? Seems you are more upset that you should be."

I suppose, to be fair, I really didn't know how upset I should have been. It seemed like the comments warranted a fair amount of indignation and anger, but perhaps for the sake of Dr. Don't-Know I could have been more of a racist, which in turn would have tempered my reaction. Stunned, I can't remember saying much. Fortunately, Dr. Don't-Know proceeded to intervene with his primary intervention—nonstop self-disclosures about his life that invariably moved further and further away from the topic at hand. Working with Dr. Don't-Know, I learned the concept of narcissism and fully developed the skill of a good head nod. This set of sexist and racist experiences taught me about a different form of White male privilege—that is, one where White men will disclose their true sexist and racist thoughts and feelings to other White men under the belief that everyone thinks like them. It also illuminated for me that many supervisors were uniquely and profoundly multiculturally incompetent—something I believe continues to run rampant in the present day.

My final incompetent supervisor, Dr. One-Trick, was my primary supervisor on my internship, the final year of my doctoral training. As with my previous supervisors, each of whom had a default or favorite supervisory intervention (no-show and self-disclose), Dr. One-Trick's favorite intervention was the statement, "What is it about you that ...?" Perhaps I should have been savvier by this time in my training, but I suppose I really wanted to believe that there were competent supervisors in the world (like ones I had had earlier in my training). But I threw caution to the wind and told Dr. One-Trick about the sexist and racist experiences I had had a few months earlier. His response was, "What is it about you that has a hard time with those comments?" The accusation was clear: There was something wrong inside of me because I was unhappy with sexist and racist comments. Dr. One-Trick's hope was that he could fix me so that I would accept these comments and learn not to react poorly to them. Unfortunately for him, and later for me, I could not wrap my head around his warped notion of counselor training. The semester proceeded with this pat intervention to the point where I pressed for some feedback about my counseling work. Dr. One-Trick did not believe he needed to listen to recordings of counseling sessions and could evaluate interns based on his experience with them in supervision. His response to my query about feedback was, "What is it about you that needs feedback?" Unwisely perhaps, I responded, "Why don't you try it and we'll find out"—to which he got quite angry and after further discussion yelled, "Why can't you just be happy being an intern?!"

Unless the reader is one of my aforementioned supervisors, I suspect that these experiences are disconcerting, if not completely unsurprising. Among many of the lessons and outcomes from these experiences, the overarching result was the development of inner passions that fueled my program of research in supervision. As a result, my research has, in part, validated my experiences but also has expanded upon the topics and ideas brought forth by these experiences (e.g., supervisor self-disclosure, trainee nondisclosure, supervisor multicultural incompetence, supervisor ethics; Ladany, Friedlander, & Nelson, 2005; Ladany, Walker, Pate-Carolan, & Gray Evans, 2008). In addition, my lifelong professional experiences have led me to believe that it's pretty clear that incompetence is not uncommon among supervisors and counselors. My own estimate is that approximately one-third of supervisors and counselors are very competent, one-third are adequate, and one-third are incompetent (Ladany, 2007). Of course, there are two overarching silver linings in all of this (the cynic's optimism coming through perhaps): From a professional standpoint, the research agenda that has come out of these experiences sheds light on some things to which the field of counseling and supervision should attend; and, from a personal standpoint, and hopefully as a lesson to others, I learned I could bend and still not break.

References

Ladany, N. (2007). Does psychotherapy training matter? Maybe not. *Psychotherapy: Theory, Research, Practice, Training, 44,* 392–396.

Ladany, N., Friedlander, M.L., & Nelson, M.L. (2005). *Critical events in psychotherapy supervision: An interpersonal approach.* Washington, DC: American Psychological Association.

Ladany, N., Walker, J.A., Pate-Carolan, L., & Gray Evans, L. (2008). *Practicing counseling and psychotherapy: Insights from trainees, clients, and supervisors.* New York: Taylor & Francis.

SILENCE
Melanie A. Nuszkowski

We sat in silence, and then we processed all that occurred during those seemingly quiet moments. Through this supervision experience, I learned the incredible skill of being with and using silence. I believe that this skill has been the most essential element in enhancing the supervisory and therapeutic services that I have the honor of providing. Years after this supervision experience, I reflect on it, wondering what ingredients contributed to the immense personal and professional growth that occurred during the year after the silence. Perhaps it was space, quietness, clarity, caring, and mirroring, though words cannot accurately reflect the experiential learning and healing that occurred. I recall trying to capture my experience and to adequately express thanks to my supervisor for this gift. The words are still difficult to find.

This supervision experience occurred during my second semester as a doctoral practicum student. It came after a difficult first semester of practicum. I was not prepared for the struggles of the first semester.

During the first semester, I was at first very open with my supervisor because this worked well during my master's internship. Thus, in my first semester doctoral supervision, I attempted to address a countertransference reaction of feeling that therapy was "stuck and hopeless" as I worked with a client who felt "stuck and hopeless" in her own life. Rather than processing this countertransference reaction, my supervisor, a predoctoral intern, suggested that I myself seek therapy. While I acknowledge that I may have benefited from therapy, I felt shocked, misunderstood, and frustrated. I became tearful as I sat there feeling "stuck" and frustrated. I recall wondering how my supervisor and I could be on such different wavelengths. Seeing my tears, my supervisor asked if I'd like to engage in deep breathing. I had no desire or perceived need to engage in deep breathing with my supervisor! However, by that point I felt demoralized and almost incapacitated. I couldn't say "No." So, we breathed together, and I walked out of supervision feeling dazed.

Luckily, I had a good friend who was also completing a practicum at the center. I relayed the story and shed a few more tears, but this time with someone who I knew understood me. We then laughed together, and I proceeded on with my day. Needless to say, I did not attempt to process any more countertransference reactions during that semester with that supervisor.

Had I been more advanced in my training, I might have handled this situation better. Perhaps I could have expressed myself more clearly rather than personalizing the situation as much as I did. But, in hindsight, that was asking a lot. I may have also shared how shut down I felt when my tears were met with the suggestion to engage in deep breathing. Or perhaps I would have declined the offer to engage in deep breathing altogether. At my developmental level, however, I internalized the problem. This translated into increased self-consciousness regarding my clinical intuition, skills, and appropriate use of supervision. I felt even more stuck and perhaps even a little hopeless about my potential to be a good clinician. I had foreclosed on clinical growth for the semester. And at this point, I did need therapy!

Luckily, during my second semester as a doctoral practicum student, I had the gift of working with a supervisor who appreciated my honesty and willingness to own and process my reactions in session. Of course, I was hesitant to again broach these topics, but my supervisor began the supervisory relationship by introducing a supervision contract. She described her supervision orientation, which included the exploration of transference and countertransference, supervisor–supervisee dynamics, and parallel process. This contract helped to facilitate a safe environment in which I could again begin exploring the clinical and personal concerns affecting my professional growth and efficacy. Although I had lost faith in my clinical abilities, my supervisor provided consistent support, encouragement, permission to make mistakes, and a gentle push to stretch my skills. Most important, I believe, was the process that occurred during these supervision sessions. It was often a time of silence, her accepting silence.

While the content of what we learn as clinicians in training is immensely important, learning the process of how to facilitate an environment conducive to healing is invaluable. I believe that I learned this "process" through my experiences in supervision. My supervisor provided space to sit quietly and to reflect. To be silent without worry. During this silence, I attended to my internal dialogue, including my thoughts about the dynamics occurring between myself and my supervisor. Then, we processed our respective experiences. After these supervision meetings, I was very present and reflective during the subsequent therapy hour. For the client, I in turn provided time for silent reflection. Eventually, I regained faith in "myself as therapist." This learning experience was internalized. That is why it was so transforming.

Looking back, what I most needed was the "space" to be heard. I needed the opportunity to voice my concerns, to examine my nonverbal behaviors and internal dialogue related to both my provision of therapy and my here-and-now experiences in supervision, to feel understood, and to have my concerns normalized. As I write this, it sounds pretty basic. And maybe it is, but so is the foundation of a house. I can't explain how much I needed those things or how much they have contributed to my development as a confident and competent clinician. This supervision experience is now an integral part of what has made me the clinician and supervisor I am today. I am eternally grateful for the impact this supervision experience had on me. I can only hope to impart this gift to future supervisees and clients.

Interestingly, my impetus for composing this "defining moment" came from my supervisee sharing her own submission of a defining moment based on our work together. I was so honored and touched that perhaps I had also imparted even a sliver of the same gift that I had received. I was inspired to share my positive supervision experience with other clinicians, supervisors, and supervisees in the hope that they may also feel empowered by the amazing capacity we have to impact the lives of others. I have been blessed to have several additional excellent supervision experiences with skilled and compassionate clinicians. I also remain grateful for the painful first semester learning experience of not feeling heard in supervision. Without this experience, I may not have realized the potential potency of my role as a clinician and supervisor.

A NOVICE, AN EXPERT, AND COMMON SENSE
Guy J. Manaster

It is hard to fathom that the "moment" I am about to relate occurred over 40 years ago. It is amazing to me how clearly I can remember the key bits that shape the incident. I was almost 30 years old, completing a PhD from the Committee on Human Development at the University of Chicago and, concurrently, a certificate in psychotherapy at the Alfred Adler Institute of Chicago. I had finished the coursework but resigned from the client-centered-oriented clinical psychology program at Chicago and had chosen to complete my therapy training at the Adler Institute, although it demanded considerable additional coursework and practicums. The theory made better sense to me, and the practice seemed more effective, more efficient, and better suited to my strengths, inclinations, values, and beliefs.

After finishing everything but the doctoral paper at the institute, which I put off to retain student status, I was invited to practice in the clinic associated with the institute. The members of the practice included some superb Adlerian therapists, notably Rudof Dreikurs, Bernard Shulman, Harold Mosak, Bina Rosenberg, and Robert Powers.

The practice was built on Adlerian theory and practices. Almost all patients were assessed through family constellation, early recollection, and dream analyses. These were interpreted for individual personality goals, worldview, *modus operandi* (way of operating), *modus vivendi* (way of living), and biased apperceptions, the sum of which Adlerians call *lifestyle*. Lifestyle is developed and interpreted with the client and forms the basis of insightful, practical, direct, and ethical counseling.

A young married couple arranged to be seen in the practice on a low-fee basis; they were referred to me. They were an attractive couple in their mid-20s. His build, strength, and memorable crushing handshake immediately impressed me, as did his strangely jovial bellicosity. She was lovely looking and politely reticent on entering the office.

He jumped right into his rendition of their problem—her. She was possibly crazy, paranoid, devious, and mysterious. She changed moods without reason. Jumped from friendly, loving, and supportive to cold and distant, evasive and absent. Hid from him with female and male friends.

She said very little, expressing mystification at her own behavior and a tentative acceptance of his. She appeared scared; I didn't pry about this in his presence. I proposed that we meet separately so that each could be open and we could explore each one's personality issues, or lifestyle. They agreed.

For the next couple of weeks my conversations with the wife confirmed both her fear and bewilderment. She did leave their home and try to find safe havens. He suspected she was sleeping with everyone she visited. He followed her and hid near her friends' apartments, keeping track of whom she was with and for how long. He confronted her, interrogated her, welcomed her, and forgave her in no predictable pattern. He was as likely to meet her belligerently when she came home from work as he was to hand her flowers and take her out for a nice dinner. She couldn't figure it out. She did not know what was her responsibility, her fault.

The husband was adamant that all his behavior was warranted. Each zig and zag in his position or behavior was vigorously and logically defended. Questions about his behavior, motives, or intent were met with dismissal, denial, or agitated and not believable acceptance. His logic seemed sound in each instance, but the underlying assumptions were fluid like quicksilver.

I can't remember all the specifics of their lifestyles, which I interpreted with each of them after data collection. Suffice it to say that hers was clear and simple: a girl who wanted to be good and taken care of. She agreed.

Every attempt I made to interpret and communicate his interpretation to him was contradicted and resisted. I never felt confident in the interpretations as I read them to him and discussed them with him. (Though I have felt more and less confident in the lifestyle interpretations I have done in the 40 years since then, I have always felt that my interpretations were in the ballpark, and every client has understood and accepted at least the drift of the interpretation and has worked with me to perfect it). After 4 or 5 weeks, not only had I made no progress with the husband; I was also lost.

At the practice, no one saw clients on Wednesday afternoons. Everyone met in a conference room to discuss practice issues and cases. Anyone could present a case, and anyone could discuss and comment on it. I needed help, so with some trepidation, I prepared to talk about the husband. I went over his family constellation, early recollection, and dream materials, as well as my interpretations. Before the consultation meeting I listened again to all of our sessions. I could summarize what I had in about 10 minutes and thought the form was adequate even if the content was not.

At that Wednesday's case conference, I jumped in to be first. My memory is hazy here too, but I think I had been speaking for about 3 minutes when Dr. Dreikurs interrupted. Here too I can't remember the particulars. He asked, "Does he do this …?" "Does he do this …?" "Does he say this …?" To each question I responded, "Yes." He asked a couple more questions, which were perfect descriptions of my client's conduct. He concluded by saying, "You are so confused because he is a 'confuser.'"

The group may have talked about the case for another few minutes; I can't recall. I was startled, blown away. I could see Dr. Dreikurs's label in everything my client did. He surely and absolutely confused me. He kept his wife confused and off balance. His evident self-assurance was based on setting up an uneven playing field where only he knew the terrain.

I sat through the rest of the meeting going over a short list of "I should haves." I had not trusted my feelings and reactions to the client. It is fundamental to Adlerian practice to assume that people move toward their goals. It is also basic that people are good at that. If I felt flummoxed when with this client, that was because it was his goal. I should have seen that. If his wife was bewildered, it was another indication of his goal and should have reinforced my understanding. Sitting there reviewing stories I had been told in sessions, I recognized instances with his friends and at work, as well as with his wife, when he marched through as if his direction was clear. If he knew so well, what had I missed? How could I have been so obtuse? Probably just lack of ability, talent, sensitivity, knowledge, basic social intelligence, I guessed.

When the meeting was over I slunk away. The conferences were to be constructive and cooperative. No one said anything derogatory, and all left with the usual goodbyes. I dragged myself to the train and home.

My expression must have been pretty hangdog when I walked in because my wife made me a drink and waited for me to recount my experience. She knew what I was going to do that afternoon and how important it was to me. We sat and I told her, without mentioning names, the story in detail.

At the end, I just told her, "Maybe I shouldn't be doing this. Maybe I can't do it."

After my afternoon's anguish, without pause, Jane asked, "How long has Dr. Dreikurs been doing this?"

I had to adjust to her question and think. "Probably 50 years," I replied.

And Jane asked, "How long have you been doing this?"

"Four months."

"Maybe you'll get better," she pronounced.

Adlerians refer to the client's reaction when he or she "gets it," or understands at a gut level the personal and deep meaning of the therapist's interpretation of his or her lifestyle, as a "recognition reflex." That's what I received from Jane. I thanked her when I stopped laughing.

As a young therapist, this moment changed me, inspired me, woke me up, and gave me the reassurance I needed to go on and "get better." A number of implications can be drawn from this moment. I realized the importance of analyzing and understanding my clients through theory—to trust my gut reactions to my clients. My clients, at some level, are probably getting from me what they want to get, unless and until I understand the client's goal or what he or she is after.

As a professor and supervisor of counselors in training, a key message I drew from this moment was to let it all hang out, do my best, and make mistakes. Through the years the supervisees I trusted least were the ones who knew it all, never were in doubt, and never thought they made mistakes. It takes stumbling to stand upright, making mistakes to discern what is correct, and having doubts to find clarity. I don't trust the ones who know the truth. Give me a searcher to find the way. "Maybe you'll get better."

"GO HAVE FUN WITH THIS SESSION"
Kelly A. Bailey

As I was leaving my supervisor's office, she said, "Go have fun with this session." Upon hearing this statement, I felt trusted. I cannot say for sure what she truly meant by her comment, but what I took from her words was an understanding that I was functioning as an effective therapist, despite the concerns and questions about my practice I often brought to supervision. Her encouraging expression influenced me to realize that to have the most fun with my work, it was time for me to shelve my anxiety. Similarly, it was time for me to trust my personal style of providing therapy. I could not expect myself to know everything—every theoretical orientation, every empirically supported treatment (EST), every assessment for every client problem or population. Afterall, I was a student with more education and supervised practice ahead of me. I interpreted my supervisor's words as trusting, which resulted in my trusting myself. This was a defining moment in my development as a counselor. I knew there was more to learn, but I also realized that I was practicing competently. I knew I could trust the words of my supervisor to "go have fun" because our relationship was built on trust that manifested regularly. Our relationship was strong, and there was a mutual respect that was powerfully validating. My anxiety was reduced, which allowed me to decrease my attention toward myself and increase my focus on my clients. I felt I could cultivate a similar relationship with my clients that I experienced with my supervisor.

I walked up the stairs to my office and stopped on the stairwell to gather my composure. For a moment, I could not recall my client's name, and I was about to see her in the waiting room! The last hour of supervision had been particularly emotional and transformative. "How are we, as therapists, different from supportive friends?" was a question I brought to my supervisor. Rationally, I knew the answer to this question, but my lack of experience was causing my emotional self to feel slightly insecure about my therapy skills and level of competence. My insecurity surprised my supervisor. I had lots of doctoral-level training, but most of my supervised training had emphasized cognitive-behavioral therapy (CBT) and ESTs. As I became exposed to therapists who practiced from other orientations, I learned that I wanted to practice as an integrative therapist. However, doing so was challenging because my knowledge of theoretical orientations other than CBT was mostly limited to information gained from a few readings and conversations among my peers. Furthermore, my training had led me to question the possibility of having any significant effect on my clients' desired goals for treatment without the provision of an EST. Following rapport building with a client, I felt anxious if I was unaware of data to justify my therapeutic approach. My supervisors, especially those with an integrative orientation, had told me I'm warm, empathic, genuine, respectful. "But are these nonspecific or common factors enough for therapeutic change?" I asked. Unfortunately, at this point in my education, common or nonspecific factors had received insignificant attention as variables responsible for change, at least relative to ESTs. Our conversation within supervision led me to consider the factors that I have most appreciated as a client in therapy. With my answer in mind, I knew I would have no problem having fun in session with my next client. I recognized that an hour in therapy, similar to an hour of supervision, could be fun, with moments of joy, laughter, pleasure, engagement, support, comfort, and relaxation. The act of self-improvement is one worthy of celebrating, even when it can be difficult at times.

Like many psychologists in training, I am a scientist–practitioner. The idea of having fun while being a scientist sounds as if it could be difficult, a bit geeky perhaps. Some might argue that it is the art of psychology that makes practice fun. But I love the science of psychology, in addition to the art. I love helping others improve their lives while knowing that research supports my chosen intervention or vehicle for change. In other words, my desire to implement ESTs comes honestly. Notably, in a collaborative class effort, my colleagues have jokingly, yet warmly, represented me in a sociogram with the symbol "$p < .05$." My genuine interest in providing therapy supported by evidence has been both useful and detrimental. It has been detrimental because the idea of providing therapy without using my behavioral training has caused me anxiety. My interest in using CBT and ESTs has been useful for at least two reasons. First of all, my practice has been guided by a convincing rationale. Secondly, with my toolbox of techniques within reach, I have been able to invest my attention to areas within therapy that may be more important than technique. I have been freer to be a genuine person within a therapeutic relationship. I am freer to listen. Being aware of CBT and ESTs has allowed me to be more genuine while I practice as a therapist because I have been guided by research that I value. Today, I have become interested in learning the evidence that supports nonspecific or common factors in therapy and other orientations to providing therapy, including an integrative orientation. In the end, I function as a therapist who is both a genuine scientist–practitioner and a genuine person. I believe that being genuine to one's character is a recipe for having fun and being satisfied with life.

As my client and I entered my office, I thought about her treatment goals discussed the previous week. I had already searched my toolbox and reminded myself how to implement systematic desensitization for social anxiety. I had also been reading about CBT for insomnia. My client had agreed to complete a sleep diary over the past week, and I was about to interpret my first one. I had some basic training on these ESTs, but limited or no practice under supervision. Feeling like an expert with these interventions would take more time. Nevertheless, it felt okay that I did not feel like an expert in these areas. I knew that I was still functioning as a competent, enthusiastic, effective therapist. I was able to allow myself to trust that I was providing evidence-based practice, even if I chose not to pull a tool out of my box during that particular session.

I spent the next hour enjoying the therapeutic alliance with my client. I listened, reflected, reassured, respected, and accepted. At the end of the hour, my client said with a smile, "It was really good to be here. Thanks." A "thank you" at the end of a therapy hour has such a powerful effect on my well-being; it feels deeply satisfying. I was feeling grateful too.

I feel incredibly grateful to have my practicum this year, which is in a university counseling center with supportive staff members who have multiple, effective, therapeutic orientations. Powerful moments that contribute to my development as a practicing psychologist occur regularly in this setting. I am glad that I heard my supervisor's words that led to my defining moment described here. I am also appreciative that my supervisor heard these words from her former supervisor. I recently learned that the clinical training director, who at one time supervised my supervisor, recalled expressing to my supervisor, "Go have fun with this session."

ANANSI, REBECCA, AND ME: A TRANSFORMATIVE LEARNING EXPERIENCE
Anissa L. Moody

When I was growing up, my favorite stories were West Indian folktales featuring the spider Anansi, a cunning cultural heroine who represents the rebellion of native peoples by changing the world through invention or discovery. As a child, I never quite understood the full magnitude of Anansi stories, but I did identify with this character's resilience and desire to make lasting changes.

Growing up on a small island, I had the unfortunate experiences of witnessing the mental pain of others. Like any small town in America, those who were different stuck out like a sore thumb, especially those who suffered from mental illnesses. At that time, I understood that most people attended to obvious physical hurt but was often confused by the refusal of some to deal with the more covert inner sufferings or psychological turmoil. This type of behavior was even more pronounced in women, who seemed to believe that a woman must be everything to everyone while at the same time absorbing punishing messages about their bodies, their abilities, and their purpose. Meeting goals, especially academic ones, seemed to be the salve that covered the wounds of hurt for many girls. My mother would often say, "One monkey don't stop no show," meaning that no matter what happened you just have to keep moving, keep doing. After many years of "moving and doing," it would take an encounter with a difficult client to bring me full circle to seeing myself as one of the women whom I thought I had left behind.

When I entered graduate school, I was excited about all the new possibilities. I recognized that I was getting closer to my lifelong goal of becoming a psychologist and relished every opportunity to learn new theories and ideas. I eagerly approached this process with intense intellectual curiosity. I asked how I could apply what I was learning to what I witnessed as a child. What I did not expect was the opposite: how my early experiences would positively influence my professional work.

When beginning my first practicum, I did not know an experience there would be instructive for all my training years. I was working at a community center that provided services to families infected and affected by HIV. One of my individual clients, Rebecca (pseudonym), was a young woman in her late teens who was HIV-positive and severely depressed. During our first meeting, she reported a significant history of sexual abuse including being "traded for drugs" by her mother to several men, one of whom infected her with the HIV virus. In the sessions with her, she insisted that these horrific events had nothing to do with her current depression; the past was behind her, she *survived,* and she was stronger because of it. She often stated that *crying* over the past would make her weak and would certainly diminish her resolve to deal with the troubles that were sure to come. During every session, she would discuss current crises that seemed to me to be so obviously connected to her experience of being abused. She often presented as angry and withdrawn and described using dissociation as her main coping skill. Most of our sessions were spent problem solving current crises and practicing distress tolerance skills.

I was baffled by Rebecca's resistance to talk about her feelings and past experiences and summed it up as therapeutic resistance. In supervision, I would discuss feeling overwhelmed and helpless and often stated that I was not equipped to help this young woman. I soon recognized that my role as a problem solver colluded with her desire to not address any feelings. When pressed in supervision, I was able to identify that my collusion was not only about my desire to problem solve but also related to my own struggle with personal vulnerability. This supervision work was arduous but very helpful.

Meeting Rebecca was the start of my self-exploration into understanding how I experience and express feelings. Over the years of school, several supervisors echoed the same message: "Allow yourself to be more vulnerable." I always had a strong reaction to this suggestion. I interpreted my supervisors' comments to mean I was ineffective or that my presence with clients was somehow problematic.

Further, I had no clue what they really meant, nor did I understand the therapeutic value of "being more vulnerable." I believed in working hard and applying the *right* theories and ideas. I also felt like my supervisors did not understand the cultural nuances of my emotional expressions.

At the same time, I realized that something was missing in my work. I often felt like I was not doing enough for my clients and was prone to frustration with their level of progress or lack of movement. Most importantly, it was extremely hard for me to sit with my clients' pain and not feel responsible for making them feel better. I frequently struggled with feeling tired and overwhelmed and, similar to my interaction with Rebecca, often worked harder than my clients. I interpreted their failures as my fault; I was not doing the right thing or not doing enough. Finally, after experiencing a bout of severe emotional burnout, I stopped focusing on my desire to do things right, and was able to see that the intensity of my reactions to my supervisors' feedback was worth exploring.

When I cried or expressed any strong negative emotions as a child, I was told to be quiet or I would "get something to cry about." As I got older, my elders explained to me the need to learn how to *handle* things or to *take care of* things because no one else was going to do it for me. I soon learned that it didn't matter how hurt I felt because crying never got the job done or got the good grades; in fact, crying often led to being perceived as weak or incapable. I also recognized the cultural bounds of this behavior. Similar to other ethnic groups, West Indians often view life as something to be endured. For generations, parents have taught their children that their survival depended upon strict adherence to the rules no matter how one felt. This resulted in parenting styles that focused on discipline rather than on emotional connections and feelings of love and affection.

In time, I had to acknowledge the benefits of being the quintessential Strong Black Woman (SBW). I certainly liked being regarded as unflappable. My opinions and support on clinical matters were often sought out by peers. I also saw myself as another SBW whose stoicism was a proven inoculant in personal and professional environments that were threatening. Sometimes, our emotional expressions can be misinterpreted with dire consequences. I never cried and often judged others harshly when they expressed soft or vulnerable emotions within professional realms.

Now I recognize that it was Rebecca who gave me the opportunity to learn the healing powers of crying. When I learned to appreciate and acknowledge the range of my emotional experiences and responses, I found that my therapeutic relationships deepened and that my work was much more fulfilling. I was no longer looking at my clients as people whom I was responsible for fixing; rather, I recognized that the possibility of growth and change were inherent in relationships where there was intimacy and mutual connection. I often think about Rebecca. I wish I could have helped her more at the time and wonder what the outcome would have been had we allowed ourselves to leave our SBW armor at the door. Would she have been more able to discuss her pain?

Since discovering this part of myself, this well of emotional vitality and expression, I have made it a point to discuss this matter when supervising students. I want them to be able to access their emotional selves. I am more aware of emotions, especially the vulnerable emotions, within the therapeutic process. When I am in a teaching role, I discuss the impact of culture on expressing and experiencing emotions including the stereotype of the SBW. I continue to be surprised by not only the number of female students who can relate to being in the *strong woman* role but also their resistance to consider how this specific role can impact their work and relationships. I often encourage them to step outside of their familiar roles and to start a path of self-discovery. I help them to understand that resilience can be witnessed in many forms. I tell them about how a spider, Anansi, influenced my desire to do this work. I tell how we can continue to make changes in the lives of others through our own *self-discovery* and *reinvention*. And at those times, I quietly thank Rebecca.

HOLISTIC AND CONTEXTUAL COUNSELING: LOVE, WORK, AND EVERYTHING IN BETWEEN
Mary J. Heppner

As a counseling psychology graduate student in the 1970s, I was trained to think about vocational development and psycho-emotional development as two separate worlds; we had separate courses, separate counseling centers, and almost entirely different skill sets. The vocational world was one of "test and tell," of huge, technical resource books like the *Occupational Outlook Handbook* (U.S. Department of Labor, 2008). Parsons (1909) first described the process of career counseling as "matching men and jobs." In its purest form, the counselor assessed the client, described job options that fit that assessment, and helped the client with the steps needed to get the desired option.

The psycho-emotional counseling world was about the rest of the person's life—his or her relationships, psychological health, emotional journey. There was much more emphasis placed on developing the working alliance and on getting to know clients and how their presenting issues intersected with the rest of their personhood. These two specialties were conceptualized at the time as separate with little overlap. As a product of such training I was, like most of my peers, much more excited about the psycho-emotional counseling world.

A defining moment for me came in the person of Amanda, who helped me to understand the falseness of this dichotomy and the importance of context and holism. This defining moment has literally changed the way I have approached every client since and has profoundly influenced my journey as a practitioner and scholar. Let me introduce you to Amanda.

Amanda was a 27-year-old, White, married woman with two boys aged 7 and 9. Amanda had recently moved to my community from a factory town in the Northeast. She grew up in a blue-collar family, and no one in her extended family had attended college. Her husband had worked in the steel mills and now had found another factory job in our community. Amanda had found a position at a local college, working as a secretary in a dean's office. This small college was very committed to encouraging all of its employees to obtain a college education, which it paid for as one of the benefits of working there. The dean had personally described the educational benefits to Amanda and had offered flexibility with her work schedule so that she could pursue the degree of her dreams. He had asked about her progress a number of times. Had Amanda decided when she would start? What she would major in? What she wanted to be? As much as the dean had encouraged Amanda to take advantage of this wonderful opportunity, Amanda was ambivalent and somewhat resistant. Baffled, he referred her to me for career counseling.

When Amanda came in, I did all the things I had been taught. Using the most state-of-the-art assessment measures, I helped her examine her interests, skills, and values, and I helped her look at occupations that would use these attributes. I worked with her to integrate these personal attributes, providing a more complete picture of her vocational being. Yet it became increasingly clear that there was a lot more going on with Amanda than what was captured by the traditional career counseling process. This was most behaviorally evident in her reticence to take action and put to use the information she had gained about herself and the world of work. So finally, I took a step back and just began to talk to Amanda, to try to understand her life narrative and how she was making meaning out of her life journey.

As I began talking more with Amanda it became clear that she had virtually no confidence in her ability to complete a college degree. She had never had anyone indicate they thought she could do it, and she saw herself as very different from the "smart people" who went to college. She also was very fearful that if she became "a professional," which is how she labeled anyone with a college degree, she would lose the support and love of her husband and family, who would think she was trying to "be better than them." She feared the loneliness that would come from being different. She had heard the way her family talked about others who did things that set them apart from the family, and the thought of that level of social ostracism was terrifying for her. As we worked at unfolding all the psychological and emotional elements that were keeping her from pursuing a college degree, I was struck by the intertwined nature of Amanda's emotional and vocational lives. These were not two separate worlds, but truly one and the same.

This encounter with Amanda also taught me a great deal about the importance of context in our lives and that vocation truly is an act in context. Amanda taught me how much the systems and subsystems that make up our lives—from the macrolevel influences of gender and class scripting and ideology to the more microissues of confidence and control—impact our lives and the way we view our options.

With these realizations, my work with Amanda changed dramatically. We focused on developing our working alliance and seeing it at the core of the counseling process. We spent much more time focused on her worldview and how that worldview developed in her own unique cultural context. We examined how all her systems from the macro to the micro influenced her perceptions of her place in the world. We talked a lot about her being the author of her own life story, an analogy that seemed to engage her thinking. She kept saying, "I thought about what I want the next chapter to be like in my life, but I need help in figuring out how I can make it happen without driving the people I love away."

This process critically influenced my own thinking about what it takes to be an effective counselor, and it also impacted many other aspects of my professional life. It had a dramatic effect on the way I teach career counseling courses and how important I came to believe it is to help trainees personalize and contextualize career development theory and practice within their own lived experience. It was an impetus for me to coauthor a text on holistic and contextual career counseling, *Career Counseling: Contexts, Issues, and Techniques* (Gysbers, Heppner, & Johnston, 2009), to create an instrument that measures internal psychological issues in the career planning process (the Career Transitions Inventory, CTI; Heppner, Multon, & Johnston, 1994), and to help me to develop the Ecological Model of Career Development with my colleagues Ellen Cook and Karen O'Brien (Cook, Heppner, & O'Brien, 2004). Perhaps most importantly, my work with Amanda prompted me to change the way I approach any counseling session, regardless of the presenting problem.

This defining moment helped me to see how essential it is to treat people holistically and not as some pieces that are about work and other pieces that are about the rest of life. It also taught me about how critical it is to have an understanding of individuals' ecological contexts to appreciate the many choices that make up their life stories.

As for Amanda? Well, she did go back to school in social work and received not only her bachelor's but also a master's degree. She now works as a clinical social worker helping birth mothers with adoptions. She loves her work and has inspired several other young women in her extended family who are now also in college.

References

Cook, E.P., Heppner, M.J., & O'Brien, K.M. (2004). An ecological model of career development. In R.K. Coyne and E.P. Cook (Eds.), *Ecological counseling: An innovative approach to conceptualizing person–environment interaction* (pp. 219–242). Alexandria, VA: American Counseling Association.

Gysbers, N.C., Heppner, M.J., & Johnston, J.A. (2009). *Career counseling: Contexts, process and techniques*. Alexandria, VA: American Counseling Association.

Heppner, M.J., Multon, K.D., & Johnston, J.A. (1994). Assessing psychological resources during career change: Development of the Career Transitions Inventory. *Journal of Vocational Behavior, 44*, 55–74.

Occupational Outlook Handbook (2008). Department of Labor, Bulletin 2700. Indianapolis, IN: JIST Publishing.

Parsons, F. (1909). *Choosing a vocation*. Boston: Houghton Mifflin.

FINDING HOPE AGAIN
Laura E. Sobik

I sit here about to begin writing, and I find myself wondering why. Why do this *now*, 23 days after my client killed herself? Maybe to optimistically force closure. Maybe to assure that I will remember. Maybe out of the hope that I can gain insight and answers from a situation that will never be anything but conjecture. I know that right after she died I obsessively searched for other peoples' stories, other therapists whose clients had suicided, other people who had experienced this early in their careers. There were few stories I could find that pertained to me, so I am adding mine to the pile, though not without fear. Fear of how I will be perceived by my colleagues. Fear of how I will perceive myself as I write this and rewrite and reread it over time. Even fear that I will someday be writing something like this *again* if I lose another client to suicide.

At the time she died, I was at a great place in my career. I had found my home in the counseling center setting and was thrilled to finally be working in a wonderful environment with role models I truly admired. At that time and now, I can say that I absolutely love being a therapist. I don't know how to say it without the clichés and the cheesiness, but this is what I was meant to be, and I love what I do. But my work is not my "everything." I take my down time very seriously; I have excellent boundaries (I am known to leave the building at 5:00 sharp, barring an emergency or a responsibility); I can almost always leave work at work. I have been intentional about finding this balance after many pressurized and overextended years, and it has served me well.

So I was 29 years old, about a month and a half from finishing my internship at a site that had been my first choice and thus completing my doctoral degree in psychology. I had successfully defended my dissertation and was pretty close to being called "Dr. Sobik." I had found a job! And it would pay me! I had been getting strongly positive feedback from my supervisors, and I was feeling pretty confident as a therapist and supervisor, starting to allow myself to believe that I was becoming a professional—someone valuable, with something to say, something to contribute. Generally I was feeling good, confident in my decisions and interventions.

I met this client approximately 2 months before she killed herself. She was seeking help to talk about some mild feelings of depression and anxiety related to academic performance. I had some pretty strong countertransference toward her, most of it positive, all of it talked about in supervision. I identified with some of her struggles and admired her resilience through a severe trauma history. I felt connected to her as a client and as a person, and I believe that she felt connected in return.

I had been working with her for a few weeks when she became depressed, severely depressed. It came on quite suddenly. When she began to talk about suicide, we (my supervisors and I) did everything "by the book." Within the span of about 2 weeks, we contracted for safety daily, got her on meds, got her evaluated numerous times, tried several times (unsuccessfully) to get her involuntarily hospitalized, called for welfare checks at critical times. Near the time of her death, we were trying to transition her care from our counseling center to a longer-term treatment plan, but financial and logistical constraints slowed the process. In the meantime, I saw her or was in contact with her almost every day for nearly 3 weeks. I spoke with her close friend on a daily basis, trying to increase her support system and to ensure safety. I stood up for her when colleagues and other professionals subtly suggested I was being dramatic or overly involved. I fought for her and genuinely cared about her, even when treatment became exhausting and terrifying. Do I sound defensive? Do I sound angry? I am.

My training director called me on a Thursday night and asked if I was at home, if I was alone. I told her that I was home, that my partner was with me. I knew. In those last moments before she said it, I started bargaining and begging out loud. "Please no, please no, please no, please no." She said, in her kindest, softest voice,

"Laura, I need to tell you that she ended her life today." At this point I was already kneeling on the floor, head on the ground, bracing for the impact. When she told me, everything went blank. "Oh fuck, oh fuck, oh fuck." I thought that I might vomit. I wouldn't let my partner touch me. I got up and moved from room to room, alternating abruptly between sobbing and trying to ask her questions: When? How did she do it? How did you find out? Were her pets okay?

I imagine that my reactions were frightening (they were frightening to me), though all of us psychologists know it as a textbook "acute grief reaction." It felt like I was dying. A part of me *was* dying. I knew that I would never be the same as a therapist. My training director arranged for one of the senior staff with whom I was close to come over that night. I didn't know, but she was on her way even before my training director called me. She and my partner both sat with me on the floor and held me, rubbed my back, let me cry and yell and drip snot and tears all over them. Deep sadness and anger came and went in waves. Occasionally I found words; a few times I even laughed. But overall I felt raw and bleeding and exposed, and I hated it.

I received phone calls that night that I couldn't make myself answer or return. My immediate supervisor under whose license I saw clients. The director. My fellow interns. At that time I could feel nothing but shame and fear and sickening sadness. I slept very little.

It was so hard to force myself to get up, get ready for work, and later get out of the car and face my colleagues the next morning. I knew that my emotions would surface upon seeing them, and I dreaded their faces looking at me. With pity. With relief that it was not them. Not knowing how to deal with me, what to say. I do not say this to blame or chastise them; I would have felt the same way. But I was the only one in the agency who had a client kill herself. Many years had passed since the last agency-related suicide (this fact had been stated with pride throughout my time there), and here I was breaking the streak. I felt that acutely and angrily. I hated myself. I hated my client. I felt so fucked up, and at the same time I feared that I had no right to feel so upset. I wondered if I should not feel that way as a professional, as a "grown-up" therapist. I began to doubt my own objectivity and ability to maintain "proper therapeutic boundaries." Why was I unable to become clinical in that moment—see the facts, assess my work, and feel sad but somewhat unaffected? I felt shattered.

I walked into the building, and the director hugged me. The other interns and staff offered their support. I remember little of what was said because I was too sunken down into my own pain and guilt and grief. We held a case review meeting that morning, both to process emotions and to communicate the legal and ethical implications of what had happened. I repeatedly apologized despite their reassurance that I and everyone else involved had done everything possible to protect the client. On some level I knew that. But I couldn't help thinking about the last time I saw her, about the first time I saw her, about our entire therapeutic relationship.

As the days went by, I internally analyzed every word I had said throughout our therapy relationship, every intervention I had offered, every moment we had spent together. I thought about my supervision in which I had talked about her, and I wondered if I had asked the right questions. Had I shown the right videotape? Had I come off as too competent to my supervisor (thus not allowing her to "see" that I really was incompetent to continue seeing this client)? The questions sliced me internally, emotionally. I couldn't let them go. I lost weight, having previously always been a stress eater. I slept intermittently during this time, often having disturbing dreams about her. In one dream, she was alive and reassured me that all was okay. I wished I were the kind of person who could take that dream to mean that she was telling me that she was finally at peace, that she was finally okay. But I felt no comfort upon waking.

The month that followed was dysthymic at best. Most of my colleagues returned to work as usual, and I resented this. I felt like everything in my world, all of my schemas, all of my reality had changed profoundly. How could they just be talking about something inane and stupid like other clients with their annoying problems? Yet I wanted to join them. I wanted to deny the suicide and return to my confident, competent, fulfilling, well-planned life. I resented my own unexpected tears and the hypersensitivity to anything related to the topic of death. I walked into rooms alert and anxious, half expecting to see a dead body or some such horrifying scene. I became very angry and morbid for a while. I hated every community mental health and law enforcement agency that had failed her (and, consequently, me). I obsessed over the details of her death and researched everything I could about the method by which she suicided. I hid these obsessions until other colleagues confessed to thinking about similar things. Processing this together was enormously helpful.

Slowly I began reaching out. I think that, at first, I was searching for someone who could give me the magic words that could finally help me find some relief from the constant self-doubt and self-hatred. A fellow intern and I had a conversation about our shared anxiety, hyperarousal, identity questions, and morbid thoughts. I tentatively began to renew my faith in the power of talking, processing, and friendship. I called my former supervisor and (now) close friend. I called my new boss, partly out of fear that she would no longer want me. I talked to the client's psychiatrist. I was invited to and attended the memorial service, during which the speaker kindly asserted, "There is nobody in this room who is to blame for her death; there is no one here who could have saved her." From all of these people—reassurance, kindness, encouragement. I held it and slowly began to feel it sincerely.

The care, compassion, and love I received helped. The assurance keeps coming, and at one point it may become internal. I have found some footing as a therapist again, after several slips and false starts. But I have not made my peace, I have not integrated her suicide into my personal and professional identities, I have not been able to get through the monthly anniversaries of her death without remembering, every time remembering. I am immutably changed by her death.

However, thus far, I have found one piece of comfort, one fact, one truth: I know for certain that I would rather be the kind of person who feels this loss too deeply than one who can move on without being touched. There are clients walking into my office every day, and I don't want them to sense that I am afraid. I would rather stumble with this unwieldy hurt for a while, carry it, and begin to sand the rough edges of it so the cuts begin to heal. And there are people in my life who believe, as I do, that this is the kind of therapist I want to be, this is kind of person I want to be.

THE CHINESE WOMAN WHO WANTED TO LOSE HER ACCENT
Marco Gemignani

When I was a practicum student, one of my clients, Mei-Li (pseudonym), was a woman from China who came to the United States because her husband enrolled in a PhD program here. She was in her late 20s, and her presenting concerns were consistent with descriptions of acculturative stress. I met with her for counseling regularly, once a week, for more than 2 months. In therapy, we talked about her cultural adjustment, homesickness, loneliness, and identity as an overseas bride. As an international student myself, I felt I was able to understand Mei-Li and to establish a good working collaboration with her. Therapy, I thought, was progressing smoothly.

Mei-Li was cheerful when she came to what became our last meeting. She said that she had found the solution to her problems: She just needed to lose her accent. She realized that her sadness was not psychological, but social. Once she acquired a perfect American accent, she would feel part of this society. She would find American friends, and she would no longer feel the shame of not being understood by her American interlocutors.

I went speechless, not because I did not know what to say but because the whole situation appeared to be so overwhelmingly complex and hurried I did not know where to start. I was afraid she was acting impulsively, without thinking carefully about this decision. On the one hand, I was pleased to see Mei-Li take such a resolute stance after feeling inactive and depressed for weeks. On the other hand, I was deeply skeptical about the behavioral intervention she had identified for herself. I knew, for instance, that her goal was almost impossible to achieve and too grandiose in its implications. I also knew that Mei-Li's social isolation and acculturative stress extended well beyond her accent.

Nevertheless, her "salvation plan" was somehow attractive to me. It spoke to me and about me. Being an international student myself, I shared her fantasies and her concerns, like feeling angry for not being understood and feeling frustrated about communications that were never as spontaneous or expressed as meaningfully as I had intended. I missed the comfort of a shared culture. I feared losing my native language and the physical and figurative relations it allowed. At the time I was seeing Mei-Li as a client, I wrote in a personal journal a sentence she said in therapy: "I feel like a singer who has lost her tongue." Like her, I doubted my communication and social skills. In my home country, I considered myself an attentive listener and a subtle speaker, but those skills were seriously hindered by my tentativeness with the English language.

In the midst of the mixed emotions that Mei-Li's proposed solution opened up in me, I did not know what to tell her. "Wouldn't you like to lose your accent?" she asked me. "No," I replied. I was lying. I then recited the words of some book on multicultural counseling about the need to celebrate diversity rather than to strive to blend in, but I was not persuasive either to Mei-Li or to myself. She thanked me for my work and left the room. I invited her to come back the next week to talk more about her plan. She said she would call me if she needed to see me again. As expected, I never saw her again.

Why was I so unprepared to process Mei-Li's resolution with her? Different attempts to answer this question left me puzzled at first and disappointed later. I did not realize the dynamics that were established between her and me. In the second year of my professional training as a doctoral student in counseling psychology, this therapy experience suddenly and directly provided the ground for eye-opening reflections on concepts and processes that, since then, have become integral aspects of my understanding of psychology, psychotherapy, and research. Some of these theoretical concepts, like reflexivity and countertransference, are quite general to therapy. Others, like social construction, dominant discourse, and cultural identity, are quite specific to the postmodern approach to counseling psychology with which I identify (Gergen, 1994).

I thought I knew Mei-Li, this woman from China. I could relate to her and her psychosocial concerns. I was an international student with a marked accent (which I still have). It was easy to develop empathy with her. Yet it was challenging to keep close contact with her psychological and social world because it brought forth my own emotional struggles. I was her therapist, but inevitably her concerns dialogued with my fantasies, challenges, and cultural background. Working with Mei-Li helped me realize the importance of reflecting on my emotional and unexpected reactions to clients, including my partial identification with her. Here, in living form, was my own countertransference.

Even though therapy with Mei-Li was over, the analysis of my countertransference with her shed light on themes and processes that became central in my training and practice. First, it encouraged me to step down from the position of professional detachment and scientific objectivity that was impossible to keep and quite useless as a psychologist. It became somehow necessary for me to think about the ways my position, identity, and interpretations were part of my therapeutic work and its outcome. Both Mei-Li and I felt oppressed, but we failed to engage each other in the process of recognizing our shared experience. My "No" to her question regarding whether I wanted to lose my accent was a missed opportunity, dictated by my inexperience at the time as well as by a therapeutic discourse that divides counselors and clients, expert and needy individuals, providers and receivers of service. Reflecting on these power dynamics made my work more humble, human, and enjoyable. Eventually, it also helped me choose therapeutic frameworks that were openly collaborative, like constructivist and narrative therapies.

The analysis of my relationship with Mei-Li also allowed for another defining realization: Her acculturation was not an intrapsychic process that could have been isolated from the social, political, and cultural contexts in which she lived. This case changed my view of culture from that of a set of identifiable values and dynamics to a shifting system of practices and relations that are not simply found but constructed. I started wondering about the political aspects not so much of culture in itself but of the identification and recognition of a specific system of values and practices as representative of a group, population, ethnicity, or geographical territory. In other words, I realized the importance of shifting my view of *culture as an existing structure* to *culture as politics of knowledge.* In my training, this move was key to understanding my client's and my participation in a process that Foucault (1975) called "subjectivation"—arguably a form of countertransference. Mei-Li did not just experience stress-related issues. She internalized her concerns to the extent that they became part of her sense of self and her possibilities. She came to recognize herself through the dominant and normative system of power and responsibility in which her life was located, including the "duty" to follow her husband overseas and the social constructions of a "foreigner life" in the United States. In her life context, her identity and relationships interplayed with dominant dynamics of power, recognition, social status, and access. The construction of her psychological issues resulted from such an interaction. Mei-Li internalized the social responses and meanings concerning her accent. Her speech pattern went from being part of her uniqueness, diversity, and culture to become a psychological problem, which was symbolically linked to her perceived "inferiority" as a nonnative speaker of English. Her accent was an issue from which she needed an illusory liberation.

For both Mei-Li and me, moving to the United States was associated with a certain anticipation of success, however we defined it. Whether it meant fulfilling her identity as a good wife or my identity as a PhD student and future psychologist, it came through conforming and partially assimilating to the values and expectations of the dominant discourse (e.g., the request posed by my client to blend in or the ideological values implicit in my training). To understand Mei-Li's feelings and "solution," I needed to understand the ways her values, relations, cultural practices, and their objects were socially constructed and responded to the pressure to assimilate—a pressure to which both of us were subjected.

I realized that, had I been frank and open with myself, my supervisor, and even my client about what was taking place internally for me during my work, I would have learned about the ways Mei-Li's concerns were also, at the same time, my experiences and concerns. More or less willingly, the two of us were simultaneously actors and spectators of the complex play of cultural identity formation, in which new margins and center were created and challenged (Hall, 1996). We were both making sense of our diversity and becoming subjects to it. In my own personal life as well as in therapy, I was right there. I was with her, at the same place of challenge and dialogue in the formation of my cultural identity. She gave me a chance, but I was unable to say "me too." It was too difficult to tell her that I as well felt marginalized by language and, more broadly, by never-ending negotiations of culture.

This experience was a defining moment for my development as a therapist because it persuaded me of the importance of exploring psychological meanings within social and cultural systems of power, culture, identity, and subjectivation. I learned to use my presence in therapy to promote openness and transparency with clients as well as to recognize and challenge power dynamics that presume that therapy is the expert's performance on clients. At the same time, in line with the work of relational and feminist therapists, I have learned that my reactions in therapy are usually telling of the client's experience. If I engage with my reactions rather than dismiss them, they provide a domain in which to ground the therapeutic relationship. Since that clinical experience with Mei-Li, critical reflections on social constructions and politics of truth have enriched my work as a psychologist. Mei-Li's accent and her resolution to get rid of it were as true to her as they still are for me. Now, however, I feel comfortable sharing this place of marginality that she experienced. Our accents, our diversities, our dis-locations are problematic not because of personal or intrapsychological dynamics. Even when it is we who construct them as issues, they entail our subjectivation to cultural dynamics of power and identification. Interpreting psychological concerns as shared (instead of personal) responsibilities is an empowering process that allows for alternative constructions of issues and provides some relief from individualistic ideologies. As a psychologist dedicated to cultural diversity in the international context, the location of psychology inside culture is crucial to avoid ethnocentrism and to keep a humble and critical reflexivity in my practice.

References

Foucault, M. (1975). *Discipline and punish.* New York: Vintage.

Gergen, K.J. (1994). *Realities and relationships: Soundings in social constructionism.* Cambridge, MA: Harvard University Press.

Hall, S. (1996). Introduction: Who needs identity? In S. Hall and P. du Gay (Eds.), *Questions of cultural identity* (pp. 1–17). Thousand Oaks, CA: Sage.

MY TIME WITH JUNE: OVERCOMING MY GRIEF AND LOSS "EXPERTISE"

Jeffrey A. Rings

I've been treating June (pseudonym), age 62, for nearly a year and a half now, mainly to help her address a shopping addiction that she had developed over the past decade. We've developed a strong rapport due to our mutual admiration for honest and direct feedback, our attention to the therapeutic process, regular laughter, and our occasional salty dialogue. However, she came to my graduate program's counseling clinic this past Monday afternoon for her first session in nearly 2 months.

In the 3 months prior to that, June had to cancel about half of her scheduled weekly sessions due to some lingering flu-like symptoms. A few trips to her doctor had yielded minimal results, other than the usual recommendation to take some time off from work to catch up on her rest. To be frank, I gave her illness little thought at first. While I certainly cared for her well-being, my finding out that she had canceled our appointments usually quickly resulted in my turning to the next most pressing matter on the never even close to ending to-do list of grad student responsibilities always floating around in my mind.

While June was absent, she and I kept in contact through periodic phone sessions. She discussed often her increasing frustration with being sick yet without having received any diagnosis that could determine an appropriate course of treatment. As her symptoms worsened, she and her doctors suspected that she was suffering from a more serious ailment. Further medical visits and tests followed, and an MRI soon revealed something much more definitive. It was probable that June had lung cancer. A biopsy could confirm the diagnosis; however, her long-standing bout with emphysema greatly complicated matters by making such a procedure too problematic to attempt until the disease had progressed. Finding out about this, I certainly didn't have to work hard to appear empathic. Paraphrasing, feelings reflections, probing, nonverbal encouragers, and so on—if it was in the textbook, I did it. But in retrospect, I was simply going through the motions—I definitely wasn't *being* empathic.

Until recently June was always an active person, keeping particularly busy lately in an attempt to distract herself from her impulse to shop. She continued to work as often as she could; however, she began to leave work early and cancel our sessions because she was too tired to continue on with her day. Over the phone, June discussed regularly how bored she felt because she could not maintain her typical highly active pace. Our talks also started to consist of her addressing her own mortality. She was learning to accept the possibility that she might die from this at some point in the near future. While other family members shied away understandably from such talk that they viewed altogether as too grim, June and I spoke of this topic as one of stark reality; she's facing the most existential of existential crises, one that's filling her with senses of both purpose and genuineness. Such conversations left me initially with a sense of pride for being able to not shy away from the topic of death, all the while remaining otherwise unaffected personally by her situation. However, I'm starting to realize that I've been working hard to avoid my own feelings about her terminal illness, and I can say with confidence that I've been pretty successful at doing so. Today, in no way is that the case.

June presented for her session this past Monday as increasingly frail. I greeted her in the waiting room, smiled, and paused for a second before asking if she would like any help with her water bottle, her purse, or her newly necessary portable oxygen tank. "No, thank you, I'm not an invalid yet," she snapped half-jokingly, indicating that she had grown sick and tired of others' constant offers of assistance that indirectly reminded her of her illness. Once in my office, June begrudgingly acknowledged that her doctor informed her that she has rapidly spreading, terminal lung cancer. At best, she has only a few months left to live. I cannot say that her illness actually felt real to me previously. While June knew already that she was facing death, nevertheless it had appeared to me to be somewhat avoidable for now, or at least somewhere off in the distant future. As of today though, her death is absolutely imminent.

As an advanced doctoral student, I consider myself to be fairly well versed on the topic of grief and loss. During the years that I spent supervising a suicide hotline prior to returning to school for my doctorate, I heard literally hundreds of calls from those whose grief experiences were profoundly affecting them. This work experience led me to seek out therapy clients who were often in the midst of their own struggles with grief. I've performed a few dozen trainings and lectures on the matter. I'm writing my dissertation examining prolonged grief responses and suicidality as well. Clinically, I might know a great deal about the grief and loss process. But be that as it may, I sure as hell cannot say that I actually understand what it is like to be profoundly bereaved. Personally, I feel fortunate in that all of my immediate family members are still alive. All four of my grandparents have died; however, our living in distant parts of the country may have kept me from feeling much of a connection with them. A close friend of mine nearly died recently; however, she made a full recovery.

Therefore, as of now it's safe to say that when June dies, she'll be the closest person to me to have died. Because of this, June is teaching me more about what it is like to grieve than any textbook or journal article ever could. Two important lessons that being a therapist has taught me over the years are (1) to work on becoming comfortable with the uncomfortable (Epstein, 1999) and (2) that while we always want to work *toward* understanding another's personal experience, we can never *truly* understand it. These two mantras have always been freeing for me as a psychologist in training, but right now, as I write this, they're goddamn scary. I'm goddamn scared.

But please allow me the indulgence of intellectualization for just a moment. In thinking about June, I'm reminded of the intricacies of Erikson's (1982) eighth stage in his theory of psychosocial development, *integrity versus despair.* Now experiencing this nonnormative life event, June appears to have been rushed into this stage as she works to gain the wisdom that comes from accepting what she has done throughout her life and her impending death in an effort to gain a sense of peace. As therapy has progressed, she's been brutally honest about her actions and feelings, both in the present and past, for what she has described as the first time in her life. She's coming to terms with her fate and is trying to forgive herself for the pain she's caused both herself and her family due to her shopping addiction.

Since finding out that her time is more limited than previously believed, she's become increasingly conscious of her own feelings and existentially has come to recognize that there's no time like the present for her to do what she feels she still needs to do in what's left of her life. As we addressed this in session, she vocalized her desire to spend significant amounts of time with her grandchildren, to spend a long weekend with her adult children pampering themselves with spa treatments at a local high-end resort, and to continue to pay off as much of her shopping debt as she can in the meantime. In what I thought at first was a random statement, she noted that her boss rides a Harley-Davidson motorcycle. Having always wanted to ride on one but never having the opportunity to do so, she decided that she would ask him for a ride next week. As she mentioned this, a large smile came across her face while her eyes began to water, ultimately releasing a couple of teardrops.

More than a couple of teardrops are being released from my eyes right now. I'm so honored to have been randomly assigned to work with June and to help her gain a sense of integrity. The personal changes that she has made in therapy are so much greater than just curbing her addictive behaviors, although doing so has certainly been no small feat. Instead, our work together is helping her to address the last of life's major crises. June is certainly more honest with herself at this moment than I am. Only now am I starting to realize just how uncomfortable I feel as a result of her impending death. I need to continue to allow myself to feel as I do; I deserve to grieve as well. More than anything personally, June is giving me such an important gift right now, one that is going to become only more painful for me but one that I will absolutely not avoid.

References

Epstein, M. (1999). Going to pieces without falling apart: A Buddhist perspective on whole-
    ness. New York: Broadway.
Erikson, E. (1982). *The life cycle completed.* New York: Norton.

RESISTANCE: THE CLIENT OR THE COUNSELOR?
John Danna

"How many psychologists does it take to change a light bulb? Only one, but the
light bulb has to really want to change." This is a classic joke about psychotherapy
that I have enjoyed for years. I have found that people tend to be drawn more
toward humor when there is some truth to it, and this was the case for me with this
joke. However, during my clinical training one of my graduate professors alluded
to this joke to argue a contrasting point: that change, as we understood it, is not
what our clients are seeking from therapy. He said that although our clients may
initially present with a desire for relief from their symptoms, they do not actually
want this. He went on to explain how it is ultimately up to the therapist to instill in
clients a desire to make meaningful change in their lives.

When I first heard this I thought it was preposterous. "Of course the client
must want to change if therapy is going to be effective," I thought. "I would not
want to work with a client who does not want to change." However, my experience
with my own clients in therapy has taught me otherwise. The clients I have had
typically come to therapy because their defenses and system of coping have broken
down in one way or another. The kind of change they are seeking, if they desire
any real change at all, is for me to either assist them in "fixing" or "repairing" their
existing network of defenses so it works like it used to or to have me simply fix it
for them. It is rare that a client will come to me for therapy initially seeking change
on any "deep" level. It reminds me of someone who takes an old and trusty but
problem-ridden car to a mechanic in the hopes of salvaging it rather than consider
buying a new car. I will usually have to go along with this desire for a while, though
I will never offer to "fix" my clients, if I want the therapy to continue. Once we have
firmly established a collaborative therapeutic alliance, I will then attempt to guide
my client toward considering alternative, healthier methods of coping. Both sides
of this can be seen through a few case examples.

Sarah (pseudonym) was a 26-year-old African American female who said she
was coming to counseling because she felt "stressed" and "anxious" about "everything in [her] life" and said she had not gotten over the death of her mother a few
years prior. She reported feeling "sad" all the time and had been crying constantly
for what seemed to her no reason. Sarah also said she had been "snapping" at
her 2-year-old daughter more frequently, which concerned her. Her assessment
feedback suggested attention should be paid to her depression, anxiety, obsessive–
compulsive tendencies, hypervigilance, and underlying anger.

Sarah expressed a constant need for control and often thought in all-or-nothing
terms. She said she often felt anger and even rage toward others but kept it inside
and rarely showed it out of fear of what others would think of her. Her goal for

therapy was for me to make things "normal" for her again and help her to regain control of her life. She pleaded with me at least once a session to "fix" her and give her "the answer" or a "magic pill" that would make her life return to the way it was, despite my repeated explanations as to why I could not do so. She frequently asked me, "How long is this going to take [for me to be 'fixed' or 'better']?" We actually had a discussion in which she said she wanted me to fix her coping styles and make them work again rather than to help her consider other options. Sarah never returned for therapy after our fifth session, two and a half months after her intake session. Throughout our brief work together, I felt perpetually frustrated and constantly struggled to establish a collaborative alliance with her without undermining her agency and taking the entire therapeutic workload upon myself, as she apparently preferred. I learned from this case that sometimes clients are too attached to their defense styles to consider other alternatives, or they are not in a place where they feel ready to do so yet. In retrospect, I have often wondered if there were ways I could have aligned with Sarah more to keep her engaged in the work without compromising my own therapeutic values.

For another example, I would like to turn to a different client with whom I worked for just over 2 years. Jane (pseudonym) was a 59-year-old Caucasian woman who came in for therapy saying she was becoming increasingly frustrated and depressed due to her "toxic" work environment, specifically because of an altercation with her boss. She initially sought therapy because her boss demanded she do so. Jane described herself as "rigid" and prided herself on her "professionalism." Her assessment feedback described her as rule conscious, dutiful, serious, restrained, accommodating, practical, and solution oriented. Jane stated on several occasions that she neither had the desire to change nor thought she could change because she was "too old," "stubborn," and set in her ways. During the intake interview and in our first session, she refused to discuss her childhood and her past in general. "Why talk about it? It's the past," she once asked rhetorically.

Most of our early sessions consisted of Jane's complaining about either her coworkers or her family. I initially honored her request for me not to pry into her past. However, after several months into therapy we had established a working alliance, and Jane began bringing up memories from her past and childhood on her own. We came to discover that her family dynamic, which was filled with conflict and emotional repression, had considerable relevance for the current struggles in her life. I eventually noticed that Jane increasingly became more open to taking on different perspectives and healthier, more effective approaches to the situations she encountered in her life, particularly with regard to her interpersonal style. She was able to increase satisfaction in her personal and professional relationships. My work with Jane often challenged my patience and personal desire to move the therapy along in the direction I deemed to be most helpful to her. In looking back, I believe a large part of this struggle had to do with my own yearning to feel like a good and effective therapist by producing visible change within my client. Contrastingly, I attribute at least part of the fruitfulness of our work to my willingness to let go of that yearning, to meet Jane where she was, and to work at her pace—all the while still challenging her to consider different perspectives along the way without making her feel she would have to sacrifice too much of herself or her own safety to do so. I found that this often involves a considerable amount of discomfort and risk taking on the part of both myself and the client and that the only thing that makes this tolerable is our shared confidence in my ability as a therapist to manage our discomfort and to establish a working environment that makes us feel safe enough to take risks.

What I learned from these cases is how, even though clients may come in with a strong resistance to change, they can eventually move toward productive transformation if they are provided with the appropriate kind of therapeutic relationship and space. I also learned that pushing clients to do therapeutic work they are not ready to do or interested in doing can effectively push them away as well. This led me to the realization that what we as therapists refer to as resistance in our clients can often be understood alternatively as our own resistance as therapists to meet our clients where they are. What we experience as their resistance is a reaction to our trying to force them to go somewhere they do not want to go. I often use a metaphor when discussing this concept with colleagues. Imagine yourself on one side of a roaring river and your client on the other side. Your goal is to help your client make it over to your side of the river where you feel it is safer and happier. You may help your client consider various options to facilitate this, such as swimming across, building a raft, searching for a bridge at another part of the river, and so on. You may come to find only that your client cannot swim, has poor building skills, is afraid of heights, or perhaps does not even have a desire to cross the river and may want to go somewhere else entirely. However, since the roar of the passing water makes it difficult to hear, the only way you will discover these things is by making your way over to the other side of the river, meeting the client there, and walking with the client as a guide of sorts as he or she navigates his or her own way. We may be hesitant to venture to the client's side of the river because it seems safer, more comfortable, and less of a risk to stay on our side, but shouting directions over a noisy river is a poor substitute for meeting our clients where they are and genuinely joining them in their struggles.

By using this metaphor I am not suggesting that we refrain from challenging our clients. Much to the contrary, I believe that doing so is an integral part of therapeutic work. I also understand that it may seem counterintuitive to suggest inspiring our clients to change by meeting them where they are because what if we find that they do not want to change? To answer this question I would point to what my training experiences have taught me about the importance of providing a space where our clients feel safe enough to consider change, to be challenged, and to challenge themselves. One helpful approach I have found with clients who are adamantly against change is to join them in exploring the dilemma they face between the difficulty they encounter in trying to reach their goals and the ways their current coping style might be serving as an obstacle to achieving those goals. However, the clients then face the difficulty of weighing out whether it is worth it to let go of the inherent pleasure they have derived for many years from their current coping style in favor of another one that is potentially more healthy and useful but heretofore unproven. It is often up to us, as therapists, to instill within our clients the courage to take that leap and to provide them a space in which they feel comfortable doing so. Yet in carrying this out I believe it is also very important to be mindful of our own therapeutic agenda and to do our best to make sure our therapeutic goals align with the clients'.

I also learned how helpful it is to acknowledge that in the larger picture of individuals' therapeutic journeys, we may be able to join them for only part of their journey or to do a piece of the work with them along the way. We may have to leave other pieces of work for our colleagues when clients feel compelled to return to therapy. I do believe that the impetus for therapeutic change often lies more with us as therapists than with our clients in that it is up to us to be willing to meet them where they are, to align with them in a working therapeutic alliance, to provide a space that is nurturing and conducive to change for them in their unique situations, and to challenge them to try out different and more adaptive perspectives, styles, and ways of being in a manner that is appropriate and productive.

WONDERLAND
Mary Kathleen Hill

> You take the blue pill, the story ends, you wake up in your bed, and believe whatever you want to believe. You take the red pill, you stay in Wonderland, and I show you just how deep the rabbit hole goes. –*The Matrix* (1999)

There are days I wonder if I should have just taken the blue pill and lived the remainder of my life ignorant of terms such as *process, introspection,* and *transference.* For me, graduate school was like taking the red pill. It opened up a whole new world of regular self-reflection, involving satisfaction from areas of strength and pain from areas of perceived weakness. At this point in my development, I still struggle with learning how to control these wonderful yet overwhelming analytical skills of mine. And, I believe, I am not alone. My purpose here is not to cure our tendency toward excessive self-exploration but, rather, to bravely acknowledge that this seems to be a normal occurrence for therapists, especially those of us just beginning our careers in the field.

When graduate school began, I naïvely thought I could sit in a room with other human beings and not be personally affected by their stories. I had no concept of how captivating our clients' life stories could be and how, at times, our clients' narratives might hit a little too close to home. I originally fought my instinct to open myself up to the intense emotional connection that binds a therapist and client. I even convinced myself that I needed to be a "professional" and that professionals do not get personally involved. Don't get me wrong; It is not that I did not have good rapport with my clients but rather that I chose to predominantly connect with them cognitively. I endlessly analyzed their cases by rationally considering their behaviors and conceptualizing the reasons behind them, but I avoided relating on a deeper level. Though it took some time, I eventually conceded that my hesitancy to connect emotionally with my clients was out of fear—a fear of looking inward.

We ask our clients to take us down their dark rabbit holes while allowing us to witness the emotions that accompany such a trip, so it seemed fair that I go down my own rabbit hole too. This became especially apparent after I was presented with my first anxious client—as I have struggled with anxiety throughout much of my life. My work with this client, whom I will call Mark, was a critical point—a defining moment—in my development as a therapist.

Going down the rabbit hole is a scary, exhilarating ride that I recommend professionals in counseling take if they truly hope to join with those they wish to help. In fact, I worry about those who finish graduate school without ever swallowing the red pill and taking their own personal journeys. Through introspection I was better able to connect with my clients by accessing the deep, dark parts of myself that I was normally skilled at avoiding. I learned to appreciate vulnerability and the power of self-realization. However, unlike my clients, my training and insight into the human mind are what helped guide me out of my own rabbit hole with a newfound sense of self and what I stand for. For me, my initial self-reflections were a complex combination of painful healing that affected not only me but also my clients and even my loved ones.

While working with Mark, who embodied so many of my own neuroses, I learned the most about painful healing, or reconciling my own inconsistencies. It was amazing how I so easily pinpointed the negative effects of his intense anxiety and felt such compassion for his struggle, yet I continued to have difficulty cutting myself the same slack I so easily gave to him. His fear of failure, desire to be perfect, and self-deprecating thoughts were all areas I had struggled with from time to time, so I initially wondered how I could help him when I could not even help myself. It was eventually because of our similarities that I gained a glimpse from the outside in and began changing my perspective. I finally began the journey toward self-acceptance and began giving myself the same respect I so readily gave to my clients. The more I acknowledged my fault finding and embraced the power of self-acceptance, the more comfortable I became with experiencing intense emotion with another person and the better therapist, friend, daughter, wife, and person I became.

The realization that *accepting ourselves as we are can be more profound than searching for who we think we should be* has become my own personal motto as well as an aspect I incorporate into therapy. The goal for me seems to be finding a balance between critical introspection and unconditional self-acceptance, as unfortunately for me and many of my clients it seems that finding our perceived faults tends to be the easier of the two. Learning how to modulate my analytical skills is a work in progress, as I still analyze the world around me without realizing it and am still easily consumed by my own thoughts. Most often it actually takes more courage to accept myself as I am than it does to identify my perceived faults. The courage to accept myself requires that I let go of control.

As a therapist, I often feel pulled to monitor the process in the therapy room as well as my own reactions to my clients' stories. In a sense, I sometimes feel obligated to be in control of my every action in the therapy room for the sake of my clients, particularly those who have relatable stories, as I place each of my client's needs before my own. However, the professionally relevant self-control that helps me monitor the interpersonal process within the therapy room occasionally bleeds into my personal life and only exacerbates my tendency toward critical introspection. Instead of initially asking what I am doing right, I am more likely to ask what I need to do to improve. It is here, in the Wonderland of Analysis, where I need self-acceptance the most because without a positive anchor it is too easy for me to get lost and overwhelmed and thus disconnected from the very people with whom I want to connect. In a sense, my Wonderland reflects the dichotomy that exists within me, and possibly within all of us: On one hand, I am full of wonder because I question, probe, and explore the possibilities, while on the other hand I must remind myself that I am wonderful just as I am.

Therefore, as each of us continues down our respective rabbit holes and on into our personal Wonderlands, I think it is paramount to remember that our personal journeys occur simultaneously with the journeys of our clients. Our clients constantly challenge us; accepting that challenge is a difficult but rewarding task. Allowing ourselves the chance to accept who we are in any given moment is perhaps one of the best gifts we can give ourselves as well as our clients.

THE TRUE MEANING OF EMPATHY
Annette S. Kluck

During my graduate training, my supervisors repeatedly asked, "What are you feeling?" as they watched my session tapes. I learned that it was hard to read my reactions from the tapes and that my supervisors questioned if I felt connected with my clients. After receiving similar feedback from multiple supervisors, I came to accept that they perceived me as emotionally distant from my clients. I began to question if I truly had empathy or could connect with others in the way that most therapists do. I believed that I cared about my clients and I could talk abstractly about empathy and its value in the therapeutic relationship, but I wondered if I lacked the emotional awareness needed to be a good therapist. Faculty members had described empathy as putting yourself in someone else's shoes but still recognizing you are a separate person. I liked to think that I had this capacity, but I wondered how it would be possible to know if I actually did. I knew that I was passionate about research and teaching, and I sometimes felt relief when clients canceled because I had more time to work on my teaching and research obligations. At the same time, my silent sense of relief left me with a burning question about whether I had what it takes to be a counseling psychologist who can provide quality clinical services.

For much of my training I grappled with feelings of doubt about my ability to be empathetic. I was drawn to research and teaching before starting to experience uncertainty about my ability to connect with clients. However, I also began to see my clinical skills as lacking in comparison with my competence in research and teaching, which made retreating into those activities appealing.

As I approached the last few months of my doctorate, I got an answer to the question of whether I was capable of feeling true empathy for clients. I worked in a setting with clients with severe mental illness, some of whom had committed crimes they themselves and society would call heinous. Frequently during my training, students and professionals would comment that they could not work with a client who had committed a crime like sexual assault. Students were encouraged to think about the types of clients they *would* like to see. Having a plan to specialize in the treatment of depression, romantic relationships, or eating disorders was acceptable. As a student, I had not questioned this perspective. It seemed logical and rational to have a preference for working with clients whose psychological difficulties evoke a feeling of sympathy. I was drawn to the idea of working with women's issues, and I had not planned to work with individuals with severe mental illness, especially those who require long-term hospitalization. However, it was when working with these clients that I found the answer to my question about my ability to be empathetic.

During my time providing psychological services for individuals with severe mental illness, I worked with a handful of clients who had criminal histories. I most vividly recall becoming aware of the power of empathy and my own ability to empathize when I sat across from a client whom I'll call John. This client had committed a crime that changed the life of another. In my first meeting with John, he shared his struggle with guilt over involvement in a violent crime several years earlier. He was involuntarily hospitalized, and his discharge was contingent upon demonstrating that he was no longer a threat to himself. He wanted to be released from the hospital, so my goals were to reduce his depression and suicidal ideation, the factors contributing to his involuntary hospitalization. As such, my initial response was to employ cognitive restructuring, focusing on the fact that John had served the sentence for his crime based upon what society thought was necessary punishment. During the initial meetings, I was emotionally distant from John. I was uncertain about whether he would engage in therapy or whether he wanted anything from his time at the hospital. I wanted to spend my time with patients who were invested in therapy. I was focused on quickly returning him to a status where he could be discharged to the community. I was a bit surprised when John informed me that he hated when people attempted to console him by pointing to time served in prison. He explained that he didn't see his punishment as sufficient reparation for his crime. I realized that he struggled with existential guilt over the crime he had committed. He felt he should be punished, and his suicide attempts were actually his attempt to right the situation.

As I sat with John, I knew I had to help him find value in his own life. I had planned to employ a cognitive approach that would address his automatic thoughts in hopes of reducing his feelings of depression. When he rejected my initial approach, I experienced discomfort and uncertainty about how to respond. Though he never said it, he was correct in his message that I was dismissing his feelings. I felt embarrassed that I, as his therapist, had responded in the same and unhelpful way as everyone else. We struggled for several minutes with the issue, as I reflected his feelings and tried to connect with his extreme guilt. There we were, John sitting across from me expressing disgust about an act he had done and me unsure how to help him reframe his perspective. Eventually, it occurred to me that John needed to believe he could contribute to society more than he had taken from it rather than to change his perspective of the past. John seemed to agree and gravitated toward the idea that making life better for other people was a reason to live and something he would be unable to do if he died. I also knew that if I were to truly help John, I also needed to believe he could contribute to society, and I needed to step out of what felt emotionally safe and get to know him as a person. I had to find a way to connect with him while maintaining awareness of the crime he had committed and the consequences of that act.

It was not nearly as difficult to establish a connection and positive regard for John as I would have predicted it to be. In listening to his story, I found so many examples of how his life situation may have led him down the particular path he took. I could appreciate that John had created a lot of pain for others but had also experienced a lot of pain himself—pain he needed to heal. As I thought about his personal history, I found it easy to connect with him while still hating the crime he had committed. I felt sadness over John's history of rejection from family, teachers, and peers. In fact, I had a hope for him that he lacked for himself. My concern for his survival was not a simple reflection of ethical obligations but a genuine concern for him as a person. I believed that he could create a better future and be the type of man he aspired to be. As I struggled to help John face his existential concerns, I realized that I was capable of feeling empathy toward my clients. I had clearly connected with John, who perceived himself as undeserving of life, as we delved into his pain, laughed at life, and grappled with his guilt. My empathy for John was critical as he experienced multiple setbacks during the course of his treatment, likely reflecting his difficulties with trusting others that had resulted from his own painful developmental history.

When teaching beginning counselors about empathy I often think back to John and my realization that forming a strong connection was essential for helping him to create any real change. I challenge students to be patient with their development. However, I also ask students to challenge themselves to have empathy for people whom most of society would cast aside or for someone they would typically not meet during the course of their daily lives. It is not that, as counselors, we must have empathy for a client who has engaged in heinous acts to be empathetic; rather, the mark of empathy is our ability to connect with those who are not like us, whether due to severe mental illness, criminal history, or cultural background. It is easy for us to connect with clients who remind us of ourselves, and we have preferences about which types of clients we treat. However, if we can challenge ourselves to connect with clients whom we perceive as lacking common experience on which to build a relationship, we can learn about ourselves and have the opportunity to observe the extensive reach of the foundation of the therapeutic alliance. It is in those situations where we connect with clients we would likely never encounter outside of our offices that our empathy shows most clearly.

FROM HOPELESS TO HOPEFUL: A JOURNEY TOWARD BELIEF
Ruth Chu-Lien Chao

"Your Happiness Project, Ruth, made me find joy I have lost for decades. Now I *believe* in myself; *I'm* the person making me happy," a dear client of mine, Mary (pseudonym), confessed regarding her homework called the "Happiness Project."

Her joy in her newfound self-belief opened a new chapter of life for us both. Her usual sad face was nowhere, now replaced by a shining face and vibrant voice. That vision remains vivid today in me, her counselor. I cannot help but ponder many questions this raises: What made her change? What does "believing in myself" mean? How powerful is belief, especially self-belief? She gave me in one session a lifelong insight—the power of belief. It has taken years to explore what this belief means.

How did I come to see belief as an essential component of counseling? In China, there is a saying that life's saddest tragedy is death of the heart. I saw in Mary's new beaming smile hope in new life. That is belief: a seed in a desert, fighting a windy drought to thrive. Mary's smile taught me that her belief was a seed, inside her tired self, that sprouted a new beginning in life.

When we first discussed this homework assignment, Mary said that the Happiness Project was too simple to have a promising outcome, not realizing that simplicity was the spirit of the project. We talked in depth about it before I asked her to conduct this homework. She was to watch her favorite movie and reflect on when, where, and with whom she watched it. Mary was then supposed to write down any changes in her thoughts, emotions, and remembrances the movie evoked. Our detailed initial discussion failed to convince her how watching a movie could make her happy. She must have thought, "This Taiwanese intern must be struggling with practicum. Poor international student! Why don't I just do her a favor to help her pass her practicum?" So she watched her favorite movie, as a favor to me, with a long-time friend she'd known since childhood.

Watching the old movie reminded her of her happiness as a child and rekindled her cherished friendship. Mary and her friend laughed about their shared sweet childhood, and she noted how precious it was to watch the same old movie with the same old friend! She remembered what a resilient girl she used to be. Her friend was still amazed at Mary's big heart, reflecting, "Remember how you saved a kid's life? Every day you followed him. He lived just a few blocks away, with an unknown disease. You insisted on following him home, he fainted one day, and you called 911. That saved his life!" Mary responded, "Yes, I am still thankful; I saved him!" Then she pondered, "It took me so much to help him. If I could do so then, why can I not help myself now? Why should I lose my belief in myself? Can I believe myself to be tough again now?"

Going through such self-inquiries, Mary decided to give herself a chance by believing that she could rediscover her positive self. From that moment, she enjoyed foods, laughing, and every little story she read. She wrote down her positive thoughts whenever she experienced moments of newfound meaning. Returning to counseling in her next session, she expressed her happiness by repeatedly reporting how much she enjoyed watching the movie. Beyond happiness at revisiting the movie and her friendship, her joy expanded to other areas such as reading books.

Is belief a magic pill that lifts us overnight from hellish sorrow to heavenly joy? It is not, of course. Belief lifts us slowly but surely. "At first, even after I decided to believe in myself, I heard little voices of doubt, insecurity, fear, and need," Mary said. And then, it seems, she also heard another voice—that of belief—saying, "It's okay, we will see what happens next. It's okay to feel insecure at first." The voice of belief told the insecure voices that she would know when the new happiness arrived. Mary spent a week learning to believe in herself and spent one session teaching me the life-transforming lesson to which I had to devote many years of thinking to digest.

As we counselors are often inspired by clients' change, I noticed that Mary's change stimulated my own new self-reflections. I wondered, How do I work on belief with clients? From what Mary taught me, I began to appreciate the power of belief both in myself and in my clients. If I do not believe in my clients, who else does? If I don't believe in myself, in whom else do I believe? Giving myself and my clients that chance allows belief to begin sprouting; I thus invite both myself and my clients into belief.

This invitation amounts to permitting oneself to succeed as well as to fail. My projects may fail, but clients must risk much to accept my invitation to believe. I cannot forget the big moments when clients take risks to accept themselves, based on my suggestions. I remember Mary's suspicious tone in saying, "Okay, I will try," even as she told me that she was also trying to do me a favor. We both had a good laugh when she revealed her motivation—helping a struggling international trainee. What a special moment of decision that was! Was it due to her happy memory of helping that boy when she was a tough little girl?

After that powerful session with Mary, I deeply examined myself. If belief was so powerful as to lift Mary out of sadness, couldn't I benefit from belief as well? This question has been with me for years. I took it to my practicum and diversity classes, to working with advisees, and to interacting with colleagues. My use of belief grows richer as I try it in new and varied areas.

I have learned that belief is important in many settings. For example, in the diversity class I teach, I have learned to believe that my White students are quite willing to examine their biases, to work through cultural barriers, and to deepen their awareness. When I pour my belief into collaboration with advisees, new light and new hope dawn on their desperate struggles with dissertations and theses. And their feedback, quite commonly, is, "Thanks for believing in me, for in the world, only you, Ruth, believe I can do it." To believe is to see the face of hope, to envision success. I have also found that belief accumulates as my clients' and students' appreciation of belief adds to my own! Now looking back, I am not sure if I am more thankful or if my clients and students are more thankful, for I owe *my* belief so much to *them*!

How does belief heal? Belief is a moment of decision. At this moment we make a new contract with ourselves. We are committed to new behaviors, new lifestyles, and thus new identities. In my Happiness Project, clients commit themselves to a new perspective by engaging in their favorite activities. With belief in their new life, they challenge their old selves that said, "I am always sad no matter what." However small a success they achieve, this self-challenge makes their belief grow.

Frankly, I doubted if I was a good enough counselor for Mary. Her shining face said she helped herself; I was there just to facilitate her self-help, which was a birth of belief. Belief is made of new vision, new perspective, new gestalt, new way of doing, and, thus inspired and convinced, a new push, new thrust, to living it accordingly. Belief *makes* the world; new belief revolutionizes the world. That is what Mary taught me. Mary showed me that those without belief lose vision and that their lack of vision crumbles into further self-depreciation. They are dead while drawing breath. The Happiness Project asked Mary to do something simple such as laugh over a joke. The laughter opened her vision and turned the world upside down; "I am dead" became "I am happy."

Our reopened vision creates a new belief to turn hopelessness into hopefulness. Belief is life; to live vigorously, we must embrace belief wholeheartedly, starting with laughing at a simple thing.

MY EXPANDED BELLY GAVE LIFE AND MEANING TOO
Jenelle C. Fitch

I never guessed that a semester in practicum would provide me with such a profound learning experience. The event that occurred pushed me to explore my identity as a therapist, to define my theoretical orientation to therapy, and to help me to understand how my personal life can intersect boldly with that of my client. Through all of this, I developed a deep awareness of how I could be a therapist who is not leery of using herself as a quiet and nondirective agent of change in the therapy process. I became a therapist who is now open with my clients about the process of therapy, the dynamics of the therapeutic relationship, and the close connections between client's and therapist's life and circumstance.

During one semester of practicum, I, as a 25-year-old therapist in training, was assigned a 50-something-year-old client, Edith (pseudonym), who was diagnosed with a pernicious cancer. Based on Edith's reports, she was uncertain about her future and came to therapy because of her fears of death and dying, including how it would affect her family. At first, I agonized about how I would be able to help Edith. I worried about our age difference and our dissimilar life circumstances. It was difficult for me to understand how to relate with her, because she was dealing with her impending death, while I was preparing to give life to my first child. I was 14 weeks pregnant when we met.

As our work progressed over the course of the semester, a statement by Lazar (1990) resonated with me: "I think every pregnant therapist is faced with a sense that she is introducing a gradually increasing intrusion into the patient's analytic space" (p. 213). This statement was so true, because as I continued to meet with Edith, I felt my very personal life becoming more and more visibly apparent in our therapeutic relationship. I wondered how this would affect my work with her, especially because she was dealing with her own death. I struggled with how, and when, to tell Edith about my pregnancy.

Some theorists (e.g., Stuart, 1997) recommend that it is important for the therapist to address these issues early in therapy. Furthermore, researchers suggest that how and when a therapist discloses the pregnancy can have an important impact on transference reactions from the client (Fallon & Brabender, 2003; Uyehara, Austrian, Upton, Warner, & Williamson, 1995). As a result, to decrease the transference reactions that might have occurred and to also deflect any hindrance to therapy, I decided to disclose my pregnancy to Edith before it was readily apparent. I felt that my giving life by having a baby was the antithesis to Edith's impending death. As I disclosed this personal experience to Edith, she reacted kindly and with joy. She gained life in the session and wanted to know about my pregnancy, my experience, and more about my life. I responded with great authenticity, because during my disclosure I realized that these circumstances could have positive therapeutic implications. Hence, I hoped to use this experience to help Edith move toward a place of peace and understanding. As I later found out, my hope for her was realized.

Theoretically, I considered Edith's impending death to be a "boundary situation" (May & Yalom, 2000; Yalom, 1980; Yalom & Lieberman, 1991), which forced her into the realm of confrontation with an existential situation. During many sessions, she would weep and explain that she was disappointed in her unfulfilled dreams and wishes and that she was terrified about leaving her children without any guidance or wisdom. With Edith's intense need to talk about these concerns, I used a more nondirective style in therapy, where genuineness, empathy, and warmth were pervasive (Rogers, 1959). This was different from what I tended to do with most of my clients, with whom I would be more directive and provide more guidance. Edith would frequently respond to my humanistic interventions, saying things such as, "It is nice to not have someone tell you how to feel." To me, this was a sign that this approach was appropriate in timing and was tailored to her needs.

As a caveat to Edith's issues of death and subsequent existential anxiety, she would frequently state that her life had no meaning. During one session, she stated that even as a mother she "failed her children," because she felt that she (financially) had nothing to leave them. Theoretically, I conceptualized her manifest references to her poor financial situation as a latent reference to her poor health and the overwhelming situation related to her cancer diagnosis. In an attempt to help Edith make meaning out of her life, particularly in her role as a mother, I discussed the concept of *priceless wisdom*. I told Edith that the wisdom that she will leave her children is priceless, something that no price can pay. Edith did not clearly respond to this intervention. She readily turned the discussion back to her finances and lack thereof. Her minimal response did not lead me to the conclusion that it was a poor intervention, but perhaps one in which the timing was less than ideal (Weiner, 1998).

As the semester came to a close, I had to terminate my relationship with Edith. This was something that I was not ready to do, because I truly felt close to Edith and felt the impact of her life on my own professional and personal experience. Consequently, for her, the impact of my pregnancy became apparent. Two sessions prior to termination, Edith began to discuss the cycle of life. She reported that even though her progress through therapy was at times difficult, she realized that life would continue once she had died. Edith reported that this revelation made her feel strength by knowing that her family, namely, her daughter and granddaughter, would be well and would persist in moving through life. I processed this with her and asked her how she came to this revelation. Edith responded, pointed to my expanded belly, and with tears in her eyes said, "You—and this." I then realized how impactful my life circumstance had been for her. My agony, worry, and fear all dispelled. I was then able to appreciate that it was my presence; the sharing of my life, that helped her. I myself did nothing profound or creative, but it was the serendipitous pairing of us together that set this experience in motion. It was amazing. Even now, it is something that is beyond words to describe.

Over the course of my time with Edith, I felt that we both experienced respective life cycles, not only the cycle of life but also the life cycle of therapy. We met at the beginning, worked through many challenges, and finally ended our relationship in a natural and peaceful way. Through this experience, I found that my approach to therapy changed. I became less active in therapy and more engaged through active listening, employing the presence of empathy and learning to maintain separateness from the intense emotions. It was a learning process for me, one that challenged my skills and former beliefs of what therapy was. I came to the realization that I cannot completely contain my clients' emotions. I have to let them feel the pain, sorrow, and happiness, because these emotions are essential to growth (Curran & Kobos, 1980).

Overall, my role as a therapist is to be present; to let the client know that he or she has been heard; to give the client an environment in which it is safe to feel the pain; to provide an environment that facilitates growth, warmth, genuineness; and most of all, to open a window through which the client can view the past, present, and even the future.

After our termination, I often wondered how Edith's life continued and how her subsequent death occurred. I wondered if she continued to hold and carry the peace that she had in that one session when she pointed to my expanded belly and with tears in her eyes said, "You—and this." I wondered how she spent her remaining days with her family, how she continued to give her priceless wisdom, and how she made sure to give her love, all that she had left, to her family. I will never forget Edith. She not only touched me professionally and enhanced my development as a therapist, but she also truly affected my heart and my being as a person.

References

Curran, M.C., & Kobos, J.C. (1980). Therapeutic engagement with a dying person: Stimulus for therapist training and growth. *Psychotherapy: Theory, Research, & Practice, 17,* 343–351.

Fallon, A.E., & Brabender, V.M. (2003). *Awaiting the therapist's baby.* Mahwah, NJ: Erlbaum.

Lazar, S.G. (1990). Patients' responses to pregnancy and miscarriage in the analyst. In H.J. Schwartz & A.S. Silver (Eds.), *Illness in the analyst* (pp. 199–226). New York: International University Press.

May, R. (Ed.). (1969). *Existential psychology* (2nd ed.). New York: Random House.

May, R., & Yalom, I.D. (2000). *Existential psychotherapy.* In R.J. Corsini & D. Wedding (Eds.), *Current psychotherapies* (6th ed., pp. 273–302). Belmont, CA: Thomson.

McGoldrick, M., & Walsh, F. (1999). Death and the family life cycle. In B. Carter & M. McGoldrick (Eds.), *The expanded family life cycle: Individual, family, and social perspectives* (3rd ed., pp. 185–201). Needham Heights, MA: Allyn & Bacon.

Rogers, C. (1959). A theory of therapy, personality, and interpersonal relationships as developed in the client-centered framework. In S. Koch (Ed.), *Psychology: A study of science: Vol. 3. Formulations of the person and the social context* (pp. 184–256). New York: McGraw-Hill.

Stuart, J.J. (1997). Pregnancy in the therapist: Consequences of a gradually discernable physical change. *Psychoanalytic Psychology, 14,* 347–364.

Uyehara, L.A., Austrian, S., Upton, L.G., Warner, R.H., & Williamson, R.A. (1995). Telling about the analyst pregnancy. *Journal of the American Psychoanalytic Association, 43,* 113–135.

Weiner, I.B. (1998). *Principles of psychotherapy* (2nd ed.). New York: Wiley & Sons.

Yalom, I.D. (1980). *Existential psychotherapy.* New York: Basic Books.

Yalom, I.D., & Lieberman, M.A. (1991). Bereavement and heightened existential awareness. *Psychiatry: Journal for the Study of Interpersonal Processes, 54,* 334–345.

MY FATHER, MYSELF

Sara M. Fier

My father died 2 years ago from leukemia, at the age of 61. During the eulogy, the priest spoke about visiting him in the hospital. The priest described how beforehand he would think about what he could say to comfort my father. He would enter the hospital room and ask my father how he was doing. Within the first couple of minutes, the focus of the conversation would turn toward the priest, and the priest would end up talking about himself. He said that he would always leave the hospital amazed at how good he felt and how he spent the entire time talking about himself and his concerns rather than my father's concerns. The priest said that it was always evident that my father cared more about others than himself.

The priest's words were a great comfort during a rough time. Yet these words additionally struck me, because I thought that my father's technique of focusing the conversation on the other person sounded a lot like what I do as a counselor. My father was a farmer with an eighth-grade education but was very skilled and knowledgeable in many areas. Prior to the priest's words, I never would have made the connection that my father may have had a large role in my choice of profession. In that moment, my reaction was, "That sounds like a counselor … and if that sounds like a counselor … that sounds like me." As I later reflected on the priest's words, I began to see many connections between the man my father was and my career choice. The priest's words were a wonderful gift that further connected my life to my father. I do not know if I would have ever figured that out on my own. I always thought that any genetic predisposition toward counseling and helping had come from the females in my family, many of whom are teachers.

My father's values are exemplified by his favorite sayings, which are, in many ways, examples of counseling attributes. He always encouraged my siblings and me to see the good in people and often said, "If you don't have anything good to say, don't say anything at all." No matter how frustrated we were about a situation, he encouraged us to view things from another perspective and to acknowledge the positive qualities in the other person. My father had high expectations and would say, "If you're going to do it, do it right," but he believed in giving people second chances, because he had faith that people could realize their full potential. He attacked life with an almost manic energy. He worked from sunup until sometimes long after sundown ("Don't put off until tomorrow what you can do today"), but if someone needed his help, no matter how busy he was, he would drop what he was doing and help. Whether he had been asked for help or not, he would be there to help figure it out with twice the number of tools as he needed to do the job. When it was time to have fun, he played with equal zeal.

I often had real, genuine conversations with my father. He was the first person I turned to if I had a problem. If I was not looking for a solution and just needed to talk, he sensed that and just listened. I knew that whether he agreed with me or not, he sought to understand things from my perspective and withheld judgment if his perspective was different.

I specifically remember the last time we had the opportunity to spend time alone. I am the oldest of five children, and there are 11 grandchildren, so the times when he and I were alone were limited. He was making a trip with a semi and trailer to get some construction supplies. I needed some patio stones, so I rode along. A topic of conversation came up on which we disagreed, and his response was to just shrug his shoulders and smile. My father had a natural ability for genuineness, empathy, and acceptance, which are among the first skills taught in counseling programs.

Six years before his death, my father had internal bleeding that the doctors could not stop. We were told that he was going to die. A tenacious doctor was finally able to stop the bleeding, and my father eventually returned home after a long hospital stay. My father was physically never the same person after that. The experience took a lot out of him, and it marked the beginning of a series of health difficulties over the next 6 years, until his death. Around a year after the problem with internal bleeding, he was diagnosed with hemochromatosis, a genetic disorder in which the liver does not metabolize iron correctly, causing damage to the body's organs and systems. There were several other hospital stays for everything ranging from kidney stones to recovering from an accident in which he was pinned under the steering wheel of a tractor underwater in a farm pond. A year and a half before his death, he was diagnosed with chronic leukemia and, finally, with acute leukemia a month before his death.

In many ways, my development as a counselor paralleled my personal development. At the time of my father's initial hospitalization, I had just started the internship for my doctoral degree and was working toward autonomy and finding my niche professionally. Personally, my father's health difficulties brought about the realization that he was not invincible and would not always be there for me. He was still my father, but he could no longer do as much as he had in the past, which on a personal level forced me to individuate and become more autonomous. He certainly lived another of his favorite sayings, "Never give up." I do not claim to have my father's resolve and fortitude, but personally and professionally, I try to remember that there is nearly always another option or a different way to look at a situation. As my father said, "It's never so bad that it couldn't be worse!"

Even when faced with the reality of approaching death, my father maintained his sense of humor. During his last hospital stay, there were times when he was really confused. He was heavily medicated and had not slept much in days. Several times a day, medical staff asked him questions to assess his confusion: "What's your name? Where are you? What is the date?" Sometimes he had an easy time with the questions, and other times he had more difficulty. One time he was asked, "Who is the president?" and my father answered, "Well, [Dwight] Eisenhower of course!" I knew he was joking, but the medical professional took him seriously. Sure enough, when the medical professional turned his back, Dad winked at me. After the person left, I said, "Dad, you need to stop that. They take you seriously!" His response was, "Well, I have to have a little fun, don't I?"

My father's death marked the start of a period of increased reflection for me, personally and professionally. It gave me a lot to think about and in many ways modified the way I viewed a lot of things. According to Skovholt and Rønnestad's (1992) theory of counselor development, I transitioned to the individuation stage of counselor development, drawing on my past experiences and knowledge to develop an individualized approach to life and to my profession. It has been a process of defining and refining what works for me when helping others.

I try to work with people at face value rather than being influenced by how things "should" or "ought" to be. I have always been interested in helping people reach their potential, but increasingly I recognize that there are countless intermediate steps to reach that potential and that potential may be different from what is realistic based on constraints within a person's life and environment. I focus on trying to make a difference in my own little corner of the world. I try not to get caught up in overwhelming situations but take things one step at a time. I try to focus my activities on areas that fit well with who I am and my personal and professional goals. I have confidence in my ability to help people, but I recognize my limitations and realize that people also have to be willing to work hard to help themselves. I try not to take things too seriously and look for the humor and irony in even the bleakest situations, which is often enough to gain some perspective on a situation. My father always teased me about being a "professional student" through my long educational process, but I am sure he would be proud to know the impact he has had, and continues to have, not only on my life but also on the lives of others.

Reference

Skovholt, T.M., & Rønnestad, M.H. (1992). Themes in therapist and counselor development. *Journal of Counseling and Development, 70,* 505–515.

PERSONAL PAIN AS TEACHER
Michelle Trotter-Mathison

On March 2, I woke up to a phone call from my dad. A phone call that I had been expecting but wasn't ready to receive. My grandfather—one of my father's best friends, a role model to me, my grandmother's love—had died in his sleep the night before. He had been battling with a variety of health problems, and, at the age of 80, he died. I was scheduled to go home to see him in a week, to see him before he died. I was away from my family, and on my predoctoral internship. I wanted to be with my family during this time of loss, but I needed to go to work before I could go home for the funeral and to be with my family.

I had experienced loss before, but this felt like my first major loss, as an adult when I was able to fully comprehend its meaning. I grew up with my grandfather and grandmother very present in my life. My grandparents lived in the small town where I grew up. My summers were spent at their house playing at the lake. Each time my parents went out of town, my brother and I *got* to stay with Grandpa and Grandma. My grandfather was an honorable, modest, and kind man. I enjoyed a playful and rich relationship with him. Losing him created a sadness and a hole within the family. In the first few days after learning of my grandfather's death I needed to put on my emotional "blinders," so to speak. Using the language of dialectical behavior therapy, I needed to live in rational mind to move through my work days, to be present with clients, to continue to attend to academic projects, and to prepare for my trip home.

Like all of us, I have experienced sadness, disappointment, and loss in my life. All of these experiences have reminded me of my connection to humankind and have bolstered my sense of compassion for others. There was something about this loss that felt like a punch in the stomach. It was the kind of loss that stopped me in my tracks and asked me to pause for a while and feel it, really feel it and all of the emotions that accompanied it. I felt so much—the sadness and grief for the loss, the flooding of positive memories from my childhood, the sense that a part of history is now gone and the emerging sense that a layer of my foundation is no longer there and that I am transitioning into being that foundation for others someday.

As my extended family and I looked through 80 years of photographs of my grandfather's long and happy life, what emerged for me was the renewed sense of what was important in my life. Reviewing the photographs of my grandfather's life told a story of a man who prioritized family, love, and goodness to others. His life did not necessarily start out easily or begin with rich blessings; he decided upon his priorities and lived them out.

This significant loss has impacted my professional life. I believe that the pain I felt helped me to once again connect to a sense of priorities in my own life. It also helped connect me to a deeper sense of my own humanness in the room with clients. As a therapist in the months following my grandfather's death I believe I grew more present with my clients. I felt as though I was better able to sit with clients and listen as things for them were "falling apart," or unraveling or just fraying a bit. My capacity to sit with my own feelings of pain and loss prompted a growing capacity for mindful attention with my clients. Namely, I felt better able to set aside my own daily thoughts and be more attuned to my clients in addition to being bolder in helping clients to identify salient themes in our work together.

As a student in what Rønnestad and Skovholt (2003) term the *Advanced Student Phase,* there was a lingering sense for me of wanting to do things perfectly. Experiencing a loss like this helped the artifice of wanting to do it exactly right to drop away and helped me return to my natural sense of sitting with clients as an authentic human being. I asked myself what is really important here: that I "do it right" or that I have an authentic interaction with this client and work to provide an environment that is healing? I believe this layer of needing to do it right can present like a wall in therapy. A developmental task for me was to work on removing that wall and become more authentic in the room with clients. In the words of Parker Palmer (2004), I was working on joining "soul and role," and this loss woke me up to the importance and urgency of this task. I also felt more connected to the emotional richness of each moment and felt a continued commitment to sit with clients in their pain without a need to fix it or make it go away.

Grief and loss, as I am learning, comes out and up at different times and in varying ways. As I write this narrative I feel gratitude that I could take away yet another lesson from my grandfather, even in his absence. My hope throughout my life is that I can continue to use life's pains as teachers in and out of the therapy room. It is also my hope that the emotional pains, the things that break my heart, help me to open myself to the rest of the world.

References

Palmer, P.J. (2004). *A hidden wholeness: The journey toward an undivided life.* San Francisco: John Wiley & Sons, Inc.

Rønnestad, M.H., & Skovholt, T.M. (2003). The journey of the counselor and therapist: Research findings and perspectives on development. *Journal of Career Development, 30,* 5–44.

THE BUMPY ROAD TO MULTICULTURALISM: LESSONS ABOUT THE LESSONS IN A CLASS
Catherine L. Packer-Williams

As an African American woman who grew up in an ethnically diverse community, I have always held a strong interest in multicultural diversity. I was born and raised in a small town across the Hudson River from Ellis Island. My childhood friends included second-generation Polish, Irish, and Italian Americans whose grandmothers still spoke their native languages. Although my religious background was Protestant, I attended a Catholic school with a host of other non-Catholics. During elementary school, my classmates were first-generation students from South Korea, the Philippines, Libya, Egypt, France, India, and Pakistan as well as White American and African American students.

My school fostered an appreciation for diversity through activities that centered on the sharing of traditional foods and participating in cultural festivals. I vividly remember the excitement and pride of being able to wear traditional African clothing on these special days and standing next to my classmates dressed in the traditional clothing of their homelands while we smiled for pictures. It was also at this time that I first gained an understanding of the impact of slavery and why African Americans were able to identify only with their continent of origin. We could not identify with a specific country like many of my classmates did when talking about their ancestral roots.

Through sharing and educating others on the parts of my ancestral history that I did know, I discovered an early desire to teach. Participating in these events as a young student also set the groundwork for my interest in discovering ways to make connections with diverse groups of people and my desire to learn more about other cultures in addition to my own. Throughout my K–12 educational training and college experiences, I purposefully sought out and engaged in multiculturally diverse exchanges in an effort to learn more about my own and others' cultures. In particular, I developed an interest in sharing my passion for multicultural diversity with young people. My early educational experiences helped me to understand the benefit of having multiple perspectives and voices in the room. It is essential for one's personal development as a citizen of the world.

This path flowed smoothly into a career as an elementary school teacher in a diverse community while possessing a strong interest in multiculturally responsive teaching. Later, I became a school counselor with a budding interest in multicultural counseling. When considering doctoral studies, I chose counseling psychology particularly because of the field's emerging leadership in multicultural counseling competency training. From my earliest educational experiences to my graduate studies, my interest in multicultural diversity continued to blossom. I had great hope that my doctoral studies would help to nurture and cultivate this growth and development both personally and professionally.

Upon entering the doctoral program, I eagerly anticipated engaging in rich and lively discussions in the required multicultural counseling course. I realized this multicultural diversity educational experience would far surpass the food and festival cultural appreciation activities from my youth. I welcomed the idea of having my values and beliefs challenged in an effort to broaden my worldview.

The class consisted of four students of color and four White students. It appeared to be the perfect class size and demographic composition to facilitate personal dialogues on sensitive issues. The diversity of students in the class was reminiscent of my earliest constructive and affirming educational experiences with my classmates from different parts of the world. This similarity was comforting to me as a new doctoral student about to engage in the hard, and often uncomfortable, work required on the journey to become a multiculturally competent counselor.

My experience in this course served as the most defining moment in my development as a counselor and a human being in this rapidly changing, multiculturally diverse world we occupy. What I remember most from this course is not the rich, engaging conversations with my classmates that helped to promote my development, for these conversations never took place. Instead, what I remember most was the staggeringly powerful silence of my White classmates. The silence seemed to create a fortified wall of resistance that could not be easily penetrated. It had the power to keep me (and the class) from being able to engage in the conversations that I had hoped would be key elements of my doctoral training. I became disillusioned by the experience. I had such an optimistic expectation of the process that the lack of participation led me to feel disappointed and confused.

The course instructor, a supportive, empathetic individual who was highly sensitive to the needs of all the students in the class, recognized the tense dynamic in the classroom. He was cognizant of the needs of the students of color who desired to share and process their experiences. He was equally mindful of the needs of White students who were apprehensive about discussing taboo issues of race. He familiarized us with the topics of racial identity development, White privilege, and unintentional racism. Through the use of technology (e.g., webcams and teleconferencing), he introduced us to leading scholars in the field of multicultural diversity and offered us opportunities to share our thoughts, concerns, questions, and ideas on our training with them. Most importantly, the instructor provided an intimate opportunity to discuss and process our thoughts through the use of journals. He connected with each of us through our journals by sharing rich, encouraging feedback. Leading by example, as a White American male, he appropriately self-disclosed when he first became aware of the disparities that exist based on race and ethnicity in this country. He shared stories of his continuous journey to become a multiculturally competent counselor. However, he did not force any student to break his or her silence and fully engage. He openly addressed the issue of silence in the classroom and expressed his philosophy that resistance is created by pushing against an opposite force. He explained that instead of using himself or the class as an instrument of resistance, he would instead work hard to build an open, safe environment where students would be equally respected for where they were on their journey to becoming more multiculturally competent.

Eventually, the silence began to decrease. Whenever the silence still remained, it was better understood as an expression of fear or uncertainty. I learned that the journey to becoming a multiculturally competent counselor is an imperfect experience. It is a bumpy road. Each step of the journey is different for everyone. What is most important is that everyone is on the journey and stepping forward at his or her own pace.

After experiencing my colleagues' silence in that multicultural counseling course and witnessing the efforts of my instructor, I knew my identity as a counselor would need to include that of a vocal advocate for multicultural diversity competency and training. As an advocate, I embrace the significance of attending to the silence in a way that fosters empathy and helps to encourage all students to not fear the bumps in the road to multiculturalism. Today, it is this identity that shapes my entire career and directly influences my teaching philosophy, research agenda, service activities, and counseling practice. Now, *I* am the voice that works to sensitively interrupt the silence and help students understand why that silence sometimes occurs.

FAITH IN CRISIS: AWAKENING TO SOCIAL JUSTICE THROUGH RELIGIOUS CONFLICT
Chad V. Johnson

I can say without exaggeration that becoming a counseling psychologist has been the greatest transformative experience of my life. I entered graduate school representing almost every group with privileged status. I was White, male, from a middle-class background, Evangelical Christian, heterosexual, politically conservative, young, and nondisabled. I believed that individual merit and effort resulted in personal and professional achievement and progress. I most certainly believed there were universal principles and objective criteria for living virtuously, defining the good life, and understanding human interaction, growth, and healing. While I believed cultural issues should be understood and considered, I mostly viewed these through a traditional and nomothetic lens; that is, culture could be equated with different tastes and preferences such as food, clothing, and music, but generally people possessed mostly similar psychological and spiritual needs.

I entered graduate school with trepidation, as the program I was entering was renowned for its commitment to multicultural training. I thought I might be criticized and discriminated against for my group statuses and viewpoints—especially my religious and political ones. What I was unaware of was how much my privilege, power, and assumptions of the world were deeply unconscious and desperately protected. My first semester was a telling one. While attending a departmental softball game before beginning my first semester, I remember feeling highly anxious when meeting an African American student. Though I grew up in Houston and San Antonio and was comfortable relating with people of color there, I felt she would see me as an imposter—as a White person who "didn't get it." Of course, we just exchanged pleasantries and went about the game, but my fear was palpable. In my first-semester research methods class, the instructor asked who believed there were objective truths to be discovered. I remember being the only one who raised my hand. Everyone else apparently held relativistic or pluralistic perspectives on the world—something I found quite at odds with my Christian worldview. Finally, I remember a discussion with a fellow student about Evangelical Christian beliefs and psychotherapy. She wondered how I could keep from evangelizing in sessions when I believed Jesus was the only way to salvation. Was it ethical for me *not* to try and convert clients? Was it ethical for me to do so? I remember not having an answer but recognizing the disturbing logic in her questions. I felt I was straddling two worlds—that of secular psychology and that of my faith. Indeed, I felt my spiritual center was a safely guarded secret from the faculty and students. I felt I was hiding a major part of who I was from those around me, and it was taking its toll emotionally and psychologically.

Several factors contributed to awakening my sociopolitical consciousness and recognizing my own cultural identity. First, the faculty and course work in my program were committed to understanding counseling from critical multicultural and social justice perspectives. The curriculum integrated these components throughout, but I was most deeply affected by the course on multicultural counseling and theory that emphasized deconstructing my beliefs about the world and myself. It was here in a process-oriented context that I exposed my fears of being seen as, for example, racist, heterosexist, and Christian, and confronted through theory and praxis my deeply held and profoundly contextualized beliefs about others, the world, and myself. It also helped that my fellow graduate students, faculty, and the counseling center staff where we did most of our counseling training were diverse in terms of race, gender, religious faith, and sexual orientation. I developed personal relationships with a diverse group of people that were based on mutual respect and trust. These relationships profoundly challenged my worldview (e.g., that gay and lesbian individuals were depraved, unhappy, and in need of Christian salvation).

Second, through self-reflection, personal counseling, and relationships with my peers, I discovered that I was most conflicted by my heterosexism. The area of sexual orientation was one that created great conflict for me, particularly in the religious arena. I was finding it increasingly difficult to reconcile my counseling experience with people from various sexual orientations, the compassion I felt for these clients, the respect and admiration I felt for faculty and fellow students who were gay and lesbian, and the religious doctrine of my faith. This doctrine, I believed, taught that homosexuality was a sin—a transgression against God's universal laws.

I decided to take a risk and disclose my conflict concerning sexual orientation in my multicultural theories course. I explained that this was a difficult area for me but that my faith taught that homosexuality was wrong and harmful. I expressed my conflict as to how to honor my faith and another person's sexual orientation as a counselor. My worst fears—that I would be attacked, ridiculed, and disliked—were realized. My peers reacted strongly. I felt assailed, misunderstood, angry, ashamed, and distressed. Had I damaged my relationships with my peers? Would I be dismissed from the program or forced to do remediation? Would my views be respected as I thought multicultural theory promoted?

The conflict continued with several of my peers following the class. I had a shouting match with one student about my apparent lack of compassion and my views regarding God's unwavering, objective truth. I hotly debated the scripture and religious perspectives regarding sexual orientation with another. I heard and felt the disdain and disapproval of still others. Upon reflection, I cannot blame my peers for their reactions or the passion with which they felt them. I feel a similar passion regarding this issue today. Unfortunately, these initial reactions were not helpful in providing me space to explore my conflict and be where I was. I felt polarized and misunderstood. I felt I had to defend my deeply held religious beliefs and, more importantly, my relationship with God. I felt very little room to hold the multiple, conflicting thoughts and feelings I was having.

This was not an intellectual exercise. My religious faith was my strongest and most cherished identity. I felt like I was coming apart, and indeed, I was. It was a painful but transformative process of reconstruction and reconciliation through my graduate training (and beyond) that allowed me to come to terms with my privilege and eventually become an advocate for social justice, particularly in the realm of equal rights for lesbian, gay, bisexual, transgender, and queer (LGBTQ) individuals.

Fortunately, I had recently begun therapy at the time as an adjunct to my counseling training. My therapist created a space for me to hold all these feelings and thoughts and to eventually realize that I was not betraying God, as I most feared, but was actually expressing my faith deeply and genuinely. Furthermore, my peers stayed with me. Though they reacted initially with confusion and anger, they eventually softened to accept me where I was and began to listen to my heart and my anguish. To the surprise of some, I began to read literature contesting the conservative view of homosexuality in scripture and literature describing the history of religious and societal oppression for sexual minorities. I also began to trust my heart and compassion over my cold rationality. My experiences and my intellectual studies began to create a murky gray where there was once black and white. My views shifted; indeed, my entire worldview transformed through my attempts to resolve this issue. I began to doubt the conservative theology and positivistic framework I had been taught; I began privileging compassion, relationship, pluralism, and humanizing action over scripture, tradition, and objectivist/positivistic views of the world. This did not happen overnight but over the following 3 years of therapy, graduate study, and internship.

Shortly after my confession in class and the ensuing conflict, anguish, and reconciliation of my spiritual identity with an understanding of sociopolitical realities for sexual minorities and other oppressed groups, I sought out and contacted a previous spiritual mentor of mine. I considered him one of my dearest and most trusted friends, but we had lost touch. When I finally made contact, I discovered that he had come out as gay, which resulted in divorcing his wife and being excommunicated from our shared faith community and friends. My heart was ripped open. I felt deep compassion and acceptance for him, something I may not have been able to do a few months earlier. I felt deeply grieved and angered by how he was treated by our faith community and friends, many of whom he had mentored and loved. I was able to provide support for him and a connection with our shared past that until our reconnection he had thought was totally lost to him. It was a deeply touching moment and reunion to say the least.

I now work as an advocate for LGBTQ rights locally and nationally. This work includes activities such as participatory action research, facilitating support groups for LGBTQ individuals with religious conflicts, and serving on the board of directors for a statewide LGBTQ advocacy group. Social justice is no longer just a concept in a textbook; it is woven into the very fabric of my being.

OF RELIGION AND RELIGIOUS IDENTITY
Amina Mahmood

I began graduate study in counseling psychology a year after 9/11. Why is this an important marker? I am a visible South Asian–American Muslim female. Visible, as I currently choose to cover my hair with a traditional Muslim headscarf known as the *hijab* as a symbol of the faith I follow. After 9/11, American Muslims and Muslims in general were constantly in the spotlight and viewed unfavorably. The larger societal context definitely impacted my personal and professional interactions. For me, as a visible South Asian–American Muslim woman, this meant constant awareness of my ethnic and religious background when working with my clients as well as my clinical supervisors.

During my practicum and internship experiences, several of my clinical supervisors made it a point to have a conversation regarding my choice of dress (i.e., the headscarf) and how it might impact my clinical work (e.g., would it make my clients uncomfortable?). Additionally, I recall two supervisors initiating a discussion about whether I would be comfortable working with certain clinical issues (e.g., coming out issues) or client populations (such as veterans) due to religious beliefs or values as well as the current sociopolitical climate. Although I was taken aback by these comments, I was able to remind myself that my clinical supervisors were merely exercising their multicultural sensitivity by recognizing me as a unique individual with different cultural and religious beliefs and values than theirs.

Members of the lesbian, gay, bisexual, and transgender (LGBT) community considered one of my practicum placements (a women's center) to be a safe site; therefore, we served many individuals from this population. It's interesting how in a society such as ours that proclaims to be open-minded, religion continues to be a topic that is avoided or, if approached in discussion, is approached with caution. I was somewhat amused at how delicately my supervisor approached the issue of religion and the possibility that my religious identity might prevent me from working with members of this population and the issues they bring to therapy. My supervisor's approach contrasts with that of my clients at a homeless shelter as well as children with whom I have worked at other placements who have bluntly inquired about my religious identity. These direct inquiries seemed to be a result of a genuine curiosity and a simple awareness that I am different from others in the way that I dress. Additionally, clients whom I have seen in federally qualified health-care clinics have merely inquired about my religious identity out of curiosity. I find this attitude of my clients very refreshing. I have noticed though that adult clients from higher social-class statuses and those with higher educational degrees—like my supervisors—tend to dance around the issue of my religious identification rather than directly asking the question.

The issue of being Muslim has hardly ever served as a barrier to service provision. In fact, I think clients' curious inquiries about my religious identity and my responses have helped to further build a relationship or alliance with my clients. My clients have been more interested in having someone to listen to their concerns and assist them in resolving their issues. My religious identity for the most part did not appear to deter them.

There was, however, one instance that served as a defining moment in my clinical career. Once during my clinical training a client refused to accept services from me due to my religious identity. This occurred when I was scheduled to conduct a neuropsychological assessment for a client who identified herself as an Orthodox Jew. Protocol at this clinic permitted clients to decide whether the practicum student could participate in the clinical interview. This particular client walked in, took one look at me, and appeared to know I was Muslim. Although the client had not said anything to me at this point, her mannerism toward me indicated to me that she did not want me there. My introduction by the neuropsychologist most likely confirmed this for her, as my name is a very common Muslim name. The client's demeanor toward me was icy cold, something I had never experienced in my clinical work. She immediately requested to have the neuropsychologist conduct the interview privately. I respectfully left the room to afford her privacy but had a gut feeling that had already been somewhat confirmed by the client's behavior that she would probably not want me to conduct the assessment.

My somewhat flustered supervisor confirmed this suspicion approximately 30 minutes later when she came to the office to inform me of the client's reluctance to have me complete the assessment. The psychometrist on staff was not available at that moment. My supervisor thought that assessing this client, due to her cultural and religious background, would be a unique experience for me. I was uncertain whether my supervisor chose to ignore or was unaware of the tension that tends to exist among some individuals of the two religious groups (i.e., Jews and Muslims), primarily due to the Israel–Palestine conflict. Perhaps my supervisor chose to ignore the fact that the client, an Orthodox Jew, was refusing to accept services due to my religious identification. I remember being very calm in the situation and explaining to my supervisor the larger sociopolitical context as well as cultural beliefs and values that likely influenced this particular client's decision to refuse my services.

I was quite shaken up by this experience, yet it helped me reflect upon my own cultural and religious beliefs and values. For example, I choose to seek medical treatment from female providers, and whether this choice is discriminating against male providers is not a question or issue that I had considered. This client's decision initially surprised me, because I am not from the Middle East and I have many friends who are Jewish. Nevertheless, my religious identity influenced this client's comfort level. She would not have benefited from my involvement in her case.

My supervisors wanted to make sure I was not offended by this client's response toward me. As we processed this case, I recall taking on the role of educating my supervisors about the client's cultural context and how this likely played a role in her attitude toward me. I realize that to some her behavior toward me may indicate prejudice, but I think it runs deeper than that. There are some beliefs and values so deeply inculcated in us, whether right or wrong, that we have to choose carefully about when to challenge them. This client chose not to.

Overall, as a visible South Asian–American Muslim female, I have been pleasantly surprised at how accepting my clients have been of me, despite concerns expressed by supervisors that I should be prepared to address client questions or reservations based on my ethnic or religious identity. At times I have thought about how I would be perceived by clients due to my ethnic or religious identity, but my clinical experience has indicated that other factors are more important in developing a therapeutic alliance. My clients have appreciated my openness about addressing religion and spirituality in therapy. A few have heaved sighs of relief when I have inquired about their religious or spiritual affiliation and stated that they were unsure whether I would understand how important religion and spirituality are to them. In my work with these clients, we actively incorporate religion and spirituality into treatment. We discuss their religious or spiritual tradition's perspective on coping with the struggles they are experiencing. These clients appreciate my recognition of their religious and spiritual beliefs, despite the fact that my own religious and spiritual beliefs are different from the ones they follow.

It is through clinical work that I continue to grow toward becoming a culturally competent professional. I attempt to recognize and respect various cultural beliefs, values, and contexts that are important to my clients regardless of how different they might be from my own. My clinical work has also prompted me to implement changes in my personal life to become a more socially conscious individual. For instance, I work to educate others and myself about opportunities to help eradicate poverty, and I support agencies that provide health and social services to underserved populations. In the end, my efforts have also helped me to become a better American Muslim.

KALEIDOSCOPIC CULTURAL IMAGES OF SELF AS A COUNSELOR
Michael Mobley

As a master's student in a counseling psychology program in 1990–1992, I experienced several critical turning points related to multiculturalism and diversity that significantly influenced my development as a counselor. Being enrolled in Dr. Portia Hunt's Race, Gender, and Class in Psychotherapy course at Temple

University offered me stimulating engagement of how culture influences the counseling process as well as my own personal and professional development. One defining moment in this course was reading William E. Cross's (1991) *Shades of Black: Diversity in African American Identity* and being exposed to several racial/ethnic and minority identity development models (i.e., Atkinson, Morten, & Sue, 1989; Helms, 1990; Sue, 1981). In this material in the course, I felt that the sociocultural and political contextual variables influencing one's racial identity awareness, attitudes, knowledge, feelings, and behaviors captured a large part of my self-concept. I'll never forget reading about the emersion/immersion stage, which is associated with an intense anger and disregard for Whites along with a distinctive desire to associate only with other Blacks. As a 25-year-old African American male, I was deeply troubled by the characterization of this stage. It did not seem to represent my experience. I had not experienced any intense anger toward Whites, nor did I limit my personal and social interactions only to Blacks. I began to question the essence of my racial identity. Was I truly Black? What were my feelings toward Whites?

In an effort to resolve my confusion, I reflected upon critical messages and values based on experiences within my family and sociocultural background. I realized that indeed I was "Black." Although race was not openly discussed within my immediate family during my upbringing, I had engaged in conversations about race with Black peers during middle and high school as well as during an Upward Bound Program, a summer educational and cultural enrichment program held at Swarthmore College. I understood the history of slavery and Jim Crow laws in the United States, the effect of past and present racism in America, and the social inequalities experienced by Blacks across institutional arenas including politics, economics, employment, education, the legal system, and housing. Equally, I understood that my mother had close friendships with Whites. I had never heard her make disparaging comments about Whites despite historical discrimination, killings, and assassinations of Black people in the United States.

Like my mother, I, too, had formed close personal interactions and relationships with Whites during my schooling and collegiate education. In essence, I recognized the validity of Cross's (1991) notion in *Shades of Black*, that diversity exists within and among Black people. Thus, my racial identity development process did not need to conform strictly to any espoused models, that is, progression via each status. My sense of racial identity and self-concept represented the uniqueness of my own family and sociocultural experiences, both of which I could feel proud. A central part of my racial identity and my relationships with Whites at this time in my life was my committed relationship with a White male.

At this time, I began to reflect upon other sociocultural influences affecting my overall self-identity: that is, being male, being gay, being from a low-income family, and being from an economically depressed community. In attempting to understand the intersectionality among race, socioeconomic status, gender, and sexual orientation based on racial identity literature, African-centered psychological perspectives, as well as cultural messages from my family and African American community, I asked myself several questions: Does my romantic relationship with a White male reflect a form of internalized hatred or disregard toward Blacks as suggested within identity models or by African-centered psychologists such as Na'im Akbar (1991)? Did my White male partner "really" understand what it means to be "Black" in America? And, finally, how might my expanding racial identity consciousness impact our relationship?

In responding to these questions, I recall experiencing a range of feelings from excitement to disappointment. I was excited that I could talk with my White male partner about racial issues. At times, he appeared to be understanding and accepting. Yet I also was disappointed by his limited engagement during such conversations, which raised the question about the depth of his understanding or genuine interest. During this period in my life and our relationship, the characterization of the "gay [read: gay White] community" as being biased, prejudiced, discriminatory, and racist toward Blacks surfaced for me. Although it was challenging to integrate this new cultural knowledge, consciousness, and perspective, within both my personal and professional development, my cultural worldview was being transformed.

Being in Dr. Hunt's class was a defining moment in my emerging consciousness about gender, race, and class in psychotherapy. Indeed, this class forged my interests in multicultural counseling and training. I continued with this focus as I began doctoral training in counseling psychology in 1992 at Penn State University. I believed it was important to increase my self-awareness, understanding, and sensitivities about my own intersecting cultural identities as well as others'. I recognized that being exposed to new knowledge about racial identity development models as well as gender and sexual orientation identity models influenced not only my personal self-identity but also my professional identity. I decided to focus on multicultural counseling competencies and training as a specialization concentration area during doctoral training at Penn State.

In the initial doctoral practicum, I worked with two clients who facilitated both my personal and professional self-understanding and growth relative to my intersecting cultural identities and the therapeutic process. The names and other identifying information have been changed in the following accounts. The first client, an 18-year-old White female named Traci, presented with deep sadness about the ending of a romantic relationship with her boyfriend. As a developing multicultural counselor, I cognitively and conceptually understood the importance of gender and relational issues based on readings, especially Gilligan's (1982) work. I recognized that Traci's White racial identity was not critically salient to her presenting issue given that her ex-boyfriend was also White. Yet I understood that her White racial identity may have been salient, if even at an unconscious level, in regards to the formation of *our* therapeutic relationship because I was an African American male therapist.

While I demonstrated a genuine concern about Traci's loss and sadness during the counseling process, my White female supervisor helped me to understand that I was unaware of the significance of a young woman's "first love" and what it meant to have such a relationship end. From this experience, I discovered that my male gender identity limited my understanding of the depths of Traci's reaction. In addition, further self-reflection suggested that my sexual orientation identity, and my consequently delayed dating and romantic relationship history as a gay male, also restricted my capacity to understand the devastation of this loss for this

White, heterosexual, female client. To aid in understanding Traci, I imagined my own sense of hurt, sadness, pain, and loss when my relationship with a White male ended during high school. I recalled beginning my freshman year of college with a feeling of emptiness. I longed to be connected with my former boyfriend. Through self-awareness and self-knowledge I was able to better understand my client's experience. Then, I could foster deeper empathy with my client.

The second practicum client was a 22-year-old White gay male, Andrew. From him, I learned how intersecting cultural identities influence my personal life and professional role as a developing multicultural counselor. I had met and interacted socially with Andrew during our undergraduate college years. We had attended similar gay social, cultural, and political activities on campus. After my first counseling session with Andrew, I immediately had flashbacks of seeing him at a gay, lesbian, and bisexual dance off campus during my undergraduate experience and thinking to myself, "He is really attractive." Yet we never had any direct one-on-one conversations during our undergraduate days. Thus, my supervisor and I concluded it was fine for me to proceed with the therapeutic relationship.

Andrew's presenting issues included significant emotional distress and relationship concerns. After several weeks of counseling, Andrew acknowledged being attracted to men of color. Andrew also carefully articulated personal qualities and characteristics of the type of man with whom he desired a relationship. In that moment I recall feeling quite uncomfortable with Andrew's description. I was keenly aware of my own present feelings of attraction toward Andrew throughout the therapeutic process. I was working hard to appropriately deal with my internal feelings and thoughts. However, this critical exchange between Andrew and me during the counseling session immediately led me to show this portion of videotape to my supervisor. She smiled and commented, "I was waiting for us to discuss this issue. It has been obvious to me for some time now." I responded in a somewhat joking manner, "I wish you would have warned me."

My supervisor and I discussed how I would proceed in therapy. We reviewed several options always with the focus being on what would be of most benefit to Andrew. The work with Andrew proceeded by affirming his interests in men of color and processing dynamics within our therapeutic relationship. From this work, I learned how sociocultural identities of race, gender, sexual orientation, sexuality, and professional role as a developing multicultural counselor could significantly influence the work. It helped me to recognize the power of the unknown cultural dynamics and issues that may inevitably surface during the counseling process.

From that first course and many other experiences, I have discovered the intersections of cultural identities and how they influence the role of a professional multicultural counselor. Multicultural counseling theory (Sue, Ivey, & Pedersen, 1996) posits that the tenet of "self-in-relationship-to-others" within a sociocultural environmental context is highly important to comprehend and integrate into one's practice to develop multicultural competence. These experiences have helped me to recognize how "multiple cultural identity selves" in relationship to others not only influences the counseling process but also expands a person's cultural worldview. The capacity to grasp how and when intersectionalities of cultural identities become salient strengthens the counselor's ability to help the client. And that, after all, is the whole point of this work. Thank you, Dr. Portia Hunt, for your course.

REFERENCES

Akbar, N. (1991). Mental disorder among African Americans. In R.L. Jones (Ed.), *Black psychology* (pp. 339–352). Berkeley, CA: Cobb & Henry.

Atkinson, D.R., Morten, G., & Sue, D.W. (1989). A minority identity development model. In D.R. Atkinson, G. Morten, & D.W. Sue (Eds.), *Counseling American minorities* (pp. 35–52). Dubuque, IA: William C. Brown.

Cross, W.E., Jr. (1991). *Shades of Black: Diversity in African-American identity*. Philadelphia: Temple University.

Gilligan, C. (1982). *In a different voice: Psychological theory and women's development*. Cambridge, MA: Harvard University Press.

Helms, J.E. (1990). *Black and white racial identity: Theory, research, and practice*. Westport, CT: Greenwood.

Sue, D.W. (1981). *Counseling the culturally different: Theory and practice*. New York: Wiley.

Sue, D.W., Ivey, A.E., & Pedersen, P.B. (1996). *Theory of multicultural counseling and therapy*. Thousand Oaks, CA: Sage.

LUMBER RIVER IMMERSION
Mark B. Scholl

During the summer of 1987, I became more aware of my Native American identity through my involvement in an historical drama called *Strike at the Wind*. The drama was affiliated with the University of North Carolina at Pembroke (UNCP), which was originally founded as Croatan Normal School. The amphitheater where we performed was bordered by the scenic Lumber River. I gained feelings of ethnic pride from the drama's true story of Native American strength and resilience. The musical outdoor drama tells the story of the Lumbee community's 7-year fight for civil rights during the Civil War and early Reconstruction Era. At the beginning of the play, Henry Berry Lowry is confronted with the murder of his father and brother by the Confederate Home Guard. Lowry is portrayed as a Robin Hood type of outlaw who protects and provides for the impoverished Lumbee. He prevails as a result of resources including intelligence, skill as a marksman, and physical courage. By the end of the play, Lowry and his compatriots celebrate Sherman's victory in Atlanta and their successful fight for the right to own land. Today, Henry Berry Lowry is revered as a heroic figure in the fight for the civil rights of Native Americans. While performing in this production, I was also working as a counselor intern in a nearby mental health center and I now realize how my participation in the drama contributed to my counselor identity development.

Growing up, I was largely unaware of my Native American heritage. This heritage comes from my mother's side of the family, but it was something that was rarely acknowledged by my family. I had been raised by my parents in a mid-sized town that was far removed from Native American life. Through my participation in the play, I gained an appreciation for the struggles of the Lumbee and also for their optimism and resourcefulness.

There was an interesting parallel between Hector, the character I portrayed, and my role as a counselor intern. Hector was a highly visible participant in the activities of the Lumbee community. Similar to a skilled counselor, he spent a good deal of the play listening to members of the Lowry family discuss their personal concerns and problems. His high level of involvement in the lives of the Lumbee effectively communicated that he was caring, loyal, and trustworthy. Like the character Hector, I was a highly visible participant in the activities of the Lumbee community. My role in the play was a major character part, and I performed in 48 shows. I also accepted invitations to attend picnics and parties hosted by Lumbee families. As a result, I believe that my clients viewed me as more accessible and trustworthy. Portraying Hector helped me to realize that by becoming involved in the cultures of my clients I am effectively communicating my accessibility and cultural responsiveness.

Because the drama was about a diverse community, the actors included African, European, and Native Americans, and they also ranged in age from young children to older adults. I soon felt a strong sense of community and that I was a welcome member. I came to understand that the Lumbee participants enjoyed being a part of the outdoor drama and that it was a natural extension of their fondness for artistic self-expression. Through the drama we were called upon to act, sing, dance, play musical instruments, and tell jokes. Collectively we were using all of these talents to tell the true story of how the Lumbee people used their strengths to gain their rights as American citizens. A new world was opened up for me.

During the mid-1980s, several major events contributed to a climate of mistrust and hostility among African, European, and Native Americans in the Pembroke community. In 1984 and 1985, after a 26-year absence, the Ku Klux Klan held two rallies in Robeson County. In 1986, a European American deputy was charged with the murder of a Lumbee citizen. And in 1987, modern-day Lumbee activist Eddie Hatcher was collecting evidence of corruption in local law enforcement and was calling for investigations by state authorities. In stark contrast to the town community, the drama's community of artists, technicians, and directors demonstrated how diverse people could coexist harmoniously.

Several times during my internship, I realized that as an intern I was performing similar acts (e.g., supporting someone who felt isolated and depressed) to those performed by my *Strike at the Wind* stage character, Hector. One of my clients was an 18-year-old African American male named Patrick (pseudonym), who had recently attempted suicide. I was successful in helping this client work through his feelings of isolation, depression, and shame. I believe that in working with Patrick I was effective; I still reflect upon the experience to recall how I can be a potent change agent with my current clients.

An important component of my work with Patrick was the quality of the relationship that we established. I have come to appreciate the fact that Native Americans rely on nonverbal communication a good deal. During my counselor training, and subsequently, I have recognized that I value the power of nonverbal listening in establishing a good therapeutic relationship. My penchant for nonverbal listening frustrated some of my internship supervisors, who urged me to interject more with verbal reflections of feeling and content. However, I have come to appreciate how my Native American heritage has probably contributed to my predilection for interrupting less. I also believe that my cultural heritage explains my relatively high degree of comfort with therapeutic silence or wait time.

In my work with Patrick, I was nonjudgmental and communicated that I trusted him and believed his account of the events that contributed to his decision to attempt suicide. I wanted him to feel comfortable confiding in me without feeling a need for censure, and I also wanted him to feel that I respected him as a person. Further, I wanted him to understand that I felt a stronger sense of loyalty and responsibility in fostering *his* well-being than I did to the authority figures in his life. On a couple of occasions I argued with parties who had questioned Patrick's honesty in recounting the events leading up to his suicide attempt. In this way, I demonstrated my loyalty through my actions, and I observed an interesting parallel between my counselor role and my stage character's loyalty to the Lumbee citizens. I believe that my actions fostered my client's ability to trust me and feel comfortable in our work together and led to a deeper level of client self-disclosure.

Patrick soon revealed to me that he had an artistic side, and I intuitively encouraged him to share this side of himself in our counseling sessions. One of his definite strengths was his sense of humor, and I encouraged him to use humor as a source for promoting his resilience. For example, I asked him to draw a picture of himself and his parents. He drew his parents as vampires controlling him as if he were a marionette. The picture was amusing in the way it poked fun at his parents, but it also clearly communicated the anger he felt toward them. We shared a hearty laugh at the expense of his parents, which I believe strengthened our relationship. Through the use of expressive drawing and humor he was able to express the anger he had been holding back and turning inward. Working through his feelings of anger and expressing his feelings verbally became an important focus of our work together. In addition to the use of art, he also expressed himself by sharing his poetry and by singing original rap lyrics. Throughout our work together, I affirmed his artistic talents. I encouraged him to express himself artistically and verbally, and he became progressively more and more self-confident and optimistic in his outlook.

I credit my self-understanding regarding my preferences as a counselor to my early immersion experience at Lumber River with the Lumbee Tribe. Upon reflection, the characteristics of my counseling style that contributed to my success with Patrick were a reflection of my Native American background and values. These characteristics include my preference for approaches that are relatively nonconfrontational, that emphasize nonverbal listening and the quality of the relationship, that embrace diversity, and that incorporate the expressive arts. Portraying Hector taught me that when I am establishing a good relationship it is important to communicate my trustworthiness and loyalty to clients through both my words and my actions. My primary approach to counseling entails using strength-based approaches to help clients enhance their resilience.

I recently moved to New York City from a small North Carolina town of approximately 15,000 people. The culture shock was nearly overwhelming, but I adapted by participating in stand-up comedy workshops and performing in clubs. By writing material and performing on stage, I was able to foster my inner resilience and soon felt more comfortable living in our nation's largest city. Recently, while teaching a master's-level class on counseling skill development, within the context of a role-play, I modeled effective listening for a group of students. At the end of the role-play, a student grumbled, "But you were *just* listening." I surprised myself when I proudly replied, "*Just* listening? I am a listening artist!"

I HAVE NEVER TOLD ANYONE THIS BEFORE
Ryan J. Quirk

During my first years of graduate school, I did service work in Belize during summer vacations and spring breaks. Belize, formerly known as British Honduras, is a country in Central America that is comparable to the size of Massachusetts. Gaining its independence from Britain in 1981, Belize is a popular tourist destination known for its rain forests, coral reefs, and Mayan ruins. It is a beautiful country, but my interest in traveling there was to work at the Belize Central Prison.

Located in Hattieville, Belize Central Prison is the only prison in the country. During my first visit, I learned that it was considered one of the most poorly operated prisons in the world. Conditions were deplorable: There was no sewer system and no potable water, and there were approximately 300 beds for 900 prisoners. When I returned 2 years later, the situation had dramatically improved due to John Woods and the Kolbe Foundation, a nonprofit organization, which had received permission from the Belizean government to manage the prison. The focus of incarceration had shifted from punishment to rehabilitation. I was very fortunate to have had John Woods and the Kolbe Foundation facilitate and support my interest in conducting research and doing counseling with the inmates.

While volunteering in Belize's Central Prison I have been able to gain experience conducting research and counseling with individuals of a different culture. Due to a history that includes colonization, slavery, and immigration, Belize contains a diversity of ethnic groups. These groups include Maya, Garifuna, Creole (or Kriol), Mestizo, and Chinese. My research project, exploring predictors of inmate violence, allowed me the opportunity to come in contact with the entire inmate population. I was impressed by the inmates' willingness to speak with me and help with the research, even though I was a complete stranger. At one time there was a rumor that spread among the inmates that I was actually an operative of the Central Intelligence Agency (CIA). Apparently some inmates believed that my questionnaires were intended to identify an individual or individuals for extridition back to the United States. I noticed that there were a few inmates who eyed me with more suspicion than usual, but fortunately most were willing to still participate. In the end, I accepted the CIA rumor and its effect as a learning experience. It was one of those unforseen impediments to research conducted in a different culture.

One inmate, whom I had met while recruiting research subjects, asked if we could meet to talk on a daily basis. The inmate's name was Barrington (pseudonym). His ethnicity was Creole; he was of average height and possessed an intimidatingly large physique. However, his most defining feature was the long scar on his face that ran from the top of his head, through his right eye, down to his cheek. The right eye was blind, milky white, and surrounded by red, exposed skin. I would learn later that this scar and disfiguration on the right side of his face was the result of a car accident. Barrington had not been wearing a seat belt when his friend collided into another car. Barrington was immediately ejected from his seat, head first through the windshield. The left side of his face offered a clue as to what his entire face once looked like. Barrington rarely made eye contact and claimed that he had never used a mirror to assess the damage that had been done to his countenance. His build alone was imposing, but I had the thought that Barrington may have been used to people looking away from his face and being afraid of his appearance.

Not knowing what Barrington was eager to talk about, or if I could be of any help, I told him that I was certainly open to the opportunity to listen. We agreed to meet in his cell after his work was completed. His job was feeding and taking care of the chickens that provided the eggs, and sometimes the meat, for meals at the prison. Most jobs at the prison are done by the inmates. I once witnessed four inmates ironically making repairs to the metal bars for a cell.

I visited Barrington nightly in his cell, which was in the medium-security area. The outside of the concrete building was a mess of hanging clothes and wires coming out in every direction. It was as if the wires were desperately searching for electricity to power the inmate's radios, televisions, and hot plates. After walking up the steps, the one guard for the entire building unlocked the door to the entranceway and locked it behind me as I walked through. Unlike in the United States, each individual cell was not locked by guards; only the single entrance to the building was. Each cell had the classic metal bars, but the inmates held the keys to their own cells to keep others out, not themselves in. To see Barrington I traveled past the loud, sweaty common room and down the dark hallways toward his cell. I was unaccompanied and thought to myself that back home nobody knew where I was at that moment. I was there to help, however, and had faith that my good intentions were recognized by all of the inmates.

As I approached Barrington's cell, he would hurry out the two or three roommates who happened to be there. He would then immediately provide me with an overturned bucket to use as a chair. While he sat on his bottom bunk, Barrington often started off by talking about his son. It was easy to discern that Barrington loved his son. Sadly, Barrington had not seen his son in over 2 years. It became clear that Barrington believed his appearance would scare the little boy. I had initially thought that Barrington's appearance was going to be his most pressing issue during our meetings, but I was mistaken. By actively listening and asking difficult questions, I learned that Barrington had other concerns. Even though he had worked for most of the day, Barrington said that he had trouble falling and staying asleep. He explained that when the environment around him was quiet, his head was filled with thoughts. I delicately attempted to gain a better understanding of what he was experiencing. After meeting with Barrington four times, he prefaced what he was about to say with the phrase, "I have never told anyone this before." That sentence indicated to me that what I was about to hear was sacrosanct. What was once a deeply buried secret would now be shared between two people, hopefully providing the freedom and relief that is often associated with such disclosure.

Barrington confided in me that as a child his stepfather had sexually abused him. Thoughts about the incidents and feelings of shame were frequently disturbing his sleep. Barrington said that he was relieved to have finally told someone about his past. I was grateful to him for choosing to share this painful part of his life story with me. Over the remainder of our meetings, Barrington discussed the incidents and the associated shame in greater detail. It was difficult for him to discuss these events and his feelings, but the bond of trust that we had established facilitated it. As the sessions progressed, he reported that he was having less trouble falling and staying asleep.

When I met with Barrington I noticed how strikingly different my present surroundings were from what I was accustomed to in the United States. More importantly, however, was the recognition of the similarity of the human condition. Despite the unfamiliar environment and differences between Barrington and me, he still needed and benefited from the support, understanding, and compassion I would have provided to a client in the United States. As I listened to Barrington speak, I was struck by how two people from such different backgrounds, from different countries could connect. I believe that this connection, during our interactions, was possible because I had been sensitive to his cultural perspective and identity as a Belizean. In addition, my willingness to support him along with a nonjudgmental attitude, a demonstration of trustworthiness, and listening ability was integral in quickly establishing rapport. The importance of deep, caring listening cannot be overlooked. It allows for the crucial understanding of a potentially different worldview and experience. Barrington taught me that these skills and sensitivity could be successfully carried into any interaction with anyone and in any place.

LEANING INTO DISCOMFORT
Aida Hutz

I taught multicultural counseling for the first time when I was a 25-year-old doctoral student. As I reread my midterm student evaluations, which I had initially tried to ignore, I felt vulnerable and a little panicky; there were many distressing comments I had to face. A central goal of my course has always been to provide students with an opportunity to recognize how their race and culture impacts who they are as well as how they are perceived by others who are socioracially different from them. Throughout the years, I have found that when intense classroom discussions that are personally and emotionally revealing begin to take place, many counselors in training of European American descent admit to having thought very little, if at all, about their own race and culture. And, often it seems they experience some degree of difficulty, reluctance, and umbrage as they begin to uncover what being White means to them.

After wrestling past my initial defensive reaction to those first midterm evaluations, I stepped outside of my apartment, intending to go for a walk, and ended up pacing in the courtyard. As I processed my thoughts and feelings, anxiety began to fill my chest, and two intimidating questions settled on my mind: Is

there something fundamentally wrong with my approach as a counselor educator in training? Should I go down a different path and teach this topic in a less
controversial manner?

I reluctantly realized that it was important to face the feedback to answer
these questions, yet I still wanted to have control over my thoughts and emotions.
Until that point, although I was willing to read my students' comments, I was not
willing to truly consider them. My intention was to protect myself and to fit the
feedback into my preexisting belief structures. Ultimately, however, I took a risk
by entertaining the idea that the negative feedback might be as valuable as the
positive.

I carefully considered the comments that were the hardest to digest, such as,
"The instructor is angry," and, "She is imposing her agenda on students." Eventually,
I realized that my primary intention as an instructor was focused on stirring up
White, European American students to feel uncomfortable rather than facilitating
awareness and growth, all the while acknowledging and accepting that discomfort
was likely to arise along the way. Furthermore, I became aware of an entrenched
belief that White people willingly caused pain to people from other racial and
ethnic groups, and thus I felt that my anger and desire to make White students
uncomfortable were justified. As I began to shed light on these previously hidden beliefs, I felt shame. Also, I realized that, like my students, I was also going
through a process of racial and culture identity development.

I immigrated to the United States when I was 16 years old and was quickly
encouraged to assimilate by my mother, who is also an immigrant, and by European
American peers in high school. I felt ashamed of aspects of my cultural background,
especially my accent. During college, I had experiences that brought race and culture to my awareness, but I was motivated to push them away so that I could see
myself as "normal" and like "everyone" else. However, during my master's program
in community counseling, I began to question messages I had internalized about
race and culture, and, when I started my doctoral program, I held a great deal of
resentment toward "White America." Those feelings surfaced through strong ethnic identification and rejection of all that I perceived to be acceptable and valued
by White culture. Throughout the years, issues of race and culture have remained
salient in my life both personally and professionally; however, with continued
exploration, anger and resentment no longer drive my racial and cultural paradigm. Moreover, I have come to make fewer assumptions and have more realistic
discernment in my commitment to social change.

Surprisingly, as I reflected on my students' comments and faced aspects of
myself that I had previously resisted, they became less threatening. Instead of
being weighed down by negative feedback, I felt both calmer and clearer about my
role as an instructor committed to multicultural advocacy. By having the courage
to embrace the image that my students reflected to me, both negative and positive,
I experienced the settling of a cornerstone that continues to help guide me to this
day. I realized that I was able to endure the tension and pain that comes with the
process of genuine self-reflection. I also found that I was willing to pursue this
path, one that would likely include uncomfortable emotions, because I saw that it
led to greater understanding and compassion not only for others but for me as well.

Most importantly, however, I found that, if I was willing to let go of my need to define my identity and be in control of my image, I gave myself room to be a more authentic person.

This process was not only enlightening; it was also healing. I felt a greater connection with others who write about their multicultural experiences, most of whom I have never met. Theoretical essays, once merely intellectually stimulating, became alive, and I experienced their message in other human dimensions—the emotional and spiritual. I immediately had renewed energy and a stronger sense of purpose for my work, as a Brazilian, White, female immigrant who was also becoming a counselor educator.

Today, 9 years later, I often tell students that if we want to be able to join our clients on their journeys we must develop a willingness to be uncomfortable and to look at parts of ourselves that are more easily left ignored, denied, or repressed. This is also the foundation of the multicultural counseling course that has shaped who I am as a teacher and, to an extent, as a person. In addition, while I used to look at most White European Americans with harshly judgmental eyes, I now look at them more compassionately. My experience has shown me that many White counselors in training experience not only some guilt and pain as a result of their unearned privilege but also a genuine desire to transcend the oppressor role when challenged with the realities of racism and discrimination.

Although I would like to say that when I receive difficult feedback today I have learned to be immediately open to it, this is simply not always the case. I have learned that our egos are automatically defensive and that they obstruct higher parts of our selves from examining potentially threatening information. Nonetheless, after years of going through this process, I have programmed myself to be aware of these initial reactions and to face the emotional discomfort instead of following my natural tendency to ignore it to return to a more comfortable state. And each time I move into, and through, an area of discomfort, I understand more deeply that I do not need to skip over these areas as if they contain something that is harmful and must be avoided. Nor do I need to figure them out. I simply need to have an openness and willingness to continue moving forward, and a higher level of understanding will happen as a natural, organic byproduct of the process.

HOW WE TELL OUR STORIES: REFLECTIONS ON FIELDWORK IN LIBERIA
Janet Shriberg

Early in March 2006, 3 months into my dissertation fieldwork, I was riding in a Land Rover from Monrovia to Lofa County in Liberia. We were on our way to a workshop, where the teachers with whom I was traveling would train other Liberian teachers in classroom management skills. Three hours had already passed, and the 12 of us, riding in a vehicle that comfortably sat no more than 6, were playing a game of "Who am I?" to pass the time. My companions laughed as I struggled to select a famous person in history for them to identify. Frequently bumping against each other, we continued down the winding, unpaved road. Numerous times, our journey was interrupted by deep puddles that forced us to get out and push the car forward.

As the day wore on, I noticed my travel companions becoming quieter. At first, I figured that we must all be weary from the long, crowded, and bumpy ride. Then one of the older male trainers, RK, touched my arm and pointed out the window at a forest. In a soft voice, he told me about the time that he had spent hiding there during the war. "The bush," he explained, had concealed him for months. He had dared move only at night, fearing that daylight might lead to recognition and death. He described his narrow escape from his village after rebel forces had rounded up most of the residents and taken the lives of his family and friends. After the massacre, RK had walked barefoot for more than 60 days, hoping to cross Liberia's border into Guinea, where he might find refuge. As he spoke of the horrific events he had witnessed—such as rebels murdering his father and tossing his body into the water "like garbage"—I noticed the other teachers nodding. Soon, they were sharing their own stories of surviving war. Their voices overlapped as they recounted experiencing torture, losing their families, and enduring long periods of starvation.

I asked them if they often recalled these tragic events when they traveled. RK told me that the current trip marked the first time that my companions had returned to Lofa. Five to ten years had passed since these teachers had traveled "north," where most of them grew up. They described how, while living in internal displacement camps inside and outside Monrovia during the war, they had found jobs with international organizations working in educational reconstruction programs there. Monrovia, the capital, is located along the Atlantic Ocean and is the most urbanized city in Liberia with the largest population of all 15 Liberian counties. While much of the city structures and roads were destroyed during the war, being the capital, it had many more social and health resources than other counties in the country. By contrast, rural Lofa is the northernmost county in Liberia and, because of its proximity to Guinea and Sierra Leone, was the site of some of the heaviest fighting and widespread destruction during the war. Even though the war had ended, many teachers had remained in Monrovia to earn money, living in rented rooms and crowded shacks. They had depended on their positions with the educational programs to earn enough money to care for immediate and extended family members. For some, this had meant spending long periods separated from loved ones who lived in rural areas far from Monrovia's city center.

During the week prior to this trip, the demands of preparing for our travel had kept us all busy with logistical concerns. As we drove on, I wondered about the teachers' own psychosocial well-being as they pushed forward to "get the work done." For over a decade, I had worked as a counselor and researcher in diverse contexts affected by armed conflict. My professional training had helped me to consider the varied ways people experience and react to traumatic events. However, this long drive reminded me of the important responsibilities that counselors and researchers must meet when reinterpreting another person's story of pain and suffering—as well as the limitations in so doing. In their studies of social suffering and violence, Kleinman and colleagues (Kleinman, Das, & Lock, 1997) argued that the language of pain should not be shrouded in silence and that the language used to describe pain should not be limited by conventional representations.

On the trip to Lofa, I grew as a counselor and a researcher. I realized that working with peoples' stories of pain and trauma requires a degree of flexibility on the part of the counselor that is not always developed in the regular course of professional training. Western models of training often keep counselors tightly bound to predetermined categories in defining and diagnosing trauma. Similarly, these models prompt counselors to rely on certain strategies for coping with their own and others' pain. This ride led to an important shift in my professional development. On this long trip north with the teacher–participants who were informing my research—which occurred outside the conditions of a conventional counselor–client encounter as well as outside the boundaries of a predetermined research protocol—I realized that I needed to reshape my understanding of trauma and coping so that I would not neglect any definition, experience, or representation. Here I recognized that being a counselor (and ethnographic researcher) can involve being present for people in natural and varying spaces. In this case our overcrowded vehicle became a space for teachers to describe their own traumas and share in each other's grief. As I listened to the teachers share their dark memories and haunting fears, I thought about how they had displayed unimaginable courage in the face of horror. Though they were themselves survivors of war, they were working tirelessly and often without pay to help rebuild the country that had almost destroyed them. Observing them over the months that followed, I noticed that little attention was paid to the suffering of these teacher–caregivers as they worked to improve the future of their students.

In writing about this research within the conventions of a doctoral dissertation, I struggled to describe the multiple ways that these teachers coped in their jobs while silently suffering the aftermath of their own experiences of violence. From this experience I enhanced my understanding of my role as counselor and researcher in relation to the people with whom I work. As counselors and researchers, we should never assume that we are capable of truly capturing others' pain (Wilkinson, 2005). However, by expanding our research methods and our notions of spaces for counselor–client interactions to occur, we honor the complexity of others' pain, suffering, and resiliency.

References

Kleinman, A., Das, V., & Lock, M. (1997). *Social suffering*. Berkeley, CA: University of California Press.

Wilkinson, I. (2005). *Suffering: A sociological introduction*. Malden, MA: Polity Press.

RESEARCHING CLIENT SUICIDE: A PERSONAL JOURNEY OF NAVIGATING THE UNKNOWN

Julie A. Jackson

I clearly remember hearing "rumors" about the suicide of another practicum student's client during the first year of my graduate training. Silently, I wondered about the details of the event. What exactly happened? How would the department handle the situation? What were the legal implications? I also recall thinking about the well-being of my colleague. What was this experience like for her so early in her training? Would *I* ever be involved in a similar experience? I just couldn't fathom what she must have been thinking and feeling. I had several unanswered questions. The unknowns related to the work that counselors do felt very lonely and somewhat scary. Exposure to the intensity of the work resulted in questions about my own competence and preparedness to work with suicidal clients and to personally cope with the aftermath of a client suicide.

Although my classmate's situation was acknowledged within the graduate department, I do not recall it ever being discussed in great detail. I understand more fully now the potential reasons why, yet I continue to question whether both the other students and I could have benefited from more fully processing this experience, with specific attention given to how to prepare for and deal with the aftermath of a client's suicide. During my training, both within and outside the classroom, the process of assessing for suicidal ideation and treating suicidal clients was discussed and reinforced on numerous occasions, but few talked about the impact a client suicide might have on a trainee. I recognized that each individual reaction may be unique, but my anxiety fueled my urge for us to talk about this experience more generally. I wanted to know more about what to expect. I wished we had talked about how we, as trainees, should attend to both self-care and professional needs and how we could best use our support systems. I would learn later that these types of conversations are unlikely to buffer the emotional toll wrought by a client's suicide. Even so, they have the potential to realistically prepare students for the possibility that they will experience such an event. Talking about it beforehand can also provide a context for feelings, thoughts, and competence-related questions that naturally arise in the aftermath of a client's suicide. I believe this would have been a valuable lesson to learn that may have helped ease the burden of the unknown with which students and early career psychologists often grapple.

Somewhat ironically, later in my graduate training, I was invited to participate on a research team that qualitatively investigated experiences of therapists in training with a client suicide, focusing specifically on the implications that this experience has for clinical supervision. I eagerly jumped at the opportunity. I was aware that client suicide is often a painful process for therapists, particularly for those still in training, and I recognized from my own experience that trainees may look to their graduate programs and supervisors for guidance and support when such an event occurs. I felt strongly that the results of such a study could facilitate valuable discussions and benefit students, supervisors, professors, and directors of training as well as me. If the information we learned and disseminated could aid one other person, I felt the project would be worthwhile.

One of my roles on the team involved interviewing several of the participants about their experiences. I found this project to be very powerful. Talking with the trainees was insight provoking. As trainees shared their private experiences in the interviews, I learned firsthand about the reality of losing a client to suicide. I also learned about what the trainees identified as "helpful" and "unhelpful" supervisor responses during an especially challenging time. Compounding the influence of this experience was the fact that, as a graduate student, I was simultaneously learning about my roles and responsibilities as a supervisor. I asked myself: What type of supervisor do I aspire to be? Would I be able to handle this type of situation and how would I do so? If I have yet to personally experience a client suicide, how could I effectively help my supervisee deal with the aftermath? I had shifted toward looking at the complex experience of client suicide through a different lens—from the supervisor's perspective. From this research experience, I learned that supervision plays an invaluable role in a trainee's overall experience of such an event. As a result, the responsibility and intensity of the supervision relationship became much more evident.

As an early career psychologist working with a dually diagnosed residential population with complex mental health and medical diagnoses, I continue to wonder about the personal and professional toll of a client's suicide. I have initiated several discussions with my clinical supervisors and colleagues about the questions I raised throughout my graduate training in an attempt to ease my anxiety and to learn whether others who have not yet lost a client to suicide feel the same. Perhaps this has been a further attempt to normalize my fear of the unknown. As prompted by my research experience, I continue to view the issue of suicide through two lenses: that of the therapist and that of the supervisor. But today I am living the experience rather than studying it. I strive to assess my level of comfort in working with supervisees around issues related to suicidality, and I routinely discuss my clients' suicidality with my own supervisor.

My research experience has also reinforced for me the need for the types of discussions and training about suicide in counseling psychology that I hungered for as a graduate student. I have been inspired to share what I learned from participating on the research team and have led discussions with my colleagues, particularly with those at my place of employment involved in our training program, about their training and readiness to manage such an event. Perhaps most importantly, I recognize that it is imperative that I address the topic of suicide with my supervisees—to normalize, educate, and provide reassurance. Perhaps I can help to assuage their fears of the unknown. I now have a better understanding about how this type of critical experience can influence a supervisee's development as a counselor as he or she transitions to becoming a professional.

For me to continue to grow and challenge myself, I must embrace the natural fear about the intensity of the work that I do. Clearly, I learn more and more every day about my own areas for personal growth as well as about my level of comfort in working with and supervising trainees who serve suicidal clients. My clinical and research experiences in graduate school have provided the foundation from which I can now face my fears and navigate the unknown, armed with the knowledge that candid discussions and a willingness to learn about myself will lead naturally to personal and professional growth.

MY FIRST PUBLICATION: A LESSON IN PERSISTENCE
Mark Pope

My first publication was the culmination of a long and rather rocky road. My entry into counseling began with a master's degree in counseling in 1974 from the University of Missouri–Columbia. After that, I worked at Northwestern University's Institute of Psychiatry as a mental health worker on their adolescent unit. I had been thinking about returning to study for a doctorate, but I was working in the field getting excellent experience and did not really want to leave Chicago. Then, Northwestern University decided to begin a doctoral program in counseling psychology to complement their other psychology programs. In 1978, I began this doctoral program at Northwestern.

The two professors in this new program were Solomon Cytrynbaum and Gus Rath, with a visiting professor, Richard Schulz. Dr. Schulz was a young professor on leave from the University of Pittsburgh whose main area of research was gerontology. As part of my doctoral program, I took his course in gerontology where he had the students, as one of the course requirements, propose a research project. I proposed a project to survey a group of aging gay men about their sexual behavior to see if there were any changes (in frequency and type) from one age cohort to another.

Dr. Schulz liked my proposal so much that he funded it. Now, I had to do it. I contacted a social group for older gay men in Chicago, called Maturity, and they allowed me access to their mailing list of members. I received over 100 completed responses, a 50% response rate. I could not believe my good fortune. This was my very first research project, and I was already a success. I worked with Dr. Schulz to analyze the data and prepare the final report.

Everything was going like clockwork. Then, I stopped because I fell in love with a wonderful, new partner. But he was moving to California. I was not going to allow my "one true love" to move to another place without me. I had to go, and I did. However, everything—and I mean everything—got put on hold while I adjusted and found a job in the San Francisco Bay Area. This took some time.

When I finally got back to research and completed the manuscript, it was 1980—2 years after collecting the actual data. I thought the data were very old, but I had contacted Dr. Schulz and he had encouraged me to submit it. I submitted the manuscript to the *Journal of Homosexuality*, the premier journal in this area of research, and waited—and waited.

It seemed as if took forever (actually only 4 months). When I received the letter with the return address of *Journal of Homosexuality,* I was quite excited. It was my very first submission of a manuscript to a professional journal. I believed, no, I "knew" the data were unique and that I had done a good job in the manuscript preparation. There was nothing like it in the published literature. I could not imagine that after all my work my article would not be accepted for publication.

My expectations were very high, and I was not prepared for a rejection. Yet it was, unfortunately, "Reject." Not even a "Revise and resubmit." It was just a flat rejection of what I had studied and written. I took the rejection quite personally. I was devastated and embarrassed, so I put aside the letter, reviews, manuscript, and data. And, although my thoughts were not spoken, I was unsure at that time if

I would ever again submit anything. What kind of masochist would want to participate in such a cruel process? Okay, so I did not deal well with this rejection. Let's just say I was deeply hurt by this incident and did not choose to continue writing at that time.

Ten years later, as I returned to doctoral studies with renewed commitment and career clarity, now at the University of San Francisco, I thought of that manuscript and the data and decided to return to it. I knew that it was going to take the right editor to see how important these data were. I revised the manuscript based on the reviews and decided to submit it to (once again) the *Journal of Homosexuality*.

By now it had been 8 years since my rejection (notice how I say my, not the manuscript's). But I was determined! I believed in these data and their importance in the research on aging gay men. About 6 months after my submission of the revised manuscript, I received another letter with the return address of *Journal of Homosexuality*. I was hoping that the editors did not remember that I had previously submitted the manuscript. If they did, I was sure they would reject it again. As I opened the letter, I let out a scream of delight when I saw that the manuscript had been "Accepted with revisions" (Pope & Schulz, 1990). This time the letter was signed by John Alan Lee. Unbeknownst to me, Dr. Lee had recently proposed a special issue of the *Journal of Homosexuality* focusing on aging. My manuscript had been forwarded to him by the journal's editor. Even though my data had been collected 10 years earlier, he said it was a good study for two particular reasons. It had been collected before the AIDS epidemic struck and was therefore especially valuable from that perspective. It was also the first study like this to define standard age cohorts and would likely set a trend in the literature.

I was shocked, delirious, and ecstatic. I knew that all it took was an editor with the right eyes looking at my manuscript at the right time and the right place. My belief—in the data, my writing, and my vision—had been vindicated.

I learned a very important lesson from this journey: Persistence is the key to success. I believed in this work so much that I persisted. It took me a while to work out the feelings of rejection and hurt and to gain some perspective, but I did. And I came back to this manuscript, persisted, and was rewarded. I learned that, if you believe in what you have studied and written, you should persist. It was truly a great lesson—one that I have never forgotten and that has shaped my entire career.

Postscript

Later, I became a journal editor myself (*Career Development Quarterly*) and used this first publication experience as I developed responses to authors who submitted their manuscripts for review. Hopefully, this first publication experience gave me sensitivity to others who submitted their manuscripts. This experience allowed me to write, I hope, better and more positive review letters. I never called them "rejection" or even "disposition" letters. As editor, I tried to elicit both an honest critique and sensitivity from the editorial board members as they evaluated manuscripts for publication and developed their reviews. Based on this first experience, this innocent opening of a letter from a journal, I learned that it is not what you say but how you say it that is most important.

Reference

Pope, M., & Schulz, R. (1990). Sexual behavior and attitudes in midlife and aging homosexual males. *Journal of Homosexuality, 20,* 169–178.

UNITED CULTURES OF COUNSELING
Valerie Stephens Leake

Ruth Riding-Malon

Yuh-Jin (Jean) Tzou

Monicah Muhomba

Our group's collective defining moment was the moment when we realized that we had each other for support, friendship, mentoring, and exchange as we forged through our doctoral programs. This defining realization emerged from shared experience and a connection that has had a profound influence on the personal and professional lives of four women from very different cultures. In 2003, Valerie, a middle-aged, middle-class, married-with-children, White, female, nontraditional doctoral student in counseling psychology was assigned to mentor an incoming doctoral student with whom she had some characteristics in common.

Monicah was married, a mother, and a nontraditional student. Here, however, the similarities, at least those most easily identified, ended. Monicah was from Zimbabwe, carrying all the rich cultural traditions from that country, and studied in the United States with the goal of returning, after school, to help those in her country. The mentoring relationship formed between Monicah and Valerie was the foundation of what became an informal mentoring group that supported the continuing multicultural development of four women from four different continents throughout graduate school. In 2004, Yuh-Jin from Taiwan became part of the group, and then Ruth, originally from Belgium. We spanned three cohorts in our program. We tried to meet at least once a semester, but usually settled for once a year, to review everyone's progress through the program. We laughingly referred to ourselves as the "United Cultures of Counseling." We were training to become counselors; by sharing our daily stress and by examining change through each other's eyes, we learned about our own strengths, and weaknesses, and ultimately gained the insight to become better helpers.

Valerie

I entered the initial mentoring relationship with Monicah because I was immediately drawn to her warmth and kindness and to her passion for learning all she could to help those in Zimbabwe deal with the HIV/AIDS epidemic. From Monicah, I learned that while I might understand intellectually the experience of racial prejudice and White privilege in the United States, I had no clue as to what it was like to live these experiences. I was the director of a summer program for children in a tiny rural area, and Monicah applied for a job one summer. Following all the interviews, I worried how the community, which was quite racially divided, would handle having a counselor who was not only dark-skinned but also spoke with a pronounced accent and if this would impact her ability to interact with the parents of our clients. I also worried if Monicah would find herself the target of abuse or disrespect. When I finally worked myself up to talk to her about it, she looked at me very kindly and said, "It would be no different from my experience every day."

From Yuh-Jin, I learned that the values underlying a culture can be as powerful a factor in someone's processing of an experience as the overarching effects of that experience. At the beginning of one semester, with tears in her eyes, Yuh-Jin related an experience when she had been berated for some innocuous deviation in an assignment during a class. As I listened, I felt anger for her and struggled to understand why her focus seemed to be on others' reactions and her inability to fully contain her own reaction while the incident happened. It wasn't until she named what she felt as shame that I recognized that, for Yuh-Jin, the biggest difficulty in this experience had been what felt like public humiliation. That would not have been the most difficult aspect for me.

From Ruth, I learned that although someone may look and sound like me, the cultural values and assumptions they hold may be quite different. Ruth came to me feeling very discouraged after a few weeks as a new doctoral student teaching an undergraduate class. When we discussed her struggle, which sounded fairly similar to my own experience, I was somewhat at a loss to understand why she felt so discouraged. Then she remarked that her students in the United States treated her very differently from how she had treated her own professors in Europe. It became clear that the differences in classroom culture, particularly involving behaviors that denote respect, were exacerbating the stress of learning to be a college instructor.

Ruth

Valerie was my very first contact in our graduate program, when I had been drawn to her encouraging, cheerful attitude. Since then, her informal mentoring has played a significant role in my life. Valerie became my American cultural broker—the person who helped me understand puzzling cultural norms and practices. As a fellow teaching assistant, she listened to my frustration and struggles with the process of fitting into the educational system of another country with its foreign values and expectations.

I am originally from a bicultural, bilingual family in Brussels, Belgium. After spending many years in the United States, I enjoy being able to move from one culture to the next. I thought that my background kept me open to other worldviews so that I was generally able to enter into other people's worlds with relative ease. As assistant director of our program's clinic, it was my job to find an appropriate referral for a client. The client needed a therapist able to work with complicated family dynamics involving siblings from several fathers. Monicah had a background in family therapy, but I wondered if, coming from a more traditional African society, she could handle a complex American stepfamily structure. I still remember how Monicah gently, yet matter-of-factly, rearranged my view of herself and of her world by saying, "Bigamy is common in my country. My father had two wives; my mother was the younger; I have many half-brothers and half-sisters. I think I can work with this family." And she did, masterfully!

Yuh-Jin and I became friends early in our training. Being more senior in our program, I was glad to encourage her as she gained more confidence in her clinical skills. It was fun watching Yuh-Jin creatively negotiate her own bicultural identity as she developed as a counselor. I admired the way she chose to overcome insecurities learned from the American youth-driven culture that surrounded her by proclaiming a celebration of a milestone birthday. Truly, I was reminded how being a multicultural person is not a destination but a journey that I continue to pursue.

A very dear friend once told me of her experience with a group of women making a mud hut for a family in Africa. She fondly spoke of the imprints each woman's hands made on the hut walls as they dried. Valerie's, Yuh-Jin's, and Monicah's multicultural handprints are on my life and on my counseling.

Yuh-Jin

Living half of my adult life as an immigrant in the United States with all the members of my family of origin in my home country, I have come to adopt many of my close friends here as my family. Valerie, Ruth, and Monicah are among them. I met Valerie as my first practicum supervisor when I was a master's student. I remember how she prepared me to walk into the therapy room for the first time. I called Valerie my "training wheels." The image of her running after me and holding her arms wide open, keeping me safe while letting me ride my bike alone was a defining moment in my journey to becoming a therapist. She is the supervisor who not only taught me that taking risks is necessary to build my confidence but who also was there ready to catch me when I fell. As I now look back at those early interactions, I realize that our supervision relationship blossomed into a friendship of a lifetime because of her acceptance and respect for my cultural background and its influences on me and my work.

I remember Ruth's agreeing to observe my session during our practicum. She took notes and gave me good feedback, but what I took away the most from that experience was the idea that if I find myself working too hard in a session, it may be time to take a step back and examine the dynamics of the therapeutic interaction and the working relationship. From her I learned the importance of patience and paying attention to a client's pace and readiness for change.

Monicah was a year ahead of me in the doctoral program. I got to know her better when we were assigned to work as a team at the in-house clinic. I was surprised to learn that although we come from opposite sides of the globe, Monicah's cultural values and attitudes were similar to my own. After the project ended, we each went our separate, busy ways but made sure to meet occasionally to catch up. Monicah was consistently a selfless friend who never hesitated to offer what she could to help me. Through her kindness, I learned about the importance of *not* underestimating the impact of any small gesture we can offer to others.

As my culture is inseparable from who am I as a minority member of this society, I often doubt the sincerity of friends who have no interest in my culture.

Valerie, Ruth, and Monicah have shown their genuine interest in seeing me as a cultural being. My friendships with these women are testimony to the value of recognizing the sociocultural context as an integral part of relationships. The women in our United Cultures of Counseling group have never failed to lend me their help and support whenever I am in need. They continue to inspire me to be a better helper to others, because through them I have reaped such benefits of being on the receiving end.

Monicah

I was born and raised on a completely different continent; therefore, my adjustment to U.S. culture was not an easy process. My interactions with Valerie, Ruth, and Yuh-Jin helped me to understand that I can still relate to and identify with people from other cultures. From the very first day as I interviewed for admission to my doctoral program, Valerie's warm and inviting attitude surprised me, made me feel comfortable, and even reduced my level of anxiety. At the end of the day, as I sat needing a ride home but feeling reluctant to bother anyone, Valerie sat with me and somehow figured out that I needed to call my husband. She offered her phone and even waited for more than 30 minutes until my husband came to pick me up. Coming from Africa I never imagined that a Caucasian woman would have anything to do with a Black, foreign woman with a pronounced accent. When I was admitted into the program I hoped Valerie would be my mentor and was excited when I was assigned to her. Valerie struck me as a hardworking student who still remained very involved with her family life even though she was very busy with graduate school. Given my cultural background, I did not want to neglect my motherly and wifely duties just because I was in graduate school. Valerie demonstrated to me that it is possible to balance school and family life, and she therefore soon became my role model. Through my relationship with her I learned to be sensitive to people who are different from me and to challenge my own biases about people who do not share the same or similar values, beliefs, skin color, or cultural background.

Ruth was one of the few people in my cohort with whom I easily connected because we were similar in a number of ways. During those moments when I thought, "Nobody understands me," Ruth was the person I would go to and vent my emotions without feeling judged. She was always prepared to listen, providing words of comfort as she helped normalize my situation. At the busy end of one semester, I missed a couple days of school because I needed to be at the hospital with my daughter, who was sick. Ruth took the time to check on how I was doing; she visited my daughter in the hospital and brought us food. Her care touched me deeply as I did not have any family members around.

Yuh-Jin struck me as someone who was genuinely concerned and willing to help me as an international student. Like me, Yuh-Jin was a busy woman, but she was among the few people who took the time to listen. Since she had been in the department and in the United States longer, Yuh-Jin was a great resource for me. Yuh-Jin also surprised me by how much she expressed appreciation at something I considered to be very small. I have applied this to therapy and am amazed at how some seemingly small acts in a therapy session with clients have brought about amazing results.

The women in our United Cultures of Counseling group provided the help that I needed as a nontraditional, minority student from a different country who speaks English with a pronounced accent to adjust to being in graduate school. Despite our different looks, accents, and cultural backgrounds, our relationship was uniquely fulfilling and enriching. One of my unique and greatest strength as a therapist and supervisor, namely, the ability to be nonjudgmental in my relationships, grew out of my relationship with these three women.

Conclusion

Through our serendipitous association, our little group discussed struggles within and between our different cultures and customs, encouraged each other with insights from our course work, and applied these insights to the rest of our lives. While each of us had a foundation of multicultural awareness, stemming from personal experience, professional course work, and training, our experiences and time together put a "face" on various cultural differences and similarities and made us better therapists, teachers, friends, and family members. Our connection challenged and supported us as we negotiated the student phases of our training and developed into therapists open to those around us. Our hope for the future, though distance separates most of us and outside commitments tug at us, is to continue our friendship and to encourage others to develop such valuable professional associations and relationships.

CHAPTER SUMMARY

Advanced students know a lot. They also know that there is so much more to be learned. In their quest to learn more, they discover knowledge from multiple sources: clients, supervisors, peers, teaching and research experiences, and their personal lives. They appear to be in a state of flux, moving beyond the basic lessons they learned as beginners while opening up to the enormity of what they do not know. However, if they take "time to digest," as Chao puts it, they are likely to learn, simply by paying attention to, and reflecting upon, their experiences.

Working With Clients

From work with clients emerge great triumphs and aching sorrows, sometimes simultaneously. Kluck shares the transformative experience of allowing herself to deeply empathize with a client who had committed a crime, while Bailey notes the affirmation she felt when she heard "thank you" from a client. Sobik tells us gut-wrenchingly about the extraordinarily painful experience of losing a client to suicide. Clients can also touch our lives incalculably, as did Ring's client, whose terminal illness and increasing frailty bubbled up his personal grief at the prospect of losing her.

Advanced students recognize that individuals are more than the sum of their parts. Their conceptualization of clients' presenting concerns becomes accordingly more complex. Heppner exemplifies this process as she talks about her growing understanding that clients need to be viewed and understood within the full context of their lives. She reminds us that we cannot consider an individual's vocation without also considering his or her life. Gemignani similarly discusses how to broaden our view of clients by examining the influences of social construction, dominant discourse, and cultural identity.

Sometimes we get caught up in work with our clients; our identification or involvement with them can act like stones in a river, subtly guiding the flow of the therapy in certain directions but not in others. Gemignani talks about the overlap between his experiences as an international student therapist with those of an international client, an overlap that created a strong countertransferential response. Hill points out that we can use the times when clients stir up our own issues as prompts for personal and professional growth. She notes that "… accepting ourselves as we are can be more profound than searching for who we think we should be."

Therapists Are People, Too

Who we are as people is also inextricably linked with who we are as therapists, and personal experiences can have profound influences on professional endeavors. Early interests interact with later experiences, culminating in powerful learning, as Packer-Williams describes in her account of her multicultural learning journey. Fier notices that, following her father's death, she was forced to individuate; this occurred around the same time as when she was reaching for increased autonomy in her clinical work. She points out that our development as counselors or therapists often parallels our personal development; by no means are these processes mutually exclusive. Trotter-Mathison also poignantly describes the influence of the death of someone close to her—her grandfather—on her personal and professional selves. She speaks of opening herself to the deep pain associated with her loss and, in turn, becoming more present with her clients as they experience and share their own pain.

There are also times when, try as we may, it is impossible to subtract our selves from the process of therapy. Fitch describes a case of this in her account of the influence of her pregnancy on her work with a client with terminal cancer. At other times, our personal lives overshadow our work with clients. We get busy with the business of being a student and can miss the significance of interactions with clients, as Rings writes, until they wallop us over the head. Luckily, our human connections can offer support and reassurance when we become overwhelmed by the work, as Riding-Malon, Leake, Muhomba, and Tzou write. Like the Beatles, they remind us that we all "get by with a little help from [our] friends."

Learning From Supervisors

For better or for worse, supervisors and mentors remain an important source of learning for advanced students. Sometimes we are humbled by our mentors' seemingly infinite knowledge, as Manaster was. Sometimes our supervisors calm us, as Bailey writes, reminding us that, even though we are not yet experts, we can do this work; we are on our way. And, at other times as Ladany notes, supervisors provide our most important learning not through pearls of wisdom but rather by poor example. Advanced students often experience both healing and harmful (or at least uninspiring) supervision during their training. Nuszkowski discusses how she moved from a harmful, misattuned supervision experience to one in which she felt heard and supported. She outlines the critical role of safety within the supervisory relationship if we are to continue to grow as therapists.

Leaning Toward Multicultural Competence

We are all cultural beings. Advanced students approach and integrate this awareness—as therapists, students, researchers, and teachers—in multiple ways, and from multiple points on the continuum of racial and cultural identity development. Fortunately, course work addressing multicultural counseling competencies seems to promote development, as intended. Johnson speaks about undertaking the difficult work of challenging our own worldviews as a student in a multicultural counseling course. Mobley similarly notes that reading critical texts can be a catalyst for cultural identity development. Empathic teachers soften tensions that can sometimes arise during cross-cultural interactions in class, as Parker-Williams describes. Hutz demonstrates in her role as a teacher that challenging ourselves to remain open to others' feedback, even when it is critical, can be crucial to learning more deeply about our own multicultural development as well as to promoting that of others.

Both *etic* (culture universal) and *emic* (culture specific) ways of knowing are salient for advanced students. Quirk, in his account of cross-cultural research and counseling experiences, acknowledges the etic perspective: Although the differences between our clients and ourselves may be great, there are still some similarities upon which we can rely, such as the importance of "deep, caring listening." Shriberg highlights the importance of relying upon emic knowledge. When research participants have been affected by trauma, it is important, she writes, to capture their experiences using their own unique "language of pain."

Learning about how to be a multiculturally competent counselor is clearly not confined to the classroom. Scholl tells us about how immersing himself in the local culture as an actor in a community play informed and facilitated his therapy with clients. Work with clients is also an important prompt for examining our development as multicultural counselors. In her account of her experiences with clients as a visible South Asian–American Muslim woman, Mahmood reminds us that multicultural contexts expand beyond race and ethnicity, as she discusses the role of religion and religious identity in therapy.

Letting Go

Authors writing about defining moments that occurred during their time as advanced students describe various instances of "letting go." Hutz talks about letting go of her need to control her image with her students and clients, while

Jackson discusses relinquishing her fear of the unknown. Moody acknowledges that letting go of the need to "do it right" and "fix" others leads to vulnerability—a vulnerability that can be healing. Similarly, Danna describes a seeming paradox: Letting go of our impatience for clients to change can sometimes lead to unexpected transformations. He talks about his struggles that originated from his "own yearning to feel like a good and effective therapist by producing visible change within my client." There can be a dark side to letting go, too. Ladany reminds us that we can be dealt blows of disillusionment throughout our training as we let go of the idealistic notion that all of our teachers are competent.

The Importance of Early Experiences

Those more experienced professionals who reflected upon and wrote about defining moments that occurred when they were advanced students exemplify how significant and enduring these early experiences can be. Relatively early defining moments prompted Ladany's subsequent program of research and Heppner's career-long interest in holistic career counseling. Pope describes how his first experiences with publication as a doctoral student influenced his actions as a journal editor many years later. Manaster remembers the moment when he "woke up" and realized that there is no such thing as instant expertise. He states, "It takes stumbling to stand upright, making mistakes to discern what is correct, and having doubts to find clarity." Here is an apt message from these last defining moments for advanced students who are struggling with being in flux, in between beginner and professional: Keep struggling, keep reflecting, keep learning. You are on your way.

QUESTIONS

1. In her narrative, Jackson describes her conviction that graduate students need to be prepared for the possibility of experiencing a client's suicide. Sobik writes about what it is actually like to lose a client to suicide. Have you considered what it might be like to have a client seriously attempt or complete suicide? If you have had a client attempt or complete suicide, what advice would you give to other practitioners who have not had this experience? How do you cope with these kinds of "unknowns" that are inherent in clinical work?

2. How do you imagine the theme of "letting go," evident for some writers at the advanced student phase, might manifest in other phases of counselor/therapist development? Do you think that it has the same salience during other phases of development? Why or why not?

3. For readers who have some clinical experience, what lessons have you learned from your clients? How have clients influenced your work and professional development? For readers who have more extensive clinical experience, which clients stand out in your mind? Why?

4. Contrast your own instances of meaningful learning in supervision with those that were more disappointing. What did you take away from the meaningful experiences? What conditions facilitated this meaningful

learning? What contributed to the disappointing supervision experiences? What did you take away from these?

5. Multiple advanced student authors wrote about experiences that prompted them to examine previously held beliefs about themselves, the therapeutic process, and others. What experiences have prompted you in this way? How have your beliefs changed over time?

6. In what ways has your personal development interacted with your professional development? How do you conceptualize or make meaning of the overlap between who you are as a person and who you are as a therapist, teacher, or researcher?

7. Having read about advanced students' defining moments, what advice might you give to individuals at this stage of development? You might tailor your answers to address encounters with clients, interactions in supervision, multicultural counseling considerations, or experiences in classes.

8. How have you grown as a multicultural counselor during your own development? What experiences have promoted this growth? What experiences, if any, have hindered it?

9. In your development as a counselor/therapist, who has provided support, reassurance, or mentoring? What are some particularly important moments that you have experienced with these individuals? How have they affected, promoted, or inspired your work?

5

The Novice Professional Phase

N ovice professionals have graduated from their professional training. The transition to independent practice, without the safety nets provided by graduate programs and mandatory supervision, is an important milestone marker in this phase. This sense of being on one's own comes with both "good news" and "bad news" sentiments.

Rønnestad and Skovholt (2003) found that following graduation, novice professionals undergo a sequentially ordered transformation. Early attempts to confirm the validity of one's training tend to lead predictably to periods of disillusionment, during which novice professionals question not only their professional training but also themselves as practitioners. If, in their searching, individuals at this phase of development uncover disappointment in their qualities as therapists, or find that client progress is lacking, feelings of inadequacy may result. Finally, rounding the curve past disillusionment, novice professionals transition to a period of more intense self-examination and exploration of the professional environment.

Novice professionals focus strongly on professional identity development. They are faced with challenging tasks such as learning to work with managed care companies and marketing their independent practices. Personal experiences continue to provide salient fodder for professional development, as novice professionals' capacity for the integration of personal and professional identities increases during this phase. More and more, novice professionals learn that their own personalities are expressed in their work. In this way, and others, novice professionals gain an ever-increasing grasp of the complexities of the work. As Matt Hanson states in his essay in this chapter, perhaps they begin to "expect the unexpected."

Reference

Rønnestad, M.H., & Skovholt, T.M. (2003). The journey of the counselor and therapist: Research findings and perspectives on development. *Journal of Career Development,* *30,* 5–44.

THE CLIENT WHO DID NOT RETURN: A PAINFUL GIFT
John C. Dagley

I've had the good fortune to work with a wide range of individuals, couples, families, and groups in my years as a therapist. I have learned a great deal from my clients about pain, misery, and the darker side of human life. Yet, on balance, I believe that I've learned even more about the more positive, constructive side of life—about courage, resilience, ego strength, and the human capacity to transform real or imagined ugliness into beauty. Looking back over my decades as a professional "helper," it's relatively easy to see cumulative ways my therapeutic experiences and relationships have shaped not only my clients' lives but also my own. Interestingly, the experiences that have probably had the greatest influence on the positive process and outcome trajectories of my therapeutic work have not been the successful interactions but the unsuccessful. It is one of those poignant encounters early in my career that serves as one of my most "defining" moments.

At the time of this encounter I was in my third year as an assistant professor of Counseling and Personnel Services at a large state university and also was in the early stages of building a small, private practice. As a part of my work I served as a therapist in a departmental clinic, the Child and Family Guidance Center. I did so in part to inform my teaching but, more importantly, to provide our doctoral students opportunities to serve as cotherapists. The nature of the presenting problems dictated the appropriateness of student involvement, so at times, such as with the case that follows, students were not assigned as therapists, cotherapists, or observers.

Context is always important in therapy, and particularly so in this case. A shifting social dynamic set a backdrop for understanding this client's particular situation in the early seventies. Amidst the many societal changes that characterized the decade between 1965 and 1975, my first decade as a counselor and professor, were civil rights protests and marches, antiwar rallies, the women's movement's struggles with efforts to achieve equality and opportunity, and various shifts in social morés attached to the free-love, drug-inspired, tune-in, drop-out days of the hippies. Importantly, it was also the time of a dramatic increase in divorce rates and the introduction and increase of cohabitation alternatives to marriage. On campus, it was a time of unrest, the demise of *in loco parentis* as a guiding administrative principle, and the beginning of sit-ins, demonstrations, and eventually, shootings. Unfortunately, it was also a time when traditional relationship boundaries between professors and students began changing; today such dual relationships would be considered wholly inappropriate, exploitive, and unprofessional on the part of the professor. This was part of the social context for my client and for me. Of particular relevance to this client and her husband's demand for an "open marriage" was the growing dismay with male power and privilege.

There was also a "professional context" for me in this case. My doctoral program, as well as most in counseling and psychology in those days, did not include any special training in marriage and family therapy, even though couples (with one or both present) were increasingly becoming a large part of any community practice. I attempted to extend my expertise in that area through professional workshops and postdoctoral supervision. The strongest challenge for me was to develop a "systemic" point of view. The modal "marriage and family therapy" approach was to focus on the system, the couple as a whole, rather than on the two individuals, singly, as my supervisor felt I was prone to do. It was seen as being critically important to work with the couple together, as a unit. Issues were to be seen as a function of the relationship's dynamics. Because women tended to initiate couples therapy most often, it was especially important for male therapists to encourage both partners to participate in therapy. In fact, my understanding of the emphasis was such that if I worked with only one individual, and if that one was the woman in the relationship, then I risked serving as an "enabler." Worse yet, in the spirit of the times, I would be guilty of being sexist and of being the kind of male therapist who simply contributed to the continuing suppression of women by helping them become better "submissive" wives. Instead, the goal was simply to get both partners to make changes in the dynamics of their relationship. It was easier to accomplish if both were present.

A young woman in her mid-30s came into our clinic asking to see a senior staff member, preferably a male. My first impressions included an observation that that she was attractive, modestly dressed, and visibly tense and appeared somewhat proper and reserved. She opened with a shaky-voiced, "I would like to know why a happily married man would have an affair with one of his students," and quickly dissolved into tears, followed by sobs and deep groans. Not much else took place for several minutes. Once she seemed to approach physical exhaustion from crying, and with her lap almost filled with tissues offered her, she unfolded layer by layer her perspective of her situation. She had begun to suspect something was adrift over the previous 6 months because of her husband's noticeable shift of time away from home. At first, upon her questioning, her husband simply stated that he was putting in late hours at his office to finish a project, but he eventually grew tired of her inquiries and openly admitted that he was involved with one of his graduate students. Apparently, he had said to my client something like, "I love you, and I love her; I do not want a divorce, and I do not want to end my relationship with her. You can take it or leave it, but just quit hassling me. I want an open marriage. I don't want to talk about it. It's up to you." With silence as an exclamation point filling several moments after her replaying of that pronouncement, she finally looked up and pleadingly asked if I would help her learn how to become a "better wife."

Amid the rush of thoughts that you might guess such a question would induce, I wandered through a minefield of silent thoughts such as the following: *My goodness, what an awful thing to hear from your partner.* This new term *open marriage* tends to be neither. I wonder why she requested a male therapist; I think I'd be down on males after that exchange. How can I work on this marriage with one person in the room?

With all of this chatter in my head, I actually said something like, "Could I be helpful? Yes, I think I can. I'm confident that I can help you 'process' what you're experiencing and explore what you might do in your situation. I'm not sure exactly how I can help you 'become a better wife' or that I even think that might be a good plan, but I am confident that if you can persuade your husband to come in with you, we can work on this together." She thought about this for a bit, smiled appreciatively but wanly, said she'd try, got up, and left. She did not return. That is a defining moment that has shaped my therapy in profound ways ever since. Let me explain.

It was in the perspective of each of these social and professional contexts that I said, yes, I would help her as much as I could but that I truly believed that it would be much better if she could persuade her husband to come in for couples counseling. An unsettling discomfort arose within me almost immediately after her departure and continued throughout the following week, peaking at the time of her appointment. Over time, therapy inevitably provides many defining moments, but for me this session with the client who did not return was the most poignant and powerful in that it enabled me to free myself from the cocoon of the shoulds and oughts of theory and supervision and to find my own voice in therapy.

As Rønnestad and Skovholt (2003) described in their writings about a novice professional, and as Levinson (1986) identified as the period of life when a male "becomes one's own man," I began to trust my own sense of how I was going to be helpful as a therapist. With my client who didn't return, I feared "appearing" sexist or nonsystemic and, as a result, served neither my client nor my profession. For the next 30-plus years of therapy, I never again let a "theoretical construct" or rule get in between my client and me. From that encounter forward, I was vigilant about focusing on the needs of my clients over any favorite therapeutic principle or imagined rule. With this client, I failed to use my skills to help simply because I was trying to demonstrate to myself, to my postdoc supervisor, and to "posterity" that I was a legitimate marital therapist and was not a sexist enabler. As it turned out, I was simply self-focused, theory bound, and unhelpful.

At that moment, with that client, I was so intent on doing what I thought I was supposed to do (i.e., focus on the couple) that I failed to be helpful to a person in pain and in need of my help. I wish my response would not have included the clause "if you can persuade your husband to come in with you."

References

Levinson, D.J., Darrow, C.N., Klein, E.B., Levinson, M.H., & McKee, B. (1978). *Seasons of a Man's Life*. New York: Random House.

Rønnestad, M.H., & Skovholt, T.M. (2003). The journey of the counselor and therapist: Research findings and perspectives on development. *Journal of Career Development, 30*, 5–44.

ON BEING NEEDED

Jim Guinee

I first met Peter (pseudonym), a young student in the United States from Malaysia, on Depression Screening Day. I remember that he seemed to be taking an unusually long time (even for someone whose first language was not English) to read and answer the depression inventory. He slowly pulled a dictionary out of his book bag, and I realized that he might appreciate some assistance. I introduced myself and asked if I could help. He stated in very broken English, "I do not know—how do you say—the meaning of these words, so I look them up." "That's fine," I responded.

As I turned to walk away, he quickly whispered, "I cannot find this word." He pointed to the questionnaire, and I saw the word: *constipated*. I started to smile but then looked in his eyes and realized he was ashamed. I sat down with Peter and explained to him (quite reluctantly) what the word meant. I could see in his eyes that he deeply appreciated this help.

I was pleasantly surprised the next week when Peter made an appointment at the counseling center, requesting me as his counselor. Though I was barely out of graduate school, I had experience working with international students and welcomed the challenge. After the first few sessions, I found myself struggling to understand or help Peter. His English was very poor, and he spent a lot of time in session just sitting quietly looking at the floor. Sessions with Peter were like riding the bus for 50 minutes sitting next to a stranger who says nothing. The silence drove me crazy.

Finally, I went to my director for some consultation. I reluctantly admitted that I still didn't know why Peter was in counseling and that I was having a hard time understanding his speech. My director gave me some useful suggestions and tended to my bruised ego. After my meeting, I admitted to myself (but not to my director) an additional problem: I didn't *like* working with Peter. I found him resistant, difficult to understand, and worst of all, boring. I blamed him for the lack of progress in therapy. I found myself hoping he would give up on me and not come back.

A supervisor once told me that occasionally we make painful discoveries about ourselves when we are providing therapy. When these revelations involve our clients, it is imperative to be honest and deal with our feelings and then to figure out how to communicate them in session. I wasn't sure that would work with Peter. What could I say to him? "Peter, can you be a more interesting and verbal client for me?"

Then I hit upon an idea. For starters, I needed to focus on Peter's feelings, not my own. All good counselors know this, but sometimes it's amazing how quickly we forget. Second, I knew deep down that Peter had a lot to tell me; I just wasn't helping him find an effective way to do that. I decided to ask him to write daily entries in a journal. I told him I wanted him to write whenever he felt sad or did not like himself. I also told him to write the entries in Chinese and then the day before our session to translate those entries into English. I wanted his initial thoughts and feelings to flow out onto paper without any barriers to restrict them. I knew Peter might have to take a long time to translate his homework into English, so I assured him that he didn't have to write very much.

When Peter shared his entries with me, it became very clear that he was not only depressed but also had a horribly low opinion of himself. His entries were replete with statements like, "I hate myself," and, "I am so, so stupid." I couldn't imagine how anyone could loathe himself so much. No wonder nothing I did with him in therapy had any impact; I had never addressed the source of all of his distress. Here was someone who did not like himself, did not like his family, and did not like his life.

In our next session I told Peter I wanted to know more about him. After some silence, Peter started talking. He stated that he had always lacked self-confidence and that he did not trust other people. I asked him to describe an incident that could explain his distrust of other people. "Think back," I said. "Was there a time in your life when someone hurt you?"

Peter began to talk about school and how well his brother had done in math—so well, in fact, that his brother was captain of his high school math team and continually excelled in math competitions with other schools. When Peter reached high school, the math teacher immediately put him on the team. Peter stated that he had never been particularly good at math but was afraid to speak up. At this point he began to talk more slowly, and he stared at his feet. He stated that he did very poorly at the first competition, and the teacher announced his poor performance in front of the entire math team. Peter didn't remember what the teacher said, but he recalled clearly having to look at his classmates and thinking how stupid he must be. It wasn't long before he was kicked off the team.

Peter related more incidents in his life during which others had criticized him for being "stupid." He stated that his father and older brother were currently paying for his education and that he feared they were becoming increasingly disappointed in him. As he spoke, I realized I was coming to care more and more about Peter, because he was so sad and because I appreciated his courage in trying to overcome his distrust in others enough to let a strange American like me into his life.

In our next session Peter caught me off guard. "I want to ask a question," he said after a period of silence. I was the one who always seemed to initiate the questions. Peter very simply asked me, "What is the point of life?" I gave him what I thought was a decent answer: that each person had to figure that out for himself or herself. Then he stated, "I was told that being a Christian would make me happy." I told him I was a Christian, too. He did not react to this statement, only replying, "I say I give my life to Christ. I'm not sure what this means."

I learned that Peter had come into contact with some well-meaning but perhaps misguided religious students who had "shepherded" Peter into their flock a little too quickly. Peter explained that he had been attending church with these students and that he was uncomfortable with people speaking in tongues, raising their hands, singing happily. He said he felt stupid because he could not do these things, he did not feel happiness inside, and he was sure that the people in the church thought he was stupid.

I told Peter about the first time I had seen someone raise her hands in church. I had been raised in a more traditional church where people just didn't do that, and it scared me. It felt good to find we shared a similar experience. Peter sat intently and nodded as if I was finally beginning to really understand how he felt inside. I thought back to his experience with the math team and imagined the wound it created and how each time he felt awkward around others that wound was reopened.

As time went on, Peter spaced his appointments farther apart. He seemed to be doing better—not great, but better. He was making friends. He had found a part-time job. He had started "sampling" other churches. One day he told me that he was trying to trust people more and to learn to like himself, but he stated, "It is so hard!" Progress was still slow, and there were times that he seemed discouraged about his difficulty with meeting people and making friends. It occurred to me: I had seen him on and off for 2 years, and he had stuck with *me*. He could have given up early on—at times I wanted him to—but he didn't. I really admired him for that.

Eventually, it was time for Peter to graduate and leave school. He would no longer be eligible for sessions with me. I told him I wanted to see him before he left for good. He told me that he was moving to Chicago to live with his brother. I told him, "You are so brave. First you come to a new country to go to school, and then you move to a huge city where you know so few people. I could never do that!" He responded, "I try to work on my confidence, but it is so hard." I said, "Yes, it is, but you are getting better. It takes a long time, but you are a special person, and you can do it." In our last session together, I told Peter how much I had valued working with him. I thanked him for coming back over and over, especially when we got off to such a rough start. His reply was simple and poignant: "You are my friend, and I will miss you."

Before we took our last walk down the hallway, he asked for my e-mail address. He said he wanted to stay in touch. I gladly gave it to him, and every once in a while he sends me a short note. He asks the same questions: How are you? How is your family? Despite the occasional mistake his writing continues to improve. He has found a full-time job. He has found a local church with a strong Chinese contingent.

Peter's presence in my life came at a time when I was starting my professional career, brimming with confidence and, unfortunately, some professional and personal immaturity. This shy, young man with little confidence and very broken English attached himself to me and, through his persistent visits, helped me learn some things about myself. I had gone into the field of counseling because I cared about other people, but I realized I had to care unconditionally if I was going to help them. I also realized that I had focused too much on how much I liked or disliked a client instead of finding in each person what is likeable and valuable.

The most important lesson I learned from working with Peter is that I cannot dictate the conditions of how I help people. I cannot help just the people I like. If one wants to be a therapist, or for that matter a decent human being, one must accept the fact that some people have few needs and that some have great needs. Some people get their needs met quickly, and some take a long time. Some do not even know what their needs are. Yet it seems everywhere I turn there is someone like Peter, someone who has great needs and someone who has unilaterally decided that *I* am the one who will help meet those needs. I cannot ride the bus anymore in silence. It is much too crowded and much too noisy. And I'm not riding anymore; I'm driving.

There are a lot of Peters out there. They're not always easy or fun to work with; I may even find it hard to like them. But then again, who says they like *me*? How arrogant of me to dwell so much on whether *I* like spending time with them.

I have also learned, though, that when I find I don't feel as much fondness for a client as I might for someone else, this is useful information. It tells me that I'm not looking deeply enough to find in that person what is likeable. I know as a therapist I place a lot of value on the relationship I have with my clients and see it as an agent of change. Within this mindset I find it vital that I work at liking my clients as much as I can, because I have found it helps me help them as much as I can.

The last e-mail Peter sent to me contained the usual set of questions and updates. But he added something new this time. He told me I had taught him so much, and he called me his "big brother." I wonder if Peter will ever understand how much he taught *me* about being a better therapist.

Thanks, little brother.

EXPECTING THE UNEXPECTED
Matthew R. Hanson

Philosophically, I have lived by the notion that phenomena in this world are basically and essentially unique and that the "essence" of something can emerge only if we hold our own preconceptions, thoughts, and judgments at arm's length. I have also been one to heed the various "words of wisdom" and moments of insight shared by practitioners who've been at this work for a while. This is why I've increasingly admired and taken to heart Irvin Yalom's (2002) recommendation to "create a new therapy" (p. 33) for each new client. From my perspective, Yalom makes this recommendation as a way to emphasize the uniqueness of each client's life and situation and to downplay our sometimes natural tendency to "think inside a box." I think it gives us, as therapists, a chance to see our clients as they really are and helps us truly understand what they really need.

I've thought about this perspective a great deal over the course of my career and would like to think that I've grown much more aware of the various biases, judgments, and preconceptions that I know were more common in my earlier practice. For example, I have a number of very clear memories about a client with whom I worked during my first year of professional (i.e., postdoctoral) practice. It was during the fall of that year that a young woman, Julia, showed up on my calendar and requested help in dealing with the impending death of her mother, whose cancer had recently spread such that it was no longer treatable. I recall how confident I felt that I would be able to help this client, given how I had successfully helped other clients work through their own personal grief over the loss of a parent or loved one. Admittedly, I may have even felt a bit more confident than usual, given that I had done an extensive review of the grief therapy literature for one of my doctoral-level courses.

To my surprise, I learned during that first session that Julia was indeed experiencing great sadness about her mother, though not only because she had only a short time to live. Rather, my client also appeared to be primarily grieving the fact that her mother—whom she loved dearly—was still living and was suffering the physical and emotional pain associated with a terminal disease she had been fighting for several years. Complicating my new client's feelings was the fact that her mother was also dealing with a separate chronic and persistent mental illness (and had been for her entire adult life) and therefore had only limited capacity to help Julia deal with her anger, fear, sadness, and confusion.

I can recall quite clearly feeling increasingly anxious as I listened to my client during those first moments, knowing that I had assumed that I knew who this client was and what she might need. Listening to Julia's story, I had the sinking feeling that what I had just learned through my research would be of limited help in guiding me in what to say to help provide the kind of perspective that might help Julia deal with her intense and immediate pain.

When I first saw Julia's paperwork, I recall thinking that I would likely share with her information about the stages of grief and steps she might take to cope with, or to prepare for, the loss of a loved one. Instead, Julia described her desperate need to feel some type of hope and optimism that hadn't been available to her for most of her life. She talked at length about wanting to know that she wasn't "crazy" for feeling the way she did (and wasn't going to "end up" losing her mind as her parents had). She also quietly asked me to help her find a type of peace that her mother, as she neared her death, simply couldn't provide.

Over the next several sessions, Julia and I talked at length about how she was dealing with the emotional upheaval that had overtaken her life. I remember feeling both lost and helpless during this time in Julia's therapy, not knowing if she would she show up to session feeling devastated, peaceful, abandoned, or all of these. One day, after working with Julia for a little more than 2 months, I received an e-mail from her letting me know that her mother had finally passed, with Julia at her bedside comforting her and holding her hand. What struck me most in this e-mail was not only Julia's peaceful tone but also the way she ended the note by saying, "I think now I can begin healing in ways I just couldn't before." Most striking to me in Julia's statement was the way that it expressed so clearly what she had likely needed all along: a chance to live relatively free from the worry about what the next moment might bring.

It's hard to look back and clearly identify all that I learned, or how I specifically changed as a professional, from this experience. I do know, though, that I learned much from Julia and continue to learn new ways of understanding the depths and range of human experience and emotion with each person who walks through my door. On a basic level, Julia reminded me about how remarkably resilient people can be in the face of unspeakably tragic and trying life situations. To be honest, I always felt some level of quiet guilt after a session with Julia—and others whose life stories were equally or more difficult—that my own life story seemed so easy, so stable.

More than teaching me about how people can cope with life's unfair circumstances, however, Julia and others have clearly shown me (more deeply than I knew at that point in my professional development) that one of the few things that's predictable about the process of therapy is how uncertain and unpredictable it's likely to be. As a new therapist, I think Julia's unexpected expressions of grief—feeling both incredibly sad about a life without her mother yet also quietly wanting her pain to end quickly—created in me a level of anxiety and uneasiness that stemmed in large measure from my desire to be helpful but not knowing what to do or what to say. And while I still have occasional moments of feeling some level of doubt about what to say or do, my reaction to clients' unpredictable disclosures and feelings is much less intense. I think I've come to expect the unexpected.

In the end, clients such as Julia have helped me appreciate much more deeply how heartache and devastation are as much a part of the human condition as happiness and joy and that people routinely go about living lives of importance, meaning, and goodness despite their pain and suffering. I think I have also benefited in this regard from having—since starting in this line of work—two of my own children, who provide me with daily (more often hourly) reminders that life is indeed less predictable than I would perhaps like and that trying to exert, or will, predictability where there is none is an exercise in frustration and futility for everyone.

I also know that while my experience with Julia taught me much, two things in particular stand out. First, this experience gave me much greater appreciation that the process of therapy often works best when we're able to draw from our deepest reserves and sense of self to ground us in the face of unexpected turmoil and trauma. I can now see how my work with this client in particular, over time, convinced me to actually acknowledge, accept, and even appreciate the uncertainty and unexpected turns that I had initially feared.

Second, my experience with Julia illustrated the wisdom inherent in creating a "new therapy" for each client. In the end, it has been my clients who have taught me that assumptions (no matter how well intended) can be misleading at best and harmful at worst and that the temptation to oversimplify a presenting concern or life problem serves only to alienate us from our clients and a true understanding of what they might need to heal. The longer I practice, the more fully I recognize that all clients are deeply unique and have unique challenges, disappointments, missteps, and unresolved hurts that eventually lead them to seek help as well as unique paths to health. And it's clients like Julia—with all of her complicated grief—who remind me that the practice of therapy often works best when we rely on a type of patience and strength to let go of our own preconceptions and let our clients reveal to us— and often themselves—what they most need.

Reference

Yalom, I. (2002). *The gift of therapy*. New York: Harper Perennial.

CARING AND LETTING GO: BALANCING BOTH SIDES OF THE TURTLE
Sally M. Hage

The only thing I know that truly heals people is unconditional love. Kübler-Ross (1997, p. 15)

In the end these things matter most: How well did you love? How fully did you love? How deeply did you learn to let go? Buddha (Kornfield, 1994, p. 85)

I was a new professional counselor, fresh out of grad school, and eager to make a difference in the lives of my clients. It was my first professional job, earning me a salary of $19,000 a year. I arrived at my office each day with butterflies in my stomach, unsure of what the day would bring yet filled with boundless energy and a desire to put myself fully into my work. I saw my role as one of reaching out to each struggling student I encountered in my work as a college chaplain. Indeed, soon after I started working, the director at our center gave me the nickname "Pied Piper" and began teasing me that the number of students coming to see me each day was beginning to wear out the carpeting leading to my office. I, in turn, experienced a sense of awe at my clients' faith in me, as they shared their lives and their feelings of pain with me and at the "gift" they gave me in inviting me to journey with them in their healing process.

It was in the midst of this period of early professional development that I met Peter. He joined one of the support groups I was leading and soon after came to see me individually. My first impression of him was of a young man who was kind, gentle, caring, and somewhat shy. He told me he was exploring a career as a professional helper and that he was new to campus and somewhat lonely. I listened to his feelings—both his strong desire to help others and his feelings of isolation. I told him about community service programs through our office and encouraged him to reach out to other members of the group. Peter continued to come see me regularly. He was 19, a college freshman, yet he appeared to have maturity about him far beyond his years. I found myself enjoying the time with him, and I was inspired by his desire to share his life in service to others.

During one of my individual meetings with Peter, he casually shared with me his experiences of sexual abuse. I was stunned to learn that Peter had been both a child victim of sexual abuse and, more recently, a child abuse perpetrator. He revealed to me his feelings of grief at the loss of his own childhood and his shame at becoming who he most despised, a man who hurt young children. Suddenly I found myself having to balance several new and conflicting roles at once—therapist, advocate, resource person, mandated reporter, and protector of young children. I also found myself struggling to maintain my positive feelings toward Peter and the focus on providing a caring presence while also needing to make decisions about an appropriate course of action. I knew I was in over my head and that I needed to reach out to my cofacilitator for help.

As a counselor, my cofacilitator embodied characteristics that were in many ways my opposite. He was older, reserved, and cautious. When confronting difficult situations, he frequently sighed, which I took to be a sign of weariness. And, while he was, perhaps rightfully so, a bit annoyed by my optimism and energy, I was, in turn, frustrated by his reticence and frequently gloomy outlook. Looking back now, I am reminded of the two sides of Skovholt's (2005) turtle image, which describe the need to balance both emotional involvement and emotional distance with a client to obtain an optimal level of counselor emotional attachment. I was the "underside of the turtle," the caring side that attaches easily to a client yet was vulnerable to being engulfed by another's pain; my cofacilitator was the "hard shell," the side that has more difficulty attaching to a client yet was able to shield himself from getting hurt.

As Skovholt (2005) maintains, and as it became increasingly evident as I continued working with Peter, both sides of the turtle are necessary in our work. I learned about how important it was to provide a consistently caring presence with Peter to let him know that I would be present with him unconditionally, no matter what pain or hurt he shared with me. I also learned, as time progressed, that I needed to keep a certain level of emotional distance, to maintain a separate space for reflection and self-care, to be effective in my work as a counselor.

Over the course of the next year, as Peter faced the "demons" of his past, he unleashed a succession of negative emotions he had previously held at bay, including anger, hurt, sadness, fear, and loss. He made frequent suicidal threats, most of which were not acted upon. At one point, he left me a note indicating that he had taken an overdose of medication and would not be returning. I contacted the staff at Peter's residence hall, spent several hours looking for him, and was awake most of that night. After finding him the next morning, having slept peacefully on a friend's sofa, I was angry, and I silently grappled with feelings of betrayal. Again, I turned to my cofacilitator for support, as he helped process my feelings and gave me the perspective I needed to see my work with Peter in a larger context. I learned that it was possible to "care too much" and that I needed to let go to be most effective in my work.

A short time later my cofacilitator located an out-of-state in-patient treatment center for Peter and assisted with arranging the financing to allow Peter to be admitted for the long-term treatment he clearly needed. After Peter left, I felt what many therapists feel after the transfer of a challenging client: a mixture of sadness and relief. I missed our working relationship and the opportunity to be a part of Peter's emerging healing process, but I was also relieved to have closure to the intense struggle I had regarding responsibility for the work in counseling and how to set appropriate limits.

The "lesson" and the challenge of my experience with Peter is one that I continue to deal with almost daily in my work as a teacher, mentor, researcher, and clinical supervisor. How do I truly and fully care for my students, mentees, supervisees, and their clients, while setting appropriate limits, to ensure that the work is truly empowering instead of disabling and also doesn't leave me depleted? It seems that as professional helpers we need to learn to live with the tension of this paradox—caring and simultaneously letting go. A danger is that, to avoid the tension and ambiguity of this paradox, we may turn to self-protection and project a "hard shell" with our clients and students.

A few years after Peter ended his work with me, I made a decision to switch my career from professional ministry to counseling psychology. Like many students who enter doctoral programs, I traveled across the country, leaving most ties with my former career, to begin a new life as a graduate student. One day during my doctoral internship, I received a telephone call. I was surprised to find that it was Peter, who had somehow tracked me down at my internship site. While we spoke only briefly, he told me he had called to thank me for all that I had done for him. He explained how much my consistent care and support had meant to him during that difficult year. He indicated that he had successfully completed the treatment program and was now working at a job that he enjoyed. In sum, he gave me a gift that we as therapists rarely receive, the gift of knowing the happy ending to the story.

While I was elated to know of Peter's success and moved by his words of gratitude, I was left wondering whether I had indeed been helpful to Peter and, if so, in what specific way? All things considered, I was left with the question: What are the most important factors that contribute to positive therapeutic gains? Carl

Rogers (1995) noted that in his early professional years, his focus was, "How can I treat, or cure, or change this person?" Later, he notes that his focus changed to, "How can I provide a relationship which this person may use for his own personal growth?" (p. 32).

Skovholt and Jennings (2004) note in their study of master therapists that successful therapeutic relationships are characterized by "boundaried generosity," compassion that is expressed within limits, as such limits facilitate client empowerment and enable therapists to maintain their own vitality. My work with Peter affirmed for me that my primary focus as a therapist, supervisor, and mentor needs to be aimed at two things: Fostering positive working relationships, which includes the ability to convey a depth of care for another or "unconditional love" (Kübler-Ross, 1997), and knowing when it is important to let go. Both of these appear to be essential for success in therapy. Discerning how to balance these two goals, providing a caring presence and letting go, is an ongoing and daily challenge for me but one that I would not trade for anything in the world! In sum, I am proud to call myself a counseling practitioner. Over the years, I have experienced much positive growth and change due to the relationships I have formed with clients, students, and other practitioners. I am deeply honored to be a part of this experience.

References

Kornfield, J. (1994). *Buddha's little instruction book.* New York: Bantam.

Kübler-Ross, E. (1997). *The wheel of life: A memoir of living and dying.* New York: Scribner.

Rogers, C. (1995). *On becoming a person: A therapist's view of psychotherapy.* Boston: Mariner Books.

Skovholt, T. (2005). The cycle of caring: A model of expertise in the helping professions. *Journal of Mental Health Counseling, 27,* 82-93.

Skovholt, T.M., & Jennings, L. (2004). *Master therapists: Exploring expertise in therapy and counseling.* Boston: Allyn & Bacon.

TRUTH TELLING
Pat Donahoe with Megan Phillips

I was honored to recently sit with Dr. Pat Donahoe in his office at Montana State University's Counseling and Psychological Services, the counseling center that he has been running for over 20 years. I came to this place as a predoctoral intern just 10 months ago. I sat in Pat's office on the cusp of my own career, ready to graduate and eager to find my place in the world of psychology. I have always admired Pat and felt connected to him not only as a senior practitioner but also as an authentic person who has never tried to hide himself from me. As Pat and I talked of the defining moments of his own career, I began to remember how it is I had come to be in this stage as a therapist myself. I have become somewhat hardened over in my quest to perfect my technique and do it "right." As we spoke, some of that hardened shell started to fall away, and I came to realize what has been at the center of my own journey in becoming a therapist. I am thankful for how the story he told me helped me remember how to be good at what I do. Pat and I decided that the most powerful way to share his story would be in the first person, written from Pat's perspective. Therefore, the words below are in his own voice, telling his own story. –Megan Phillips

If we dealt in truths all of our lives, I wouldn't have a job. Learning to tell the truth—to authentically connect with and express what is at the core of oneself—is central to what I do. I'm 31 years postdoc, still doing therapy and directing a counseling center where a wide range of difficult mental health issues walk through the front door every day. The moments in which I'm able to witness or be a part of an engagement with the truth, whether it is my client's, my own, or something we've generated together, continue to be the most powerful and transformative gifts that I believe the profession has to offer. Truth telling is at the core of why I enjoy what I do and why I still do it.

I remember when I was about 4 or 5 years postdoc, and a couple in their 30s sat in my office talking about what they wanted from each other. They had been together for 3 or 4 years and were wondering if they were capable of taking their relationship to the next level. I could see that they were dancing around a larger issue of intimacy, moving around each other in circles, and trying their best to avoid real confrontation. These two were bright. They were both articulate and fairly psychologically minded. They came into my office with their own respective histories of relationships and had both been previously married.

At one point she said to him, "That's not what I want from you. That's not what I really want." I don't remember specifically what she was speaking about, but I do remember what followed. I interpreted this as her trying to avoid making her partner feel trapped. It seemed that she felt that if she were to tell him what she actually *did* want, this would create distance between them. Trying to trust my intuition and take a risk, I said, "But I think the truth of the matter is that that is exactly what you want."

She looked at me for a moment, and then she turned to her partner and said to him, "That's right. That *is* what I really want from you." Then she paused, apparently reveling in some kind of reflective, almost trancelike state. After a few moments, I asked her what was going on for her in that moment.

She said simply, "It's amazing how centering the truth is."

In that short moment, I saw how powerful the truth was for her, for their relationship, and for me. It's something I hold onto, hearing that line in my head over and over throughout the years. I consider myself lucky in my work, having had a number of excellent mentors, though, to be honest, most of them have been my clients. The most significant lessons I have learned have come from what my clients have taught me about the essence of therapy. This woman's comment, in particular, was one of the most powerful and poignant of my career. In it was the punch line to a lesson about truth and authenticity that I have been learning my whole life.

In that moment that I responded to her, I did so based on some intuition I had. Paying attention to our intuition and acting on it is the truth we owe ourselves as therapists. During my predoctoral internship, I took a tape into supervision one day. I hadn't seen clients in a couple of years and so was deeply imbedded in an effort to get back on "therapeutic track" by integrating theory and technique into my practice. Once the tape had played for several minutes, my supervisor pressed the stop button and commented, "Pat, you're trying to hammer this guy with a technique. Just be yourself. The most important thing you have is who you are in this relationship. Just do that." This was another simple pearl of wisdom. He tried to teach me the importance of being genuine in the room with my clients. I had been trying to be a "therapist" rather than a real human being, sitting with another human being.

These stories capture the essence of therapy and of good mental health. We grow up in a culture that doesn't nurture truth telling. We learn to avoid, deny, dismiss, and suppress our truths. I'm talking about our affective truths—not being able to express how we are feeling and not being able to acknowledge what it is that we need or want to either others or ourselves. When I myself spent time in the client's chair, I needed to engage with my own truth for the work to be therapeutic. That was scary, as I had to be really honest with myself and then also do that in the presence of somebody else. I was lucky to have a therapist who fostered that process for me, creating conditions for truth telling that hadn't occurred for me before in my life.

David Schnarch (1991) talks a great deal about individuation and true intimacy. Any form of intimacy has more to do with our ability to be intimate with ourselves than it does our ability to be intimate with someone else. That's where we start—inside—and it's not easy, because it can be threatening when we either try to admit things to ourselves or present these to someone else we love and care about. Schnarch talks of self-validated intimacy, which is the kind in which we learn to speak our truths. We may or may not get validation back from others, but we speak our truth all the same. When you tell your truth in the presence of someone else, such as in the therapy room, there's a high potential for other-validated intimacy. At the same time, you can dabble in self-validated intimacy. That's what my client was doing, with a little prompting.

Therapy can set up conditions that provide a safe holding place to dabble in the truth, but it still presents a risk. As therapists, we try to establish these conditions, encouraging our clients to encounter their own truths and then to speak these to us. I think we hope that they will then go on and do so with others. We act as templates for truth telling and, in doing so, try to help our clients connect with their authentic selves. Winnicott (e.g., 1971) calls this the "true self"; I call it the truth; our clients call it an "epiphany." But it's in there all the same, all the time. As therapists, we have a responsibility to be present with our clients in this way. I say this directly to my clients: "One of the things I owe you is to speak the truth in here." That's not always easy, because I have my own needs for validation by the other and to be liked. But I try to strive for that all the same.

I'm old enough to have come into this profession when there wasn't much mentoring or training in working with intense issues such as eating disorders and sexual trauma. In many ways I have been self-taught, and once I'd learned this transformative lesson, I learned to follow my intuitions when I was working with such issues. Years later I'd attend a workshop or read something and realize that following my intuition had led me down the right path. It's been a gift to learn that I can trust this intuition. Many years back a coworker who knew and loved me well said to me, "You have a lot of power, and I'm not sure you're aware of it. I would really like to see you embrace your power." I think she was trying to tell me to be truthful to my clients.

I'm constantly amazed by the courageousness of our clients and the strength of the human spirit. People ask me who my heroes are, and I have to say, without reservation, that several of my heroes are my clients. They thrive in the face of unbelievable adversity. Connecting with more heroes and being honored with the presence of their true selves is what keeps me feeling alive in this work.

References

Schnarch, D. (1991). Constructing the sexual crucible: An integration of sexual and marital therapy. New York: W.W. Norton & Company, Inc.

Winnicott, D.W. (1971). *Playing and reality*. London: Tavistock Publications.

ON BECOMING A TEACHER
Amanda Lienau Purnell

My defining moment was a complete, utter failure on my part. I was a first-year assistant professor, and I was excited to be able to teach graduate students all the wonderful aspects of being a counselor. I imagined engaging discussions about cultural factors in counseling, complex theoretical discussions of client material, and the incredible challenge of trying new skills. I forgot that I did not start out at that place.

It seems to me that my development has become so completely folded into my current experience that it is difficult to parse out the changes over time. This may help explain how I was suddenly so far ahead of my beginning counseling students without realizing it. It's as if I can see only the whole tapestry of my knowledge and can no longer find the individual fibers, or, if I can find those fibers, I can't recall how I managed to weave them together into one complex whole. My understanding of the counseling process is intricately interwoven, rich and messy, full of different paths and possibilities.

During that first year, I felt completely overwhelmed by my desire to pass on knowledge to students that I felt was absolutely necessary but was unorganized in my mind. I knew that I would be partly responsible for the kinds of counselors my students would become, and the heaviness of this task weighed on my mind. How could I share all this knowledge in a way that would allow them to learn not only the knowledge but also their own preferences and the flexibility required for each unique client situation? I was so excited! I loved counseling, and I wanted my students to see all the wonderful aspects I loved so much. I wanted them to find the same passion that I had for the process.

With this passion, I threw everything I could think of into my classes. I was shocked to find that my students were left confused, overwhelmed, and a little defensive. To be frank, I blamed them at first. I thought, "Maybe they just aren't capable of the kind of complexity that counseling requires." I felt concerned that these students would be entering the counseling profession. Then I read the course evaluations I had the students complete in addition to the standard evaluation required by the university. My students told me that I was starting at the wrong place. They told me my readings were too complex and too numerous and that I covered too much information. They needed the information broken down into smaller parts and explained in more detail.

I had failed them.

I wanted to help them develop their own rich and complex maps of the counseling process, but I had left them with only a vague image, like a reflection of something far off. They couldn't see all that I saw. Once I got over my initial disappointment in myself as a teacher, I decided to change the way I taught.

I added more structure, more encouragement, and more empowerment. I taught one skill at a time and then had them practice and receive feedback on that skill alone. I gave them more control over their own learning by letting them choose areas they'd like to learn more about and then presenting their knowledge to the class. I paired students who came from different educational and cultural backgrounds to work together so that they would personally learn more about a person from a different background. Rather than telling them how to be culturally competent counselors, I had them select core articles from differing perspectives and debate the merits of each. As a result of these changes, I actually learned more from them and enjoyed my teaching a great deal more.

It was counterintuitive for me, initially, to realize that more learning occurred when I taught less. I felt that it was my responsibility to give them my knowledge. It sounds naïve when I write it down, but that's how I felt. Perhaps it was hard to grasp because it is as paradoxical as effective counseling can be. Often, we can do more when we do less. It is important that we keep out of the way of the other's (student's or client's) development. That is what I had to learn from my students.

What's remarkable to me is that I had already gone through this process as a counselor, yet I had failed to apply it to teaching. I vividly recall the time that I realized that I could not control a client. I could not make a client be at a place where I thought she or he should be. I had to meet my client where she or he was, and we needed to take the journey together. I remember how freeing that realization was for me. I felt like I had taken a great deal of weight off my shoulders.

The realization that effective teaching is like effective counseling has freed me to be a better and happier teacher. I feel less stress and more joy. My job doesn't feel like one so much anymore. I cannot possibly weave an entire tapestry of counseling expertise for my students, and I no longer try. They must weave their own. I have tried, through my own internal process of reflection and examination, to break down what I believe to be the fundamental elements of counseling. I then share these elements with my students so they can build their own structure, and, as a pleasant side effect, I also understand more about my core beliefs of what makes a good counselor.

My reflections on my early difficulties with teaching have helped me develop more as a person as well as a professional. This joint professional and personal growth has also made me a more cohesive person. My professional self is no longer broken down into elements that have differing assumptions. Because of this, the transfer of learning from all of my ongoing experiences is greater. I apply experiences from teaching, personal life, and clinical work across domains (with an eye to appropriateness and confidentiality). I was drawn to counseling because of the genuineness of the work. Counseling requires immersion in real, lived experience, and I find that process invigorating. It was initially less clear how I would connect that genuine experience to teaching.

The core insight is that, for me, it is all a developmental process. I will always be developing as a counselor, a teacher, and a human being. Just like my students, I cannot become fully realized immediately, even if I have access to all the knowledge available. It is a continual unfolding over time—they need time, I need time, we all need time to develop. This is what my students taught me.

STEPPING INTO THE FUTURE
Edward A. Delgado-Romero

In January 1999 on Super Bowl weekend, my wife, Amy, and I made the journey from Gainesville, Florida, to Newport Beach, California, to attend the inaugural National Multicultural Summit and Conference (NMSC). The summit promised to be a historical event; it was the first time divisions of the American Psychological Association (APA) had united to focus on the issue of multiculturalism in the United States. I chose to attend the conference because my practice, research, and service interests all revolved around multiculturalism. Personally, my experiences as a first-generation Latino and a son of immigrants made the conference relevant to my life as well.

On the long plane ride to California I was nervous with anticipation, and I felt that I was stepping into the unknown. My previous professional experiences had been at regional conferences, which were student focused. The NMSC would be my first exposure to psychology at the national level. I was nervous to meet people I had read about only in textbooks and was very concerned that I would not fit in or, worse, would be judged to be an impostor. I felt both pressure and excitement.

The trip gave me time to reflect on my career. When I was in graduate school my advisor, George Howard, assumed that I would become a professor at a research-intensive university. I worked diligently on developing my academic vitae and was fortunate enough to be part of several interesting research publications. However, my heart was not in pursuing an academic career at that time. I struggled to find my own voice in research because I was not passionate about the things I was researching. Luckily I found that passion in applied work and outreach to diverse populations and in the excitement of working full time in counseling. My supervisors encouraged me to develop my voice, and I wrote a personal narrative on racism that would become part of a special issue of the *Journal of Counseling and Development* (*JCD;* Delgado-Romero, 1999). After internship I accepted a job at a university counseling center where the commitment to multiculturalism was evident. In addition, I was classified as a clinical professor, which meant that in addition to providing therapy I could teach, conduct research, or serve on doctoral committees. I was excited to work at a counseling center, but I had to break the news to Dr. Howard that I would not be an academic. His reaction was not unexpected and at the same time comforting: He accepted my decision unconditionally and reassured me that what counted was that I was a good person and professional. It was the perfect thing to say.

Life as a counseling center psychologist was exciting and fast paced. I worked at a large comprehensive university with many opportunities for clinical work and advising students. The university also had a large Latino population, and my work with Latino clients spurred an intense time in my identity development as a Latino psychologist. I loved the part of my job where I spent time advising student groups, and I looked forward to teaching, mentoring, and administrating. However, providing therapy did not energize me, and I began to doubt my decision to work at a counseling center. Thus, the trip to California came at an opportune time for me to reflect on my career and any possible options that I might have.

When we arrived in California, Amy and I gathered our bags and boarded the shuttle bus to the hotel. Any apprehension and concern I had about attending the conference immediately melted away as other psychologists who were attending the conference greeted me. The first person I met was the guest editor of the *JCD* issue where my manuscript was in press. Madonna Constantine recognized me and greeted me warmly and said very positive things about my writing. I instantly felt like I might have something to contribute to the profession. From the moment I got on the shuttle bus, I felt a warmth and personal caring that had been missing from my professional life. It was that same personal caring that Latinos call *personalismo*, which stood in stark contrast to the individualism and impersonal judgment that I had expected and was used to in interactions in predominantly White environments.

This auspicious beginning continued and intensified once I reached the conference. The national response to the NMSC was overwhelming, and it had quickly sold out. The sheer amount of attendees overwhelmed the food service, yet I remember that the cramped conditions and long lines just made it seem more special. The NMSC was the first time in my professional life where I was surrounded by those who shared my commitment to multiculturalism. More importantly, it was the first time in my career that I stood in a room where professional people of color were the majority. In my career I had often been the only person of color, and I had often gone to great lengths to meet other professionals of color. And then there I was at NMSC, both surrounded and deeply connected to a ballroom of people who understood the struggles of racial and ethnic minorities and were committed to change. I met and was warmly greeted by psychologists of all races, but what touched me the most was sharing time with other Latino psychologists. Before the NMSC I had met a handful of Latino psychologists and was unaware of the rich history of Latinos in psychology. I sat in awe of Martha Bernal, the first Latina to earn a PhD in clinical psychology in the United States, as she talked about her life and career. I met her in the hallway after her talk and thanked her. Meeting Dr. Bernal helped me understand that I had place in the lineage of Latino psychologists and that it was now my turn to leave my comfort zone and make a contribution to the profession. The NMSC provided the greatest comfort I have ever experienced as a professional and at the same time represented the greatest challenge I had received in my career. I felt pushed, called, and inspired. I received the message from the elders that I was capable of much more that I thought I could do and that I was ready to step up. This calling was not one based on the need for individual achievement, but rather I received the message that I had gifts to give to the group. This message hit me in several ways and continued to repeat after the NMSC.

The final moment I remember of the NMSC was the keynote by Thomas Parham. He had us all holding hands and swaying back and forth with the energy in the room. Dr. Parham's message is one that continues to resonate. This work was not about personalities or meeting famous people. It was about connection and transformation. I didn't feel "starstruck"; rather, I felt a deep connection to others and the beginnings of a professional transformation. After the NMSC concluded Amy picked me up at the hotel, and we went to dinner. I excitedly told her about everything that I had seen and how much the conference had meant to me. She shared my excitement and encouraged me to take that excitement and energy and do something with it.

The NMSC sparked a personal and professional awakening within me that inspired me to claim a place in the national leadership of the profession. While previously I had been hesitant to attend national conferences, the NMSC and the people who attended it inspired me to join and become intensely involved on a national level. Personally, attending the NMSC inspired me and gave me the confidence and courage to develop my own voice and eventually led to my decision to pursue a career in academics on my own terms and to focus on my passion for multiculturalism.

Now, 10 years after the first NMSC, I am a tenured professor, a fellow of the APA, and president of the National Latina/o Psychological Association. The genesis of my success lies in many experiences, but the moment in which my career came into focus was the 1999 NMSC. At the time I thought I was stepping into the unknown, but I realize now that I was stepping into the future—the future of both the profession as well as my own.

Reference

Delgado-Romero, E.A. (1999). The face of racism. *Journal of Counseling and Development*, 77(1), 23–25.

THOUGHTS FROM THE BACKSEAT: NEITHER CLINICIAN NOR ACADEMICIAN
Julie Dorton Clark

Like most people, I have evolved through many identities via my ascribed and chosen roles as a woman of Native American heritage, daughter, sister, girlfriend, wife, parent, friend, banker, marketing manager, and small business owner, all of which have shaped who I am and why I pursued the PhD. As a nontraditional student, I mostly assumed I would be a clinician upon obtaining my doctorate, as I somehow thought my age would prohibit me from getting on the tenure track. However, when offered a faculty position, rather than continuing my work as a full-time counselor, I accepted, so I am, once again, at 40-something, spinning a new version of my identity.

Upon reflection I find that one of my first defining moments as a counselor was when my predoctoral internship training director persuaded me to "*own* my identity as a psychologist." These words struck a chord with me as they helped me understand and take ownership of the role my training had been preparing me for. Three years later, as an assistant professor, I am in the role of training future counselors and counseling psychologists, and what I have experienced over the course of the last five semesters—engaging in teaching, research, and service—is the restructuring of concepts about myself, not so much as a psychologist but as an academician.

I believe some of this restructuring to be developmental as I transition from graduate student and clinician to faculty member. But sometimes I wonder if I—as a person who walks in two cultural worlds, that of Native culture and that of mainstream culture—can adapt to what I find to be the intriguing, and sometimes perplexing, atmosphere of academia. It is from this perspective that I believe I am *currently experiencing* my second defining moment, as I strive to create meaningful distinctiveness as a researcher and teacher of future therapists. For me, meaningful distinctiveness in this field will be to prepare counselors and counseling psychologists to be culturally competent practitioners, to publish research that gives voice to those who have had none in the mental health literature, and to influence others to embrace and "live" the concepts of diversity and to truly be more accepting of those who are diverse.

Recently I've been reading *Neither Wolf nor Dog* (Nerburn, 2002), a gift from a great friend and potentially a required reading for the multicultural counseling course I teach. It is the narrative of a Native American elder, Dan, trying to explain precolonized indigenous ways and postcolonial trauma to the non-Native American author, Kent Nerburn. The author shares his personal reflections as he learns from the elder. It's a fascinating book as, over the course of a road trip, the author immerses himself in the elder's world and struggles with his own ethnicity, cultural values, and concepts about the world in which he lives.

There are many days I find that my own experiences parallel the book's storyline. I sometimes identify with the elder as I try to create a sense of understanding and acceptance from colleagues and students about the Native American experience and the importance of understanding historical influences and government policy when working with Native clients. Other times I feel like the author, as I sit in the backseat of this big Buick called academia, observing, listening, and learning from all that is around me.

While sitting in the backseat of this Buick I have pondered concepts such as *ivory tower, academic freedom,* and *the professorate.* According to Merriam-Webster (2001), the term *ivory tower* is "an impractical often escapist attitude marked by aloof lack of concern with or interest in practical matters or urgent problems" (p. 622). This definition seems to be in sharp contrast to the very reason I pursued the PhD, which was to be able to empower those who feel voiceless and to conduct research and teach in such a way that the field of psychology begins to address the mental health needs of oppressed groups.

Merriam-Webster (2001) defines *academic freedom* as "freedom to teach or to learn without interference" (p. 6). I have been tactfully mentored that academic freedom, or freedom from interference does come with tenure but that, until then, I should focus on publishing my research about diversity as opposed to pushing my diversity agenda to create change within the ivory tower. On these occasions I ask myself if I am giving up the basic notion of academic freedom to appease those who will decide whether I can be a member of the elite group called tenured faculty. Is it compulsory for me to agree with them or at least not threaten them or to exasperate them with my idealistic views about diversity, equality, and multiculturalism? These topics seem to make many, both students and colleagues, uncomfortable. It seems that this discomfort stems from issues related to power; by acknowledging that mainstream society holds power over the disenfranchised, those who hold the power may feel threatened if forced to acknowledge it. This is a struggle students in my multicultural class often experience as they come to grips with how power is wielded in our society.

As for the professorate, being an instructor in the classroom and engaging in the process of "teaching" is very different from simply "guiding" along a path to wellness or being in the here and now with a client. Within that context, instructing others, or "professing," is a verbal task to which I am slowly but surely adapting. I'm realizing that perhaps the struggle has been moving from a "listening" role— traditionally a highly valued skill in my Native culture—to "talking," an activity valued after one has listened and formulated thoughtful responses. As a counselor I do not view myself as the "expert;" yet, to students, professors are expected to be "experts." For me, it means finding a balance between being the expert yet enticing counselor trainees to come into the conversation to create an atmosphere of collaborative learning. Within my culture, "teacher" or "expert" may often be equated with "elder," a status I do not yet hold. Understanding this difference may help me to wrap my head around the idea that I *am* the teacher of those wishing to become counselors and from that aspect I do have wisdom to pass along.

Despite the occasions upon which these concerns arise, I try to keep in mind my overall goal: to teach and train culturally competent counselors and counseling psychologists and, through my research, to give voice to those who have historically had none. As I navigate my relatively new role of "professor," I often ask myself: Is the importance of my research and teaching in the field of psychology so valuable that I am willing to create new ways of being to adapt to the ivory tower atmosphere?

These are the same struggles—survival and adaptation—that Dan explains to Nerburn (2002) in *Neither Wolf nor Dog*. Adapting to survive was mandated upon my ancestors; it was not a choice. Part of the struggle for me is to sustain the voice of my ancestors, those who suffered so that I could walk in both worlds: to not let my voice, or the voices of other Native Americans, be silenced as has been done over the last several hundred years. Much like Kevin Costner's character in *Bull Durham* (1988), I still believe in a list of things that motivate me at the beginning and end of every day. I believe in the ideology that if we work together, collaboratively, we can accomplish more for the benefit of all; that if we work to help others, collegially, we will also benefit, at a personal level, in untold ways; and that when I die there will be at least one person whose life I've touched who is carrying on these same beliefs and at least one person who was given a voice—to speak about all those ugly things we don't like to talk about and prefer to pretend don't exist, like racism, oppression, and inequity.

Currently, I believe my identities as psychologist and researcher to be intact, as my curiosity about human behavior and the human condition is still at the heart of what I do. I suspect that within time I will own, and embrace, my identity as a professor. I believe I can make a difference in the field of psychology, especially when it comes to increasing awareness of multicultural and social justice issues. I am hopeful that my passion to guide and mold culturally competent therapists and to create change for underrepresented groups in the field of mental health will motivate me not only to reflect from the backseat of the Buick but also to adapt and survive within the ivory tower.

Reference

Merriam-Webster's Collegiate Dictionary, 10th ed. (2001). Springfield, MA: Merriam-Webster, Incorporated.

Nerburn, K. (2002). Neither wolf nor dog: On forgotten roads with an Indian elder. Novato, CA: New World Library.

CHAPTER SUMMARY

As mentioned in the beginning of this chapter, the novice professional is plagued by two different sentiments. The good news: Hooray! One has graduated and can begin to practice independently. The bad news: Oh no! One has graduated and has to begin to practice independently. The novice professional is setting out on the road without the training wheels that were there previously. The result of this may be excitement coupled with identity confusion, uncertainty about work with clients, or—yes—occasionally even feeling like one wishes one were back in graduate school again. The following are some themes that emerged for authors who focused on the novice professional phase of their development.

The Impostor

We often hear about the "impostor syndrome," or struggling with the transition to being seen as expert or professional, and it seems that this is never felt more strongly than during the Novice Professional phase of counselor development. No longer a student under close supervision yet not a seasoned veteran, novice professionals seem to fear that their clients, students, or colleagues will "discover" that they are, in fact, incompetent and should not be conducting therapy, teaching, or acting like psychologists. In this chapter, Delgado-Romero shares with us his fears at being seen as an impostor at his first professional conference. Now in this phase, Dorton Clark continues to be concerned with her role as "expert" in academia. Lienau Purnell talks about feeling like she has "failed" her students, and Hanson says that he felt "lost and helpless" with a client.

Identity Formation

We also see the novice professional as struggling to form an identity as a professional. Delgado-Romero and Dorton Clark both discuss the ambivalence they felt on the path to becoming academics. Dorton Clark specifically mentions trying to reconcile her cultural values with the independent, competitive values and atmosphere of the academic setting. Lienau Purcell shares her struggle with becoming a "teacher" and learning that good teaching *is* like good therapy.

Practicing Independently

Novice professionals in the counseling setting experience similar struggles to those in the academic setting, often related to the transition from being a heavily supervised student to a professional expected to work fairly independently. Several of our authors in this chapter discuss confusion about how to work with a client. They talk about the need to consult with colleagues as they wavered in their decisions or judgments about how to approach a case. Hage tells about both sides of the "turtle" and learning both to care for a client and to protect herself from getting hurt. Guinee describes sessions with a client that were "like riding the bus for 50 minutes sitting next to a stranger who says nothing."

This phase seems to show evidence, too, of transitioning from being a student and working under "the rules," or, as Dagley calls them, the "shoulds," to finding one's own voice as a therapist. Hanson mentions that during this phase, he was able to discover the importance of "creating a 'new therapy' for each client." Dagley learned from an "unsuccessful interaction" that freed him from "the shoulds." After a client interaction was seemingly unhelpful, he realized that sometimes it is better to not do things according to narrow, specific, theory-driven "rules." Guinee discusses his realization that he cannot "dictate the conditions of how [to] help people."

Learning From Our Clients

One of the strongest themes throughout the narratives in this phase, particularly for those in counseling settings, seems to be that of clients as teachers or students as teachers. Donahoe refers to clients as "mentors." Several authors share illustrations of client interactions during this phase that were formative and have since guided interactions with other clients. Dagley has a client who never returns and learns to "trust [his] own sense of how [he] was going to be helpful." Guinee has a client who does the opposite—his client returns, and returns, and returns, much to Guinee's bafflement. Guinee learns to look for the "likeable and valuable" in a client. Hanson has a client who challenges his sense of comfort with a content area. He discovers that therapy is uncertain and begins to expect "the unexpected." Hage encounters a client who forces her to consider the most effective way of balancing caring for the client while maintaining a level of emotional distance. Donahoe takes a risk with a client and is rewarded with the understanding that authenticity and the truth are powerful things.

QUESTIONS

1. Dagley discusses a case where he felt that he was closely following a theoretical approach and "doing the right thing" by asking a client to bring in her husband and she did not return. Have you had any cases in which the client did not return and you felt that it might have been due to something you said or did?

2. Dorton Clark and Delgado-Romero mention their cultural identity as playing a role in their professional identity. How do your cultural values match (or not match) those in the field of counseling? Have they played a role in the development of your own professional identity?

3. Hage talks about finding a balance between caring for clients and setting limits. Have you ever had a client for whom you felt you "cared too much?" How do you find this balance in your own work?

4. Hanson shares that he initially felt fairly confident about his work with a client because he was familiar with the content area; however, he later felt differently about his competence. He said he was really challenged by the work with this particular client. Conversely, Donahoe mentions times when he was able to successfully work with a client without having specific expertise in a content area. Have you had any similar experiences? How important is it for counselors and therapists to be fully familiar with the content of clients' presenting concerns?

5. Guinee mentions not particularly liking a client at the beginning of his work with him. How important is it for us to "like" our clients?

6

The Experienced Professional Phase

*E*xperienced professionals have had at least several years of experience as counselors. As their experience grows, they adopt the belief that there is not much that is new in the field. Accordingly, experienced professionals seek out ways to practice authentically and work to develop their own style, reflecting their unique values, interests, and personality. They begin to apply techniques and methods less rigidly as they develop their unique styles. Also evident at this phase is a growing appreciation for the strong role that the therapeutic relationship plays in promoting client progress. Carl Rogers (1995) summarized well the shift in focus that occurs for many therapists as they gain more experience:

> In my early professionals years I was asking the question: How can I treat, or cure, or change this person? Now I would phrase the question in this way: How can I provide a relationship which this person may use for his own personal growth? (p. 32).

Important experiences at this phase of development may include providing supervision to more novice counselors or branching out beyond one's initial "comfort zone" to experiment with different types of counseling experiences, such as consultation or teaching. Unlike more junior members of the field, who often "take their work home," experienced professionals are much more practiced and skilled at drawing emotional boundaries around their work, such that they avoid overidentification with clients. As a part of their work with clients, they also describe increasing comfort with the ambiguity that is constantly present in the work of the counselor and therapist. In the words of John Keats (1970), they practice the art of *negative capability* as they become more accustomed to "being in uncertainties, mysteries, doubts, without any irritable reaching after fact and reason" (p. 43). Experienced professionals understand that often, there are no clear answers to the questions that are raised in work with clients.

REFERENCES

Keats, J. (1970). *The letters of John Keats: A selection.* Oxford: Oxford University Press.

Rogers, C. (1995). *On becoming a person.* Boston: Mariner Books.

HOW COULD I TRUST THE WORLD TO HOLD ME STEADY
Salina Renninger

I was 24 years old and in my first year of graduate school. I went home for the holidays to learn that my mom had been sick for about a month and couldn't recover. The medical doctor thought it was a chest cold and left for her own vacation. I ended up taking my mom to the emergency room in our small Alaskan community. They drained her lungs of fluid. By Christmas Eve, my mom could not participate in preparing meals. Instead, her best friend and I made preparations together. Soon after, she was admitted to the local hospital. On New Year's Day my dad and I flew with her and a nurse to Seattle to see if doctors there could find what was wrong. After a day or two, I returned to school in the Midwest. Within 2 weeks, I was called back to Seattle as she wasn't doing well. Driving from the airport to the hospital my dad told my brother and me that Mom didn't have long to live. Soon after, my mother passed away from a rare form of lung cancer. She died 1 week after diagnosis.

Looking back at this event I marvel that I survived as well as I did. I was always independent, but I came from a close family. My mom lived far from me, but we were in close contact. I had always put forth effort to make my mom happy. So, now, could I survive without my mom? How could I continue to believe that love, joy, and connection would be steady for me when something I thought was unshakeable was so suddenly taken? How could I trust the world to hold me steady? How could I trust that what I loved wouldn't be taken suddenly, unfairly, and without warning? And how could I make sense of the fact that coupled with the immense loss was a strange sense of freedom—a sense that "I can do anything I want and my mom can't comment"? Was I a horrible person for feeling this way? It was an incredibly confusing time for me. It was a time when I was learning so much about myself, about the profession I was newly entering, and about what it meant to be an adult. It was a time when a person needs a mom.

The death of my mom challenged what I thought I knew and what I thought to be true. Before I lost my mom, I didn't know I could survive without her. But more importantly than that, I didn't know there would also be a relief coupled with the deepest loss I'd ever experienced. How shocking to learn that even in tragedy there could be something else. The gain in this situation wasn't worth the cost. I wouldn't choose it if I had a choice. But there is no denying the gain.

What does this have to do with therapy? How has it impacted my work? It has led me to have a deep trust in the possibility for growth and gain in the face of great pain and loss. Having lost my mom and allowing myself to explore this loss deeply has given me insight and courage to sit with clients who are suffering and to trust that there is a way out. It has taught me the value of holding that faith until clients can do it themselves.

Perhaps, however, most significant is discovering that I am more effective when I hold a "not knowing" stance. I haven't always been a good predictor of my own reactions to painful life experiences, so how could I possibly hold "truth" for a client? The loss of my mom was not totally what I thought it would be. With this loss I experienced unexpected pains and gifts. Thus, when I can listen carefully to a client, when I can forget "armchair psychology" and quit making interpretations, I am more able to find the unexpected pain and the gift in the client experience. It's not that I stop using my knowledge of theory or my skills for good helping, or providing useful education to clients. But a "not knowing" stance allows me to be present to hear the full story from the client's perspective and to take in, to see, and to use all that is there.

I find that when I falter from this stance I run the risk of making inaccurate assumptions and creating misunderstanding in the therapeutic relationship. Clients can end up feeling unheard, and I end up missing data that could inform our work and make it more effective. At times it has seemed an act of courage to maintain this stance when either the client or I am calling on me to take the "expert" role. I have found the "expert" role to be an alluring one at times. It is so much easier to have the answer, the quick and ready solution, to pretend that my years of education and professional experience give me the wisdom to hold the truth for the client.

It has been my experience that managing the tension between being the powerful "expert" and holding a stance of "not knowing" is a major task itself. Self-doubt can creep in when I am in a space of "not knowing." My thinking can get fuzzy, and I wonder, "Should I know? Would a good psychologist know? Will I be judged for not knowing?" I have to remind myself that there are multiple kinds of knowing, that I can rest secure in my knowledge and skill of how to help a client seek answers for what troubles him or her. When the client wants me to give the answer, I want to meet this demand to satisfy the request and also to decrease tension in the session. But when I remember the power of allowing some tension and discomfort, allowing the client to find his or her own pain and gifts, believing that this is possible, then the client has a chance to solve the issue and to take ownership of the solution. This lets the client find his or her own path rather than the path I might choose. Ultimately, this is the most satisfying response to a client who seeks answers. It is a response that honors each person for his or her unique and individual experiences.

At age 24, I wondered how could I continue to believe that love, joy, and connection would be steady for me when something I thought was unshakeable was so suddenly taken? How could I trust the world to hold me steady? My clients ask similar questions for themselves. I have found how to be patient with myself and how to find my own way. Now I work to help clients be patient with themselves as they find their own way through the varied joys and sorrows of life.

INTEGRATING PSYCHOTHERAPY
Sandra Kosse Kacher

After a nearly 30-year career as a psychotherapist, it's interesting to look back for examples of defining moments in my development. My early training came from my family (whose doesn't?). My parents' relationship could have been the template for the Bickerson's, and I believe I took in the words *just listen* in utero. Good guidance for a therapist! I've since learned that "just listening" doesn't come all that easily. Listening is receptive, but not passive, and it demands internal silence from the therapist. Hard to do when you're so full of good ideas and helpful advice!

I've been fascinated all along by the sense that the practice of psychotherapy is evolutionary. I remember thinking during my fifth year of practice that I was finally getting somewhere in terms of ease and confidence. That happened again around year 10. Both of those times were accompanied by a feeling of reduced tension and of sighs of relief. At last I knew what I was doing. Ha. My career has taught me that those moments of ease are typically followed by periods of confusion and unrest.

A period of significant unrest occurred a couple of years later. At that time there was a great deal of background noise in my head, the theme of which was doubt. Doubt that prompted questions: Is this really helping? Don't you think someone else could do a better job with this kind of client? I responded to that voice a few times by referring clients to people who had more expertise in certain areas. Often enough, the reports that came back suggested that the other therapist didn't have any better magic to offer. So my crisis of self-confidence became a larger doubt: Is therapy really helpful, after all? I moved from doubt to pessimism and, ultimately, cynicism. All of this occurred in the context of working for a health maintenance organization (HMO)—a context that undermined therapists' self-trust by actively sowing seeds of doubt about any psychotherapy except brief, solution-focused therapy. The basic message was that if it couldn't be fixed in six sessions or fewer, someone was malingering (probably the therapist). Thus, my personal crisis of confidence was abetted by a system that fundamentally mistrusted and misunderstood the therapy project.

As I look back on that period I think there was a kind of backlash happening. I think in the previous 10 to 20 years, therapy was overconfident. It took on more and more issues and suggested it had larger solutions than it actually had. A similar thing happened in the late eighties and nineties with the introduction of selective serotonin reuptake inhibitors (SSRIs), a new class of antidepressant medications. In our zeal to relieve suffering we overestimated the power of our product. As with psychotropic medications, therapy was overprescribed, and when it didn't deliver, people became disappointed and angry. I think the withdrawal of faith and funding for behavioral health in the HMO for which I worked was an expression of that angry disappointment.

On the other hand, I think that the nagging voice that keeps asking, "Is this really helpful? Is what I'm doing with my clients of real benefit?" is an important one. Even though the context in which I worked eroded my confidence in myself as a therapist and in therapy itself, there was still value in those questions. I remember two particular sessions. One was with a woman who was very depressed and whose conversation was pretty much one self-deprecating statement after another. I remarked that she seemed to have trouble accepting herself. Well, duh! Although it was almost worthless as a therapeutic intervention for her (akin to saying, "Well, you should probably try exercising" to someone who's too depressed to get off the couch), a light bulb did go off for me. I realized that most of the troubles my clients had could be traced to alienation from themselves or to self-rejection. Similarly, around that same time, a client and I were tracing the history of some of her painful feelings. We nicely identified family dynamics and early messages that set her up for these difficulties. It was a rather brilliant assessment, I thought, but then she looked at me and said something like, "So now what am I supposed to do?" These two moments challenged me in a fundamental way and began a process that changed not only how I practice psychotherapy but also where I practice it and with whom I collaborate.

There is much in my personal life that contributed to a sense that what I do could be better done by someone else. It turns out this is completely true when it comes to washing my kitchen floor but absolutely not true when it comes to practicing the work that I love. However, these two sessions highlighted for me the need to (1) get more pragmatic in what I offered clients (attending more intentionally to the "What do I do?" question); (2) work in a setting that is consistent with my beliefs; and (3) enlarge the team of people I work with.

In Tennessee people talk about rhododendron hells. This refers to places where the shrubs are so thick and interconnected that you really have to struggle to get through them and you sometimes doubt that you will. The years following those two sessions were like that. I was challenged to leave a secure employment and enter private practice at a time when it was a very insecure way to work. I also began to learn more about nutrition, meditation, and bodywork so that I could incorporate that knowledge into what I bring to clients or to know when and to whom to refer clients when the talking cure needs to be amplified. Another challenge is ongoing, and that is the challenge of living with doubt. I've reframed that now and see not always knowing what to do as a good thing, as a sign that my clients and I are in uncertainty or "don't know mind," as some Zen people name it. I believe in this as a place where creativity can flourish.

I find myself today seeing therapy in partnership with other practices such as bodywork, medication, contemplative practice, and nutrition. I have the opportunity to ask myself what therapy's contribution to healing is and to not overwhelm myself with the expectation that my contribution is supposed to do it all. In addition to my own private practice, I have found a part-time professional home working in an integrated program for the treatment of depression. I see clearly that multiple strategies are much better than just one, and I am fortunate to work once again with people who are excited and genuinely optimistic about what they're doing.

LIVING WITHOUT ANSWERS
Carolyn Bershad

As I look back professionally, my most recent "defining moment" is the shooting on our campus on February 14, 2008. I had been at Northern Illinois University for only 6 months, in my new position as clinical director at the Center for Counseling and Student Development. Ironically, I had finally begun to feel as though I knew what my job entailed, and I had begun to look ahead and think about things outside my immediate path. All that changed within a few minutes after learning that students had been shot, injured, and killed a couple of buildings away from our center. No one had prepared me for this, and while I found I could manage the tasks set before me, reorienting myself to working in a place where such violence had occurred was uncharted territory for me.

I knew immediately that the ripples of this event would continue through our campus for a long time. I knew that many lives would be affected, on our campus and beyond, and that the impact of this event would last over the days, weeks, and months ahead. But I didn't know what it would eventually mean to me.

I admit that I initially found it easier to focus on what others might need in those next hours, days, and weeks rather than on what the shooting meant to me. So many lives were touched by this event, and my energies were focused on how they were affected and what we as a center might do to help. I am still trying to fully understand what it meant to me, and I know that I still do not fully understand it. I can, however, say that it changed how I see my world of work, my counseling center world. It is no longer the same place for me.

Before the shooting, even though I had grown up in a large city full of violence, I had never expected to experience a campus shooting and had always thought of campuses as safe places; "bastions of learning," not "shooting galleries" where lives could be taken so easily.

Right after the shooting, I often felt fearful for my own safety, and for the safety of my staff, and wanted to find ways that I could make our center feel more secure. My mind went to thoughts of shooters coming into our offices, something I had never imagined in the past. Knapsacks were filled with bombs, knives, and guns. What was in those bags? What is that person holding behind his back? Why is she hiding her hands? Each person who came into our center was a potential terrorist. Even today, I sometimes wonder whether someone else will visit us again with violence.

This event painfully reminded me of how tenuous life is and that I should live as fully as possible. I keep thinking that "we should live as though each day is our last." But what does that really mean? I certainly know the fear of each day possibly being my last, worrying that another shooter would visit our campus and perhaps would even come to our center.

For me, the shooting was a reexamination of what it meant to work in a university counseling center. Work was no longer a safe haven. Being vulnerable and open became even more difficult and challenging, as the need for protection and safety came to the fore. My workplace became just another spot where I couldn't figure out what had happened, because what had happened just didn't make any sense to me. I've known people (including myself) in pain and have understood their pain, but I don't understand the kind of pain that leads to killing others.

Over the next few weeks after the shooting, as we focused on trying to help our students, staff, and faculty come to terms with what had happened, I had to continuously remind myself that some things cannot be understood. Instead, I had to find ways to actively make meaning from what had happened, and it has been a challenge. As a psychologist, it is strange to say to myself, "I just don't understand people."

And I found myself saying just that over and over again.

Ironically, I went into the social sciences, and ultimately psychology, because I like to "figure things out." But now I had to allow that not everything was understandable, or explainable. Growing up, I wanted to understand what led others to do things that I found hurtful or shaming. "Why?" was a central question for me and still is; it probably led me to this career. When I was young, I wanted to know: Why did that person hit me? Why did that person yell at my friend? Why would anyone want to hurt another? People intrigue me, and I enjoy working to understand what motivates others. I thought that if I could understand, I could make things different.

But sometimes there are just no good explanations and no good reasons why. As a child, I used to spend many hours reading at the public library after school, waiting for my parents to come home from work. I read story after story. The stories I read helped me make sense of the world by elucidating others' perspectives. Reading helped me develop my understanding of others. Yet stories also demonstrated that many bad things could happen to people who did not deserve them and that the world would continue on regardless.

It has helped to remember those stories about the limitations of understanding on my more difficult days, when no answers present themselves to explain why someone would come into a random classroom and shoot people. The scientist looks for answers, but they are sometimes not there or are not present in ways that make sense to us. Certainly, I can create hypotheses regarding what happened—I could make educated guesses. But I don't believe that I can *know*, and what I wonder about is how to empathize with the person who causes so many others so much pain. What I continue to grapple with is how to not consider the person who killed our students a monster, because doing so would be so much easier for me. I want to understand so I can have empathy, but I am not able.

Instead, I hope that, each day, what we do with our clients—the love and understanding we foster and develop—shows others how to live with their own pain, without the need to inflict their pain on others. I hope that our work shows that it is possible to be vulnerable and open with others and to risk one's safety, even in the face of great danger and fear. I hope that our responses to violence will become our defining moments, outpacing those violent acts in importance and weight.

I hope that we remember that it still important to ask why—and that it is even more important to learn how to live, and to live fully, without any answers.

COUNSELOR AS COMPASS: LIVING AND LEARNING IN THE STORM OF SUFFERING
Richard F. Ponton

In October 1997, I was standing alone in the brisk night as I watched our dog run in the yard. The events of the day were seeping into my consciousness like water into a sponge, gradually yet certainly. It was the first moment I had stopped since the early morning. The day passed before me, more like a slide show than a movie. My wife of 25 years, waking up to find that she could not speak. The look of panic on her face. Dressing our 4-year-old daughter and making the short trip to the hospital. The long wait in the emergency room. The parade of physicians, nurses, and technologists, followed by another long wait for test results. The nurse's announcement that she would be admitted, followed by the long wait for a room upstairs. And finally, the consult with the neurologist. He was an old Greek physician, a bit brusque, with the confidence of an expert and the bedside manner of Attila the Hun. "We are trying to schedule the operation with the surgeon for Tuesday morning; it will be Wednesday at the latest. Your wife has a brain tumor.... We won't know for sure how bad it is until the surgery."

There in the night, the images of the day passed through me like shards of broken glass. Oh my God, I thought, how will I do this? My wife, my daughter ... no family nearby ... and my job ... indeed, my two jobs. How will I do this all by myself? On that October night, in the midst of the pain and fear, I knew that I would not be doing it by myself. At that moment, in blind faith, I knew that I, my wife, and my daughter were all held in the hands of God. All that I had learned, all that I had professed to believe, and all that was promised in the faith that I hold enveloped me in a real and tangible way.

That was the first night of an 18-month journey that eventually led to Carol's death. She was diagnosed, after that first surgery, with a very malignant form of brain cancer. She suffered through two surgeries, stints in rehab centers, and learning how to talk and walk again. She suffered through a gradual awareness that she would not see her child go to first grade. She suffered through a series of lasts. She knew when she was celebrating her last Christmas and that her 44th birthday would be her last. Finally, as the suffering came to an end, she seemed to know that she would not see another morning. She died on February 20, 1999.

A colleague asked me a short time after Carol's death if being a counselor helped me to deal with her suffering. I remember pausing, taking a breath, and thinking about me the person and me the counselor standing in one body next to her bed, at her gravesite holding our daughter, and then being alone when everyone had left the funeral. I took another breath and simply responded, "No, I think it is more like being with her in her suffering helps me to be a counselor." As the years have passed since that journey, I have come to see two main themes that have shaped the counselor I have become—and continue to become.

The reflective experience of my own journey of suffering has changed the meaning of empathy for me. Like all novice counselors, I learned about empathy in my first course in counseling. Like all counselor educators, I taught empathic listening and responding to novice counselors in their first course. In the language of Elizabeth Lessor (2005), what was "broken open" for me by Carol's death was the mystery and sacredness of suffering—mine and that of my clients. Suffering, a natural and inevitable part of the human condition, is often what brings clients to counselors. Suffering is more than pain, more than illness, more than confusion. Suffering is the person's response to those internal or external events that challenge one's wholeness, one's sense of self. There is a relatively small thread of discussion in the literature of counseling and therapy about suffering and an even smaller thread in the medical literature. Perhaps, this is because we, in our respective healing professions, somehow look on suffering as tangential to the actual problem. Indeed, the surgeon is less concerned with the patient's fear about how life has been and will be changed by the malady than with the malady itself.

Likewise, we as counselors concern ourselves with this or that strategy for change for our clients. They, however, may suffer as their very understanding of themselves has been shaken by the events, internal or external, that have brought them to us. Beyond empathy is the compassionate affective response to this suffering in clients. This response invites me, the counselor, to stand with my clients in the midst of the confusion and fear. It invites me to feel the weight on the chest, the shoulders, the back, the neck, and the legs as they carry the burden. The compassionate affective response allows me, the counselor, to understand that all the rational cognitions in the world, while helpful in the development of problem-solving strategies, won't take away clients' fears of losing what they know of themselves and having to replace it with some unknown. Clients' intrusive thoughts are not some symptom of an internal dysfunction; they are part of suffering. Suffering is a process of letting go. The dying patient lets go of life, dreams of the future, and the illusion of control. The suffering husband lets go of wife, mother, friend, dreams of the future, and illusion of control. The client suffering with addiction, the unemployed, the depressive, the grieving, the divorcing—each lets go of something, and all let go of dreams of the future and the illusion of control.

The second theme that has emerged from this reflective experience is that of hope. The resilience of the human spirit seems often to partner with suffering. Having been privileged to walk the journey of suffering with so many, I have been astounded that the letting go of dreams is so often followed by the weaving of new dreams and new hopes. The "I can't go on" of suffering is replaced by the "I must go on" of hope. The motivation for the change varies from one person to another. For one person it is some transcendental meaning; for another it is the common good; for another the children she is raising or the pet that needs him. Each person finds his or her way from letting go to creating anew.

By Christmas 1998, Carol could not talk or walk. She was in constant pain, and her body was clearly breaking down. That year (like most), there was a particular toy that was the rage, and parents were lining up at 4:00 AM to get one. At her bedside, I told a friend that I just couldn't add fighting other parents for a toy to my list of things to do and that our daughter would live without the toy. With that, Carol shook her head no. I, with some guilt—but convinced I was right—explained again that I thought this item would not be missed. Again, Carol shook her head. Two days later, in time for Christmas, I found not one but three of those toys in the closet. In the bag was a receipt from the previous August, a testament to Carol's "I must go on" of hope.

It is perhaps an outgrowth of this journey of suffering and hope that has reinforced in me a deep and cherished sense of humility. It is not I who makes change happen. It is not I who transforms experience. It is not I who comes to inspiring or inspired insight. Indeed, in the client's life and journey, I am powerless. I am powerless, but not ineffectual. The role of the counselor is that of compass. We do not steer the ship through the storm; rather, we provide information that allows the client to chart a course. Like the compass, we can know that, no matter how awful the storm, north doesn't change. If, with the client, I can find "north"—that reality within and beyond the client that, although threatened or obscured, will not change through the suffering—the steady announcing of its presence allows the client to build new dreams, without the illusion of control.

In October 2001, a new dream began for me as I married for a second time. Sharon and I have two children who are now teens. The new dream brings new hopes and new challenges with no illusion of control. My true north remains the same: "We are all in the hands of God."

Reference

Lessor, E. (2005). *Broken open: How difficult times can help us grow.* New York: Random House.

SAYING GOODBYE: ONE GEROPSYCHOLOGIST'S PERSPECTIVE
Tammi Vacha-Haase

When you specialize in working with older adults, and more specifically those who are at the most frail stages of life, therapy often ends due to the natural process of death. Thus, saying goodbye can happen in the last days or even hours of patients' lives. It can happen during a therapy session, as the patient is aware he or she will not be alive by the appointment time next week. Or the goodbye can happen later, and silently, after the patient has passed away.

Saying goodbye to each patient is unique, just as therapy with each patient is unique. No two persons are alike during life, and, thus, no two persons are alike at the time of their death. Each goodbye has helped me not only to understand but also to internalize that "you can't die if you don't live, and you can't live if you don't die."

What does this mean? It means that some people waste time worrying about the end of life, while others do not seem to focus on it enough, for if they were cognizant that time was finite, they might spend their time differently. Death is not something to fear; it is a natural consequence or outcome of being alive. As I have heard so logically stated, "No one gets out of this life alive." So my work as a geropsychologist stems from a perspective, a basic belief in the importance of focusing on the value of each and every day, and the significance of every interaction.

I remember the first time I had to say goodbye to one of my patients who was dying. He was a man in his 80s, whom I had known for only several weeks. As I was closing the session, he started to tell me the value of our short time together, wished me well, and shared that he would no longer be on this Earth by our appointment time next week. He eloquently spoke of flying with angels and having loving thoughts of the world that he left behind. I walked out of his room with tears in my eyes; it was only the beginning of the learning I would have ahead of me as my patients taught me the most important lessons of all: how to face death with courage and dignity and how to say goodbye to those who have cared for you.

Since that time, I have said goodbye to many of my patients; some situations were more emotional than others, and there are some that I will never forget. The woman who was sleeping, so I thought I would check on her later in the week—she died that night, without my having had the chance to say goodbye. She taught me the importance of never taking time for granted. Do not wait to see someone or do something that is important, as there may not be a second chance.

Or the man who planned his death down to the hour, writing out a daily chart of whom he would have come to visit, what activities he would do, and how and when he would restrict liquids to end his life. He shared with me the letters he had written to family and friends, outlining his reasoning and timeline. A very successful large-scale event planner prior to retirement, he taught me that people often die as they live and the importance of recognizing the congruency between the act of living and the process of death. As he said until the very end, "I am who I am."

I have one patient's favorite book from when she taught English at a community college; having no family, she offered it to me. I still enjoy reading her short notes in the margins of the pages and thinking about her courageous struggle at the end. I remember the final laugh with another patient, who called me a "head shrinker" at our first meeting. Years later she would refer to me as "Blondie," and no matter how ill, she could muster up the strength to say "hello" followed by one of these favorite nicknames. These patients taught me the importance of valuing time together and savoring the bonds that are formed.

I believe that saying goodbye has an ultimate value in providing closure for both the patient and me. But it can be tiring, and at times I start to feel sorry—not for my patients but for me. This, of course, is never an admirable position to be in, nor do I like the negative light I shine on myself. But it is hard to lose these wonderful older people, especially those who embraced death with incomprehensible strength and grace, as well as those who made the world a better place by their unique contributions, as on more than one occasion, the world has seemed different or less without them on this Earth.

In darker moments I have asked, "What about me?" or said, "I'm tired of losing people; I'm tired of hurting." But then I remember that I am a geropsychologist and that letting go of people and saying goodbye is a part of what I do. If I am successful at what I am there to do, I help older adults to live each day with the highest quality possible. Whether someone is 8 or 88, quality of life matters. And regardless of whether there is one more day, one more month, one more year, or one more decade to live, life matters. It is my role to help bolster my clients' emotional well-being in any way possible.

Thankfully time does have a way of healing, and so does remembering the natural developmental cycle of life. That is, as human beings our lives come full circle, and death and life are intricately intertwined. If I am happy that my clients have lived, I must also be accepting, if not happy, of their deaths. I know it is strange or even frightening for many to consider the word *happy* in relation to death. However, perhaps focusing on the value of life helps me to put the end, and thus the goodbye, into perspective. This is so simplistically highlighted by Dr. Seuss, who wrote, "Don't cry because it's over. Smile because it happened."

How do I continue to do this? I must simply practice what I preach. At times it is easier said than done, but I strive to see the value of each day and the significance of every encounter, including meeting new patients. For if I am overly saddened by the loss of a previous patient, then I cannot be fully present and will not be at my best for the next. They too deserve my full support and care at this time in their lives. I must let go of my sorrow, for if I wallow in it, I may lose today and tomorrow. The next patient needs me, or I would not have been asked to see him or her. It is always interesting how doing things for others can give us the strength we need to do for ourselves.

Over the years, I have learned more about myself and what I need to do for self-care in saying goodbye to my patients. I often take a minute after patients' deaths to think about them and what they shared during therapy sessions. I silently thank them for our time together. I end with my wishes for them, based on what I know of their individual beliefs about the end of life on this earth. And then a final word: goodbye.

I am sure that the saying, "It is better to have loved and lost than never to have loved at all" was not meant for the relationship that a geropsychologist has with patients. Yet I find meaning for my professional role in that well-known quote. Regardless of the loss I feel with each goodbye, I would rather have had the opportunity to work with my patients than never to have met them at all.

As I think about my work as a geropsychologist, it is clear that there has not been just one defining moment but many, each having a similar theme. The moments that I have said goodbye to patients have coalesced into an impactful experience in my development as an individual and a therapist. I have changed because of the time I have spent with patients who are no longer on this Earth. Although I believe that I will always struggle at some level to say goodbye, each ending is a part of my defining moment. And with each goodbye, I am grateful that I was there and that my patients are now a part of me.

Providing psychotherapy to older adults has been a wonderful opportunity to help those in need while also learning firsthand about living and dying. I would encourage therapists beginning to think about working with an older adult population to ask themselves why they want to work with geriatric patients. I would tell them to make sure to be clear about their views on life and death. And, I would ask them how they are at letting go and saying goodbye.

WITH GREAT TRAGEDY COMES GREAT STRENGTH
Elizabeth A. Garcia

Valentine's Day 2008, I immediately felt a sense of excitement upon waking—that is, after I picked myself up off the floor from tripping over two dogs that like to sleep a little too close to the bed. My husband took the day off from work so we could have dinner at a restaurant in town (one of those restaurants that you never go to unless it is a special occasion). I decided to wear heels that day, something I never wore, especially at work; I wanted to look special for my husband. You see, we never really celebrated Valentine's Day before; he has a history of bad luck with the day, but I wanted to make sure this one was special.

I have learned over the years to never take him for granted; his job in law enforcement is dangerous, and he puts his life at risk every day to protect the lives of others. I didn't want to miss an opportunity to celebrate our love, and I wanted to make this Valentine's Day a day to remember.

I headed to my university counseling center job at Northern Illinois University (NIU). The day went on as normal: clients, phone calls, progress notes. I was in a meeting that afternoon, and my mind was wandering to what delicious meal I might have that night (no disrespect to my supervisor, but I was hungry). A coworker knocked and opened the door before being asked to come in. He was pale, but relatively calm. He spoke quietly but with intensity. "A student said the police are not allowing anyone to cross the street. There was some kind of shooting." I laughed at my coworker and stood up. "This is exactly how rumors start," I said out loud. And then the "bat phone" rang—you know, that phone in your boss's office that *never* rings unless there is an emergency.

I went to the atrium of our building to do "rumor control." Staff members poured out of their offices, and as they looked out the window they began to hypothesize about what was happening. Because I am highly skilled at glaring, I did my best to show my disapproval in how their uncontrollable rumors were instilling panic in those around them. Unfortunately, they looked past my glares, so I moved to phase two: I stepped outside to prove to them that nothing was wrong.

I immediately regretted the need to prove them wrong; it was cold outside, and I had left my jacket in the office. I was grateful, however, that the expected snowstorm had not started. After only a few seconds, the pain from the cold began to dissipate, and I realized that something was *terribly* wrong. There were ambulances everywhere, and their sirens were so loud they echoed painfully in my ears. Not knowing what to do, I started pulling students inside our building and directing others to go straight home; we had threats of violence the previous semester, so I really thought this was just another threat. I soon realized that a campus shooting was no longer a rumor. While I desperately hoped it was some kind of drill, the undeniable pain and fear I saw on the students' faces in the ambulances confirmed otherwise.

I later learned that a graduate from Northern Illinois University returned to our campus and opened fire in a lecture hall injuring 21 people, killing 5 students, and then killing himself. My life, in that brief moment, changed.

After I came back inside the building, I volunteered to cross campus to go to a residence hall close to the location of the shooting. I had just talked to my husband, and he feared for my safety; he wanted me to come home, and, when I said no, he begged to come to campus. As I think back, I know that, at the time, I still didn't fully understand what was happening; I was in "crisis mode." As I rushed across campus to get to the residence hall, I wondered, "Why in the world did I wear these shoes today?" And then I remembered: It was Valentine's Day, a day to celebrate our love and a day to prove to my husband that his bad Valentine's Day luck had ended.

I spent several hours in the residence hall; I went door to door checking on students. Some were crying; some were obsessively looking at the television waiting for answers; others were looking out their windows describing to their friends what they saw as they ran from the building to their rooms. Yet others played video games and acted like it was any other day of the week. Everything seemed to be in slow motion, and time lost its meaning.

Hours later, physically exhausted and emotionally drained, the adrenaline of the immediate crisis was starting to fade; I decided to return to our office. As I stepped outside the residence hall, there were spotlights everywhere, and the sounds of helicopters echoed in the lit-up sky. It was dark, but I had never felt so exposed and so vulnerable. There were police officers everywhere with guns, *big* guns, *lots* of big guns. I thought about my husband and the irony of the situation. He is the one who has the dangerous job. It is supposed to be my husband who has to worry about people shooting one another, not me. And a sense of guilt crept over me; I wanted this Valentine's Day to be memorable, but not like this.

In the days that followed, my coworkers and I functioned on very little sleep. The time we spent at home was in the arms of our loved ones, and for me it included hours of playtime with two dogs that had no understanding of my heartache yet had every intention of helping me forget the pain. Parents held their children, partners embraced, and prayers and questions to higher powers were abundant. I went to church that weekend and asked my pastor why; he didn't really have an answer.

At our counseling center, our daily tasks and responsibilities were multiplied. We saw more students, heard more traumatic stories, and lived through more threats of violence. But the most challenging task was helping a community heal, a community that survived the very trauma I experienced with them. I felt helpless, and I too was hurting.

In the field of psychology, we all learn to be empathic and genuine, and we all understand the importance of good listening skills; we even practice them in school. What the textbooks don't teach us is how to be committed and empathic to others when we experience our own tragedy, when we ourselves are having our own emotional reactions to trauma. Someone said to me, "This is what you went to school for." While I know the person was trying only to be supportive, I thought to myself, "Well nuts, I must have missed the Your Campus Has a Shooting 101 class." When our personal safety is at risk and when we feel vulnerable, we as humans need to turn to those who nurse our wounds. For me, it was my husband, my friends, my colleagues, and, of course, my dogs.

Within a few days of the shooting, I was given an opportunity to work with the Animal Assisted Crisis Response Team, a nonprofit volunteer organization that specially trains human–canine teams to respond to disaster and trauma and to promote emotional healing. Being given the opportunity to share the gift of canine healing was a dream come true and something I will never forget. I had been interested in animal-assisted therapy for quite some time and was open to this experience, but I wondered how the NIU community would respond to therapy dogs. Would people experience the unconditional love that I had experienced with my own dogs? Would they think it was "cute" but not truly effective? Prepared with dog bones and bottles of air-freshening spray, I opened the office doors and welcomed the human–canine teams. Before I could fully introduce the team to the counseling center staff, I found myself tripping over my coworkers who were on the floor holding, actually *squeezing* the dogs. I stepped back and heard gratitude being expressed, and that was just from my coworkers.

It is hard to fully explain the reaction that the community had to the presence of the dogs. Our students flocked to them and would often call our office not necessarily wanting to talk to counselors but wanting to know where the dogs were. They were even "profiled" in the student newspaper, everything you could want to know about them: their nicknames, their tricks, their favorite toys. The dogs were recognized everywhere: on the buses, at the basketball games. The students even honked their horns and called out their names as they drove by them on the streets.

For me, witnessing the power of the human–canine bond redefined what therapy is and can be. The dogs provided safety, normalcy, a reason to laugh, and a reason to have hope for the future. As people nuzzled their faces in their fur, they would tell the dogs their painful stories, and the dogs willingly accepted their pain with *honor*; they were committed to helping us heal. While nothing can ever take away the pain the community experienced from the shooting, these dogs eased our heartache tremendously.

Saying goodbye to the Animal Assisted Crisis Response team was particularly difficult. The team not only had a positive impact on the community but also provided the counseling center staff with endless support and encouragement during the weeks following the shooting. I became anxious as I wondered if I could effectively reach the community in the same way. I soon realized that I needed to trust myself. I needed to trust my training. I needed to believe that with this tragedy, a strength developed within my core to guide me as I helped my community heal.

Following the tragedy, the campus and the surrounding communities were plastered with memorial ribbons and the words, "Forward, Together Forward." Sometimes these were reminders of those who lost their lives and those who lost their innocence, and, other times, they were symbols of the strength we inherited to move forward in our lives as stronger men and women. As the university community approached the close of our first year following the shooting, the ribbons were not as noticeable and the words, "Forward, Together Forward" seemed to blend effortlessly into our campus surroundings. I was reminded of the once hazy details—the details that transformed a terrible tragedy into a defining experience, both professionally and personally.

I will never know what my life would be today if the individual who opened fire in a classroom on Valentine's Day at 3:06 PM had acted differently. While I would erase this experience and the pain it caused if I could, I know that this is simply not possible. But what is possible is sharing the lessons I have learned to help other professionals heal after tragedy. I have learned the importance of turning to those who can nurture our wounds. I have learned to live each day to the fullest and never take life for granted. I have learned that comfortable shoes will take you far and that it is okay to take time to sit with a dog and look deep into its eyes to be reminded of a more innocent time. I have learned to never forget the past but to use the memory of the pain to find the courage within to move forward. And I have learned that with great tragedy comes great strength. I am honored to have shared this experience with my community, and I am committed to moving Forward, Together Forward.

WORKPLACE TRANSITION AT MIDLIFE
Sarah L. Hastings

At age 43, I am quite literally a midcareer counselor, with 21 years of training and practice behind me and—hopefully—as many years or more ahead. This midpoint in my career has been a time of transition. Two short years ago, I left my position at a university counseling center, a job I had aspired to for most of my professional life, and began a new position as an academic.

I suppose I have always had a foot in both the academic and practice worlds. Even 15 years ago, as I crafted doctoral admissions essays regarding my career goals, I struggled to choose between visions of myself as a clinician and as a professor. At the conclusion of my formal training, however, practice called to me. I had been honing therapeutic skills for such a long time, it made sense to put them to the test. I worked in a number of clinical settings but eventually found my place in a university counseling center.

Counseling center work fit me well. This setting is one of the few places left where managed care does not dictate clinical decisions and where therapists still are involved in prevention, consultation, and psychoeducation. I credit my counseling center supervisors and mentors with much of my professional fine-tuning. It was in the counseling center where I learned to balance a desire to help with attention to an internal alarm signaling someone needing more than I could provide. This was not easy for me. I struggled with turning clients away who perhaps needed more comprehensive services, especially given that they had asked for help on campus. Of course, we tried to arrange for counseling elsewhere through referrals, but often clients simply did not follow through—a referral meant they had to sacrifice confidentiality to access their parents' health insurance or that they had to drive some distance to see another counselor. Nonetheless, the services we could provide were limited, with minimal after-hours coverage and no case management support. Sometimes, the ethical responsibility of nonmaleficence or "do no harm" prompted us to turn away clients and urge them to seek a more intensive level of care. It's a difficult ethical decision for a university counselor, but I learned, with the help of more seasoned professionals, to make it.

With practice, I developed clinical judgment by integrating the professional literature with my own empathic sense about what clients needed. Over time, I developed my own style and found my therapeutic voice. I discovered a way to challenge clients that involved playfulness and calmed client defensiveness. "Let me just play devil's advocate for a minute," I would say before zeroing in on a client's problematic belief or before offering an alternative perspective. "Help me understand…" and "Tell me more about…" served as tools to nudge at tender places. I was not very good at dealing with mandated clients or with those displaying narcissistic or antisocial features. I was fooled more than once by anorexia. Many of my clients got better. Some did not. Some sent letters of appreciation months or years after termination. Overall, clients said they found me accessible, empathic, and supportive. I was helpful to some and not so helpful to others. But I had settled in. I knew what I was doing. I believed I was good at my work, and I was comfortable.

Yet when I saw an announcement for an academic position in a new practitioner-oriented doctoral program, I did not think twice about throwing my hat into the ring. I became aware of a quiet, though persistent voice prompting me to carve out more time to reflect, to read, and to think. I had learned to enjoy facilitating group discussion and thought I was good at drawing connections between ideas. I knew I liked supervising the practicum students placed at my site. I reminded myself that one does not need to be miserable in a current job to move to a new one. Counseling theory teaches us vocational growth is intertwined with personal growth. When my family expressed excitement about the move, the stars seemed aligned, so to speak, for this transition.

But the transition has been anything but easy. In some ways I am starting over. I am needing to rediscover my research legs—to move into and embrace an identity as a "scholar." The academic culture is very different from the clinical culture. In many ways, I was unprepared for that. The values that drive academic culture involve the search for "truth" and the expansion of knowledge. One demonstrates expertise by knowing a great deal about some discrete aspect of one's field. Academic culture feels very individual—each faculty member is striving to make a name for himself or herself. One's counseling skills are less relevant than one's singular accomplishments in the discipline—usually measured by the number and quality of publications.

In contrast, the values that drive clinical practice—especially in counseling psychology and counselor education—emphasize promoting growth in others, helping people meet their goals, and practicing as a generalist. Clinical work typically requires us to see first where the client is and then to craft our intervention to meet the client's needs. In an academic setting, one looks within to chart one's own course. Academia requires less focus on others' needs than on what the individual scholar wants to demonstrate. The two worlds are very distinct and seem to call upon different skill sets and to attract different personality styles.

Given that I am still in the process of making this transition, I have not yet developed a perspective that neatly resolves this tension. Having served in a clinical setting for most of my professional life and, perhaps, having a personal temperament that lends itself to humanistic practice, I am still adjusting to the demands of an academic workplace. However, in describing these cultural differences, I do not intend to communicate regret for the decision I have made. In fact, I am grateful every day for the opportunities I find here. I love learning and reading. I enjoy discussing ideas and having permission to pursue tangents both in class and in discussions with students and colleagues. I have also found that what I loved about therapy translated to what I enjoy in teaching and mentoring students. The interpersonal connection that characterized my work with clients remains my primary tool as an instructor. I strive to ensure that content resonates personally with students, because if it does not prompt students to reflect on their own experiences and to connect intellect with emotion, it has little relevance.

As I continue my third year as a faculty member, my energy is directed toward my research—toward moving from ideas and data collection to the writing and application of my findings. This feels like the hardest part of developing myself as a scholar. I am grateful the field is still wide open in the sense that there is room for discovery in so many areas. My challenge has been pruning ideas in the hopes of narrowing my inquiry to something manageable.

Because I am in the middle of this change, I cannot yet pronounce my conclusions about it. Tenure is still 2 years away. When I began this job as an assistant professor, I worried whether my students would find my lectures interesting, whether they would find me credible, whether I could manage the advising, planning, supervising, grading, committee involvement, and research expectations. That anxiety seems far away now. I am no longer consciously aware of these concerns—no longer asking myself, "Am I capable?" I am reminded that facing intimidating tasks requires chipping away at barriers a little at a time. This is a lesson the universe continues to send my way—just keep going, move ahead, keep your eyes on the road, don't be paralyzed by the fear, focus on what needs to be done now. Suddenly, I look up from the task and realize I am not afraid anymore, that life has carried on, and the fear that previously gripped me is no longer that salient.

I am also reminded that change spurs growth, whether that change is invited, as in my case, or it is thrust upon us. Significant, meaningful growth takes time, and often we don't know exactly where it will take us. In many ways this is counter to our Western notions about how change occurs. We are trained in counseling our clients to articulate concrete, measurable goals and to work toward these. While I do believe in the value of goal setting, of planning, and of monitoring one's movement in a desired direction, I also believe that sometimes life provides unexpected excursions that have something more powerful to offer. Until we emerge from those excursions, however, we will likely lack the perspective to know exactly what they have had to teach us.

LIFELONG CHALLENGE: RECONCILIATION OF VALUE DIFFERENCES
Changming Duan

As a Chinese American who immigrated to the United States as an adult, I found myself in a field of learning and service that was challenging and inspiring in a unique way. I felt I was being continuously tested to see if I was able to truly appreciate the cultural values of the people I served. Interestingly, I felt challenged and motivated to test myself to see if I could adequately address the value conflicts among the people I work with, our profession, and myself. My journey toward recognizing the role of different cultural values in counseling and reconciling value conflicts began with my very first experience of counseling and continues until this day. Every interaction with clients and students reenergizes my quest for this reconciliation.

I am ever indebted to my very first client, a 21-year-old White female commuter college student, whom I will call Amy. As an only child reared by a single mother, Amy and her mother were emotionally very close to each other. One issue we dealt with in counseling was her feelings of being torn between wanting to stay more involved in campus life and needing to drive 30 miles home every day to keep her mother from feeling lonely. After a few sessions, my supervisor suggested that I discuss the idea of moving away from home with Amy and roleplay with her ways in which she could start this conversation with her mother.

I lost sleep that night. To me, it was absolutely wrong for a daughter to move away from a mother who loved and needed her. The suggested intervention was way too individualistic in my opinion. This recognition of the difference between my values concerning the self and family and those of my supervisor (probably of my client as well) and our profession made me troubled. I even questioned my career choice. As a newcomer to the United States and to my training program, I had no courage to bring the issue up with my supervisor. So I did what I was asked while keeping the bad feelings about the intervention to myself. To add to my confusion about my role and what is success in counseling, the client brought me flowers at the end of that semester, thanking me for assisting her in pursuing the transition from living at home to living in an apartment near campus.

It became really clear right then, in the work with Amy, that I had to reconcile value conflicts as part of my training to be a counselor. I accepted the idea that I would need to leave all my values at home when working with Americans. In fact, I did just that, or at least attempted to, in the following years of training. However, several years later while working as a university counseling center staff psychologist, I realized that my solution to value conflicts only provided me with a false sense of comfort. Value-free counseling was neither desirable nor possible for me.

It happened when I began seeing an "angry" 19-year-old White college student who was required by her professor to receive counseling as a condition of being allowed to stay in the class. This client, whom I will call Erin, started the first session with the angry remark, "I hate counseling!" She subsequently disclosed that she had never received counseling but that her mother had. As a result of counseling, her mother felt "more independent" and "happier" and then divorced her father. Erin said that she and her three younger siblings were very angry and had not forgiven her mother for leaving or the counseling profession for separating her family.

This incident hit my "value-free" mindset head on and woke me up to a new challenge. I began to question my thinking about the role of counselor values again. Although I never knew exactly how the mother felt, I did learn that her children's anger and rejection did not allow her happiness to last. Perhaps at the time of counseling, needing to be independent and happy was what the mother reported to her counselor as the goal. I started to think, however, that simply delivering what she wanted at the time without sufficient consideration of possible consequences was, to say the least, irresponsible or even negligent. I realized that my operation of value-free counseling was over. I was determined to find a nonintrusive but facilitative role in counseling for my values while fully using myself as a helping agent in the therapeutic relationship. This has turned out to be a lifelong search and learning process.

In some ways, my processing of the work with Erin has lasted for a long time. I have continued to ask: What is the goal of counseling? How should we define desirable "outcome"? Shouldn't we see adjustment as more of an individual-in-relation phenomenon than an independent-individual phenomenon? Such questions provided a context for me to ponder the role of values in counseling and to reach a newer level of reconciliation between the counseling profession and my Chinese cultural heritage.

There have been many times when I worry that my values are sources of potential biases and even prejudice, from the perspective that the counselor should deliver what the client desires. However, when I view this issue from the angle that an effective counselor will help the client learn new ways of perceiving the world and of coping with life challenges, I believe that certain values of mine have contributed to positive therapeutic outcomes for my clients.

One key to the value reconciliation at this phase was when I began a deeper level of self-examination and recognized that the core of my biases was due to my tendency to see my values as better than those of others. I started pursuing a value-based understanding and enrichment approach, in which my values were used as references for understanding others. Without being "judgmental," my value-based perspectives could help clients see alternative possibilities.

As I have become more genuine in respecting different values, I have become a more comfortable and competent counselor. Yet the recognition that in a multicultural society, everyone is multicultural and changes constantly in their cultural orientations brought me new challenges. I am from a culture where sameness is desired and stability is preferred over differences and changes. Moreover, I am a middle-aged woman who values history and resists changes in values. My approach toward new reconciliations of values has been to expose myself to diverse experiences and to position myself as an old "young learner." The recent internationalization movement in counseling psychology further challenges and motivates me to become both internationally as well as multiculturally competent. There is much more to do to reconcile differences related to my Chinese cultural heritage, my Western educational background, and my professional obligations to the global community. My journey continues.

CHAPTER SUMMARY

Experienced professionals are at a midpoint in their careers, often with years of experience, knowledge, and practice behind them coupled with years of practice stretched ahead of them. They often have well-developed energy streams for the profession. They have integrated their professional and personal identities to develop their own unique counseling styles. In the words of Parker Palmer (2004), their developmental task is to join "soul and role."

Living the Questions and the Value of Not Knowing

What we hear in the defining moments of the authors in the experienced professional phase is a greater tolerance for ambiguity and more value placed on the role of "not knowing." We hear much less anxiety about "doing it right" and more of a focus on life's larger philosophical questions. Renninger speaks of the major task of "managing the tension" between the expert role and a stance of not knowing. She describes her belief that she is often more effective when she is fully present with a client and holds this stance of "not knowing." Kosse Kacher echoes these sentiments as she explains how she views "not always knowing what to do as a good thing." She explains that, for her, this is a space in which "creativity can flourish."

Bershad, in attempting to make sense of a senseless act, comes to understand for herself that she needs to continue to ask why and, at the same time, "to learn how to live, and to live fully, without any answers." This theme of not knowing and of living the questions is present in the stories of these experienced professionals. They are asking of themselves, and often of their clients, to do as Rilke (1993) asks us to do: "Be patient toward all that is unsolved in your heart and try to love the questions themselves" (p. 35).

The Impact of Loss and Trauma

Loss and trauma in our personal and professional lives influence us at any stage of development. However, experienced professionals may be at a unique place in their developmental arc in which they are vested enough in their professional identities to be able to more fully integrate the meaning of loss and trauma into their professional identities. Ponton writes of how the loss of his wife to cancer changed the way he viewed his clients' suffering and how he now feels moved by a "compassionate affective response" to essentially stand with the clients in their suffering. He also emerged from his loss with a sense of hope, in the knowledge that the human spirit is resilient. In the face of the loss of her mother, Renninger asks of herself, "How can I trust the world to hold me steady?" She found that she needs to be patient with herself and find her own way. She has also found that this experience of patience has translated into her work with clients; now she can be present with her clients as they work to find their way in the world.

As a geropsychologist, Vacha-Haase often has to say goodbye to her clients when they pass away. She shares the impact her older clients have had on her in addition to the lessons she takes from their passing, such as to never take time for granted. Finally, Garcia and Bershad both write about the same tragedy, a shooting at Northern Illinois University. Garcia seeks to create healing through her involvement with the Animal Assisted Crisis Response Team and strives to understand what strength can come from this tragedy. Bershad wrestles with the limits of her own understanding of the same event while challenging herself to continue to live without the answers.

Practicing Authentically

Experienced professionals are charting their own paths and finding a way to practice their profession that fits with their emerging or long-standing interests, personalities, and ethics. Hastings, after practicing in a college counseling center for nearly half of her career, found herself inviting a change and transitions into an academic position. There she crosses the cultural divide present between the academic and practice worlds. Duan, in integrating herself more fully in her professional role, found a way to effectively examine her own cultural worldview and to pursue a more multiculturally competent approach. Kosse Kacher took the leap into private practice at a time when that meant uncertainty, and, in doing so, she was able to incorporate a more integrative and, for her, authentic approach into her work with clients. Garcia incorporated a love for dogs into therapy to help heal the wounds of students and colleagues alike created by tragedy.

It is clear that these experienced professionals have the grounding that allows them to take leaps professionally and to come out better for it.

References

Palmer, P.J. (2004). *A hidden wholeness: The journey toward an undivided life.* San Francisco: John Wiley & Sons, Inc.

Rilke, R.M. (1993). *Letters to a young poet.* (Trans. M.D. Herter). New York: Norton.

QUESTIONS

1. Renninger and Ponton share how the loss of a loved one forever changed how they practice therapy. If you have experienced the loss of a loved one in your life, what lessons might you take from the loss that could influence your work with clients?
2. Several authors discuss the concept of "not knowing" or living with doubt as therapeutically significant for clients and therapists alike. Do you agree or disagree? How might this be therapeutic for clients?
3. Duan writes of her challenges in practicing value-free counseling and later decides that it is neither desirable nor possible for her. In her own process toward becoming a multiculturally competent counselor, she examines and identifies her own values and biases. What are some of your values or biases related to work with clients?
4. Garcia and Bershad both discuss their personal and professional reactions to a shooting at the university where they work. How do you think violence on campuses impacts the counseling centers/individual therapists on university/college campuses?
5. Which defining moment at the experienced professional phase strikes you as most meaningful or significant? Why?

7

The Senior Professional Phase

S enior professionals have more than 20 years of experience in the helping professions. They are well established and regarded as senior practitioners by others. They tend to have an integrated style that is authentic and individualized. In the spirit of generativity, providing mentoring to junior professionals becomes important at this phase. At the same time, loss is a resounding theme for senior professionals as they cope with the loss of their own important mentors through retirement or death. They are also confronted by the specter of future loss as they contemplate leaving the field through retirement.

A primary challenge for senior professionals is to steer clear of the twin siren songs of intellectual apathy and boredom resulting from performing routine tasks over and over again. Failure to do so can sometimes result in disengagement from client work. Finding new topics and addressing them with established skills can produce satisfying and engaging work for the senior practitioner.

THE 2004 TSUNAMI: AN AMERICAN PSYCHOLOGIST AND DISASTER RECOVERY IN THAILAND
John L. Romano

On December 26, 2004, a massive under-the-sea earthquake rocked Asia and parts of Africa, creating massive destruction and the loss of thousands of lives. Thailand was especially hard hit on its southern coast, noted for its breathtaking beaches, sunsets, and warm and welcoming people. The area is a favorite vacation destination, and on the day after Christmas, the resorts were filled with vacationers and Thai staff. During the next weeks the disaster would become a focal point of my work in Thailand and one of the most significant and meaningful experiences of my career.

My visit to Thailand had been planned for many months, as I was part of an interdisciplinary group of University of Minnesota (UM) and Thai faculty working on a Fulbright Partnership grant. My part of the project focused on the role and impact of psychology and counseling on Thai society. Little did I know how relevant this topic would be in the weeks following the tsunami. Despite my apprehension about traveling to Thailand in the aftermath of the disaster, after consulting with Thai colleagues, I decided to continue with my plans. I arrived in Bangkok on December 31.

I was warmly greeted by Thai colleagues. While the tsunami did not reach Bangkok directly, the effects of it were felt throughout the country, including among university students and faculty, some of whom had family and friends living in the affected region. Chulalongkorn University (CU) psychology faculty members, where I was housed, were making plans to assist in the tsunami-affected region. One faculty member visited the region to assess the situation. The faculty decided that a small group of graduate students and faculty members, including me, would visit one of the most devastated tsunami-affected areas, Phang Nga province, to offer mental health crisis relief and to develop plans for ongoing assistance. After nearly 40 years in the counseling and psychology fields as a practitioner, researcher, and teacher, this would be my first experience with disaster relief. It was also a first for others in our group. However, I believed that our training as counselors and psychologists would be helpful to the survivors of the disaster and that, as the most senior member, I would add support to the graduate students and younger faculty. While my planned project was placed on hold, the disaster work was certainly relevant to it. Prior to traveling to the region, we met as a group to discuss how we might assist in the recovery and also our roles, hopes and fears, and specific travel and housing details. We expressed much sadness about the loss of lives and the massive devastation to entire villages, schools, homes, and fishing vessels.

Once we arrived in Phang Nga province, Bann Nam Khem district, the real work began. All of us were apprehensive and not sure about how our work would proceed. We decided to begin our work at a larger camp, Bang Muang, where hundreds of tents were arranged to shelter over 3,000 survivors. Here we found families who had lost everything during the tsunami: loved ones, homes, and livelihoods. Many of the inhabitants were experiencing fatigue, sleeplessness, and fears associated with spirits and ghosts. Many of the children clung to their parents for security and safety. The world community rallied around the relief efforts to provide medical care, education, and sustenance.

Our team felt the pain of the survivors, and during our group meetings we discussed how we could help people deal with the disaster and their emotional anguish. We discussed how our knowledge and training in counseling and psychology could be relevant in this situation, especially since counseling and psychology are very foreign to people in this part of Thailand. As an outsider, I had the additional limitations of not knowing the language and having a limited knowledge of Thai culture. However, I also learned that several members of our group had similar limitations, as the dialect of the language and culture of the people from this region were different from other parts of Thailand. We decided that we could be most helpful by active listening as we visited the people in their tents, sat on the ground, and heard their stories and experiences related to the tsunami. I went on several of these visits, although more as support to my Thai colleagues. Periodically, one of my colleagues would give me a translated summary of the discussion, and I would participate as appropriate. Basically, we were there to offer psychological support to the people of the camp and to assess, with other mental health professionals, how to continue mental health relief efforts once people left the camp and began to rebuild their lives and communities.

The days in the camp were meaningful but also exhausting. The reports of the survivors were emotionally draining to hear, and tropical weather and camp conditions took their toll. We had a relief tent on site, where we would gather between interviews to discuss the previous and upcoming meetings with the survivors and would offer support and suggestions to each other. In addition, our team spent many hours late into the evening discussing the day's events, the reports of camp residents, and how we could assist them. The psychology graduate students told of the strong impact on them of what they heard during the interviews: for example, listening to a mother tell about her child being swept away by the wave and being powerless to help; or hearing another describe recurring nightmares and fears that the dead would reappear.

How does counseling and psychology help in these cases? As novice professionals, the Thai students asked what they could say or how they could help people feel less pain. They were searching for answers, never having faced clients with this degree of emotional distress. In fact, none of us, seasoned professional or novice, Thai or American, had had this type of experience previously. I asked them about Thai culture, and they looked to me for suggestions from Western psychology. In this situation, we were all novices. I encouraged members of our team to be mindful of the strengths that they brought to the survivors. I said their willingness to be present and listen was extremely important because sometimes "less is more." We were attempting not to probe, to diagnose, or to provide psychotherapy but to offer supportive listening during this time of emotional trauma. We were also gathering information and laying the ground work to meet mental health needs in the future. This latter goal was partially achieved through discussions with Thai mental health professionals, nurses, physicians, educators, and community leaders.

My interest and professional work emanating from my tsunami-related mental health work continues. The emotional scars on a population from a disaster like this do not end once the media headlines stop and physical structures are rebuilt. The losses and fears remain; therefore, it is important to maintain long-term connections to the people. Work continues in the region on several dimensions. A Thai doctoral student, whom I advised in the United States and who was a member of our team, was so greatly impacted by the tsunami that she changed her dissertation research to focus on the mental health needs of adolescents in Phang Nga province. She is now a psychology faculty member at CU and continues with mental health work in the tsunami-affected region. I continue to collaborate on research projects in the region.

Three and one-half years later, our research team visited Phang Nga province and conducted interviews with tsunami survivors as well as community stakeholders. Although the research team had made previous visits to the region, this was my first visit back. I was struck by the major improvements in roads and schools, rebuilt communities, tsunami warning systems, and a peaceful seaside memorial for victims of the tsunami. I was especially moved by the stories of survivors who told about their continuing struggles, including the added burdens of raising children due to the loss of parents or grandparents, the lack of funds for students to complete school, fears associated with the sea, and disruptions of employment and income due to reduced tourism. In terms of mental health, misunderstandings and stigma associated with seeking psychological help remain, as mental health professionals seek ways to provide preventive care in communities before personal situations reach crisis levels.

I continue to be impressed with the resiliency of the Thai survivors of the tsunami and the professionals who assist them. During the weeks after the tsunami, people who occupied tent shelters at the camp moved into temporary housing on the camp grounds and eventually relocated to their rebuilt towns and villages. Even in temporary housing, people were very grateful for the help received. I was struck by how quickly people began to rebuild their lives; one vivid example was flowers planted around the temporary houses. People of the region have rebounded from this terrible disaster. However, the loss of loved ones—child, spouse, parent—is not easily forgotten, nor are the fears associated with the possibility of another tsunami-like disaster occurring, especially for people who live and work by the sea. While we can see the physical reminders of the tsunami, such as the large boat washed up by the force of the tsunami in a field far from the sea, the emotional scars of surviving a disaster like the tsunami are not as obvious. Mental health work continues to address not only psychological issues related to the tsunami but also other mental health needs of the region.

Major mental health questions remain: How to identify people in need prior to their problems' reaching crisis levels? How are services best delivered? How do Western psychological theories/techniques/concepts apply in a non-Western culture? How can the stigma associated with seeking help for emotional distress be reduced? Who will supply funding to deliver culturally sensitive services? These questions are not unique to Thailand or a disaster situation, as I have confronted similar questions in the United States and other parts of the world where I have worked. However, my brief time providing disaster relief after the 2004 tsunami showed me an intensity of human suffering that I had not previously experienced, and these questions became prominent once again. I feel privileged to have worked within this context, and it has significantly enhanced my sensitivity and understanding of counseling and psychology as I apply them in my teaching, research, and practice.

CONFRONTATION AND CHANGE: GROWTH THROUGH DISCOMFORT
Susan Allstetter Neufeldt

What a shock! After nearly 30 years of continuous clinical practice and 10 years of training clinic directorship and supervision as a university lecturer, I thought I was tuned in to multicultural issues. I had attended workshops over many years and written a text (Neufeldt, 1999) for beginning supervisors with cultural ideas integrated into sample dialogues. Yet the clinical, counseling, and school psychology graduate students at the large state university where I worked had now written a plea to all faculty to incorporate culture into every aspect of training. They claimed that it was insufficiently integrated into every aspect of training, from statistics class to the training clinic. Students believed they had prepared the faculty by going to each member in advance to warn that a document was coming. One of my supervision students came to me with the advance notice, and I imagined that the actual message would be relatively benign. I didn't anticipation such a specific enunciation of where they felt we were falling down. As a person who believed she had integrated culture into her courses and the training clinic, to my dismayed surprise I felt attacked and defensive and slightly betrayed, as if my efforts had gone unnoticed.

The defining moment came during that afternoon's seminar of eight advanced graduate students who were engaged in supervision of junior students. They met with me for 3 hours in a small, dimly lit room where we routinely watched videotapes of supervision and engaged in frank critiques and discussion. The whole group, a diverse group, had formed a trusting bond. At our usual check-in, they spoke of their feelings about the faculty response to what they had presented.

Though they spoke in low voices, each person expressed deep disappointment and some anger at faculty defensiveness and criticism of the document. Some were uneasy about their advisors' responses to them, and many feared the negative reactions of their instructors and doctoral committee members. Yet they were resolute in their insistence that culture was not really being incorporated, despite the efforts instructors had made to include lessons on culture in nearly every course. They said one or two classes didn't indicate a general inclusion of culture.

I grew more and more uncomfortable and began to question them. I could feel myself grow red and sweaty and near tears as I spoke, as if I had been unfairly attacked. They listened and then made an effort to explain it to me. One African American student asked me, "Why is it that when faculty members criticize us, we are supposed to suck it up, but when we criticize the faculty, they get angry?" I considered the question and then replied, "Everyone reacts, sometimes defensively, but students feel less safe about expressing their feelings." He nodded. When we ended class, I think everyone felt heard, although we were not in agreement. I realized that their willingness to talk about their feelings with me was in itself a vote of confidence, however uncomfortable I felt. Yet as I look back, I realize how the feelings I expressed simply verified their feelings that faculty just didn't get it. In the most profound way I did not.

Over the summer, however, it must have been working on me outside of my awareness. I honestly don't know how the change came. But when I returned to teach and direct the clinic the following September, I suddenly realized that I had shifted my thinking in a very specific way. I could no longer think about culture as a single factor. Instead, I saw every exchange between people as a cultural interaction. The way we saw things, the way we experienced things, the way we lived in our families and in our society, the way we made decisions all depended on our cultural experience. Humbly I wrote my former supervision students and thanked them for making me see that everything has cultural transactions.

Though I have retired from the university, I now see that virtually everything we do has cultural implications. When talking with clients or serving on the board of our church or engaging with neighbors or reading newspaper articles, I see each aspect through the lens of culture. Once I had that lens, I could never go back.

Since my retirement from the university, I have been exploring wisdom and interviewing wise people. My wise interviewees all report some difficult challenge they encountered, whether personal rejection or a crippling bicycle accident, that led eventually to a reordering of their view of the world. In Piagetian terms, they had to accommodate their thinking to the new circumstance. Wisdom, like professional development, does not seem to come without some struggle. I believe that this uncomfortable and valuable experience moved me along the path toward the wisdom I hope to attain.

Reference

Neufeldt, S.A. (1999). *Supervision strategies for the first practicum* (2nd ed.). Alexandria, VA: American Counseling Association.

"POSITIVE"
Paul J. Schwartz

The year was 2003. The war in Iraq was beginning; Barack Obama formally launched his Senate bid; Tiger Woods was adjusting his swing. Several milestone events occurred in my life: I turned 50; I celebrated with my wife the 25th anniversary of both our wedding and our move to Brooklyn, New York, from Minneapolis, Minnesota; and I began adjusting to a new career as crisis counselor at an urban college. To use a golfing analogy, I am now on the "back nine" of life, but for the past 6 years, since finding my niche in college counseling, I've never felt more energized and alive in my profession. An epiphany occurred for me while being "roasted" at my 50th birthday party. After some critical thinking and reflection, I identified one remarkable season from my past practice that contained a "defining moment" in my professional development: working in the trenches as an HIV counselor.

I accepted a new position of social work AIDS coordinator at the Brooklyn Veterans Administration Medical Center. It is important to note that this was during the height of the epidemic in the United States—the late 1980s into the mid-1990s, before and during the advent of medicines that are now extending and greatly improving the quality of life for people living with HIV. This was an amazing time to be working in the social work and counseling fields. HIV and AIDS were very much in the news and the nation's consciousness. A sense of panic invaded urban areas. The epidemic carried with it tremendous social stigma and unwarranted fears of contagion; societal taboos of sex, including homosexuality at that time, drug addiction, and premature death demanded discussion; issues of confidentiality and disclosure were heightened; waves of loss, death, dying, and grief were continuous; and the rate of compassion fatigue among providers was huge. All of these converged on me in my new position, and due to the intensity of each issue, I grew quickly as a counselor.

I had received 5 days of intensive training at the New York City Department of Health, a requirement for becoming a certified HIV pre- and post-test counselor.

After beginning a designated HIV counseling and testing clinic, I performed hundreds of pre- and post-test counseling interventions including the dire task of providing clients with their HIV test results. Dozens of my clients tested HIV positive. These I followed as outpatients in the Infectious Disease (ID) Clinic through the course of their illness, many to their deaths. Most were Vietnam veterans, in the prime of their lives, people of color, former (and some current) intravenous drug users. Already marginalized from society due to inequality and racism, they had experienced the horrors of war and were then blamed unfairly for *that* unpopular war when returning home. Many overcame drug addiction and were living in new freedom, only to discover they had a terminal illness that carried a stigma that defined them as "modern-day lepers." It was this part of my job, the delivering and then sitting with someone after receiving an HIV-positive diagnosis, that became for me a defining moment.

Providing men and women who were in the prime of their lives news that would change their lives forever forced me into their world, confronting together our mortal condition. The training I received did not prepare me for the range of client reactions. Mr. A., with tears streaming down his face, stood up and pounded his fist into the wall, despairing over leaving behind his 8-year-old son, as he anticipated his imminent death. Usually, the news overwhelmed the client's coping abilities, especially because of the limited medical interventions at the time. I learned the importance of remaining very present with clients to counter the feelings of isolation that so often accompanied this cruel disease. Henri Nouwen wrote of healers being willing to enter into the painful condition of the wounded bringing assurance that they would not be left alone but would answer "man's desperate cry for a human response from his brother" (1979, p. 63).

An interesting dynamic developed. I discovered that in the course of an intense post-test counseling session, a special bond was formed between the client and me. This serendipitous union cemented a therapeutic relationship between us that deepened and enhanced our ongoing work together when confronting future crisis points. I learned the important truth that people cope with crises, even major ones, much in the same way they have dealt with previous crises experienced. Certainly, the veteran patients I worked with were familiar with crises. The integrity of many clinic patients was evident in those who persevered through tremendous hardships. Mr. B., a disabled Vietnam veteran, reacted to his positive test result with a stoic resolve, stating, "So what else can happen to me?" Our relationship developed over the years, during which he tried unsuccessfully to persuade his wife to be tested for HIV. She didn't want to know. One day during his ID Clinic appointment, he painfully told me that his wife was in the hospital with pneumocystic carinii pneumonia (PCP), an opportunistic infection indicating she had full-blown AIDS. Later that year, I was able to arrange for Mr. B. to receive a wish from a foundation that helps terminally ill patients. He merely asked to take his wife and the couple's four children to a fancy Manhattan restaurant and to have a family photo taken, since his wife's illness was at an advanced stage. I had the privilege to accompany Mr. B. and his family to the restaurant and to take the photo, which I had enlarged. The great meaning Mr. B. received from his humble wish, and the tears in his eyes when I presented him with the framed family photo, I will never forget.

It was back then when I first embraced the value of a strengths-based approach and began appreciating the reciprocal nature of counseling. Mr. C. was 6 years into his recovery from drug addiction when I told him his HIV test result was positive. I became a container for his pain as he struggled with how he would tell his ex-wife and much more, after she also tested positive. Drawing out Mr. C.'s existing strengths and resiliencies, he tapped into his inner resources and spiritual strength, allowing him to maintain his recovery and to remain hopeful even as he lost his eyesight due to cytomegalovirus (CMV) retinitis. I recognized how I benefited from those I helped and learned to truly appreciate, learn, and grow from people like Mr. C. Although this work was enormously challenging, it provided an opportunity for growth that would significantly inform my crisis and trauma work in the future.

Six years ago, I entered academia as crisis counselor and faculty member at New York City College of Technology, known as City Tech. My season working in the AIDS world yielded skills that I carried over into my work at the college. I learned to be comfortable in talking about sexual issues (very helpful when counseling college students!) and notably developed my "chops" for dealing with difficult, emotional material in counseling. The post-test counseling experience also helped me understand the role and value of process. How momentous and meaningful it was to join men and women in a life-changing moment and then to follow these HIV-infected individuals over time, often to their deaths, and to be a part of their inner growth and healing: reconciliation in relationships and making peace with self and, with the help of chaplains, their God. This has been called one type of "promotion" or "graduation." Now, I have the privilege of helping college students experience the value of process. This time, however, I can be part of their emotional healing and growth (both educationally and personally) over time, often to their college graduation!

Before, the challenge was fostering hope and renewing inner resources in terminally ill patients who experienced loss and isolation after hearing that fateful word, *positive*. Bolstered by those HIV counseling sessions, I can now be present to the fears of loss and isolation among college students and can help them to embrace a positive future, with possibilities.

Reference

Nouwen, Henri J.M. (1979). *The Wounded Healer*. New York: Image Books, Doubleday & Co., Inc.

GOING BEYOND BOUNDARIES: A FIVE-MINUTE CALL PROVOKES PALPABLE AND PROFOUND CHANGE
Laurie B. Mintz

When I was a predoctoral intern, I was in therapy. One moment in this therapy radically changed how I conceptualize therapy boundaries.

I had one particularly gut-wrenching session. I left the therapy room emotionally shaken. That evening, my telephone rang. Answering it, I was surprised to hear my therapist's voice. "I was just thinking about you and wanted to see how you were doing," she said. I told her that while I felt like a truck had run over me, I was actually doing fine. I said I appreciated her concern.

What I didn't say, because I didn't realize it until later, was that the phone call was profoundly therapeutic. Given the topic of my distress, a call from a caring, mother figure was exactly what I needed. It was a powerfully healing corrective emotional experience.

My therapist went beyond traditional therapy boundaries by calling me. By doing this, she taught me that sometimes these borders ought to be stretched for the client's benefit. Indeed, sometimes boundary pushing is *precisely* the therapeutic intervention needed to provide a corrective emotional experience for the client. Sometimes such corrective emotional experiences cannot be provided within the confines of the traditional therapy hour, room, or intervention. Had my therapist not called me, we would have had just another painful, yet good, session. I would have learned things at a cognitive and emotional level and eventually changed as a result. But, instead, in a flash her call provoked a palpable and profound shift in my emotional landscape. It resulted in deep, core change.

I have used this lesson in my work as a therapist. Sandra (pseudonym) is a prime example.

I saw Sandra for the first time when working at a college counseling center. On the intake form, she wrote that she was concerned about a problem with her boyfriend. During our first session, she curled into a fetal position and wouldn't make eye contact. We spent a couple of sessions like this: with her curled up in her chair with downcast eyes and me intermittently breaking the silence to tell her that I cared what was happening with her. Eventually, she spoke and revealed both present and past abuse. She was in a battering relationship and had endured abuse as a child.

She slowly told me her story, and for a long time she couldn't make eye contact as she did. Once, while she was telling her story and sobbing but still not looking at me, I asked what she needed from me. She said she would like me to hold her hands. I reached across our seats and held her hands as she told her story, continuing to look at the floor as she did. Eventually, she looked me in the eye periodically. By the end of therapy, she was fully holding my gaze and even joking about my shoe wardrobe being an important part of our early therapy.

Long before she could look beyond my shoes to my eyes, I left the counseling center for part-time private practice. The center had a policy against therapists taking clients with them, yet to end therapy at that point would have been to shatter the first trust she had developed with an adult figure. So I made arrangements to present her case to the center's director and clinical director, and both agreed that I should offer her the option to come to my private practice. Because she had no money, we worked out an arrangement for her to pay me $5 a week. There were some rough patches in her recovery, including times we needed to see each other several times a week and a couple of times that, once her own boundaries were intact, I called her to see if she was doing okay.

After about 5 years, Sandra was leading a different life. She was in a healthy relationship and had made the choice to confront her abusers. Her grades skyrocketed, as did her future orientation. She was accepted into a very prestigious graduate school in another city.

As we readied to say goodbye, we agreed that she could call for a therapy appointment anytime she was in town, pending permission and a release from any therapists she was currently seeing. We also agreed that she could write to me and I would always write back, although I would never initiate contact. We established that these letters could not be for the purpose of getting therapeutic support or advice by mail but simply for her to update me on developments in her life. As her last session approached, we discussed how to meaningfully and properly say goodbye. She decided that she wanted me to walk her to her car, hug her, and then stand behind her car waving goodbye as she drove off. She asked me to stand there and keep waving until she was out of sight and thus could no longer see me waving in the rearview mirror. She said she thought of this as her mother waving her off to college. I still remember standing there waving—and while she didn't see them, tears of pride and joy welled in my eyes as she drove away.

It has been about 18 years, and I am still in touch with Sandra. She has written to me through the years when good things, like graduation and marriage and promotions at work, happen in her life. I have kept my promise to always write back. Each year, without fail, she sends me a holiday card and updates me on her life. One year she sent me a Mother's Day card—designed for someone "like a mother." She is now a mother herself.

She comes to town once every few years, and every time she does we see each other—in the confines of my office for a therapy appointment. She takes great pleasure in paying full fee. At one point, she wanted to set up a bank account with thousands of dollars in it that I could draw from to pay myself to see a hypothetical pro bono abuse client who might contact me. I said that I understood the sentiment of wanting to give back and help someone else, but I gratefully declined.

I declined because therapy boundaries should never, ever be broken. Yet sometimes they must be intentionally stretched to allow us the ability to provide a corrective emotional experience for a client. I am eternally thankful that my therapist did so; her 5-minute boundary stretching provoked instantaneous, profound, and core emotional change, making me both a better person and a better therapist.

BREAKING THE RULES: USING SELF-DISCLOSURE TO BUILD A POWERFUL THERAPEUTIC CONNECTION
Marcia Hanlon

The jolt of a car crash and the crushing blow of a sibling death have defined my life and my career as a counselor. It's a recurring nightmare that first led me into the field of counseling and has provided a point of connection with many clients over the years.

It began my senior year in high school, in a small town outside Chicago. Two friends were killed on impact when their speeding car slid on wet autumn leaves into an 80-year-old pine tree in our neighbor's front yard. I heard the "boom" from inside my house, looked out to see what the noise was, recognized the car, and ran out the door.

As I ran toward the car, the passenger door slowly opened, and my friend Dan stumbled out. He was stunned and disoriented, so I went to him and bear-hugged him, moving him away from the car to safety. As we stood a few yards away, watching firefighters work to rescue the others still in the car, Dan slowly began to realize what was happening. He drew back and grabbed my shoulders, eyes blazing into mine as he said, "My brother has got to be all right!"

I tried to comfort him, saying, "It'll be all right, Dan." But we later learned that neither the driver nor Dan's brother—his twin—had survived the accident.

Eight years later, I was in Dan's shoes as I lay in a hospital emergency room, waiting to hear if my sister had survived surgery following the car accident we had just been through.

It was the evening of my birthday, and my sister Deb had arranged a surprise dinner gathering at a restaurant. I was running late, so she waited for me to pick her up. Deb got into the passenger side of my car, and I drove off, following her directions. At a four-way stop sign near the restaurant, I waited my turn and then drove into the intersection. At the same time, a large car from the right blew through the stop sign, slamming into the passenger side of my car, spinning us 100 yards or more.

My sister never regained consciousness. The paramedics took over, and I ended up on an emergency room cot with minor injuries while she was taken to surgery.

For 10 days, they kept her alive with machines. Having already been in therapy for a couple of months, my therapist became my lifeline. He would call daily and act as an outside person with whom I could openly share my fears and my guilt.

My therapist's presence through the trauma with my sister was much different from what I had experienced after the accident in high school. In high school, I, along with many other friends, had been the support for Dan as grief spread through our class. As the days turned into weeks and my high school friends moved on with their lives, I was left alone with a depression that came from depleting my inner resources and having no support to help me through what I had experienced in the aftermath of that accident.

The circumstances with my sister were different. Besides my therapist, my sister's pastor came to the hospital hours after we arrived in the emergency room that night, and throughout the 10 days he supported my parents and me as more of a grief counselor than a religious leader. He was present when we received word through my sister's husband that the machines keeping my sister alive had been turned off. "It's all over" were my brother-in-law's words, and my knees gave way as I began to sink to the floor, keening. But before I was halfway down, the pastor—a big bear of a man—grabbed me and enfolded me in his arms as I wept.

The next year, I entered graduate school, determined to turn a vague desire to help people into concrete skills and knowledge. My passion was working with college students, so soon after I graduated I began my career working in college counseling centers.

More than 20 years later, as director of counseling at a small private college in suburban Chicago, a professor walked into my office with a student. She explained that Tanya (pseudonym) was withdrawn and not doing well in her classes. She hoped I could help, and, with that, she left. I glanced at Tanya. She looked like she wanted to be anywhere else in the world except here in my office.

Our differences were obvious—I am a White, Scandinavian American, middle-aged woman from the suburbs; she was a 20-year-old African American woman, just a few years out of an urban housing project.

I asked about her professor's concerns but didn't push or pry. She told me she was sent to a counselor when she was 15 and she didn't like it at all. She stated that "crying is weak," while tears fell from her eyes. We agreed to meet later in the week.

When she arrived for the next appointment, she stood by the door and said she had a paper to write. I said, "Okay. Give me about a half hour." She moaned, so I said, "Twenty minutes." She didn't say anything. When I offered her a seat on the small couch, she said that she'd rather stand where she was, by the door. We talked about her paper and her life on campus. When 20 minutes was up, I gave her a card with another appointment, and she was out the door.

The third appointment, she came in, closed the door, and stood in her usual spot. I looked at my watch to let her know I was keeping track of the time. We chatted about spring break and about going home, during which she asked if she could sit down. I said, "Sure." But instead of going to the couch, she leaned her back against the wall and slid down to a sitting position on the floor. She continued to talk about home and her family, which led into a discussion about some health problems her mother and grandmother had. "So much death," she said.

Softly, I asked her, "Who died?"

"My brother. He was 9."

"How old were you?"

"Fifteen." And she began to tell her story. She, like me, had been driving when a car accident occurred, and her brother had died from his injuries.

As she continued with details of what happened, she drew her knees to her chest and held her head in her hands as tears streamed down her face. I quietly got out of my chair and sat down on the floor to her side, facing her. I gently put my hand on her arm and said, "Let it go, let it go." She sobbed, the tears and the memories shaking her to her very core.

After the tears slowed, we sat quietly, and she asked, "Do you believe in God?"

"Yes," I said.

"Do you go to church?"

"No."

After more questions about my spiritual views, she asked me if I'd answer any question. I said yes. She thought for a second and then asked me, "What's your favorite kind of ice cream?"

"Mint chocolate chip," I answered, and we both smiled.

Her choice in our first two meetings to stand by the door instead of truly entering the room and sitting on the couch was an indication of her hesitancy to invest in me or in the therapeutic relationship. When she looked at me, she didn't see a reflection of herself and probably thought, "How can this woman possibly understand my story and the depth of my pain?" Before she could open up, it was necessary for her to test my genuineness and trustworthiness. My flexibility to let her stand by the door and to respect her time limitations by ending our second meeting after 20 minutes was the first step in showing that I was there for her. It also was crucial for me to honestly answer her questions for her to believe that I could be trusted. When she finally opened up and shared the devastating tragedy that she had tried to bury deep inside her for years, I believed that my own self-disclosure was crucial to deepening our therapeutic relationship to begin the healing process.

She had run out of tears and was depleted and emotionally raw. I could feel that rawness. It felt as if she had taken me into her very soul, yet I was sitting there, detached. It was at that moment that I felt I could not leave her all alone with her heart opened, asking with her eyes, "Do you truly understand? Are you here with me, or am I once again facing this alone?"

So I said, "Have you heard the phrase, 'God works in mysterious ways'?" She nodded.

"This seems like one of those times," I said. She looked at me quizzically, and I continued, "The fact that you're here and that you've experienced this tragedy in your life seems like one of those times, because I lost my sister in the same way."

She looked at me more intensely as if to say, "Don't mess with me here." She asked, "Will you tell me about it sometime?" I told her I would.

The next week she sat on the couch and continued to for the many months we met. A few weeks after telling me her story, she asked me again about mine. So I told the story, while she sat perfectly still, hanging onto every word and welling up with tears.

"How do you get past it?" she asked, when I had finished.

"You never forget it," I said. "It's always with you. But its place in your mind becomes smaller as you let go of it and don't let it overshadow how you live day to day."

"Well, I hope that starts soon," she said, with a wry smile.

I smiled back, "Yes, I hope so, too."

Our relationship continued over a year, until she graduated, and our work together helped her grieve her loss, recognize the ways that burying her feelings had interfered in her life, and give her a start toward emotional healing. None of that could have happened without the deep therapeutic relationship we established, which was achieved through openness and self-disclosure. As new therapists, we're often taught to avoid self-disclosure because it can interfere with the necessary focus on our clients' issues. In this case, though, my years of experience in many therapeutic relationships taught me that it was crucial to build trust from the very beginning—if I wanted her to open up, I had to be open as well. Then when she did take a risk and tell her story, sharing my own similar experience provided her a sense of safety and hope—that I was someone who *did* understand.

"WE'VE GOT A LOVELY DAUGHTER"
Moshe Israelashvili

Four years ago, I entered a train in France on my way to a conference. When I got to my aisle, I heard, "Move your legs aside, Tinoket, and let this gentlemen approach his seat." It was an adult, speaking in my native language of Hebrew, to a girl who seemed about 7 years old. She was traveling with a family friend who asked her to move over. Tinoket moved so I could take my reserved seat in the train. Usually after being seated, people either look around, open a book they've brought, or simply fall asleep. However, for me, this time was different. I suddenly found myself startled while sitting in a seat next to the girl—"Is it possible that it is *her*?" I was wondering to myself. The girl's name was very unusual, but *I had heard that name once in the past.*

The story started about 11 years ago. A young woman, Bachura (all people in the story have pseudonyms), entered my university office and asked if she could talk with me. I said yes. She was a student in my class on school adjustment. During the course, she was actively involved and significantly contributing to the class discussions. Bachura closed the door, sat on a chair, and started to cry. I realized that she was suffering from a lot of pain at that moment, and I waited patiently until the tears stopped. After a while she told me that she had a boyfriend and that they loved each other and were planning to get married in the distant future.

Then she said, "Unfortunately, I discovered that I am pregnant, and my boyfriend wishes me to induce abortion." While she continued talking, I realized it was not only her boyfriend but also her parents who wished her to stop the pregnancy. Actually, they were not "waiting" for her agreement to do so; rather, they were "insisting" on her doing so "at once." I didn't know exactly why she was telling me—and not someone else—about her problem. Nevertheless, it was completely clear to me that the only issue that I should address at that moment was her well-being. But, wait a minute: In what terms should her well-being be defined? Is her welfare related to the abortion itself, or should her entire relationship with this boyfriend be considered? If she were to refuse her boyfriend's demand, would they still get married? How would she react if she knew that her boyfriend might break off their relationship if she insisted on delivering the baby? What kind of single mother might she be? What kind of relationship would she and her boyfriend have if she kept the baby and did marry him later? Speaking of the future and assuming that she might get married soon and depart from her parents' home, how important are her parents to her current well-being? What about the well-being of the newborn? In addition to the baby, is it really true that only *her* well-being should be considered? Wouldn't it be appropriate to talk to the boyfriend and the parents? Is it possible to talk to them?

In light of all these internal questions and debates, I did what I've learned is the most important, and surprisingly very obvious, thing to do to better approach the problem. I kept asking questions like, "Do you think you are ready to be a parent?" "What really attracts you to delivering the baby?"

It turned out that the more I was questioning her about her real attitude toward having an abortion, the more she was talking in definite terms against such a possibility. Moreover, gradually she started using words that labeled abortion of a first pregnancy as a risk factor. I realized that Bachura didn't care much about the pure existing scientific knowledge regarding the impact of abortion on the probability of future pregnancy; in her perception, the slightest danger of not becoming a parent in the future, due to having an abortion, was overshadowing all other potential negative implications of the decision to carry on with this pregnancy. Hence, I made up my mind that the most significant role I could play at that moment was to support her in implementing her already existing internal decision to deliver the baby.

In the following moments I found myself discussing several scenarios with her that might occur once she would announce her *final* decision not to have an abortion to her boyfriend and her parents. Meanwhile, internally, I'd been seriously wondering whether I was doing the right thing in focusing on her present well-being and ignoring all other present and future potential derivations of her decision.

After a while, Bachura left my room on her way to make her refusal announcement. Much later she called me to say that she had finally gotten married to her boyfriend, had given birth to a baby girl, and had given her the very unique name of *Tinoket*. Bachura said that for her, this baby girl was a very precious and unique person.

I did hear that name once in the past. Still hesitating as to whether I was doing the right thing, I turned to the little girl sitting next to me in the train and asked her about her mother's name. The girl answered me. "Oh," I said to the little girl, "I know your mother. By the way, please remind me of your father's name." The girl called her father by the name of Bachura's boyfriend. "Yes," I said, "somehow I am familiar with him as well."

Here I was, sitting in the train far away from my homeland, next to a girl about whom I've been involved in the decision to give her life and wondering about the role that destiny, chance, or God had in making this meeting happen. I found myself feeling such great relief. The girl was so cute!

Over the years, since the meeting in my office 11 years ago, I had intensively wondered about Bachura's well-being: What would have happened if she would have had the abortion? What price, if any, did she pay due to her decision to keep the baby? Does her joy of motherhood equal, or go beyond, the price she probably paid for standing up to her boyfriend and parents? Nevertheless, one question has not bothered me much over these years: Would I give the same advice to a "determined young female" who might ask for my advice in an identical circumstance. She was not a patient with a major mental health problem whose comprehension of reality was questionable. Rather, she was an ordinary person who found herself in normal—yet extremely difficult and stressful—circumstances and was in need of advice and support.

My personal experience as a counselor taught me that a person's understanding of what is best for himself or herself at the moment of help seeking should be seriously taken into account. Thus, from my point of view, proper counseling does not mean taking into account all potential consequences or being solely responsible for managing the client's situation. Rather, it has to do more with joining the other person and encouraging him or her to become the "case manager" who will implement the program he or she knows will work best. From a theoretical and empirical point of view, the fact that some people come to counseling to get confirmation of their attitudes and perceptions (Kelly, 2000) is not necessarily a problem. Sometimes they come to indicate their ideation of the best solution to their problem and are asking for the counselor's support in helping them approach that solution.

Upon returning to Israel, I searched for Bachura's telephone number and called her. After telling her about the unexpected meeting with her daughter (about which she already knew), I told her, "You've got a lovely daughter." She was silent for a second and answered me: "Yes, *We've* got a lovely daughter."

I didn't dare ask her who the *we* was she was talking about. Was she referring to herself and her husband? And me? The three of us?

Actually, the true answer to this question does not matter. Any answer is fine. No answer changes the profound and joyous moment of meeting the little girl on the train. It is one of the most precious moments in my life as a person and as a counselor.

Reference

Kelly, A.E. (2000). Helping construct desirable identities: A self-presentational view of psychotherapy. *Psychological Bulletin, 126,* 475–494.

THE LIMITS OF GOOD INTENTIONS
Daniel F. Detzner

It was an unusual offer and one I couldn't pass up: I was asked to permit a man convicted of double murder to take my class at the University of Minnesota where I was a young faculty member. He wouldn't be attending my class, but I was assured that he would complete all the assignments and more, if I would allow him to register. I arranged for several students to be his eyes and ears, taking notes and even telephoning on occasion to bring him up to date. Late in the semester several students came with me to the maximum-security prison to meet him and discuss the writing of final papers. None of us had ever been in a prison before, and none had ever had such close contact with a man convicted of first-degree murder. I could not have known then that I would work and collaborate with this man for more than 20 years, nor could I have predicted how much I would learn from him about the limits of good intentions.

This man was considered a model prisoner (identifying information has been altered) and was granted special privileges such as using the telephone more freely than others. He was a master at many things, including using the phone to network with prominent persons in the community. I was one of his most recent connections.

His success in the course, desire to be doing something positive while serving a life sentence, and hopes for eventual parole led him to initiate a unique nonprofit education organization within the prison walls. His contacts in the community became the Board of Directors, and over the 25 years I was involved with the organization, it became one of the most innovative ventures in the history of correctional education. Although the directors made policy, raised funds, and provided external credibility, my former student and his inmate staff handled the day-to-day administration of a higher education program that eventually enrolled 25 full-time inmate/students working toward bachelor's degrees.

The prison officials and those in the larger correctional community bragged about the program, which cost the taxpayers nothing, because it was financed through a telemarketing business, because it created a positive culture within the institution, and because it demonstrated, at least for a number of years, that something good could emanate from this unusual environment. I served on the board for a number of years, took on the title of vice president for education, and had daily telephone and monthly face-to-face contact with its leader and the student/inmates in the program. The program was such a success that when seven inmates in caps and gowns were graduating, the University of Minnesota president came to the prison to confer B.A. degrees on them to the delight of their families, the warden, and those who believed that higher education could serve as a rehabilitative force in the lives of serious transgressors.

The prisoner used the goodwill he created to engineer his release when he became eligible for parole. Everyone was certain that he was a different man from the one who entered the joint more than 17 years earlier. If ever there was an inmate who had proven himself, it was the charismatic president and chief executive officer of this unique higher education program.

A couple of years before his release I had left the board. I wanted time for other volunteer activities, and I was also becoming weary of the multiple daily phone calls and a bit concerned about some of the policies that gave, what I thought, was too much power to its inmate president. We continued to be in contact, as he considered me one of his friends although I thought of our relationship as more professional. I spoke at the release party he threw for himself at the on-campus hotel and later invited him to my home for dinner. My young daughters were intrigued by his warmth and friendliness and his delight with being "back in the world" again. As he continued to run the organization and seek my advice, I tried to maintain some distance.

Like many men and women who are incarcerated for many years, a few months after being paroled he was having more trouble adjusting to his new freedom than anyone imagined. The rigid structure and rule-bound routine of prison made the freedom and decision making of everyday life almost impossible for him to navigate. Despite the fact that he had many professional associates, a winning personality, and a well-paying job, he began drinking heavily as he had earlier in his life. He called me and others for help. I was more than a bit wary, but after years of investing in this man and the program, I found it impossible to turn him away. We discussed his problems by phone and in a series of breakfasts, over several months. His problems grew worse. The program staff tried to cover for him, but he showed up at work disheveled and smelling of alcohol. His new partner called me several times for counsel. Bills were not being paid, credit card balances were maxed out, and he was drinking all the time. I wanted to say, "This is not my problem," but thought that I could still be helpful by offering advice and a bit of friendship to a man who seemed to have lost his bearings.

The defining moment came late in the afternoon on a hot June day. His spouse called with great alarm in her voice. He was holed up in a motel near a casino, drunk, and threatening to commit suicide. When I called he told me how useless and out of control he felt, how life on the outside was not what he hoped for, and how drinking was his only solace. I knew that the terms of his parole included no alcohol and no gambling, so calling the police or a suicide intervention might land him back in jail. Maybe that's what he wanted.

I told him not to leave the motel. I was going to drive to where he was and try to talk him out of the black hole he'd dug for himself.

The motel room was freezing, with the air conditioning turned on high. A half-empty quart of vodka was on the desk, and a partially gnawed, cold pizza was lying on the bed. He offered me a swig from the bottle and a piece of the uneaten pizza. I declined. He was dressed in a way that I had never seen him before—with a glossy-looking sport coat, a wrinkled shirt opened at the neck down to the third button, and hair slicked back into what used to be called a DA, or duck's ass. Instead of the meticulous man who learned spit-shine attire in more than 10 years in the military, I was seeing for the first time a man who looked every bit the hoodlum that he was.

After trying for more than an hour to talk him into leaving the place, we both grew weary. He told me to leave, and I told him I couldn't. He made a motion with his hand to show how he planned to kill himself with a gun to the head. I told him that if he did I'd be in big trouble: My fingerprints were on the water glass and the doorknob, and people knew I was there. As I was the only other person who'd been to the room, I might even be accused of killing him. At the very least, I was complicit in his parole violation since I knew the stipulations and did not report him. "You better leave now," he said.

That's when I saw the small pistol he had holstered on his belt, and I realized that this was not false bravado. Having a lifelong aversion to guns, I was frightened by the realization that I was alone in a motel room with an inebriated convicted murderer who had a gun and who kept telling me to get out. Hoping that a change in location might change his mind about going home, I talked him into walking over to the local restaurant for something warm to eat. It worked, and I agreed to leave my car in the parking lot and drive him home in his car to his apartment and very frightened spouse. I asked him to give me the gun for safekeeping; he refused. When we arrived at his apartment, his wife was relieved but also wary. We talked for more than an hour, and I agreed to stay for what was left of the night. The next morning he was agitated, and after waking, he wanted a drink. I stood in the doorway blocking his exit, knowing full well that this very short stocky man, 10 years older than I, had training in the martial arts and survival skills from elite military trainers. I knew he could kick my ass if he wanted, and he still had the gun.

He backed down, but then he began to sweat profusely and to shake with delirium tremens. After a while he became so tired that he fell asleep. I was able to leave without knowing if my good intentions had been foolish or wise. I struggled with my thoughts of whether to turn him in to the authorities. I hoped for the best but would not have been at all surprised by the worst. Mostly I worried about whether he would hurt someone again, whether his alcoholism would overcome his more positive instincts, and whether I was trying to be heroic or simply following what I knew about suicide intervention.

I heard later that things improved for a while, but I stayed as distant from him as possible. We had an occasional phone call or meeting, and I learned that he was overdrawn and overdue on as many as 10 credit cards. He thought this was funny and that he could keep up the scam for a while, but he also realized that he was heading back to the slammer. I read and conferred with colleagues about alcoholism and sociopathic personalities and came to understand that the warm, laughing, engaging personality he presented to the world was part of a much deeper disorder that many experts thought were beyond the pale of interventions. Doing good wasn't as simple as I'd thought.

The man spent the last few years of his sad and wasted life in the minimum-security prison for aged inmates. When they told me he died a few years ago, I had no desire to attend the wake or funeral.

BECOMING A FATHER
Thomas M. Skovholt

I was sitting on the aluminum bleachers the other day with my daughter watching her daughter, my granddaughter, attempt the elusive art of hitting a ball in a summer league softball game. After my granddaughter's turn at the plate, my daughter and I had a mini father–daughter talk. It was about things that fathers and daughters talk about, like painting her deck and whether the one who just attempted the elusive art of hitting the ball would like to work on her swing with her grandpa.

It was another moment in a long life play—36 years now—of which I have been fortunate to be part. There has been great continuity in this life as a father over these years and discontinuity too. The continuity is about the commitment, bond, and some tasks that are central to being a father. I am fortunate to have two children—one of each gender. It has been a lot of fun! The discontinuity is about how the role changes as life evolves and infants become children who become teens who go out into the adult world and then in time get an even stronger grip on the adult world. That is where we are now. But time stops for no one, and this play is continuing.

The defining moment happened at 1:42 PM on December 11, 1972. After being in labor for many hours, my wife delivered a beautiful baby girl. In an instant, I became a father. It was as if a light switch forever turned from off to on and produced a permanent change in illumination. It is hard to explain the powerful, permanent change in me that happened in an instant when I saw the baby emerge. There she was! Right there, inches away! Anxiously, I looked for fingers and toes. I listened for noises and breathing. Everything was okay! In that instant, the hues of my life forever changed to richer colors.

After the birth, I eventually left the hospital and then got stuck in the snow as I left the Missouri parking lot. It was a strange experience to go from life-altering intensity to a regular life hassle of getting stuck in the snow.

Becoming a father is such a different process from becoming a mother. The process of having a human being take shape inside oneself over many months ties the mother to the child in a way that is foreign for a father. Months later, after conception, a father can be told he is a father, and he can say, "I am?" That distancing is a major obstacle in establishing the father–child bond. We didn't have that problem because I was involved during the pregnancy in childbirth classes. My wife was a maternity nurse, and that made possible an unusual exception to the rule that fathers could not be present for the birth. However, they did rush me away after the birth as a precaution. Against what, we would now ask. In those days, it was the way it was.

Being involved in the preparation over many months helped me get ready. I remember thinking that I needed all of those months to make such a major change in responsibility and focus. Probably more important for me in creating my fathering bond was the bond I received as a child. My own father and mother created the attachment path for me. I am the fortunate child of involved, caring, committed parents. I have never felt unwanted by them. Bowlby (1969) articulated, in his classic work, the important process of attachment, an area of research that is now flourishing and of great use to practitioners, teachers, and researchers.

As a note, I don't want to make all of this bigger than it is. I am not the only man who is a father! With a world population of 6 billion plus, there are at least 1 billion fathers out there. In every continent and every country there are fathers committed to the welfare of their children. We all know men who are great fathers. There are millions and millions of remarkable ones out there!

Young children take up all the space in the room, and so did our daughter. It was all engrossing early on with every day filled with a roller coaster of excitement, pleasure, hope, and wonder mixed with anxiety and worry. My first evening alone with the baby led me to give a distressed call to my wife, who quickly returned home. My distress was about the noise coming from the baby. Was something really wrong? My wife listened and then proclaimed that the noise was simply the baby breathing. Oh!

A few years later, my son was born. Here too I can recall the events as if they were yesterday. In this case, the memory includes rushing to the hospital for a quick delivery. Suddenly, there was a beautiful, healthy baby boy! This time, I felt a sacred excitement. By then, fathers weren't rushed out after the delivery. They asked me if I wanted to cut the umbilical cord and wash up the baby, and I said yes.

How do I summarize the father events—at last count it has been 9,033 days and, from the magic of my son's birth and being a father for the second time, 7,832 days? The early day intensity evolved into a march of daily events—some with Oh! experiences, some mundane, and some stressful. A grape temporarily caught in a child's throat is first on the historic father terror list. Child accidents with head cuts and bleeding in rural areas away from doctors and being burned in a city restaurant make the list of memorable stress events. To soothe my own worries about the flow of normative versus off-kilter things, I recalled my own youthful days. Watching this movie in my head of some dumb things I did calmed my father–worry energy.

My own kids give more direct reactions than others to my style and methods of going through life. It is refreshing. They have saved me from a variety of ill-conceived adventures such as a book project that had no future or a clothing choice that had seen better days. And then there is technology. Globally, we have the almost uniform experience of the young teaching the old about technology. I fit right in.

I suppose one could agonize about not being a good enough father. There has been parental agony, like "Are they safe?" but not too much wishing I would have done things differently. One wish is that I would not have been away so much at work during some of those years. But, all choices have rewards and costs. Of course, there are many things I could have had that would have helped them more—money, fame, power, unique world-class skills, better jokes—but I haven't agonized about these. I figured the basic idea was to have their welfare as a priority in my life and to give love and some guidance, and try to live my life in a positive way. And to love their children and partners too. The long-term nature of the bond and commitment, with its rich variety of experiences, has been a big part of my life. It has been a great blessing to get a part in life's play as a father and now as a grandfather. And to watch both of my children become great parents of their children—that is something to experience!

Counselor and therapist development is about a lot of things. We are in a field that attempts to promote human development by reducing distress such as anxiety, depression, and anger and by promoting positive qualities such as compassion, optimism, integrity, hope, and happiness. How does a counselor, therapist, teacher, advisor, or other helping professional learn to be proficient at the work? It is my view that as practitioners, we sit on a three-legged stool when we do our work. The legs are theory and research, practitioner experience, and personal life. All three legs give stability to the stool as we try, as practitioners, to understand and help the most complex of all species. My life as a father has given me much that feeds into the personal life leg of the stool.

Practitioners make a lot of mistakes in their work but the mistakes are usually because the work is so ambiguous and the path so unclear. Often, a path that seems right at the beginning can turn suddenly into a dead end. This is the same reality as being a father. There are lots of natural mistakes in both roles because there is no precise instructional manual for the thousands of unique situations in each role. I try to accept my mistakes in both roles and learn from them.

In counseling and therapy work, we are always stretching to understand and connect with another while realizing that each person is unique. It is always a puzzle. Our work is like a complex practice-based art form that is enhanced by research and theory. Becoming a father has enabled me to understand more. Now, at my age, I have the bigger picture of the phases of parenting: the life before when there was freedom and anticipation, the early infant intensity, the pattern of a child-filled life, and then the two-child life coexisting with very demanding work expectations, having them grow up with their friends becoming so important, and then various launches into the world. And now I have evolved into a relief pitcher, rather than a starter, in the game of raising children. I know all of these phases and can use this information when working with parents and their urgency. I am able to be encouraging to younger males as they get overwhelmed by the adult world of multiple family and work demands. Becoming a father has enabled me to enter these client worlds and to offer understanding, support, and occasionally tips.

One counseling/therapy area with which I have worked over the years relates to client distress over insufficient fathering. I think by knowing the richness of the fathering bond as child and parent, I have a sense of the magnitude of loss when it is not present. I have had adult male and female clients who are stuck in time, waiting and hoping to have a responsive father. Sometimes people wait for years and years for the sufficient father to show up. It has been painful work to stay with these clients as they do important grief work—start to "see life as it is," start to free themselves from the frozen grief, start to mobilize themselves, and start the process of going on.

Sometimes I have been struck by the indifference that clients who are fathers express regarding their own children and grandchildren. These are moments of tension for me; I try to understand the roots and reasons for their indifference, want to encourage their bonding with their children/grandchildren, and also try to keep from giving unsolicited simplistic advice. I am usually aware of being pulled at the same time by all these directions. That awareness means, to me, that I am being mindful.

Fathering reminds me of rivers. For some people the fathering river is frozen; sometimes it is polluted; sometimes it is dry and devoid of life. Engaged fathering is like a flowing, vibrant river, like the Upper St. Croix River that threads across Wisconsin and Minnesota. It is pristine, teeming with nature, and a naturally protected area with quiet water and rapids taking turns around the next bend. I love to canoe on this river. For me, the gift of fathering has been like the Upper St. Croix River.

The whole fathering deal has been a lot of fun! It was years ago, on a December day at 1:42 PM, when the intensity of a life-changing event was permanently sketched in my mind. I can recall the sights, sounds, smells, and emotions as if it were yesterday. It was a defining moment in my life. Oh yes, now I am back on the aluminum bleachers, in the innocent world of youth softball. We need to find a time to work with a child on the elusive art of hitting a ball with a bat.

Reference

Bowlby, J. (1969). *Attachment*. (Vol. I). London: Hogarth.

FACING MORTALITY: LIVING WITH CANCER
Samuel T. Gladding

His voice seemed incongruent with his message. His tone was upbeat like he had just won the grand prize in the North Carolina lottery.

"You have cancer" was the message. Specifically: "You have prostate cancer."

For a moment I was caught off guard as I tried to separate the fact from the intonation. My physician was not telling me with his cheery voice that I had a clean bill of health. He was not saying I was one of the most physically together 62-year-old men he had ever seen, which until seconds ago I had believed. Instead, he was telling me I was mortal. There was something dangerous growing in my body, and, by implication, I needed to do something about it.

My response was grave (no pun intended) as I solemnly began to question him about the implications of the news he was delivering. Naïvely I was conscious that I was acting, as if in a play, for I did not know what other role to take. My hope was there might be less drama and more reality if I pretended I did not know much and was depending on his expertise (which was true whether I acted this way).

Thus, I shot off a volley of questions: Was it possible that the biopsy he had received was wrong? After all, I was seldom sick, except for a winter cold every now and then. What did I need to do now? I thought there must be something other than waiting and worrying in which I could engage. How serious was this? Had the cancer spread? These last two questions were to ease my mind as much as to find out additional information.

As if he had a shield, he deflected my most pointed questions quickly by saying, "Come in next Friday, and we will talk."

The message I heard beneath his words was, "This is serious, and you need to do something about it. The matter is too complicated and complex for a phone conversation."

The exchange ended with my agreement to make an appointment; however, I wrestled quietly with the message after putting down the receiver. I was now in new territory as if walking in a field of land mines. I did not know which way to go or exactly what to do besides keep the appointment. I was afraid that one false step could lead to disaster, and I knew I had important choices to make soon. Thus, I just sat stunned and silent until a colleague disrupted my thoughts by knocking on my door.

The noise caused me to move, and in the movement I realized I was still alive. "Funny," I thought. "What would existential therapists like Viktor Frankl and Rollo May say about this situation?" Pinching myself, I responded with an internal answer. "I think they would say, 'Be glad you're still alive and live in the now.'"

With that I turned my attention to the door and entered into a conversation with the colleague, in which I knew my counseling skills were in full force as I concentrated on her concern. Yet, beyond the exterior, I began to think about what to do next. Almost automatically, it came to me: "Call Claire!" So after bidding adieu to my colleague, I used the speed dial on my cell phone and momentarily was in touch with my wife.

I told her the news I had received as calmly as I could. I then listened for her questions, which were so similar to the ones with which I had bombarded the doctor that I almost laughed. I realized that 22 years of marriage can make you more alike than you might ever dream. Finally, I responded to her barrage of queries by saying, "Let's talk when I get home, and I'm coming home now."

So with finesse and the fake excuse that I was a bit tired and had caught up on all my work for the day, I explained to my fellow professors that I was going home for some rest and relaxation. They congratulated me for leaving early—something I never did. On the outside I accepted their good wishes, feigning a laugh or two, but inside I was aching as I realized the news I had been given was not just about me. It was about we—my wife, my three children, and my future with friends, colleagues, work, and the profession I love, counseling.

My talks with Claire, which started that day, were not so much informative as they were liberating. There are a lot of emotions surrounding sharing the news of having cancer. After all, what I had been told had a permanent ring to it. It was forever. I was being informed that my number might be up—not that my number had been drawn as a sweepstakes winner.

When the feelings had settled down and the pretending had ceased, it was time for action. The first act was to visit the cheerful doctor and soak in the facts about what he had found and what he recommended. Realizing I would hear it selectively, I took Claire and a notepad and pencil with me. The report he gave, while bad, was not as bad as I had anticipated. Yes, I had prostate cancer, but it had been detected early and did not appear aggressive. Yes, I would have to have some type of treatment—surgery or radiation. I was a good candidate for either. Yes, I would most likely survive and could thrive—be back on the golf course in 2 weeks after surgery! No, I would never be the same again, and there might be some permanent secondary effects, such as erectile dysfunctions or sudden urges to void when I was in the midst of an activity or in a place where there were few, if any, facilities.

Following the facts, came a question: "What do you want to do?"

Finding my footing, I replied, "Think, talk, and read."

Thus, I left my physician's office that day mulling over the words I had heard and inquiring from Claire what she had heard to confirm reality. After lunch that day, and several times afterward, we went to a bookstore, where we could read undisturbed among the latest books in the field.

All of this happened in the month of May. As fate would have it, an entering student in our counseling program was also a radiation oncologist, and since I knew him on a personal level as well, I called to ask if I could speak to him about the matter. He sent over materials, and we met at a coffee shop on a warm June night for a couple of hours of lattes and conversation. He provided me more information than I could furnish him coffee. Upon leaving, I felt more empowered, less anxious, and with a greater ability to not just meet but also to defeat the growth in my body. Shortly thereafter, I saw a second physician to discuss other options, and I broke the news to my late adolescent children. I also told my best friend, who is in the news bureau at Wake Forest University. Other than that, I kept the news confidential, realizing that to announce what I knew would cause more concern and possible consternation than it would constructive interventions.

As I write this piece it is now late April; 11 months have passed. I lived with cancer in a "watchful waiting" period for about 6 months before starting treatment. The circle of those who knew was tight: my physicians, my wife, my children, and my best friend. That was it. However, the number of people who have become aware of this matter has now grown quite large. After Thanksgiving I let my colleagues at work, church, and elsewhere know that I would undergo radiation treatment (I ruled out surgery) after the university's winter break. I expect the news was a bit shocking for many of them since I had not shown any outward signs of the disease. Nevertheless, I received an outpouring of good wishes that made my approach into therapy easier.

At this time, as spring leaves and flowers brighten the landscape with their newly minted colors of green, pink, and yellow, I cannot help but think of Randy Pausch and his talk and book *The Last Lecture* (Pausch & Zaslow, 2008). In his lecture, which I have now watched several times for cathartic reasons on the Internet, Dr. Pausch does pushups and appears to be in the best of health knowing his fate is terminal. What appears externally is not what is going on internally in his body. I have been more fortunate. The "southern," or lower, part of my body is still recovering from the 42 radiation treatments I had from early January through mid-March, but that was the worse part of the experience (besides two MRIs, a CAT scan, and a couple of biopsies—ouch!). My cancer was not insidious. I was inconvenienced, fatigued, a bit nauseated, but not incapacitated. Besides being frustrated that my body does not exactly work as it did before, I am adjusting and recovering. Hopefully I will continue to be productive for years to come.

However, I will not be the same person as previously. I have seen mortality and now realize my time on Earth will not continue forever, which I think is a common fantasy I have shared with many others. I will, as William Cullen Bryant wrote in *Thanatopsis* (2009), "join the innumerable caravan which moves to that mysterious realm where each shall take his chamber in the silent halls of death" (p. 33). Yet, before moving on, out, and under, I have a chance to have more meaningful experiences. My thought is, "I am fortunate. I have time that is to come. Cancer is a shot that has been fired across the bow of the ship that is me. I have heard the noise and taken notice. But I am alive!"

How will I be different? That is an elusive and serious question that cuts across many domains. Physically, I do not know. I can only speculate. I do know my empathy for others who have noticeable physical disabilities will be higher than previously. Furthermore, I will most likely be more attuned to individuals whom I perceive to have less observable limiting conditions. Mentally, I know I will change because I have already begun to move in a different direction. No longer will I, or can I, be more intellectual. It is vital to know facts and figures, and as a counselor educator I will continue to read and absorb the research literature. However, I will be more affective and behavioral as well.

I realize even on a deeper level that to be alive is to have the opportunity to "give back" to others, to the community, and to my family in a variety of ways. I am a counselor, but I am more than just a man with a professional counseling license and ability. I am one who can contribute to people in many ways—emotionally, physically, and behaviorally. So the journey in and through life continues. For however long and regardless of how strong or weak I may be, living with cancer has awakened within me more of a commitment than ever to serve, as a servant to learn, and as a learner to grow. Now, with the realities of time and age, I may face death as I have lived life, with "an unfaltering trust" that because I was alive, others had a chance to live more fully.

References

Bryant, W.C. (2009). Thanatopsis. In *Poems* (p. 33). Charleston, SC: BiblioLife.
Pausch, R., & Zaslow, J. (2008). *The last lecture.* New York: Hyperion.

BEING 65
M. Carole Pistole

In the United States, you cannot turn 65 years old without knowing it. Medicare-related mail assails you, thereby letting you know that you are officially "old." Even the airlines give you a "senior" discount.

I came to my career as a midlife calling. As a faculty member, with program training director (TD), publication, and clinical and research training responsibilities, I felt overworked and was surprised by my 65th birthday. In May of the previous year, I had completed an accreditation self-study, then welcomed site visitors in the fall, and spent a spring sabbatical responding to the Site-Visit Report, writing papers, and "catching up" with data that had been waiting on and pressuring me. In summer, I completed my last semester of TD responsibilities, with a 7-page narrative response to the accreditation report. Despite the program's 7-year reaccreditation, I felt burned out. Then I had my "now you are officially old" birthday and went off to a conference.

In conversations with professional friends of 20 years, I decided that, actually, my return to a regular faculty role was coinciding with a normative midcareer transition point. At the same time, I was reaching retirement age. In wondering how I bundle my self into a future nonprofessional self, my only certainties are (1) not wanting to die at work, (2) wanting to finish my students (i.e., graduate them and publish our work), and (3) not yet being ready to wake up without something to think about. Interestingly, with my 65-year-old perspective, I feel more confident of making peace with my career "errors" than I do of transitioning into a nonworking self. Both, however, are linked—still—to my childhood, divorce, and dating experience.

My father died at work; my brother went from work to the hospital, where he died. Although both ended their lives while fully engaged and highly successful in doing what they loved and found meaningful, I have lived longer and expect to retire. They died relatively young (ages 61 and 41, respectively), left their work unfinished, and left me without the benefit of their career guidance. Unlike my career- and family-oriented brother, I was raised to "find a good man who can take care of you and get married," which I did, for about 20 years. Being successful in corporate careers, my father and brother had to have understood work politics, but both died before they could teach me that politics are inevitable and can be managed effectively. I needed their guidance, because I am an introverted, work-focused, nonnetworking person. I also naïvely thought that personal issues affect family, not work, interactions. So I made some career choices without being aware of doing so.

For instance, from my recent "old" perspective, I notice that I, perhaps, avoid work interactions that can take me into the deep, dark, dank, depressing, dungeony places in my psyche and soul, where I am devastated, paralyzed, and bereft of my competence. At least, this idea is how I currently account for my "quirky" career, reflected in my 39+ refereed journal articles not sufficing for promotion to full professor. I first thought that I could "sit out" the politics. Later, I sometimes misunderstood work politics, and, particularly with other women, I did not even recognize a conflict. I also avoided the few personality-related, professional "fights." Unlike conflict, fighting resonates with childhood battles with my mother and takes me into a desperate, alone, and lost place. Although I made peace with and appreciated my mother before she died, I am convinced the dark places still exist. For now, I find it important and worthwhile not to visit them. Visiting those places with my mother was unavoidable yet essential to gleaning the benefits of being her child; visiting those places in my career—not so relevant. Compared with the dungeon, career consequences are easier to weather, perhaps due to having some perspective on where I started and the meaning my career has for me, including doing what I wanted or needed to do.

Recently, a barely older colleague asked me, in an almost whispering voice, "Do you think about when to retire?" Indeed, yes. I am on the cusp of my career becoming a life phase. I want to finish my work and my students. My current career demand, which is linked to pay increases, is to submit grants. I enjoy the reading and thinking required to develop new scholarship. I feel pressured, however, by the 20 data-based, student-coauthored projects waiting to be written. And I worry about how to retire and still have something passionate to think about and do. I am beginning to realize that I choose, nonconsciously, to eschew grant writing to finish my students. My career time is limited, and I feel it running out. I question if it is wise to make new investments now. I do not think I can go full-tilt and then retire. I need to withdraw gradually and transition into whatever is next.

My work concerns attachment themes in peoples' lives. In conversations, I often respond to people's stories with "That's attachment." I have two examples from my life. My granddaughter, early on, marked her mother's leaving the room with heart-rending crying and could only rarely be comforted or distracted by anything or anyone. My son recently had to leave his young cat for 2 days; he returned to find her toys around her water bowl, her voice hoarse from having cried for him, and her then latching onto his leg for days.

Some people may become aware of attachment forces when they become a parent. Not me. I discovered attachment theory during my doctoral program, which I entered at 40 years old. Until then, I was unaware of the two seemingly opposing attachment positions: (1) the profound, "I can't survive without him/her" emotion; and (2) the possibility of a meaningful, enjoyed life without a central love relationship. Nonetheless, to pursue my calling to counseling psychology, I violated my highest, strongest values: I found myself divorced, without believing in divorce, and thought that I had lost my children forever. I had a great deal of support from family; friends, who became voluntary family; an excellent therapist; a reflective graduate student community; and George Gazda, my doctoral program advisor, who told me, "People have to *learn* to live alone." Still, following my childhood directive to organize my life around a (another) good man and marriage, I also dated. I managed to choose men who could help me live, see, breathe, and meaningfully understand personality and relationship theories and patterns. My love-and-broken-heart experiences were extremely painful, often numbing and paralyzing. They were also the source of enormously rich learning that allowed me to better know myself and better understand attachment theory. As a result, I no longer cry myself to sleep at night over a romantic attachment hurt, and I am delighted to be comfortable as a single adult who values and is valued by her adult children.

Open discussion about retirement seems not entirely okay. It somehow counters the norms in my work setting. But as I feel more physically vulnerable, while being the oldest person in the room doing turbo kick, hip hop, zumba, and step aerobics, I remember that "Fear's not a reason *not* to do something." This command has been with me since I was a child needing my father to talk me through my fears while doing math homework. I can now appreciate his wisdom and the influence of history in the present.

My career is narrowing. My mentors are retired and are seemingly missed by me and a few others but are not so much missed professionally, despite their contributions to the field, to students, and to colleagues. I am no longer in tune with young professionals' passions, nor do I feel their excitement. I worry about the economy, a fixed retirement income, declining health, Medicare, and keeping up with technology. I am amazed that I link to my family on Facebook and think I am cool when I "chat" with two of my sons at the same time. It is as if the world has begun outpacing me. Then, I remember, with wonder, that my grandmother came to Texas in a covered wagon.

For me, 65 feels different. I have begun to look for perspective, like my career being something I did for me, as a way of being in the world. I question whether I can withdraw gradually while finishing what is important to me and simultaneously contribute to my program, or must I "break up" with my work? My unsolved dilemma is how to have an active, passionate, and intellectually engaged life, with structure but without work. I understand my dread and "stuckness" when thinking about retirement. Having been a stay-at-home housewife and mom for nearly 20 years, I well remember the sense of needing something intellectual to do. I like to wake up thinking about work, which is perhaps the fit of an academic career despite being, at heart, a therapist. On occasion, I remember that counseling psychologists and professors Naomi Meara (University of Notre Dame) and Kathy Davis (University of Tennessee), whom I knew "of" rather than knew, told me at a conference after they retired, "Don't worry about what you will do. You'll be busy. Worry about where you want to live." I want to live in Texas, where I came from. But, you know, Texas is a big state. And it could become water or even desert, or maybe the resource for discovering a third life mission.

REFLECTIONS ON BEING A COUNSELOR
Abdalla M. Soliman

I spent 47 years within counseling: some 6 years studying and 41 years in professional work within it. At the age of 76 years I am still active, a professor of counseling psychology at Cairo University in Egypt, my home country. I often reflect on what fostered my "attachment" to counseling, what made me pursue it as a profession, and what made me fall in love with it. I feel that I was compelled to choose psychology and counseling psychology. I still remember threads of my psychological thinking in my early childhood. Sometime I would amuse my friends and tell them that I was a psychologist before I entered grade school. This was probably due to the kind of upbringing with which I grew up and the kind of environment in which I grew up.

In my local culture, parents were uneducated. Children were left to themselves, to play in the streets or house yards. When they misbehaved, like spoiling their clothes or quarreling with each other, they were punished severely. Ours was a traditional culture that demanded conformity to traditional values and expectations. Two elements of my father's behavior affected me. He was punitive and harsh with me and my mother. In addition, he was not adequately providing. I feared him and hated him and did not feel guilty about it. On the other hand, I had a loving mother and a loving aunt who tried to do their best to make me happy. More importantly, they confirmed my feelings toward my father and accepted them. In middle childhood I tried to process my feelings toward my father and to understand why he behaved the way he did, an example of my psychologically minded thinking at this early age.

From threads of ideas I knew that my father was managing the inherited estate of his two maternal uncles. When these uncles separated, he was left in the air not knowing what to do and continued in a state of inertia, depending on a small amount of revenue from a small inherited land, which he rented to other farmers. As I was growing I never saw him work. Had he worked in this land and planted it himself, he would have increased its revenue, and we would have lived in a better condition. When I completed elementary school, I wanted to continue my education in the secondary school. This meant that I traveled and stayed in the capital of the state, where the only secondary school was located. Attending this school required more expenses, and my father resisted. With pressure from one of my uncles, he submitted, and my maternal aunt traveled with me and stayed with me 5 school years until I completed my secondary education. My father's rejection and impatience with me continued through my college years. From my early childhood I knew that there must be reasons for my father's behavior that were beyond his control, but I was angry that he did not make an effort to provide for his family. At Cairo University I majored in philosophy. The program espoused courses in psychology and sociology. When I graduated from the university and began to earn my living by working, my negative feelings toward my father diminished. What remained was a cognitive understanding of his behavior. A feeling of duty and obligation to care for him in his aging years replaced anger and hate.

How did my father affect my behavior? I learned that I have to work hard to earn a living. I also learned that I should not be ashamed or feel guilty of my feelings. Honoring responsibility grew early in me. I learned that I should not submit to the expectations of others; therefore, I thought that the culture's imperative of submitting to the wishes and whims of authorities was absurd.

In my college years I realized the value of psychology in helping people understand themselves and change. Acquiring knowledge and skills of psychology was facilitated by two professors who permitted students to become close to them and learn from them at a deeper level. The second factor was my success in helping clients who were assigned to me in the psychological clinic in Cairo in which I began my training. My relationship with these two professors and their caring for me provided an introduction to the U.S. culture and thus facilitated my adjustment in the United States when I left to study counseling at the University of Minnesota.

My move to the United States was a significant period in my life. Being a graduate student at the University of Minnesota, where professional counseling psychology was born, and working under C. Gilbert Wrenn helped to shape the kind of person and the kind of counselor I became. Ashley Montagu was right when he said that education and schooling must be based on love (Montagu & Matson, 1979). The learning climate at the University of Minnesota was a climate of love. Dr. Wrenn was a professor who loved counseling and loved his students. In April 1974, he gave the keynote address to the Sixth International Roundtable for the Advancement of Counseling, held at the University of Cambridge. He said he was very happy to address the conference and to see his former students, who were now university professors, present, and he mentioned us by name (there were four of us present: J. Krumboltz of Stanford University; W. Johnson of Michigan State University; R. Ripley of Arizona State University; and me, of Cairo University). He went on to say, "Guidance is an American product."

On the professional side, Dr. Wrenn was an example of the professor who radiates love and learning to his students. His concern for them can be revealed by many examples. When I was a student, he held a seminar in his house for his students to discuss issues of their interest. Love has been defined as "the active concern for the life and growth of that which we love" (Fromm, 1956, p. 22). Such a definition is applicable to counseling. Dr. Wrenn's creed has been to help his students grow and mature. He certainly helped counseling grow and mature.

On the personal side, Dr. Wrenn and his wife, Kathleen, adopted me and my family. They cared for us and helped me make adjustments to graduate school. They called us their children and our daughter their granddaughter. Dr. Wrenn symbolized the loving father who accepts his children, makes them feel important, and motivates them to do good work. In his classes he related the professional to the personal; he would have us reflect on our lives, capture significant moments, and reflect on them. From him we learned to activate our *experiencing ego*, to be open and spontaneous, but to always let our *observing* ego reflect on our experiences. I explained this in a comment during the Ninth Minnesota International Counseling Institute, held in 2005.

I said I grew up in three cultures: the culture of Southern Egypt where I was born and grew up until I graduated from high school. This culture is known to be a conservative culture. The second was the culture of Cairo, the capital of Egypt, where I spent my college years. Cairo is a somewhat liberal culture. Then I left for the United States, a more liberal culture, where I did my graduate education. I added that with 6 years of graduate school at the University of Minnesota, one year of visiting scholarship at the University of Georgia, and several summer visits, I am more "American" than many of the immigrants who lived continuously some

25 or 30 years in the United States. In every culture I have lived I have assimilated and integrated the positive aspects of that culture that facilitate and enrich my development and left the negative aspects of it. My mission became helping my clients become aware of this whole *process of becoming*, the process of growing and maturing, and letting it spontaneously emerge.

I acquired several learnings from each culture I grew up in, while transcending it. From my father's treatment I learned the art of self-reflection, to process experiences, to try to understand them, and to find a solution. Thus, I learned the art of self-counseling at an early age. I also learned not to feel guilt or shame about my feelings toward others, especially when it is their behavior that is responsible for such feelings. From Dr. Wrenn I learned self-acceptance and caring for the self and others. He always related to us an authentic, genuine, and transparent person that one hopes to emulate. We hoped that such learning would transfer into our teaching and counseling with our students and clients. It still remains an ideal to achieve and to preserve.

In my extended family, in the Egyptian universities, in Minnesota, and in Georgia, several people cared for me. Here comes the understanding of the essence of counseling. It is a science and an art. Counseling is the scientific art of caring.

I learned and applied the principles and strategies of counseling in my teaching, practice, and functioning. I always felt ecstasy when I helped someone understand himself or herself and to plan a path that is full of light, joy, and productivity. Working with counseling has always been a joy for me. It has been love made visible, as Arab sage and philosopher Kahlil Gibran (1964, p. 28) says about work: "Counseling is love made visible."

References

Fromm, E. (1956). *The art of loving*. New York: Harper Colophon.
Gibran, K. (1964). *The prophet*. New York: Alfred A. Knopf. Originally published in 1923.
Montagu, A., & Matson, F. (1979). *The human connection*. New York: McGraw-Hill.

AT 60, I FINALLY FOUND WHAT I WAS PUT ON THIS PLANET TO DO!

Arnold R. Spokane

I've never cared much for South Florida. I prefer the seasons and feel most at home in the deep greens of the Appalachian Mountains. But I loved my father, unequivocally. Though he was impatient and frequently overstressed, our bond was strong. He never completed high school, but he worked tirelessly to ensure that I was well educated. I had no mixed feelings about my father. So when my parents moved to Pompano Beach, Florida, I visited as often as time permitted, despite my penchant for northern climates.

One dreaded visit to Florida that eventually changed my career as a counseling psychologist occurred in September 1998. Hurricane Georges had been moving on and off the Florida panhandle for 17 days. Having hospitalized my father following a rapid decline from Alzheimer's and intermittent bouts of depression and then, reluctantly, moving him to hospice care, my siblings and I made what we knew would be the last trip to the hospice. The first floor had flooded from the Georges storm surge, and I waded through ankle-deep water to my father's room. There, we spent our final peaceful hours with Dad—time that I will always cherish. The funeral was unremarkable (though wet), and I gave a brief eulogy. As I spoke, through tears, I silently but resolutely vowed that I would do something to help those who suffer and decline, as my father had, from the ravages of Alzheimer's.

For the remainder of 1998 (I had just turned 50) and most of 1999, I read everything I could find on gerontology generally and Alzheimer's specifically. I attended a training institute in gerontological psychiatry and began conversations with local physicians and colleagues who specialized in medical and psychological issues in aging. After having been a vocational psychologist (person–environment career theory) for nearly 25 years, my professional career was in the process of a 180-degree turnaround. I did not realize then that, in many respects, the turn was actually back to my intellectual roots.

My university sends me weekly e-mail notices of federal grants and requests for applications (RFAs), which, during the period following my father's death, I read scrupulously. One RFA on the environmental contributions to health disparity caught my eye, and I began to think in terms of a longitudinal study of Alzheimer's decline and what social or living environments might have slowed the cascade I saw occur in my father. I called two colleagues to discuss collaboration. The first wondered why I was thinking about a project so far afield of my area of expertise. The second said, "Let's talk. When can you come?"

A multidisciplinary group of psychologists, epidemiologists, architects, and gerontologists convened by my colleague, José Szapocznik, read the RFA and met (in Miami, how ironic) for a day of fortuitously heuristic discussions. As these discussions unfolded a remarkable and unusual idea emerged. We realized that we could blend two streams of research and apply them to this RFA. The first body of work was the finding that social support has a beneficial effect on mental and physical health. The second was work begun in the 1950s and 1960s on the effects of the physical environment on behavior. Work in an impoverished community in Miami had begun to explore the role of the built environment on the behavior of residents. In 2000, after several months of conceptual work, we submitted a grant to National Institutes of Health (NIH) for the transdisciplinary study of the built environment and behavioral health disparities among Hispanic elders in a small community in South Florida.

Fortunately, I had taken Spanish in junior high school, had corresponded with a pen pal in Argentina, and then had continued Spanish for 4 years in high school and 2 years in college. I also made multiple visits to Latin America as a vocational psychologist and had broadened my international perspective through our international programs at Lehigh. My Spanish was far from fluent but was of significant benefit in our longitudinal study, which was conducted entirely in Spanish. The measures had to be translated, bilingual assessors trained, and participants recruited—all in Spanish. In another twist of fate, at the time our proposal was being considered at the National Institute of Mental Health (NIMH), the Bill Clinton administration was struggling with a decision about what to do with a small Cuban boy, Elian Gonzalez, who had been brought to Miami into the very community in which we had proposed studying—Little Havana. Elian was sent back to Cuba, to the dismay of the Cuban American community and with a flood of bad and politically sensitive press.

Whether the fallout from the incident had anything to do with our funding is unknown, but we were later told that funders actually argued over the table for a piece of the project. We were awarded $3.3 million and subsequently were refunded for an additional 3 years. Our collaboration with the architects on the team was particularly stimulating. As a result of my involvement with these architect colleagues, I was, in 2002, selected as a Knight Fellow in Community Building and spent the year studying with eminent architects and urban planners. I had background in person–environment interaction from my work on Holland's theory and on contributions of the work environment to occupational stress, but the Knight opportunity opened my thinking (at 55) in novels ways. Architects and urban planners who believe in applying design principles at the human level do so using an interactive urban design process called a *charrette*. The charrette actively seeks community input in generating design possibilities and exchanges ideas with community members about what elements are needed in the design. The process is unique and blends the social sciences and urban design.

During the Knight year, I moved and, while packing my files, discovered my undergraduate thesis on the design of my college campus as a contributing factor to the student riots of the 1970s using the urbanist theories of leCorbusier (along with Jane Jacobs, a precursor of modern urban design and community building). I was stunned when I realized that my 180-degree turn was actually a return to roots even earlier than my vocational psychology days. The effects of environments on behavior had influenced my thinking from the outset. How much so, I would be surprised to learn.

During this same period, having participated briefly in community efforts following the World Trade Center disaster, and in the aftermath of Katrina, I trained and participated with the Department of Health and Human Services and Substance Abuse and Mental Health Services Administration as a mental health counselor (on the recommendation of another colleague) in the worst-hit areas of Mississippi. As it turns out, all of these agencies fall under the aegis of the U.S. Public Health Service—the implication of which I did not fully understand until later. Application to the public's overall health drives the research and the activities of even the most "pure" scientists at NIH—a stunning similarity to the scientist practitioner model we embrace as counseling psychologists. Two tours (one on a cruise ship and the other on the ground in Mississippi) and two additional study visits later, I trained in disaster mental health with the American Red Cross and for the past 4 years have volunteered in local and national disaster relief efforts. In addition, I designed and implemented a new graduate course in disaster mental health. These two efforts—built environments behavior and health, and disaster relief—are now combining. For me, positive human outcomes after disasters depend on restoring and reconstructing the physical and social environments in synchrony.

While all of this may seem foreign to counseling psychology—and especially to vocational psychology—every bit of what I learned and understood as a counseling psychologist was directly applicable in my work in built environments behavior and health and in disaster mental health. Our profession emphasizes the normative adjustment (across a range of domains) of basically healthy individuals to stressful external circumstances. The public's health, then, is counseling psychology's goal as well as that of NIH. My turn is evolution to a more ecological perspective and, in retrospect (things are always better explained in reverse), to an understandable amalgamation of personal and professional experiences. In our built environment work, basic mental health and cultural concerns of "normal" individuals were always considered in studying the health of inhabitants. In our Katrina work there were always vocational issues, educational concerns, and family issues exacerbated by the high levels of postdisaster stress and cultural vulnerabilities. The natural extension of counseling psychology paradigms to novel situations and human conditions not only is logical but also may be imperative to the continued vitality of our professional identity as mental health professionals.

Although I have been too busy to think much about the vow I made when my father died, I believe that I am fulfilling the promise I made and integrating lifelong intellectual and research interests at the same time. In any case, at 60, I believe that I have found the work for which I am best suited and for which I was placed on this planet, at this time, to do.

THROUGH OTHERS' EYES
David McGraw Schuchman

I am a 58-year-old White, American man. Culturally, I am Jewish. My father didn't speak English until he went to school. His mother never learned to speak English. I grew up near the University of Chicago. This was a diverse area (we called it "integrated" back then) surrounded on three sides by Black communities and on one side by Lake Michigan. My family was active in the civil rights and peace movements. Some time in my childhood there was an international peace conference in Chicago. My parents invited people from Russia and China to stay with us. I couldn't speak with any of them, but I remember being fascinated, knowing they were from different countries and cultures. My father was a social worker, and my mother taught eighth-grade science in inner-city Chicago. Through elementary school my classrooms were diverse. I remember one year a Chinese student joined the class. His English was hard to understand, but we had fun together. I had Black and White friends at school. My high school had 2,000 students; I was one of 50 White kids.

In spring 1968 I was a senior in high school, and Black power was energizing the African American community. In April, Martin Luther King, Jr., was assassinated. In June, Robert F. Kennedy was killed. Both of these events enraged the Black community. On the day Dr. King was killed, students started throwing plates, trays, and chairs in the lunchroom. Much of the anger was directed at White people. Some of my Black friends found me, escorted me away from school, and told me to go home.

My first 18 years were filled with diverse and multicultural experiences. Then I went away to a mostly White college, thereafter attended a mostly White graduate school, and ended up working in predominately White nonprofit organizations in the Twin Cities of Minnesota. White people, doing good work, primarily staffed these organizations. Yet there was a limited commitment to the idea of a diverse workforce. All of these organizations valued the idea of hiring people of color but, when they received no qualified applicants, hired White people. Working in these relatively homogeneous settings was comfortable and safe. There were few cross-cultural challenges.

In 1992, I applied to work as a mental health supervisor and program manager in a community mental health clinic in inner-city Minneapolis. Arriving for the interviews, I was uncomfortable with the large numbers of people of color and refugees in the waiting room. In addition, some looked poor and dirty. By this time, I had been away from people of color for almost 25 years. I didn't know how to talk to them, and I was uncomfortable with the differences between us. I didn't see them as individuals. I thought of them only as a group of people whose needs seemed vast and overwhelming. Working with these people, it seemed to me, would not be rewarding—only sad and frustrating.

I had to decide whether I wanted to be comfortable in my work, as I had been for the 15 years since earning my master's degree. At the time, I was unaware of the reasons for my discomfort. I focused on whether I would be able to do community organizing, instead of working directly with clients. I wanted to continue the contact I had been enjoying with community groups and community education. I was offered, and then declined, the job, thinking I wouldn't be able to do the community work. Looking back it was really because of my discomfort with the people with whom I would be working.

Fortunately for me, my soon-to-become boss called me back and talked me into it. When I accepted the job I didn't have much insight into whether I would be able to help clients who were so different from me. On some level, though, I knew it was the right thing to do. It was the best professional decision I've ever made.

Once I started working there, I found that this clinic had a very diverse staff and clientele. As I got to know people who were different, I found more commonalities than differences. One thing I learned about myself is that I have the skill to find these commonalities with others. With this insight and added confidence, I no longer feared people who were different. In fact, it became very exciting to get to know people who seemed so different.

In the mental health program where I worked, over half the staff were people of color or identified as gay or lesbian. I was neither. This proportion was also reflective of the client population served. There was a real commitment to hiring diverse staff. If there were few applicants for jobs, many nontraditional ways of finding staff were used. This included using relationships in the various communities to find qualified applicants. This also meant being creative about adapting job qualifications to best meet client needs. The mission of the program was to help others, to promote justice, and to treat people equally. This commitment and other factors made it a place that reflected my values. To be able to work in a place that matched my values was a wonderful experience.

For the past 17 years I have worked primarily with immigrants and refugees. First it was with Hmong, Cambodian, Lao, and Vietnamese. For the last 11 years I've also worked with Latinos and East Africans, primarily Somalis. Even when I was young, it was easy for me to understand another's worldview. Growing up I had the remarkable good fortune of living and playing with people of different cultures. Now, as an adult, I work side by side with people from very different backgrounds. The people with whom I now work are deeply committed to helping others. I learn from both colleagues and clients. In return I share my experiences and values. In this way, meaningful relationships have been built and maintained.

This transition to work in a truly diverse environment wasn't always easy. In my first years of this multicultural work, I supervised a Cambodian mental health worker. When a male client had been kicked out of his house, she invited him to stay with her. She was single. How would this reflect on her and, as her supervisor, on me? Another time a Hmong worker collected money from clients to buy food for a group. These things would never be allowed in mainstream settings. In these and numerous other situations, I sat with the workers to try to understand their perspective. Was this a scandal? Was it inappropriate handling of funds? Or was it a culturally appropriate activity that I did not understand? And if it was the latter, could this kind of activity be allowed in a mainstream organization with many licensing and regulating eyes on us?

In each case, and countless more, I learned something new: We could not provide culturally sensitive services to immigrants and refugees if we insisted on mainstream rules. I also knew that if we did not follow mainstream rules we wouldn't be allowed to provide services to anyone. There was great tension between these two poles.

The diversity of my lifetime experiences and my ability to see others' perspectives helped me make my way through the maze of conflicting influences. As a supervisor, my role was to bridge the gap between immigrant and refugee providers and mainstream culture and rules. I no longer think that there is a right and wrong answer for every situation. Perhaps a better way to say this is that the ill-defined area, between the so-called right and wrong, has gotten bigger. I also learned that often the solution lies in the relationships of the people involved. If, for example, I didn't have a good relationship with the Hmong worker, it would have been that much more difficult to find a solution that worked from varying perspectives and was, therefore, culturally appropriate.

Working with so many people of different cultures has been a life-changing experience for me. It has become more than a job; it is a calling. It is something I am meant to do. By way of helping others, I have changed as well. I have taken in the worldview of others and am a better person as a result. I am frequently moved to tears by the stories that colleagues and clients tell me about their lives. That they are still strong and able to laugh after their experiences amazes me. I do not know whether I would have the same strength in the same experiences. I am also incredibly honored that they share parts of their lives with me. I no longer see the sharp delineations among mind, body, and spirit. I no longer believe that science can explain everything.

I have been greatly enriched by my relationships with so many people, both coworkers and clients. As a result, I am a better person and am better equipped to help others. I am better connected with parts of me of which I wasn't previously aware. In my own way I am carrying on the values of my family's activity in the civil rights and peace movements. Now, in my life in the helping professions, I have rich and layered relationships with people who at first seemed very different but who now seem like brothers and sisters. I believe that I am making a contribution to a vision of the world as a just and safe place.

CHAPTER SUMMARY

The intensity of professional life and personal life keeps pulsating. That is what a person feels when reading the defining moments at the senior professional phase. The pulsating intensity of life at this point is one of the classic surprises a person may encounter when going through the $N = 1$ experiment of living life.

The Senior Professional Phase is the longest phase in counselor/therapist development, perhaps equaled only by the Lay Helper Phase. If the Senior Professional Phase can start at age 50 and end at—who knows when—that is a lot of time with a lot of possible change. For example, we were tempted to ask one practitioner, age 81 and still at work, to write a defining moment, but he seemed too busy for the task.

What is the motivation for all this senior energy? Erickson says with simplicity and clarity that it is integrity versus despair (1968). How much more motivation does one need? Of course, we have to add into the equation that defining moments are by their nature intense, life-altering experiences. No one sent in a senior defining moment about sitting in a rocker all day with automatic deposit of the Social Security check and other retirement funds. Just sitting all day and letting nature sing. Yet, sitting quietly can be quite internally meaningful. So this issue about the elements of growth and development can be complicated.

Here is an overview of the defining moments at the Senior Professional Phase.

New Experience as an Energy Jolt for the Senior Practitioner

The senior defining moments speak to the power of new experiences. Suddenly, Romano is in Thailand 5 days after the devastating tsunami in 2004, scrambling with Thai colleagues to respond. Neufeldt reports being taken aback and insulted by graduate students—this was after she had taught for 20 years—when they questioned her multicultural competence. She went on from there and was, in time, transformed by what she described as a great learning experience. A new chapter in Schwartz's work began during the senior professional years, when he started working with clients who had HIV. The result: His work as a practitioner was injected with new energy.

Beyond the Rigidity of the Early Professional Years.

For the sake of being ethical, Mintz questions narrow, conventional, safe rules of professional behavior to better serve her client. To help a traumatized client,

Hanlon talks about her own intense suffering years earlier. She uses this intense suffering from her own life as a powerful gift to her client. She demonstrates, for the rest of us, how the life of the therapist, and perhaps the suffering that comes with life, can be a powerful ally in the work.

The Senior Time Benefit

So much of human development takes time: time for things to unfold, time for new experiences to counter old ones, time for reflection to kick in, time to see the mature tree after having planted the seed much earlier. The graduate student counselor is often in such a hurry and has trouble being patient so that things can unfold. Going from a first graduate school year to a second seems to be a big deal. Yet from the 40-year perspective it isn't much. Mountains for the beginner are more like hills to the veteran. So much novice anxiety is tied to the urgency of the moment. This is, of course, natural since the immediate is the experience base. Senior practitioners, when novices, did the same thing.

Some of the senior defining moments reveal the benefits of time. The story from Isrealashvili is startling; it is a unique tribute to the sacred quality of human life and the role a counselor may play without even knowing it until many years later. Detzner reaches out to help, reaches like grasping for a scared cat way out on a limb. Suddenly he is in grave danger. The event occurred in the early professional years, but the lesson has carried itself powerfully into the senior professional phase. Skovholt has a similar experience of a powerful event in the early professional years pulsating from there on and impacting his work over decades. For him, it was the moment when he became a father.

And Now, a New Life Chapter

Gladding tells us how his life has been changed by cancer. Things are the same yet different, with a deeper perception of life and love for the counseling profession. For Pistole there is a new reality: She is suddenly 65! And now what, she asks, will the new chapter be?

The Power of the Early Internalized Mentor

Early in our career we suck up the advice, wisdom, and encouragement of mentors just as a thirsty child uses a straw to suck up a drink on a hot summer day. It feels good to have mentors during those early days when we search for the career path and how to successfully walk on it. Yet a good mentor gives even more than this. Soliman tells us how the mentor influence can be profound and last way beyond the early career weeks and months. When the impact of the mentor is internalized, the mentor, in this case the historically famous Dr. Wrenn, can be monumental because it is timeless.

Choosing Authenticity

Choosing an authentic route can be really costly because it often means giving up aspects of one's life—hence, the meaning of "hard choices." Yet choosing authenticity to one's values and deeper commitments can also give the senior practitioner so much. Spokane dedicates himself to a whole new career path as he laments the lack of dignity present in the environment when his father died. McGraw Schuchman describes his long route of coming home to the kind of professional life and values his family lived when he was growing up—multicultural caring for the dispossessed and powerless. Now, decades later, his work motivation is fueled by this congruence.

Summary

The Senior Professional Phase has both a major limit and the opposite, a lack of limits. The limit is the hourglass of time that is running out. The limitlessness is the opportunity to choose one's own path, more than even before. These vibrant images demonstrate that challenges that enrich, never end. So many people have jobs that are boring and meaningless. Not practitioners in the helping professions! We are on a 40-year career path. The long-term perspective can help the novice avoid the urgency of the sprint when the task is a marathon. And hopefully, while doing this long race, the practitioner can really appreciate the chance, all along the path, to serve the needs of others through the complex art form of counseling and therapy.

QUESTIONS

1. Looking ahead in your own professional development, what lessons can you glean from these senior defining moments?
2. Have you found ethical themes that are unique to these defining moments at the Senior Professional Phase?
3. Which defining moment at the Senior Professional Phase strikes you as most poignant? Why?
4. Which defining moment at the Senior Professional Phase has the most implications for your work?
5. If you are newer in your counselor/therapist development, how do you respond when reading these senior defining moments? Do you feel energized by reading them—or, perhaps, is it more exhausting because it seems that the path of professional development never stops?
6. Can you use these to stories to imagine a defining moment for yourself at this phase? What kind of outline could it have? What issues do you imagine it would involve? Who would be some of the key players?

REFERENCES

Erickson, E.H. (1968). Identity, Youth and Crisis. New York: Norton.

8

Defining Your Own Journey

*M*ary Pipher (2003) aptly observed that "being a psychotherapist is no Caribbean cruise with bonbons and bourbon" (p. 75). Day in and day out, as counselors and therapists, we are presented with countless variations on human suffering—it comes in all shapes, sizes, hues, and textures. We listen, we support, we challenge, and we hope for change. It's hard work. But it's rewarding too. Perhaps the intermittent reinforcement schedule of client progress keeps us coming back for more. Or maybe it's something more intrinsically satisfying about bearing witness to clients' courage and hard work. Irv Yalom (2002) touches on the meaningfulness of the work as reward itself:

> I rarely hear my therapist colleagues complain that their lives lack meaning. Life as a therapist is a life of service in which we daily transcend our personal values and turn our gaze towards the needs and growth of the other.... There is extraordinary privilege here. And extraordinary satisfaction, too. (p. 256)

Learning how to sit with others' suffering is not easy work. Counselors grapple with a developmental process that is demanding in scope, ill-defined and ambiguous, and sometimes challenging to fundamentally held beliefs. Most people in the profession would probably say that, although the process of becoming a therapist is influenced by who they are as people, the converse is also true.

Our identities become irreversibly entangled in who we are as therapists. We enter the crucible of the counselor/therapist developmental process, and, if we value continued reflection and learning, we never leave. As Rønnestad and Skovholt (2003) point out, professional development is a lifelong process. Engaging in the kind of critical reflection that is necessary for professional growth is probably not for the faint of heart.

Congratulations are in order. Congratulations to you for choosing to seek out the "noble goals" of "understanding others' points of view, alleviating human suffering, and enhancing relationships" (Pipher, 2003, p. 179). Congratulations for joining us on this journey of self-exploration and self-discovery as we learn from others' most important developmental experiences—their defining moments—about how to grow as a therapist and as a person.

VOICES FROM THE FIELD: BEGINNINGS

In 1988, Skovholt and McCarthy published a collection of 58 "critical incidents" written by a wide variety of individuals in the helping professions. These critical incidents were aimed at energizing and inspiring readers. We found, in discussing this book with colleagues, friends, and peers, that the term *critical* seemed to have negative connotations. Thus, over the past few years, the term *critical incidents* evolved for us into *defining moments*. Also, many of the books that focus on critical incidents are case-study books in which the client is presented and students are expected to deliberate on the features of the case, such as diagnosis, treatment strategies, or ethical issues. In our experience, these case studies miss the central element of a compelling story. It takes courage and vulnerability to share one's story. They are not fictional case studies; they are real experiences. The reality of the authors' writings in the original 58 critical incidents is what energized us and inspired us. We decided that defining moments, written by those who experienced them, more accurately captured what we wanted to convey—those singular moments or experiences that are so important to our development as practitioners.

As we proceed in our professional work as counselors and therapists, we are often alone. In the aloneness, we struggle with making sense of our experience with questions such as Am I doing this right? Why is this work so confusing? What method is best? Are my peers doing better than I am? We have fears about many things (Skovholt & Trotter-Mathison, forthcoming).

As our project began to crystallize, we found others to have immediate, positive, and emotionally laden responses to the concept of defining moments. Even when discussing the book with friends or family members outside the field of counseling, the project seemed to resonate; teachers, attorneys, nurses, and individuals in other fields were able to immediately understand the importance of defining moments. As we sent out the call for contributions or invited authors to participate, we realized that there was a hunger for these types of narratives. As contributors submitted their narratives, they spontaneously told us things such as "Thank you for the opportunity to share this" or "I have been looking for a place to tell this story." Later, as we worked with the authors through the editing process, we continued to hear, "I am so glad that I was able to take the time to reflect on this." It was evident to us that practitioners can benefit from a place or venue in which to share these types of stories.

DEFINING MOMENTS THEMES

Contributors seemed to find this process personally and professionally meaningful and shared that they were usually able to think of a defining moment immediately. It was amazing to us that as we asked contributors to scan through the hours, sometimes hundreds or thousands of hours, of experiences in their training and professional lives to come up with the most engaging and important moment, they were able to do this—and with alacrity! Actually, this is perhaps the most important reason why the defining moment writing exercise works so well: The author gets to choose a highly personally meaningful experience to describe. So, it is natural that authors were motivated to write about the values of that one crystallizing moment for them. Compiling all of these authors' contributions has resulted in a collection of episodes that are saturated with meaning and intensely energetic.

We also found that a wide range of events were meaningful for contributors. Defining moments in the book related to such topics as a therapist's pregnancy, client suicide, and attraction to a client. Events that authors shared fell into both personal and professional realms and the interplay between the two. Authors spoke of the rich lessons they learned from their work with clients, their interactions with supervisors, and sentinel life events, such as the death of a loved one or the birth of a child. Many narratives related to multicultural awareness—whether through international experiences, adjustment to life and work culture in the United States, or a cross-cultural encounter that was life changing.

It seemed that often the most powerful defining moment narratives were the ones in which the authors took risks and allowed themselves to be vulnerable. In these narratives we were frequently reminded of the human side of the counseling field.

We were struck by how writing the defining moments pieces seemed to be therapeutic for the authors. While in the middle of a defining moment, one may not exactly realize its significance. Even when receiving supervision or discussing an event with peers, one may be too "in the moment," or too close to the experience. Through writing the defining moments narratives and teasing out all of the intricate details of the experience, it seems that authors were able to gain some perspective. Allowing ourselves to spend time examining our experiences is part of being a reflective practitioner. Sharing these experiences with the community of helping professions is like participating in group supervision—only on a global level. It allows us to build community and to learn and grow from others' experiences.

DEFINING MOMENTS OVER THE CAREER SPAN

As we considered how to group the defining moments, it occurred to us that organizing defining moment narratives according to the phase of counselor development in which they occurred would offer conceptual clarity and contribute to the use of the book as an instructional tool. We reasoned that the types of defining moments, and the important lessons gleaned from them, would likely vary according to individuals' experience level and accumulated knowledge. However, we learned along the way that, often, people don't fit into phases neatly or perfectly. Some defining moment narratives cut across developmental phases, others tied earlier development (e.g., occurring as a beginning student) with later development (e.g., as a senior practitioner), and still others read more like a "journey" that spanned an entire career. Defining moments ranged across the lifespan from childhood events that shaped authors' worldviews to early experiences in counselor training to later stages in life and work.

Despite the wide range of defining moments across developmental phases, many of the narratives clustered around the graduate student years. Even experienced or senior practitioners described the influence of early experiences on their subsequent development. These formative experiences appear to be well remembered and to have a lasting impact. One possible reason for this is that early experiences in the field become disproportionately embedded into our professional schemas, similar to an early, intense romance in personal life. Whatever the reason, it seems that early experiences are critical to counselors' development.

DEFINING MOMENTS AS A TOOL FOR PROFESSIONAL GROWTH

Given the large number of narratives centered on the beginning and advanced student phases, we feel that this compilation of defining moments in counselor development offers important implications for training. Because so many of the defining moments focused on these early formative years, we offer extra encouragement to instructors to consider the beginning student phase and the advanced student phase as crucial points in counselor development—ones that may shape therapists' thinking and practice throughout the rest of their professional lives. We wonder what, if any, "necessary conditions" foster these growth experiences. Is it pushing trainees outside of their comfort zones? Or is it simply providing the opportunity to work with diverse clients with a wide range of presenting concerns? Certainly cultivating a reflective stance toward practice is important for therapists in training. In our (albeit understandable) rush to inculcate students with the ever-expanding wisdom of the field of counseling, we of course need to also find time to help students practice deliberate reflection. Perhaps trainees need more explicit opportunities for reflective practice in which they are able to discuss their early experiences and the meaning they have taken away from them. As therapists, we are, at least in part, in the business of facilitating clients' efforts to make meaning from their lives. As counselor educators, we can similarly encourage trainees to periodically take stock of what influences their view of the world from the therapist's seat.

We feel that the process of reading defining moment narratives in and of itself can contribute to trainee development. One of the editors of *Voices From the Field,* Tom Skovholt, has used this technique with students in a master's practicum class and a doctoral professional issues class. Reading the narratives allows students to compare their own development with the stories of others. It also allows them to differentiate their development from others' and to learn that their developmental processes are unique. Because of our varying worldviews, it seems that everyone has a different response to each defining moment narrative. For the editors, this was true when we first encountered the collection of critical incidents in the *Journal of Counseling & Development* (Skovholt & McCarthy, 1988), and it remained true as we read the contributions for this book; one of us might have found a piece merely enjoyable, while another editor was moved to tears. Sharing our unique responses allowed us to get to know one another better and to understand that while our worldviews may have been different, we all had important stories to tell and share. We have also found that reading a collection of defining moments such as this can be a catalyst for writing one's own defining moment narrative. Reading others' stories prompts recall of one's own important developmental experiences. Again, Skovholt has used this process as an instructional tool in his courses. As the students are reading the collection of defining moments, they are also asked to share a defining moment of their own at midsemester with the whole class. He has found that having a group of personal defining moments discussed at one time is a good way to process students' important novel experiences as well as the universal features of their experiences. He has found this to be a more meaningful classroom experience than having the students read about or the instructor present the same ideas.

We also feel that reading a collection of defining moments allows for greater empathizing with others. It offers the opportunity to try on another's subjective worldview; it reminds us of what often happens in the counseling process when a counselor is able to hear another's story from the inside and is able to build more empathy in this way.

DEFINING MOMENTS JOURNEY

Several years ago, three of us (Michelle, Sandra, and Julie) sat down for coffee at the end of our first year as doctoral students. It was a beautiful, sunny, May day in Minneapolis, and we found a table where we could enjoy soaking up the sun. We were there for several hours. During these hours, this book project began. A several-hour discussion generally weaves through many turns, and ours did this. Looking back, we see this time as our first "defining moments" meeting. In the meeting, the three of us discussed beginning our own collection, inspired by our interaction with the collection of critical incidents published by Skovholt and McCarthy (1988). *Voices From the Field* started to take form in that sun-drenched outdoor Minneapolis café.

We invited Skovholt, one of the original editors of the "critical incidents" issue of the *Journal of Counseling & Development,* to join us on the project. It seemed like a natural fit due to his extensive experience as a practitioner, teacher, and writer about counselor development and his warmth and genuineness as a person and mentor.

Compiling this book has allowed us to fully realize the power of the defining moment. This power is like an instructional tool, a spur for personal reflection and growth, a way to share ourselves with others, and a way to build community. Now, several years after our initial meeting to discuss the collection of defining moments, its potential has been realized. As we moved into the editing phase of the book, we again sat down for coffee. We felt that we had our own collective defining moment as we read various pieces of stories out loud to each other. We were emotionally moved by the deep humanity of the defining moments and the courage and willingness of the authors to share their narratives. We felt emotionally connected with the authors and were in awe of their openness. In many cases, the authors shared parts of themselves with us and the readers of this collection that they had not previously shared with others. We are inspired by their openness and extend our sincere gratitude to the authors for sharing the defining moments in their development with us and with you, the reader. We hope that you, too, have found this collection inspirational and provocative. We wish you well through your own counseling journey and the moments along the way that define it.

REFERENCES

Pipher, M. (2003). *Letters to a young therapist*. New York: Basic Books.

Rønnestad, MH., & Skovholt, TM. (2003). The journey of the counselor and therapist: Research findings and perspectives on development. *Journal of Career Development, 30*, 5–44.

Skovholt, T.M., & McCarthy, P.R. (1988). Critical incidents: Catalysts for counselor development. *Journal of Counseling & Development, 67*, 69–130.

Skovholt, T.M., & Trotter-Mathison, M.J. (forthcoming). *The resilient practitioner: Burnout prevention and self-care strategies for therapists, counselors, teachers, and health professionals* (2nd ed.). New York: Routledge.

Yalom, I.D. (2002). *The gift of therapy: An open letter to a new generation of therapists and their patients*. New York: Harper Perennial.

Using *Your* Voice… Articulating Your Defining Moment

A fter reading through the collection of defining moments, we wonder if you have heard parts of your story articulated or felt prompted to reflect more deeply about a defining moment in your own development. Perhaps you feel ready to begin putting words to your experience. To guide your writing, you might ask yourself the following questions:

- What particular event or events do I see as having profoundly influenced my development as a counselor or therapist?
- Why was this event meaningful to me?
- How did it change me personally and professionally?
- Why does one particular event stick out for me more than others?
- Who were the key individuals involved in this event?
- What words can I use to convey my emotions related to this event?
- How did my thinking about the field, work with clients, understanding of my role as a counselor or therapist, etc., change as a result of having experienced this event?
- What kinds of conversations have I had with others around this event? What might I like others to know about my experience?
- How have my subsequent professional experiences been influenced by this event?
- How do I feel as I take the time to reflect on this defining moment?